Published by Rajneesh Foundation Europe

THE REBEL

by Bhagwan

Editing by Ma Prem Pankaja,B.A., Ma Puja Melissa,B.A.,
Swami Krishna Prabhu
Design by Ma Dhyan Amiyo
Typing by Ma Anand Shanti,B.A.,M.S.W.
Production by Swami Prem Ramarshi, M.A.(Cantab),
Swami Antar Satlok, Ph.D.
Proofreading by Bodhisattvaa Ma Mary Catherine, Ph.D., Arihanta

Copyright © Rajneesh Foundation Europe
First Edition: July 1987 – 5,000 copies
Typesetting by Photon Graphics Pvt. Ltd., Poona, India
Printing by Mohn-Druck, Gütersloh, West Germany

LIOUS SPIRIT

Shree Rajneesh

Distributed in the United States by
Chidvilas Foundation, Inc., Boulder, Colorado

Distributed in Europe by
Rajneesh Foundation Europe, Zurich, Switzerland

Library of Congress Catalog Card Number 87-42814

ISBN 3-907757-16-5

In loving gratitude
to Bhagwan

Swami Anand Vibhavan

Talks given
to the
Rajneesh International University
of Mysticism

Table of Contents

Introduction

Rebellion is a peculiar word, and rebels are singular people. Rebellion is not a social phenomenon like revolution, but an intensely individual fire in the soul. When you stir from the sleep of ages, when your eyes flicker into wakefulness and you see the world around you – the same world you once believed was civilized – a profound friction takes place. Wherever an awakening soul looks, it clearly sees that all man's ideologies, art, religions, philosophies, politics, education, accepted social norms – in fact everything before our new eyes – is riddled with unreason and ancient humbug. At that point you can either grunt, turn over and go back to sleep, or else you can stoke up the fire of awakening and become a rebel.

As the soul awakens, alongside it a natural intelligence unfolds, and a friction arises from the interaction between the invisible walls of conditioning within which we have encased ourselves and our newly-born intelligence. As awakening grows, the inner fire takes on a greater and greater intensity, consuming everything in its path, except pure truth.

Rebellion is an alchemical process: the world is the crucible, man is the base metal, and the fire in his soul can transmute and transform him into the glowing, living gold of truth.

An enlightened being has been through the whole alchemy of transformation which leaves only pure gold. An enlightened master has not only been transformed but he has also mastered the art of alchemy. He can create a fire in your soul and bring it to the peak of intensity needed for your ultimate transformation.

Bhagwan Shree Rajneesh is an enlightened master. He has awakened many, many souls, and now they too are aflame with inner rebellion. The master himself is the essence of that fire; he is the very spirit of rebellion, the pure energy of the universe, vibrant and urgent, to awaken any soul yearning to return home.

This book is compiled from questions put to Bhagwan by his disciples, and the mysterious electricity that crackles between master and disciple provides the current underlying each word. Some of the questions in this book are from me. I cannot, in truth, call them mine, because they both echo and emphasize what is happening here in Poona for many people at this time. It does mean, however, that I can speak about how the process of interaction with Bhagwan has affected me.

It needs to be understood that this temple of meditation in Poona is a mystery school; and a mystery school is not a place where one comes for information but for transformation.

Bhagwan chooses to answer authentic questions, and that means the questions are an attempt to express an existential situation which is confusing the questioner. As the words emerge from their hiding place they often come to the surface wrapped in tears and accompanied by pain; sometimes they are accompanied by laughter and relief, but always they come not from the head but the heart – more of a birth process than a thought process.

Finding expression for a deeply subjective state, private and hidden, is hazardous, and for me to expose my inner workings took a mixture of courage and simplicity. An authentic question can only find expression in an atmosphere of loving trust.

In this mysterious inner world, language is a clumsy stranger, often too insensitive to carry its fragile burden. But the master is here to help. He knows the inner world – your wounds, your tears, your fears, your terror, your hidden springs of love, of joy – and his responsiveness to your deepest needs enables the most delicate subjects to reach him intact.

Once the question goes to Bhagwan, he responds; perhaps by throwing it away, perhaps by keeping it on ice for a time, perhaps by answering it in discourse. Whatever his response, it triggers some kind of change in the questioner.

Some of the questions I sent to Bhagwan were answered in discourse, and I am still feeling the effects. The questions he chose to answer were centered around the apparent conflict between my male-conditioned mind – my gorilla – and the subtle, sensitive, meditative self – my Buddha. Bhagwan, as midwife, clearly enjoyed the image of a disciple struggling out of his gorilla skin, and he laughingly made use of it. But this is a mystery school, and all is not just as it seems on the surface.

As he unzipped me with his reply, something actually started dropping from my usual pattern of behavior – and it looked very much like a moth-eaten, overused gorilla suit.

Bhagwan's method is definitely accurate, and the gentleness of his words laid bare the path taken by the question on its journey from my depths to the light of day. As he spoke he brought clarity and healing. His surgery is of a rare and wonderful kind, and though its instruments are invisible, the surging sense of joy and wholeness it brings in its wake is unmistakeable proof of its effect.

The questions are only a part of Bhagwan's multidimensional attack on our sleepiness; there is much, much more.

The Chuang Tzu Auditorium, where the discourses take place, has a circular, open design, and no walls, just pillars, so that even the birds and the trees can join in the celebration around Bhagwan. There is a new vibrancy in the air this time. We can all feel it. Life around Bhagwan has always been intense, but right now there is a new quality. I can see it shining in eyes newly soft and brimming; I can hear it in the music that we play and sing at each discourse as our hearts take flight; I can taste it in the delicious silence which dissolves five hundred people into itself twice every day as we all sit at Bhagwan's feet.

Is it the incredible energy Bhagwan is pouring out as he dances with us, his robes shimmering, his great beard flying madly as his arms become a blur of pure rhythm? Is this his new game? He brings the whole auditorium full of people to a peak of melody and dance; then suddenly his arms lift to the sky, and everything stops! One moment there is a roaring torrent of almost blistering ecstasy; the next, a silence beyond anything.

He is giving us a glimpse of eternity, and we are getting it.

Yes, that's the difference – right now we are actually getting it!

Bhagwan Shree Rajneesh is undoubtedly an enlightened master, and the pure, smokeless flame arising from his rebellious spirit is lighting up many souls and guiding them to his table for a taste of eternity. He is serving it up in immoderate quantities.

All you need is the appetite and the thirst – the rest you can safely leave to him.

Swami Devageet
Poona, India
April, 1987

Meditation Is The Greatest Charity

To me, charity first means the education of the inner; and only secondarily, it means education of other things. "Know thyself" must be the most precious education, and then you can become acquainted with everything else.

A man who knows himself will never misuse his education in the outer world. Otherwise, when you don't know yourself, you are going to use your education to exploit people, to create poverty.

If you know yourself, you will create a society where poverty does not exist. All your religions have failed in creating a society where poverty does not exist. And one of the most fundamental reasons is that none of your religions has been emphasizing the education of the inner – the journey into one's own self.

The moment you are at the very center of your being, you have such clarity about all the problems of life that one thing is certain: you will not create any problem, and another thing is certain: you will spread your vision, your understanding, to other people.

All problems are our own creation.

In our ignorance of ourselves we have created them. In our consciousness, they will dissolve just like dewdrops disappearing in the morning sun.

February 10, 1987,   7 p.m.

Beloved Bhagwan,

In Your vision, is charity a part of religiousness?
If so, what would constitute charity?
Following the Catholic concept, the Indian legislature specifies:
1) relief for the poor, 2) education, and
3) medical relief, as being charity.
What is the concept of charity in the eyes of a buddha?

Om Prakash, the concept of charity in the eyes of one who is awakened is bound to be totally different from the so-called Catholic idea of charity.

The Catholic idea is relief for the poor. The idea of the buddha will be: there is no need for any poverty in the world. Poverty is man-created, and it is in our hands to destroy poverty. But all the religions – and most prominent of them is Christianity – have emphasized relief for the poor. Relief for the poor is not charity, it is not love.

Why, in the first place, should poverty exist? It exists because there are a few people who are too greedy. Poverty is a by-product of greed. One part of society goes on accumulating; naturally, the other part of society becomes poor. And man has lived for centuries under this exploitation. This exploitation can be completely destroyed.

Whatever the society produces belongs to all. And the most surprising thing is that the poor are the people who produce, and the rich are the people who do not produce. Those who produce are hungry and starving and dying. Just to give them relief is a very cunning idea: it protects the exploitation; it protects the capitalists. It protects those who are the criminals, and it also protects the poor so that they go on producing and go on fulfilling sick ambitions of pathological people.

A man who accumulates money, seeing clearly that it is going to destroy millions of people, cannot be called healthy. To call him religious is a mockery – he is not even human. And particularly now, when science has developed to a point that the whole earth can be comfortably rich, there is no need of any relief for the poor.

What is needed is a revolution of the poor, a deep understanding among the poor that "It is not because of your past lives' evil deeds that you are poor; it is not your fate that makes you poor. It is a few people who are pathologically sick, who have lost all compassion, all sensitiveness, whose hearts have become inhuman – it is because of these people you are poor." And just a great understanding among the poor can bring a revolution in the world.

I don't advocate any violent revolution. There is no need, because the poor are in the majority, and the rich are very few. Just by democratic means, the power can be in the hands of the poor, and we can create a society which is classless, where everybody's needs can be fulfilled.

Greed is not need. And there is no way to fulfill greed, it goes on growing. Just for a few people's sickness, the whole society suffers. But the priests are servants of those who are rich. Naturally, in a country like India, where for thousands of years poverty has existed, there has not been even a philosophical idea of revolution, to say nothing about an actual revolution happening. There has not been even a single philosopher to say that a revolution is needed.

Just to go on giving the poor a little relief keeps them alive at survival level. I would not call it charity. It is really to keep them alive so that they can go on producing for those who are rich and want to be richer.

I agree totally with Karl Marx on this point, that religion has been the opium of the poor. It has drugged them with hopes for a better life in the future, after death, if they remain content with their poverty now.

Naturally, the rich people have been the protectors of the priests, of the missionaries. They have made great churches and temples for God, because they have seen the point, that if religion prevails over people's minds, there is no possibility of any revolution. What you have been told up to now is charity, is simply the suicide of all those who are poor and suffering. It has been in the service of the rich; it is not in the service of the poor.

I teach you love. And love is not blind; love can see the whole structure – how poverty happens. And love can bring the revolution; a revolution brought by love,

not by violence, is charity to me.

The Catholic concept also says "education." But what education? In the advanced countries, almost everybody is educated, but that has not transformed man. Man remains as miserable as before – lives a life of anxiety and anguish.

Education is not bringing peace and silence and blissfulness to people. There is something missing in it; it is only education in subjects which do not touch your interior being at all. They may make you doctors, engineers, professors, but they do not give you the insight that can create a Gautam Buddha in you. The true meaning of the word "education" is "to draw out." But all that your so-called education does is to force in. From outside, borrowed knowledge is being forced into the minds of innocent children.

In my vision, education is nothing but another form of meditation. All that usually goes on in the name of education is secondary. The priority should be given to meditation – education of the inner. Unless you become acquainted with yourself, all your knowledge is useless.

So before education I would put meditation. Education is trivia: geography, history, arithmetic. It is good as far as the mundane world is concerned, but it is not good as far as your interiority is concerned. You go on accumulating degrees and inside you remain empty. Your degrees can befool people, may even befool yourself, but you cannot have the joy, the blissfulness, the peace, the silence, the compassion of a Gautam Buddha.

And unless education has two wings, it cannot fly in the sky in total freedom. Right now it has only one wing; the other wing is missing. Why is it missing? Because the priests don't want you to become meditators.

Once you are in meditation, you are soon going to be free from all priesthood, from all churches and synagogues, temples and mosques. What is the need to go to a church when you can go inside yourself – to the *real* temple of God? What is the need for a priest?

What is the need for a pope, when you experience God directly, immediately, within your own being?

When God becomes your personal experience, naturally you are free from being a Christian or a Hindu or a Mohammedan; hence, no religion wants you to be meditators. They want you to be educated in physics, in chemistry, in biology. No university in the world has a department for meditation. And without meditation, a man remains incomplete. This is one of the root causes of our misery.

To me, charity first means the education of the inner; and only secondarily, it means education of other things. "Know thyself" must be the most precious education, and then you can become acquainted with everything else. A man who knows himself will never misuse his education in the outer world. Otherwise, when you don't know yourself, you are going to use your education to exploit people, to create poverty.

If you know yourself, you will create a society where poverty does not exist. All your religions have failed in creating a society where poverty does not exist. And one of the most fundamental reasons is that none of your religions has been emphasizing the education of the inner – the journey into one's own self.

The moment you are at the very center of your being, you have such clarity about all the problems of life that one thing is certain: you will not create any problem; and another thing is certain: you will spread your vision, your understanding, to other people.

All problems are our own creation.

In our ignorance of ourselves we have created them. In our consciousness, they will dissolve just like dewdrops disappearing in the morning sun.

And third: Catholic charity has the idea of "medical relief." There is nothing wrong in medical relief, but why do so many diseases exist? Look at the wild animals and you will not find a single deer who is suffering from cancer or from tuberculosis or from any psychological problem. You will not find a deer murdering another deer, and you will not find a deer who is trying to commit suicide.

It is strange that man, who is the climax of existence and consciousness, suffers so much. Perhaps we only help to remove the symptoms and we never remove the causes.

For example, when I was in America they passed in Texas a resolution that homosexuality will now be a crime, because of the fear of AIDS. And the whole of America must have been shocked, because one million homosexuals protested outside the state legislature of Texas. Texas is a backward state in America. One would never have conceived that one million people are homosexuals.

They declared, "If homosexuality is a crime then we are going underground." You cannot write on anybody's forehead that he is a homosexual; neither are there any signals that show that a certain person is a homosexual. And they said, "Right now, we have our homosexual clubs, homosexual restaurants, homosexual meeting places. We will go on being what we are, but no longer in the open."

A problem becomes more difficult if it goes underground. It is better to know that a certain person is homosexual. And homosexuality itself is only a symptom. But nobody in the world has the courage to say the right thing – that it is celibacy that has created homosexuality. Nobody can say it, because it goes against all the religions. Nobody wants to be condemned, like me, by everybody in the whole world. But I have really enjoyed this condemnation.

No animal in the wild ever goes homosexual. Why? – there is no need. But in zoos it has been found again and again that animals become homosexuals, because the female is not there. What are you supposed to do with your sexual energy? It is a natural phenomenon. It needs some outlet.

All the religions have been teaching celibacy as one of the greatest religious qualities, and all the societies have been respecting virginity as something spiritual – these are the causes which have created homosexuality and lesbianism. And out of this homosexuality has come the disease AIDS, for which the scientists are finding no cure.

But still, no priest in the world, no political leader in the world, no man who has any international status has said clearly that celibacy should be the crime, not homosexuality.

But I want to say it: Celibacy is the crime. Homosexuality is only a symptom.

And if you repress the symptom, then the possibility is that something worse may happen, because the same energy that has turned from heterosexuality to homosexuality can turn towards sodomy. People can start making love . . . they have been making love for centuries, there are descriptions even in the *Old Testament* and other scriptures about people making love to animals, particularly shepherds who are living in deep mountain forests where they don't have anybody else except their animals. And animals are not going to report to the police. If homosexuality has created AIDS, then sodomy – making love to animals – can create something far worse.

Medical relief is good, but it is very superficial. The man of real charity will try to find out the causes that are creating so many diseases, and those causes should be removed. They *can* be removed!

It has been found that people who eat too much live only half the normal lifespan. If they were going to live for seventy years, they will die when they are only thirty-five. But people who eat less live longer than is normal. The norm may be seventy – they may live one hundred years. You don't understand a simple thing: that whatever you eat, your body has to digest . . . it is a great labor for your whole digestive system; and if the digestive system becomes tired, you are going to die soon; and if your digestive system remains untired and young and fresh, of course you can live longer.

And there are people who are living longer. In the Caucasus, there are thousands of people who have passed one hundred and fifty years of age, and there are a few hundred people who have reached almost one hundred and eighty years. And they are still young;

they are still working in the fields. Scientists say that looking at the mechanism of the body, everybody should easily be able to live for three hundred years; but so many diseases go on destroying the possibility.

People are eating things not for nourishment; people are eating things only for taste. People are not eating things in proportion; they may be eating something which is not needed in the body and they may not be eating something which is absolutely needed. For example, vegetarians are missing certain vitamins which are absolutely necessary for intelligence and its growth. It is not a surprise that not a single vegetarian has ever won a Nobel prize. In fact, they should have won more than anybody else, because they eat the purest food. But the problem is that their intelligence never grows, it needs certain vitamins which are missing. Substitutions can be found; without eating meat, substitutions can be found.

I have been telling the vegetarians, "Just by eating unfertilized eggs, you are in a far better position than meat eaters; and the unfertilized egg is just vegetable, there is no life in it."

They have been getting angry with me, saying, "You are teaching people to eat eggs."

I said, "You don't understand. I am saying unfertilized eggs" – but they don't hear the word *"unfertilized."* Just the word "eggs" is enough to freak them out.

Right food . . . . Humanity is almost mature; it should not live on lollipops. But there are people . . . I have seen even old people with lollipops! People are filling themselves with ice cream and all kinds of nonsense, junk.

Real charity consists in making people more educated about how to take care of their bodies, how to be more loving towards their own bodies. Medical relief should be a secondary thing.

Because of this Catholic concept of charity, even the Indian constitution has accepted the idea of charity in the exact same words: "Relief for the poor, education, and medical relief." It is even more shocking that the people who made the Indian constitution are not aware of their own Eastern tradition, of their own heritage. They have not put in it anything which is their own; otherwise, how have they forgotten meditation?

The man who was mainly responsible for making the Indian constitution was Dr. Babasaheb Ambedkar. He converted thousands of untouchables to Buddhism and he wrote a great book on Buddhism, and I don't think he knows anything about meditation. Without meditation, Buddhism is just a corpse – without the very flame of life. And even Dr. Ambedkar did not add to the constitution that helping people to be more meditative is the greatest charity, helping people to become enlightened is the most important charity.

It has been a problem for us: the Indian government cannot accept our mystery school as an institution of charity because of this definition. It is so strange that meditation is not included in charity. What can be more valuable than to be a light unto yourself? And all that they have included are very superficial things.

The constitution needs something much deeper to be representative of the East. It looks as if a Catholic missionary has written it; it does not look as if we have Gautam Buddha, Mahavira, Adinatha, Kabir, Nanak, Farid. These people are not charitable; Mother Teresa is the only charitable person in India, because she goes on raising the orphans. But she is against birth control.

If you have a little understanding, you can see the point: if you don't want orphans, then birth control should be the most charitable thing. Spread the idea of birth control, distribute the pill to as many people as possible, so there are no orphans. It is a strange thing that first you prevent people from birth control, and then they create children which they cannot raise, and you come in to become a great saint because you are doing a great, charitable act. If birth control methods are used, there will be no orphans.

If medical science is not working under religious conditions and is allowed freedom from religions, many diseases will disappear.

There are thirty million people in America who are in the hospitals because they eat too much; they have gathered so much weight, they cannot even move. And it is charity to take care of them, so thousands of doctors and nurses and hospitals are engaged in taking care of these idiots. And exactly the same number, thirty million people, are dying of starvation on the streets.

If this is the situation of America, which is the richest country in the world, what to say about the poor countries? Thirty million people have no shelter, no food, no clothes, and another thirty million people are being served by doctors and nurses and hospitals and the whole of medical science because they go on eating too much. They cannot be sent back home, because at home nobody can prevent them – they will go to the fridge!

These thirty million people who are in the hospitals should be left on the road, and the thirty million people who are on the road should be put into the hospitals and should be taken care of – that would be charity! These idiots would come to their senses soon – and you would be saving sixty million people just by a small change.

Man needs to understand that our problems are our own creations, and if we want to get rid of them this superficial Catholic so-called charity is not going to be of much help. These charitable missionaries and institutions have existed for thousands of years but poverty goes on growing, sickness goes on growing, madness goes on growing. It is time to realize that we are doing something fundamentally wrong.

All these people teach something against your body, that the body is the enemy. And if this concept goes into your mind – that the body is your enemy – then naturally you are not going to take care of it.

I say unto you: The body is your greatest friend. Take care of your body. And remember, you are not suffering from any fate, there is no fate as such. And you are not suffering from your evil deeds of a past life, because each action brings its result immediately.

I was talking with a Jaina monk, and he was very insistent that it is past karmas which create poverty. It was a winter night in the Himalayas. We were sitting near the fireplace, so I told the monk, "You put your hand in the fire."

He said, "Why?"

I said, "I want to see whether you get burnt now or in your next life. That will be decisive."

He said, "Are you mad?"

I said, "This question you should ask about yourself."

Each action is related with its consequence. It does not wait so long that when you die and are born again – perhaps sixty years or eighty years afterwards – you will suffer because you have done something wrong. Each wrong act brings its own suffering, and each good act brings its own reward and its own blissfulness. But people have been deceived, and deceived by those in whom they have believed so much.

To summarize, I would like to say that charity is to make the poor aware that poverty is created by the few people who are greedy.

Those who are accumulating too much should be behind bars, and those who are producing should be the owners of their product. The land should belong to the one who toils on the land, and the garden to the one who works there, and the factory to those who pour their very life into creating things.

Just two percent of the people in India can be called rich, and these two percent are keeping ninety-eight percent of the people poor. You will not believe it, but half the wealth of the whole of India is in Bombay.

Just one city has half the wealth, and the whole country – a continent of almost nine hundred million people – has the other half. It seems we have lived in such a way, geared to such a style, that we have come to accept that those who are rich are being rewarded because of their past good karmas, good actions. I want to destroy this whole ideology.

Education is certainly needed, but before education, meditation is needed. Anybody who becomes a graduate – either an engineer or a doctor or a professor – should not be able to have his degree unless he also passes his examinations in meditation. Each university and each college should have classes for meditation for the students – and for people from outside also; they may not have been able in their youth to learn meditation, but now they can learn.

Education is a vast phenomenon. Each hospital should have a certain department where people who are going to die should be taught meditation before death – just as people who are going to live . . . when they pass their examinations in the university, they should be taught meditation – how to live dancingly, joyously, beautifully, without greed, without jealousy, without anger, without hatred.

Then comes another point, when a person is dying. When the doctors feel that only a few months are left, he should be taught meditation as a preparation for the eternal journey he is going on. Soon he will leave the body. Before he leaves the body, he *must* understand, experience, that he is not the body. Then he can die joyously.

Living joyously and dying joyously – if we can create this atmosphere, I call it the greatest charity.

And that is what we are doing here. Whether the government accepts it or not does not matter; whether the constitution goes on superficially . . . . It will have to change. We just have to create people who are evidence of right education. An education is complete when it is inner and outer both. And we have to create people who can change this whole exploitative structure with love and compassion in a democratic way. There is no need for any violence. The poor just have to be made aware: It is time for you to wake up; everything belongs to you.

Beloved Bhagwan,

In this past year, I have been apart from You for many months, living in the world.
I learned how You and Your message have become an everyday living experience in me,
independent of time and distance.
In some strange way, Your life has become my life and my life Your life.
Being close to You is utterly delicious.
When You talk of leaving us, although my tears come, I know You have done Your work well.
Your vision will live on long after Your body has returned to the earth.
I don't have a question, just a gratitude for Your tremendous efforts to wake us up.
P.S. Please tell the captain of Your ship to cruise around for a little bit longer.
He has waited so long that a few more years won't make much difference.
P.P.S. Here's my question: Am I being selfish in wanting You to be here for a while longer?

Devageet, it is not being selfish at all, wanting me to be here for a little while more. It is a simple longing, as your journey is not complete yet. You have entered on the path and you are growing well, but you still need the gardener to take care of you.

And do not be worried about the captain of my ship, because he is not my servant; he is also my disciple. He himself wants me to linger a little longer here. And there is no problem. If you need me I will be here until your need is fulfilled. And even if I am gone, if your love is deep enough I will be present for you. Whenever you close your eyes, you will find me beating within your heart.

I have sown the seed. It is only a question of when the spring will come — and it always comes. Just remain open, available. I will be here to help you. If I am not in the body, still I can be here to help you. In fact, I can be of more help when I am freed from the body. Then my consciousness will be spread all over.

Those who have loved me — they will become part of me. They have already started melting and merging with me. So the only question that should be important to you is: not to hinder the process of your merging and your melting. Whether I am in the body or not, you should not wait for tomorrows.

Today is the day. This moment is the moment.

And this is my promise: I will try to linger on this shore as long as possible. And even when my ship is gone, whenever your tears will call me, or your laughter, I will be with you. And whenever you will dance and sing, you will find my shadow also present there.

Beloved Bhagwan,

For me, after ten years of being with You, You are the most intimate
but also the most distant person to me.
What is this pain of longing caused by Your physical distance which does not get less over the years?
Is it really only desire and attachment?

Yachana, it is not only desire and attachment. It is your longing to know yourself. To be close to me is, deep down, a desire to be close to yourself, because I am nothing else than your future; you are nothing else than my past. One day I was in the same darkness in which you are; one day you will be in the same light which has happened to me. We are not apart. All distances are false.

You find yourself deeply intimate with me and yet very distant. There is not a contradiction in it, because your past and your future, although far away, are connected with one another. You find me deeply intimate with you — in your love, in your longing, in your dreams. But because you find yourself so intimate, you can also see that you have only come close to me but not become one with me. And love desires to become one.

Howsoever intimate it may be, there is a distance, a vast distance. And love does not want that distance at all. The only way to go beyond the distance is to be yourself, utterly naked of all conditions, of all expectations, just silent and pure and innocent — and suddenly you will find that you have become one with me. This is the last stage of the disciple.

His first stage is the student, where he is just intellectually interested.
He has many questions and he wants the answers, and his whole effort is to accumulate knowledge. Out of hundreds of students, only a few turn out to be disciples.

Disciples are those who become aware that just knowledge is not going to help — one needs a transformation. The disciple comes closer to the master. He is no longer interested in accumulating knowledge; his longing has changed; he wants to be more authentic, more sincere, more truthful, more himself.

There is one more stage ahead: that of the devotee, when the disciple drops the idea of himself completely and becomes only a pure presence. In that pure presence, the devotee is not distant from the master. They become one. And only in becoming the devotee does this duality of intimacy and distance disappear.

Yachana, it is going to happen. I have given you the name Yachana. That simply means: a longing for the ultimate.

Beloved Bhagwan,

There is such a sweet and delicious experience in simply being near You.
Is it possible that the very presence of You, living in the vibration of Your fulfillment,
dulls my thirst for my own enlightenment?

Devageet, this is the beginning of enlightenment, when even the desire for enlightenment disappears. That is the last barrier — the desire for enlightenment. The moment that too disappears, there is no hindrance.

You are blessed that you feel a sweet, delicious experience simply being near me. You are asking: "Is it possible that the very presence of You, living in the vibration of Your fulfillment, dulls my thirst for my own enlightenment?"

Enlightenment is neither mine nor yours. The closer you come to me, the more available you become to me, the more you will find there is only enlightenment; there is only light, eternal. It does not belong to me, it does not belong to anybody else.

Right now, it seems to you that it belongs to your master. But when you merge with the master, you will know there has never been any master and there has never been any disciple, but only an eternal delight, an eternal life which knows no limitations.

It is in our ignorance that divisions exist — I and thou, the master and the disciple, the lover and the beloved. The moment you wake up, all these distinctions will evaporate. And it is good that the desire for your own enlightenment is disappearing. It is really you disappearing; hence, how can you carry on your desire for enlightenment?

And it is not my presence — it is simply the presence. I have disappeared a long, long time ago. And the same experience is going to happen to you now. What you call my "presence" is really my absence and God's presence. The moment you also become absent, God's presence becomes your presence.

We all live in the same ocean — just that a few are asleep and once in a while somebody becomes awake. One who becomes awake knows it is one ocean. Those who remain asleep go on thinking in their dreams, in their sleep, of all kinds of separations, of all kinds of desires and goals.

Awakening is such a fire that it burns everything that is false, and only the pure gold remains.

Okay, Vimal?

Yes, Bhagwan.

The Pilgrimage Is Endless

To be a disciple is to expose yourself, not to hide your wounds. If you can expose your wounds to love and to compassion, there is no other miracle greater than that. Love heals. Soon you will not find even a trace of the wounds, and when you are healed completely, your life becomes not a burden, not a drag, but a joy and a dance.

My own teaching is: Dance all the way to God. People who are walking don't know that this is not the way to reach to God. He does not understand the language of walking; he understands only the language of dance and song and ecstasy. But if you are full of wounds, how can you dance and how can you laugh and how can you produce blossoms out of your being?

One of the main functions of a mystery school is to help you, to encourage you to open all your wounds. And the moment you open them to love, to compassion, to the presence of the master, they heal very quickly. And a man without wounds is a man who can be said to be whole. In fact, the whole man is the only holy man.

February 11, 1987,   8 a.m.

Beloved Bhagwan,

You have opened me to new heights and I hear You ahead of time. I see that You are here and then I feel that it is only Your body that is present.
When You speak of Jesus, You are he. When You speak of Buddha, You are he. When You speak of Mahavira, You are he. I see that You are all masters.
And when You spoke of time that does not move, I heard and saw. My heart is full.

Jivan Mary, there are heights beyond heights. Don't be contented. The spiritual search is an eternal discontentment, but it is sweet.

The more discontented you are for new heights, more heights, the more fulfilled, the more fruitful and significant becomes your every breath.

I can only show you the way, but you have to walk on it, alone – singing and dancing and always remembering that there is no place where you have to stop forever. It is good to have an overnight stop and wait for the beautiful dawn, and open your wings, because new heights are waiting for you.

The pilgrimage is endless.

This is one of the most fundamental things to understand – because all the religions have been teaching that there is a full stop; there comes a moment when you have reached and there is nowhere to go anymore. Life knows no full stop, it goes on and on. The full stop is only for those who are not courageous. Then just a little joy, a little light, a little song, suffices them.

I would like my people never to be satisfied. To be unsatisfied about worldly things is meaningless – with the worldly things you can be satisfied – but to be satisfied with spiritual growth is committing suicide. Contentment with the world and discontentment for God is the way.

It is true – if your heart is beating with my heart you will hear me ahead of time because whatever I am saying is nothing new: it is only dormant in you, asleep in you. When your heart is dancing with me, that which is asleep in you becomes awake. And the quality of awakening is the same, so you can hear me ahead of time. That is a very significant indication of coming closer and closer to the state of a devotee.

You say, "I see that You are here and then I feel that it is only Your body present. When You speak of Jesus, You are he; when You speak of Buddha, You are he; when You speak of Mahavira, You are he; I see that You are all masters."

Every master is all masters, because the message is the same. Every master is only a vehicle, a passage, but what comes through that passage belongs to existence itself. It cannot be otherwise. The language is going to be different, the ways of expression are going to be different, but the essential core of the message is eternally the same.

It is because I feel such a deep affinity with Buddha, Mahavira, Jesus, Zarathustra, Bodhidharma, Moses, that I feel an absolute right even to criticize them. That is out of my love.

People misunderstand: they think I have criticized Jesus, I have simply corrected him. Jesus is two thousand years old. In two thousand years the very style of life has changed; the concepts, the words, the approach to reality has changed. Although the fingers are pointing to the same moon, the fingers are different. And my love for Jesus or Buddha is so great that I don't feel any difficulty in criticizing them – just like a friend can criticize you, not a stranger.

A Christian is afraid to criticize Jesus because he is a stranger, he is not a friend. He does not know that love is capable of criticizing one he loves. In fact, the more he loves, the more he is capable of criticizing.

It is true that you have heard through my voice all the masters of the past and all the masters of the future too, because whatsoever superficial changes happen make no difference to the fundamental religiousness, it remains the same. But to have understood it is certainly a great opening, the opening of the heart, a great understanding, a great light in the house that has been dark up to now.

And you say, "And when You spoke of time that does not move, I heard and saw. My heart is full." Whenever the heart is full, everything stops: time, mind, everything comes to a stop, just like a lake which is so silent that there are no ripples anymore. It becomes almost like a mirror; and in the fullness of your heart you are also a mirror. You will be able to see the whole sky reflected in the mirror.

Rabindranath recalled a man who was of the age of his grandfather – very old. He used to come often to Rabindranath's house, and Rabindranath never felt at ease with the man because he would always ask strange questions. If you are asked those strange questions, either you have to answer them and you know you are wrong, or you have to remain silent, which feels very embarrassing.

And that old man used to laugh whether he answered or not; it did not matter. He used to say to Rabindranath, "Your answer is wrong, your no- answer is wrong. You are known to be a great poet, you are a Nobel prize-winner – and you don't know anything at all. You have written so many beautiful poems about God: Have you met him? Have you seen him?" And the man and his eyes were so penetrating that it was very difficult to deceive him.

One day Rabindranath had gone to the ocean, which was close by. In the full moon night, he saw in the ocean the reflection of the moon. The reflection was even more beautiful than the moon itself. It happens many times . . . your photograph may be more beautiful than you are in reality. You can be photogenic. There are many people who are photogenic – their photos come out very beautiful, but if you look at those people they are not so beautiful in reality.

When he was returning, full of the joy of the moonlight and the ocean, he saw small ponds by the side of the road. Just in the morning it had rained, and there were small pools of water, dirty, but the moon was reflected as beautifully in those dirty water pools as it was reflected in the vast ocean.

That opened his eyes to a new truth – that the moon is the moon whether you have a very beautiful mirror or a very ordinary mirror. The reality of the moon remains untouched. For the first time, he felt relaxed about the old man who had been annoying him. And rather than going to his own home, for the first time he went to the old man's house. His eyes were full of the beauty of the moon, the ocean, the small pools of water. And he said to the old man, "I have seen God."

The old man hugged him and he said, "I know. I can see it from your face, from your eyes. I can see it from the way you have come to me for the first time. Now I will not harass you; I will not come again. I have been harassing you again and again, because I knew your potential. I would be very happy if you can tell me how you found God."

Rabindranath said, "Looking at the reflection of the moon in the ocean, and then looking at the many reflections by the side, in dirty water pools. But the moon was not dirty, the reflection was not dirty; it was as beautiful as in the ocean. Just then I remembered you – because I have been irritated with you, I have been annoyed with you. I was blind. I could not see God in you. I only saw God in beautiful people, in flowers, in the moon. But I know now it does not matter who you are. To me now, you are also a reflection of God, and I am grateful to you that you went on poking me, pushing me towards this realization."

When your heart is full it becomes a mirror, it reflects that which is the truth. And if you see and understand that, time certainly stops. It is a great realization.

And it is true that I am only body–available to all that has been discovered and also to that which will ever be discovered about the inner being of man. I have surrendered myself to existence. I don't know myself what I am going to say. Yes, just like Almustafa, I am not speaking anything, I am also a listener. And the one who is speaking has spoken through Mahavira, through Buddha, through Confucius, through Lao Tzu– through millions of mystics. Because the mystery is the same: that the mystic becomes a hollow bamboo and allows existence to sing its songs.

Jivan Mary, you are blessed; and you will be more and more blessed. The door has opened and the ultimate has given you a challenge, and I know you are courageous enough to move. However arduous may be the path, it is beautiful–its glory is beyond words.

Beloved Bhagwan,

Soaking up everything that You give to us in discourses, being totally overwhelmed by Your grace and Your beauty–when feeling Your compassion tears come to my eyes, and it is as if You would touch all the wounds of my heart so that they can beal.
Listening to the music of Your voice, slowly allowing myself to relax more and more, and then the gaps... everything disappears, bocomes so light and silent and bright.
I have no idea what enlightnment is, but it is worth giving my whole life for it. How will I ever be able to express my gratitude to You, my most beloved and beautiful master?

Prem Turiya, I have given you the name Turiya. It is a very strange word–it simply means *the fourth*.

In the East, the mystics have disappeared again and again in the fourth. They have discovered that our consciousness consists of four stages: the waking, the dreaming, the dreamless sleep and the fourth. Very strange–they have not given any name to the final stage, but a number; because any name is bound to carry a certain meaning which is confining. But a number does not confine.

It does not matter how you are going to express your gratitude. Your experience of silence and meditation, your experience of love and joy, your experience of dancing in blissfulness is more that any gratitude can be.

Gratitude cannot be expressed through words. It can be expressed only through your whole being–your eyes, your hands, your breathing, your heart; it overwhelms you completely. And it is not possible to put it into any words, so don't try that. Nobody has ever been successful in showing his gratitude in words. That's why, in the East, we have discovered different ways of showing it–the disciple touches the feet of the master. The West cannot understand it. All human beings are equal–then why should someone touch the feet....? They have not discovered many things.

When the disciple touches the feet of the master, the master touches his head and a circle of energy is created; and that circle is gratitude.

Just your being present in deep silence is enough. You are saying, "Soaking up everything that You give to us, being totally overwhelmed by Your grace and Your beauty–when feeling Your compassion, tears come to my eyes. Neither the grace is mine, nor the beauty. It all belongs just as flowers and birds belong to existence. Do not confine them into a cage. Let your experience of my grace or beauty become your experience of the grace of the trees and the mountains and the beauty of sunrise and sunset. Spread it all over the world. And without your being alert, it is spreading; hence, tears come to your eyes.

People ordinarily think that tears come to the eyes when you are suffering, when there is pain. Their understanding is absolutely wrong.

Tears come to people when they are in pain, when somebody dies; but they have known only one side of tears. The other side is reserved only for those few whose experience of love, grace and beauty – whose ecstasy, is so overwhelming that it cannot be expressed in any other way. Tears are the most subtle expression.

Your eyes are full of tears, a silent expression of overflowing joy. Tears express any experience that is overwhelming – whether it is pain or blissfulness, whether it is agony or ecstasy.

It is unfortunate that millions of people never know the higher and the greater side of tears. They know only the lower, the very superficial, the ordinary. In their minds, slowly, slowly tears become associated with pain and misery and anguish and anxiety, and they remain unaware that tears can also become an expression of overwhelming blessings. And unless you have known your tears as overwhelming blessings and benediction, you have missed the most beautiful experience of life.

Tears are a kind of language – silent. They don't come from your head, they come from your heart. It is the heart which is flooded and cannot contain the experience any more and finds language impotent, inadequate. Then, suddenly the heart remembers it has got a language which does not speak, but still expresses.

Tears of joy are the language of the heart.

And you say, "And it is as if You would touch all the wounds of my heart so that they can heal." Yes, Turiya, people go on hiding their wounds; they are afraid of exposure. They do not want anybody to know their wounds. They pretend that they do not have any wounds; and the more you hide them, repress them, the bigger they become.

To be a disciple is to expose yourself, not to hide your wounds. If you can expose your wounds to love and to compassion, there is no other miracle greater than that. Love heals. Soon you will not find even a trace of the wounds, and when you are healed completely, your life becomes not a burden, not a drag, but a joy and a dance.

My own teaching is: Dance all the way to God. People who are walking don't know that this is not the way to reach to God. He does not understand the language of walking; he understands only the language of dance and song and ecstasy. But if you are full of wounds, how can you dance and how can you laugh and how can you produce blossoms out of your being?

One of the main functions of a mystery school is to help you, to encourage you to open all your wounds. And the moment you open them to love, to compassion, to the presence of the master, they heal very quickly. And a man without wounds is a man who can be said to be whole. In fact, the whole man is the only holy man.

You say, "Listening to the music of Your voice, slowly allowing myself to relax more and more, and then the gaps . . . everything disappears, becomes so light and silent and bright. I have no idea what enlightenment is, but it is worth giving my whole life for it."

You cannot have any idea of enlightenment. But in the presence of one who is enlightened, you become infected. Something heart-to-heart is transferred. Something transpires in you: without having any idea what enlightenment is, you start moving towards enlightenment, almost like a magnet.

Do you think the moth knows what the flame is? But the moment the moth becomes aware of the flame it starts moving towards the flame, knowing perfectly well that the closer it comes – it becomes hotter and hotter and the danger becomes very clear – that coming too close means being consumed by the flame.

Yes, if you start feeling the beauty of enlightenment you are moving towards a flame where you will have to sacrifice your life. Because this life is not the true life; this life is just a stepping stone for the true life. The moment you are ready to sacrifice it, you will be reborn. That is the meaning of Jesus Christ's crucifixion and resurrection. It may not be historical – most probably it is not – but it is absolutely true that after crucifixion, resurrection is bound to happen. The old body, the old life, the old desires, the old greed, the old structure of your whole being is consumed, and you attain to new heights which you had not even dreamt of before.

But I repeat again: the music of my voice is not my music, neither is the voice my voice. I am simply available to existence. Whatsoever it wants to say to you, I don't hinder it, I don't edit it, I don't add anything to it. Just as in a mine you find raw gold, raw diamonds – uncut, unpolished: the same way I never polish anything. I never know what I am going to say to you. I simply allow the mine – for you to pick up all the raw diamonds. They belong to existence.

And you say, "I relax more and more and then the gaps . . . ." Those gaps are almost inevitable. You may have heard many orators and many speakers: I am not an orator, I am not a speaker. The orator prepares what he is going to say: it is his own mind. And you will not find the orator leaving gaps; that is against the art of oratory.

One of my vice-chancellors, even though I was only a student in the university, made it a point that he should be informed whenever I was going to speak. No matter what, he would cancel all appointments and he would come and listen to me. And I asked him, "You are a great historian . . . ." He was a professor of history in the Oxford University, before he became the vice-chancellor in India.

He said, "I love your gaps. Those gaps show that you are absolutely unprepared, you are not an orator. You wait for God, and if he is waiting . . . then what can you do? You have to wait in silence. When he speaks, you speak; when he is silent, you are silent."

The gaps are more important than the words because the words can be distorted by the mind but not the gaps. And if you can understand the gaps, then you have understood the silent message, the silent presence of the divine.

But again I say to you, Turiya: Don't feel obliged towards me, feel obliged towards the whole existence – I am only an instrument in the hands of existence. You need not feel grateful towards me. But feel grateful towards the trees and the birds and the ocean and the mountains and the stars, because they are really speaking through me.

Beloved Bhagwan,

Dancing with You, laughing with You, enjoying the sheer ecstasy that You provoke in me,
my mind is left far, far behind. It is a delicious madness which I only allow myself in Your presence.
Please talk about how I can dissolve into ecstasy yet still live in that other madness we call society.

Devageet, it is perfectly good to be dancing and laughing with me, enjoying the sheer ecstasy – which I do *not* provoke in you, which arises on its own while you are in love and silence in my presence. It will appear to you as if I am provoking it. No gardener can provoke the flowers, but he can water the plant, give better manure to the plant, more care to the plant. Flowers come on their own.

The laughter that you feel and the ecstasy that you enjoy is not provoked by me. To you it will appear that it is provoked by me but I am simply present here. Just because you love me things start happening in you: it is a synchronicity.

It is true – when you are in an ecstatic mood the mind is left far behind. And it is also true that "It is a delicious madness which I only allow myself in Your presence." That is very sensible of you: don't allow this delicious madness in the marketplace. People will not understand it, they will only misunderstand it. It is one of the most profound facts to be remembered: that you need not tell your innermost secrets to everybody. Share your secrets only with those who are capable of understanding them. Misunderstood, they may even destroy something in you, because their misunderstanding is bound to affect you. One has to learn to keep secrets, just like a mother – who is pregnant for nine months – keeps the child growing within herself, not exposing it to the outside world until the child is mature and ready. A day comes when it is beyond your capacity to hide it; but then there is no problem, because nobody can distort it.

What you are calling "delicious madness" is the highest form of sanity; don't expose it to the ordinary people in their ordinary madness. They are in the majority. Your madness will be so strange to them . . . . They crucified Jesus for the same crime, they killed Al Hillaj Mansoor for the same crime. They could not understand the joy, the ecstasy, the divine madness – keep it a secret in society.

And it is good, because everything grows in secrecy. You put the seed deep into the earth; you don't just put it on top of the ground. There, it will not grow, it needs privacy to grow. You put it deep into the soil where no sun rays reach, but one day, suddenly you see green sprouts coming out. The seed grows only in secrecy, in privacy.

Being with my people and with me, there is no problem; nobody is going to think you mad. In fact, everybody is going to think: When will the blissful day come that I also taste of the same divine, of the same wine, of the same madness?

But it is one of the psychological facts: to keep anything secret is very difficult, one wants to tell it to others. It is said that if you want your wife to hear you, don't say it loudly and don't say it to her. Whisper it to somebody else and she will hear everything. If you want to spread news in the city – true or false it does not matter – just tell it to a woman.

We have in India an ancient parable: A poor woman purchased a beautiful bangle. She had been collecting money her whole life – only then was she able to purchase a golden bangle. And now there was a problem: she went around the city showing everybody her bangle, but nobody asked anything about it. It was a rich city, and to the people it was a poor bangle; why should they bother to ask about it? She was so disappointed that she came back in the evening and set her poor cottage on fire. The whole town gathered there and she was beating her chest and shouting, "I am destroyed!"

At that moment a man said, "It is very sad that your house is burning, but you have really a beautiful bangle."

She said, "If you had met me before, you could have saved my house from burning. It was so much in my heart that somebody should ask about the bangle that I could not find any other way to advertise it, so I set fire to my house. Everybody is bound to come, somebody is bound to ask. Although I have lost my house, I am perfectly released from a deep burden: somebody has appreciated my bangle. It was my whole life's effort."

It is difficult to keep your ecstasy, your joy, your madness a secret. But keep it a secret as long as possible, unless it starts overflowing, and you are helpless.

Al Hillaj Mansoor used to shout, "Ana'l haq! – I am God!" His master, Junnaid, said to him, "Ana'l haq is perfectly right. I also know I am God. But keep it a secret, because people are mad and fanatic; they will not be able to tolerate it."

Mansoor said, "I will try, but there are moments when it is not me who is shouting 'Ana'l haq!' I am just a watcher. I hear myself shouting 'Ana'l haq! – I am God!' and it is beyond me. So I will follow your advice; but I cannot promise that I will not shout it, because there are moments I cannot do anything – just in the marketplace, the madness grips me! And I try hard: the harder I try, the louder I shout 'Ana'l haq!'"

Junnaid said, "I do understand your problem, but try your best."

He tried but could not succeed. Whenever he saw people miserable, painful, dragging their lives somehow towards the grave, it was impossible *not* to shout, "Don't be worried! I am God and you are also God – you are just asleep. Wake up!"

But people who are asleep are not so easy to wake up. They killed Mansoor because according to Mohammedanism, anybody calling himself God is a *kafir,* is anti-religious. They killed their best flower.

In these fourteen centuries Mohammedanism has not produced another flower which surpasses Al Hillaj Mansoor – so innocent and so beautiful and so graceful. And he was saying simply the truth. He said, "What can I do? I feel God within me. My life is nothing but God. He is breathing, he is beating in my heart, he is speaking. Although my master goes on preventing me – and I respect him and I understand the problem that there are fanatic people, I am putting my life at risk – but still, a moment comes when the bud has to open and become a flower."

The juices flowing in the tree force the bud to become a flower; and the god dancing within your heart – how long can you hide it? But as long as it is possible, hide it. Or if it becomes too much, go into privacy. Move into a lonely place, shout and dance and sing and be mad – but not in the marketplace. The marketplace is very dangerous for religious people; not in the temples, not in the mosque, not in the synagogues – these are the most dangerous places. Keep yourself completely silent. Best is, don't go to such places.

And whenever the urge is too much there are still forests, still mountains, beaches where you are alone, and the ocean will not make any objection and the mountain will be very happy and the trees will dance with you.

Milarepa has sent me a joke. It is for Devageet.

An elderly man walked into a church and took a seat in the confessional. "Father," he said solemnly, "I am making love twice a day to a sixteen-year-old girl."

"Mr. Goldstein, you are Jewish, why are you telling *me?* I am a Catholic priest!"

"Not just you, Father, I am telling everyone!"

There are moments when who cares that you are a Jew and you need not go to the Catholic priest to confession? And he has not gone there for confession, he is telling everybody!

But avoid the Catholic priest and the confessional, and avoid everybody. Your secret is far greater than Milarepa's joke. Let it grow. One day you will not be able to contain it, it will explode. But let it explode on its own; as far as you are concerned, keep it secret.

Beloved Bhagwan,

I feel useless. I do not know what to do anymore and
whatever I do or plan to do turns out to be wrong or useless.
There is nothing really I want to achieve, but on the other hand,
when I do nothing and just hang out and meditate it seems everything is easy.
Things around me happen beautifully.
I feel taken care of, even spoilt sometimes. Can I just relax in my uselessness?

Govindo, it is what I have been teaching you. Be useless, because there are millions of people who are useful! Don't destroy the variety of the useless. You say, "I feel useless" – do you think I feel differently? You say, "I do not know what to do anymore" – do you think I know? And you say, "And whatever I do or plan to do turns out to be wrong or useless." That is really great! "There is nothing really I want to achieve." That's what all the buddhas have been teaching: Don't be an achiever.

You say, "But on the other hand, when I do nothing and just hang out, meditate, it seems everything is easy. Things around me happen beautifully. I feel taken care of, even spoilt sometimes. Can I just relax in my uselessness?"

Absolutely. And if you relax absolutely – nature is very abundant; it has spoilt me, it will spoil you. What else is enlightenment . . . ? Getting spoilt, finally.

Okay, Vimal?

Yes, Bhagwan.

What Binds You Is The Lust For The Unlived Life

A poor man can become respectable by becoming a beggar in the name of religion, but he will never become enlightened. Hence my emphasis is: before you enter into the inner world, be finished with the outer. Live it so totally – your life torch should burn from both the ends together. The more totally you live, the quicker you will understand that there is not much. It is only the unlived part of life that seems to be attractive. If you have lived totally then nothing seems to be attractive. And only in that state can you move inwards without hesitation and without any split.

I am not saying renounce the outside. There is no need. Renunciation is out of fear. And naturally, twenty-five centuries have passed since Gautam Buddha . . . . In these twenty-five centuries not only scientific technology has progressed; spiritual consciousness and the methods that can lead you to enlightenment have also been refined. Gautam Buddha is, after all, a bullock-cart Gautam Buddha. He knows nothing about Rolls Royces.

I would like my people to live at ease, with all that is available on the outside. Don't be in a hurry, because anything left unlived will pull you back again.

Finish it.

February 11, 1987,   7 p.m.

Beloved Bhagwan,

How is it that all the past buddhas expressed themselves against money and sex, which are the sources of worldly pleasures? You are perhaps the first buddha to stand by all of them together – pleasure, happiness, and bliss – which is causing so much misunderstanding and opposition in Your case. Did the past buddhas try to compromise with tradition and to play for safety?

Anand Maitreya, there are many things to be understood. One: all the past buddhas came from royal families. They enjoyed money, they enjoyed sex, they lived in the most luxurious way possible; and still they found a deep emptiness inside themselves. They made from their own experience a fundamental principle for all human beings.

All human beings are not born in royal families. They don't have the chance to experience money, sex, and other pleasures of the outside world.

Because they were frustrated – the money was not fulfilling, the sex was superficial, all the pleasures were repetitive and became routine – they were utterly bored. They renounced the world.

Because of their renunciation of the world – going into the forests and the mountains – a fallacy arose that unless you renounce the world and worldly pleasure, you cannot become awakened, you cannot become enlightened. Their individual experience they made into a universal principle. It is a human tendency.

It still persists.

For example, only psychologically sick people went to Sigmund Freud. Obviously, he who is healthy mentally has no need to go to Sigmund Freud. Freud came across only sick people, and he extended the principle to the whole of humanity, as if everybody is sick. He only knew the dreams of sick people, and he thought all dreams are repressive. In his experience that was so, but his experience is not universal.

It happens with you too, a very basic human fallacy: you come across a Mohammedan, and he cheats you, or a Hindu, and he deceives you – and immediately you jump to the conclusion that no Hindu is worth believing, that no Mohammedan should ever be trusted. A single instance becomes to you indicative of the universal.

In fact, all the past buddhas support my thesis. Of course, they were not aware of it. What I am saying is, unless you are deeply acquainted with the outer world, unless you have been a Zorba in totality and intensity, there is no possibility for you to become a buddha.

It was fortunate for Gautam Buddha that he was born as a prince. All the beautiful women of his kingdom were made available to him, and the most beautiful woman he married. But when he was just twenty-nine years old, he became so frustrated. He was intelligent enough to see that now his whole life was going to be just a routine: more women, more wine, more delicious food. But he was acquainted with it all.

It was his intelligence to see that all his tomorrows had already become yesterdays; there was no future, and he was utterly empty. He had to go in search of something which fulfilled his inner being.

My thesis is very simple and supported by all the awakened people of the past. Mahavira and all the twenty-four great masters of Jainism were born in royal families. One never asks: Why were all your twenty-four masters born in the richest and the most luxurious atmosphere? Why did a beggar not become a buddha? And why did a man who was starving not become a buddha?

All the Hindu incarnations of God belong to royal families, and Buddha himself . . . . Not a single poor man has been accepted by Hindus or Jainas or Buddhists as enlightened. This supports my thesis.

I have been saying to you that because Gautam Buddha renounced the world . . . . First you have to live in the world to be capable of renouncing it. How can you renounce something which you don't have? You have to be so frustrated, so nauseated with the outside pleasures that they become almost pain, anxiety and anguish. Only then can you turn inward.

But all these buddhas of the past have fallen into the human fallacy: they project their own experience. They thought perhaps a starving person, a person who has never known any pleasure in his life, will also understand them. And the result has been a tremendous calamity. The poor in the East have remained poor, thinking, "What is the point of achieving wealth, what is the point of attaining luxury?" – because they have seen all those great, enlightened people renouncing luxury, so perhaps they are in a better position: they are poor already.

Buddha became a beggar by renouncing his kingdom; but do you think he is the same kind of beggar, can be put in the same category, as any other beggar who has never known anything of delicious food, of a beautiful woman, of a palace, of all the joys that are possible? On the surface they both look the same; both have a begging bowl. But they are not the same – they belong to totally different categories.

I would like you to belong to the category of the buddha.

But . . . first he was a Zorba, and only then he became a buddha.

The other has never been the experiencer of outside reality. He can only repress his sex; he is not frustrated with it.

Buddha has no need to repress – he has lived it, over-lived it; otherwise, in twenty-nine years one does not renounce the world.

The story is that when he was born all the astrologers of his father's kingdom were called, because Buddha was the only son and he was born in the king's old age. He wanted to know exactly what Buddha's life was going to be; all the astrologers were puzzled, and nobody was ready to say anything. The king was in much difficulty: "Why don't you say something? Even if it is bad news, at least don't keep me in confusion. Say it."

Then the youngest of them spoke. He said, "The problem we are all facing is that he does not have a fixed destiny. There is an alternative destiny – and that is a very rare case such as we have never come across. It is expected that we should tell you what is going to happen to him. But he has an alternative destiny – two destinies: either he will become a world conqueror, a *chakravartin,* or he will become a renouncer of the world. They are extreme polarities, and we have not been able to find which one is weightier; they are of equal weight.

"So we cannot say anything definitively. All that we can say is that these are the two alternatives: either he will become the greatest emperor the world has known, or he will become one of the greatest enlightened persons the world has known. In any case he will be one of the greatest persons. But whether he will be a beggar or an emperor is beyond our understanding and our science."

The king was also puzzled; this was his only son. He had conquered new lands, he had made a very big kingdom – and the only successor has an alternative destiny . . . .

He asked the astrologers, "Help me. Advise me what should be done so that he never renounces the world, but *conquers* the world. That has been my dream my whole life. He is going to be the fulfillment of my dream. He is my child – he has brought my dream in his heart. Just tell me how to prevent him from renouncing the world."

They all suggested, with ordinary logic . . . and ordinary logic destroyed the whole thing. They said, "Surround him with as much luxury and comfort as possible so he never feels the miseries of life. Gather around him the most beautiful girls so he never feels any sexual deprivation. Make beautiful palaces for him in different places of your kingdom for different seasons, so that he never feels that it is too hot or too cold or too much rain." They went into every detail as to how his life should be guided: even dead leaves should be removed in the night from his gardens – he should never see a dead leaf, because one never knows, he might start asking what happened to the leaf.

"He should never see a leaf which is becoming pale, old, ready to die. In the night, all the flowers which are going to die soon should be removed. No old man, old woman should be allowed to enter into his palaces. And whenever he passes on the roads, arrangements should be made that he never comes across a dead body or a sannyasin."

All these preparations were done, and the old king managed everything that the astrologer had said. But the ordinary logic is not the only logic. There is a transcendental logic which they were not aware of.

I would not have suggested this. I would have told him, "Let him live like an ordinary human being. Let him strive for comfort; don't give it to him. Let him strive to find a beautiful woman — don't just gather women like cattle around him. Let him know the pains of desire and longing and passion." Perhaps he would never have renounced the world, because he would never have come to know the world in its reality so soon.

Those twenty-nine years were almost equal perhaps to two hundred or three hundred years. Even in three hundred years you may not be able to attain all the luxury that was showered on him. And that was the reason that he renounced the world — seeing that it is all superficial and routine; seeing one dead man . . . . In twenty-nine years he had not seen even a dead leaf. If he had seen from his very childhood that people die, he would have become accustomed to it. But for twenty-nine years he had never thought about death. The very idea was not a question to him.

But how long can you prevent . . . ? One day he happened to see a dead man, and the whole palace of playing cards that his father had made, collapsed. He asked his charioteer, "What has happened to this man?"

He said, "Master, I am not supposed to tell you; but I cannot lie to you either. This man is dead."

And immediately the question was asked which ordinarily you don't ask. Immediately he asked, "Is this the destiny of every man? Am I also going to die one day?"

And just when the charioteer was saying, "There is no way to avoid death — even to you it will happen," a sannyasin passed by. He had never seen an orange-robed sannyasin, and he asked, "What type of man is this? What has happened to him?"

And the charioteer said, "He has also become aware of death, old age, and he has renounced the world. He is going in search of that which never dies."

They were going to participate in a youth festival. Gautam Buddha said to his charioteer, "Turn the chariot back. For me now there is no youth festival.

I am old, I am dead. Just take me back home." And that very night he escaped from the kingdom.

The charioteer — an old man, a very faithful servant of the king — tried to persuade him. Buddha said, "There is no way. If you cannot prevent old age, don't try to persuade me. If you cannot prevent death, don't try to persuade me. I am going in search of that which never dies."

So it is a double fallacy. Buddha renounced and he found the truth; and he also must have thought that it was because of renunciation that he had found the truth. That was not the case. It was because of his luxurious life that the search began — because luxury had failed, money had deceived; palaces became empty, the kingdom became meaningless; conquering the whole world became pointless. If you are going to die, what is the point of bothering with killing millions of people when in the end your hands are empty? So he himself thought that renouncing the kingdom had been helpful in finding the truth. But he forgot one thing: that everybody does not have a kingdom.

And Buddha's fallacy became a universal fallacy. Others who didn't have kingdoms started moving into mountains, into forests, into isolation.

I know a man who was a retired postmaster. He was a little cuckoo, so he never managed to get married. His parents tried very hard, but because he was cuckoo he would do something to spoil the whole thing. He was trying to hide his craziness, and in that very hiding something would erupt and something would go wrong.

When he retired from his post office he became a Jaina monk. I knew in his post office account he had exactly three hundred and sixty rupees; he had never married, had never known anything you can call comfortable – luxury was a faraway star; could not even afford a servant – he used to cook his own food.

After his renunciation, he passed seven or eight years in different monasteries with different Jaina monks. And then in Calcutta, just by accident, we met again. And the people who introduced him to me said that he had renounced everything he had.

I said, "I know. He lived in a rented house, he cooked his own food, and he had three hundred and sixty rupees in his post office account – which are still in the post office account in his name. He has not renounced anything, not even that post office account."

He was very angry, and when we were left alone he said, "This is not good of you. People think I have renounced everything, and you told them that I have not renounced anything. This is true, that those three hundred and sixty rupees I have kept in my name in case of sickness, in old age. But you are destroying my reputation. They all had great respect for me."

A poor man can become respectable by becoming a beggar in the name of religion, but he will never become enlightened. Hence my emphasis is: before you enter into the inner world, be finished with the outer. Live it so totally – your life torch should burn from both the ends together. The more totally you live, the quicker you will understand that there is not much. It is only the unlived part of life that seems to be attractive. If you have lived totally then nothing seems to be attractive. And only in that state can you move inwards without hesitation and without any split.

I am not saying renounce the outside. There is no need. Renunciation is out of fear. And naturally, twenty-five centuries have passed since Gautam Buddha . . . . In these twenty-five centuries not only scientific technology has progressed; spiritual consciousness and the methods that can lead you to enlightenment have also been refined. Gautam Buddha is, after all, a bullock-cart Gautam Buddha. He knows nothing about Rolls Royces.

I would like my people to live at ease, with all that is available on the outside. Don't be in a hurry, because anything left unlived will pull you back again. Finish it. And then there is no need to escape from your house or from your bank account, because they are no longer a burden on you. They don't mean anything. Perhaps they have a certain utility, but nothing is wrong with them.

Even a Gautam Buddha needs food, but somebody else earns it. He needs clothes, and somebody else earns them for him. You earn your own food. It is better to earn your own clothes, your own shelter. What is the point to be understood? – there is nothing in them that binds you.

What binds you is the lust for the unlived life.

So live life totally and let this lust disappear.

Then you can live in a palace with the same ease as you can live in a poor man's hut. But if a palace is available, then why unnecessarily torture yourself in a poor man's hut? Just, the palace should not be your prison.

And because all these great enlightened people consistently renounced the world, it created an atmosphere in the whole of the East that poverty is something spiritual. It is sheer nonsense. Poverty is not spiritual, it is ugly. It is one of the wounds that has to be healed.

If poverty were spiritual, then there would have been millions of Gautam Buddhas in the East. But we have never heard about beggars becoming buddhas.

My approach is a discontinuity with the past. I teach you first to live as a Zorba, and only on that foundation will be raised the temple of your buddhahood. And in this way we are joining the outer and the inner in a single unity. The outer is also yours as much as the inner. There is no question of denying anything; there is no question of being against anything.

So I say to you: pleasure may be the lowest step, but it is part of the same ladder. The highest step may be enlightenment, may be blissfulness, but it is the same ladder. And if you renounce the first rung of the ladder, you will never reach to the last rung.

Just think – you are standing upon the first rung of the ladder. There are two ways of renouncing it: one is getting down, the other is moving to the second rung. Both have renounced the first rung of the ladder. Gautam Buddha moves to the second, and you are moving below the first.

You see that he has left the first rung, but you have not understood that he has left the first rung for the second. He will leave the second rung for the third, and he will go on leaving the third and the fourth for the final. But you have become afraid of the first, because you have seen buddhas leaving the first, so you never step on the first. You remain below the first.

These people have reached to the highest fulfillment of bliss, and you remain hungry, thirsty even for the shallowest pleasure that the first rung can make available to you.

And secondly, the buddhas of the past were not concerned with any social revolution. Their whole concern was with their own achievement, with their own spiritual attainment. In a certain way they were very self-centered. And because of their self-centeredness, the East has not known any revolution at all. All the geniuses became so self-centered, who was going to give the masses the idea of a revolution? At the most they can teach charity to the poor, but they cannot conceive of a world without poverty.

I conceive of a world without poverty, without classes, without nations, without religions, without any kind of discrimination. I conceive of a world which is one, a humanity which is one, a humanity which shares everything – outer and inner – a deep spiritual brotherhood . . . .

So my function is not simply finished with my own enlightenment. In fact, my work began *after* my enlightenment. Gautam Buddha's work came to an end when he became enlightened; I started my work after my enlightenment.

As far as I am concerned, I don't need to live a single moment more, because life – either outer, or inner – cannot give me anything more than I have already achieved.

But to me it seems to be selfish. I would like millions of people to be aflame with the same light, with the same vision, with the same dream.

I would like a new man to be born, a new humanity, where ugly discriminations disappear, where there are no wars, no atomic or nuclear weapons, no nations, no races; where man can share all the bounties of existence and all the experiences of his inner being.

I want this whole humanity to be one ocean of consciousness.

Whatever the buddhas in the past did was good, but not enough. They created for themselves the highest peak of consciousness. I would like to create that highest peak for everyone – at least for those who are in search of it.

And I cannot say, "Renounce the outer" – because the outer is as essential as the inner. Just don't cling to it. How can you renounce the outer? You can renounce the palace, but how are you going to renounce your breathing? Each moment the outer breath comes in. . . . How can you renounce food? – it comes from the outside. How can you renounce water? – it comes from the outside.

Looked at with clarity, there is no division between the outer and the inner, but a constant harmony – just like the incoming breath and outgoing breath.

I am giving you a new conception, a new vision, a new dream.

Naturally, Maitreya, those who are clinging to the old buddhas are going to be against me, because their whole point is that the world is sin and it has to be renounced. Pleasure is sin and it has to be renounced – even simple pleasures like drinking a cup of tea are sins.

In Mahatma Gandhi's ashram, people used to drink tea, hiding. And once in a while somebody was caught, and he was so condemned that Mahatma Gandhi would go on a fast. This is a special way of torturing people. And the whole ashram would torture the person: because you drank tea, Mahatma Gandhi has gone on a fast unto death. And he would never say that it is a punishment for you. He would say, "It is a punishment for myself, because it shows that my soul is not pure enough; that's why my disciples go on committing such sins."

He has his own logic. He does not give you even the freedom of being yourself – it is his purity which is going to be decisive. And he is fasting to purify *his* soul; he is not concerned with you. When his soul is purified, then naturally no disciple can commit any sin.

Stupid logic, because if this was the case then just a single buddha who is absolutely pure will purify the whole of humanity – why only one ashram? Then anywhere on the earth, if somebody is drinking tea, that means your soul is still not absolutely pure. And it is not only tea, there are so many sins: chocolate, ice cream – all are prohibited. In fact, taste itself is prohibited. You should eat your food without any taste. The best cooks in Mahatma Gandhi's ashram are those who make such food that you cannot eat it – so tasteless that you will feel like throwing up. But that is spirituality.

Naturally, these people are going to be against me. I accept their irritation, their annoyance, because I know the future belongs to me. They are fighting a losing battle. They may have the majority, but it is a majority which has lost its roots, which is dead, which lives only on the past – and a very ugly past.

Just yesterday I received news from Palestine. Because of the creation of Israel, many people who were not Jews left the land of Israel. Israel was a new creation after the second world war. It is a new nation – forced by the American politicians and the British politicians on the poor Mohammedans who used to live there, in order to give the Jews back their country, which they had lost long before.

There was no need. Jews were living happily everywhere else. What is the need of having a nation? In fact, they were free from all national problems and difficulties – defense and armies. They were perfectly happy. But to create a permanent trouble for them, Israel was forced . . . it used to be Palestine, but now only a small part of it remains Palestine, and the Mohammedans have escaped to that small part. They are refugees.

Just yesterday, they said to the religious authorities: "We should be allowed to eat human flesh, because we don't have anything else to eat. Because there are so many terrorists killing people, so many bombs exploding and people are dying . . . why waste their bodies? Just give their dead bodies to us, because we don't have anything to eat." And these authorities have agreed that all dead bodies from now on will be given to the refugees.

This is the twentieth century! When man has to eat other men . . . . On the one hand, such an unbelievable phenomenon; and on the other hand, billions of dollars worth of food and foodstuff is being thrown in the ocean, in America, in Europe, because of overproduction. They don't want to lower the price, so the overproduction has to be drowned into the ocean.

Are we living in a madhouse?

Just a short time before, so much butter had to be drowned in the ocean – mountains of butter – that the cost of throwing it into the ocean was two billion dollars. That was not the cost of the butter, it was simply the cost of carrying the butter to the ocean. And just nearby, people are asking that they should be allowed to eat dead bodies, human bodies; and the authorities have no other way, because nobody is willing to give Palestine food. And their land has been taken away to create a new land, Israel.

We are still living in a barbarous age, it seems.

Human consciousness needs to be transformed totally.

My concern is not only with individual enlightenment; my concern is with a collective uprising of human consciousness. Many will be enlightened, but let others also be very close to it. Not that one becomes a Gautam Buddha and another goes to eat a dead body – this much difference is unbearable, intolerable.

At least I would like my people to fight for it – for their own enlightenment, and for an uprising of the whole of humanity. Simple things, which don't need much intelligence . . . . You can see it – anybody can see it – that this is nonsense. When people are starving . . . when one thousand persons were dying every day in Ethiopia, America was drowning its food in the ocean, Europe was drowning its food in the ocean. For the same price, for the same cost, it could have been carried to Ethiopia, and thousands of people would have been saved.

But it seems we are not alert at all.

Just now there are only five countries which have nuclear weapons. Just the other day, I received the information that by the year 2010, twenty-five other countries will have become nuclear powers – India and Pakistan included – because they are all striving hard for only one thing: to become nuclear powers. It is so costly, but even poor countries like India and Pakistan are not worried about their poverty, are not worried that half of their people are going to die. Their whole concern is how to make nuclear weapons, how to be a member of the nuclear club. There are only five right now. Twenty-five more countries are going to join soon.

Thirty countries having nuclear power is a very dangerous and vulnerable situation, because these nuclear weapons will be in the hands of pygmy politicians. And the politician is always in search of becoming the greatest man in the world – every politician – that is his whole desire.

Adolf Hitler, in his autobiography, says that if you want to become a great leader of humanity, you cannot do it without war. Have you ever heard of any great leaders who were born in times of peace? In times of peace, nobody needs their leadership. When you are troubled, in danger, you need leaders. Great wars create great leaders, and there are sick people all around who want to become great leaders, even at the cost of the whole of humanity.

So my function is very different from the function of Gautam Buddha. His function is only a small part of my philosophy. I want individuals to become enlightened, but I want also the whole of humanity to rise with the enlightened people. They may not become enlightened, but at least become conscious enough so that nations disappear, religions disappear, races disappear, and we can live as one humanity, as one earth. It is not difficult. A little understanding . . . .

And if the earth is one, then there is no need for any nuclear weapons, any war, any armies. All these people . . . millions of people around the world are in the armies, in the navy, in the air force, wasting their lives. They could be put to production. But that is possible only when nations disappear.

And, Maitreya, this too is true: In the past, the buddhas, the enlightened people, never bothered to say anything against the traditional mind, because they were concerned with their own enlightenment. It was none of their business. Even many so-called saints have told me, "You are unnecessarily creating so many enemies all over the world. If you simply talk about meditation and enlightenment, nobody will be against you." But I don't see that thousands of years of talking about meditation and enlightenment have helped much. So I am ready to take all risks, because I have nothing to lose. Whatever I have gained is going to be with me even if I am crucified. And I would love it if my crucifixion could raise human consciousness just a little bit more.

Beloved Bhagwan,

I have been your sannyasin for a few months, after a long search for a master. Now I am afraid you might die, and I cannot fulfill the meaning of my life without Your presence.

Prem Felix, you are still too concerned with your own ego. You are not worried about my death; you are worried about your enlightenment – what will happen to your enlightenment.

You are not aware that this is not love; this is not trust. You are trying to use me. And love never tries to use.

You have not yet found the master; you have simply believed . . . . Because you find here so many people in such deep love and in such deep ecstasy, you have believed in them – perhaps here is a master. But it is a perhaps.

If you have really found your master, you will forget all about your enlightenment. In finding the master, you have already found the path. In finding the master, you have already found someone who is going to be with you, even after death. That is the meaning of being with a master.

One sannyasin has sent a small Sufi story from America. She was puzzled by the story. She wants to know its meaning. It will help Felix also.

The story is: one man is drowning and is shouting for help. A hand reaches to him. It is dark in the night so he cannot see whose hand it is. He asks, "Who are you?" and the man says, "A friend."

But the man who is drowning says, "No, I don't want to be saved by a friend." It is a very strange story.

Again he starts shouting, "Help! Save me." And the same hand again reaches to him, and he asks the same question, "Whose hand is this?" and the answer comes, "I am God." And the man says, "I don't want to be saved by a god."

And third time when he shouts, the same hand reaches again, and he asks the same question: "Please tell me, who are you?" And the answer comes, "I am a master." And he said, "Then it is perfectly okay. I can trust you."

The story is strange. He cannot even trust God, but

he can trust the master. It has great implications.

To be saved by a friend is not possible in the spiritual sense, because the friend is drowning himself. He is in the same boat; he is not of a higher consciousness. How can he save you?

It is not a question of ordinary saving: somebody is drowning and you can save him. It is a parable. A friend is of the same consciousness; he cannot save you. But God? – the drowning man refuses even to be saved by God, because God has no hands, no face, no body. God is a consciousness – how can consciousness hold his hand?

God is not a person, but only a presence; not a flower, but only a fragrance. How can a fragrance save him? You can enjoy the fragrance when you are saved, but fragrance cannot save you. You can enjoy God as a presence when you are saved, but the presence itself cannot save you.

But the moment the Sufi master says, "I am a master," immediately the man grabs his hand and he says, "This is the right hand. Only a master can save me" – because a master is both. He is a man and he is a god. And of course, he is a friend too. A master is all three rolled into one. He is a friend, but not only a friend. He is a god, but not only a god. In him, god has become embodied; in him, love has reached to its highest peak. He can be a savior.

The story is certainly strange and may baffle anybody. If you have found the master, Felix, then don't be worried about the death of the master. The master never dies. If you have loved, your master will live in your love forever.

And drop this lust for enlightenment, because that is a barrier. Only people who drop the desire for enlightenment ever become enlightened.

And why should you be worried about the future? – I am alive! Rather than being saved by me *right now,* are you asking for an appointment in the future?

Finding the master, in a subtle sense, is finding your enlightenment, because the very presence of the master thrills your whole being, gives you a new freshness. A new breeze passes through you, taking with it all the dust that you have gathered down the centuries.

In fact, there are stories of great disciples like Mahakashyapa who said to Gautam Buddha, "Only on one condition can I become your disciple."

Buddha said, "What condition?"

And Mahakashyapa said, "You have to protect me from enlightenment. Once I am enlightened, I will lose the master, because I will not be a disciple anymore. And at no cost do I want to lose you. I can forget all about enlightenment. You are my enlightenment."

Buddha laughed and said, "Mahakashyapa, you don't know that in this very clear understanding and love, you are giving the indication to me that you will be my first disciple to become enlightened."

And Mahakashyapa was his first disciple to become enlightened. He was very angry, and for a few days he wouldn't even speak to Buddha. Whenever Buddha would pass by his side, he would close his eyes. Finally Buddha said, "Now forget it. Whatever happened, happened. And I am not saying to you to leave me or to go away to spread my message. I will not take any note of your enlightenment. You can remain my disciple."

And there were tears of joy in Mahakashyapa's eyes, and he fell at the feet of Gautam Buddha. He said, "That's what I was afraid of: that perhaps now you won't allow me to touch your feet. And I had warned you before – but neither we listen to you nor you listen to us."

Buddha said, "It is not in my hands to make you enlightened or to prevent you from becoming enlightened. You came with such clarity that I was worried that you were going to become enlightened very soon."

A man who can desire enlightenment and can use the master only as a means does not understand love and does not understand disciplehood.

A master cannot be used.

You can simply try to dissolve into his being as deeply as possible. One day, without any warning, comes enlightenment – suddenly. It is not a gradual process; it does not come in installments. It suddenly comes, and you are gone. Only a pure presence remains. So don't be worried about my death. While I am alive, use these moments to dissolve yourself. And if you can use these moments to dissolve yourself . . . .

And forget enlightenment – otherwise that will remain a continuous hindrance. You just enjoy being here. Dance and sing. What are you going to do with enlightenment? You cannot eat it, you cannot drink it – it is absolutely useless. So just hope that it does not come too soon!

Beloved Bhagwan,

The saying goes: Close your eyes, look inside, and see the beauty. But I love to keep my eyes open. I love to see the people, the places, the things, the lakes, the mountains, the rivers, the streams, the animals and the birds – but most of all I love to see You, Bhagwan.
Is it possible to go inside and see the beauty with open eyes?

Anand Vimal, there is no harm in keeping your eyes open. Love as intensely as possible the mountains, the moon, the sun, the trees . . . love everything existence consists of.

And you want to keep your eyes open because you love to see me too. Nothing is wrong in it, but I have to remind you that there is a far more beautiful land, far more beautiful stars, far more beautiful trees, within you, which you cannot see with open eyes.

And as far as I am concerned, with open eyes you can see only my body. With closed eyes, you will be able to see my being too, which is the very essence of godliness.

So there is no need to have a fixation. And that is the beauty of the eyes. Perhaps you have never thought about it. Your ears are continually open; your eyes are naturally made in such a way that you can close them, you can open them, you can close them, you can open them . . . .

So whenever you want to see the trees and the beauty of a sunset, open your eyes. And when you want to see the beauty of the inner world, close your eyes. And it is good exercise too! You are not renouncing

the outside world; you are simply making the inside and outside both available to you. And when you can have both, why should you have only one? And the inner is qualitatively, and tremendously, superior.

In fact, whatever beauty you find in the outside is just as if you have seen a moon reflected in a lake. The outside is only reflection. The inside is the real – the existential.

There are people who are against looking out. There are religions who are against looking out. In Jainism there are two sects: one sect believes that Mahavira, their great master, used to meditate with closed eyes; and there is another sect which believes that he used to meditate with open eyes. This is the only difference between them. And on this point they have been fighting and arguing for twenty-five centuries.

I was passing by a small place, Dewas, and I saw a Jaina temple with three big locks on it. So I told my chauffeur to stop the car and enquire what has happened to this temple. And I came to know that the temple had not opened for almost fifteen years. The two communities of Jainas had made the temple together, because their number was very small in the village. No single community was capable of making the temple. Otherwise, they make their temples separately.

But they agreed to make one temple, and also agreed about the ownership of Mahavira, the statue inside the temple – that in the morning till twelve, one sect will worship; from twelve to sunset the other sect will worship. First, those people will worship who believe in closed eyes. Because a marble statue . . . either you can make it with open eyes or you can make it with closed eyes. It is not a Japanese doll that you lie down and it closes its eyes; you make it sit and it opens its eyes. A marble statue is very difficult . . . so the statue was made with closed eyes.

Up till twelve the first sect worshiped; after twelve the second sect would place two open eyes, just made with paper, on the marble statue. Then it became their Mahavira. And once in a while . . . there were always fights happening, because somebody from the first sect would go on worshiping after twelve; then the second sect would come in and push him out, and he would shout, "You are disturbing my worship, and worship cannot be done according to the clock. You can wait for a few minutes."

But why should they wait? The agreement was that exactly at twelve they should be out. And the first sect would be worshiping and the second sect would be putting the false eyes on Mahavira. And they would start fighting and boxing with each other . . . . And it is a nonviolent religion – it believes in nonviolence.

And one day things went too far. There was bloodshed. People brought their staffs and started hitting at each other's heads. The police came and the police took them all into custody and they locked the temple. Until the court decides, the lock cannot be opened.

But, fearful that the other sect may break the lock, the first sect also brought another bigger lock. The second sect brought an even bigger lock. So three locks are on it, and the court has not been able to decide yet. Because how to decide whether Mahavira used to meditate with open eyes or closed eyes?

I said to my chauffeur, "If you know the magistrate, you take me to him."

He said, "But why are you getting unnecessarily involved? I always see you unnecessarily getting involved in things, unpopular causes . . . and you jump into them. We should go where we are going."

I said, "Don't bother. You just go to the magistrate."

I reached the magistrate and I asked, "I have come to help you, because you have not been able to decide how Mahavira meditated."

He said, "You can help me?"

I said, "Certainly. Nobody else can help you."

He said, "Then just tell me."

I said, "He always blinked."

You cannot keep your eyes open continuously; neither can you keep your eyes continuously closed. You have to blink; that keeps your eyes fresh. Blinking is a natural process; it is just like the wiper on the windshield on your car. Keep your wiper moving.

Your eyes close and open. They go on keeping themselves fresh, removing all dust.

So, Vimal, both are good. Sometimes meditate with open eyes. Sometimes meditate with closed eyes. But never forget blinking.

Okay, Vimal?

Yes, Bhagwan.

The Thread Of Understanding

Just be here now – no need to understand. I am not a problem, neither am I a hypothesis. I am a living presence. Don't try to understand me.

Otherwise, if you love me you will feel baffled; if you don't love me you will become my enemy. Those are the two possibilities of trying.

If the friend and the enemy both can just be silent with me, understanding will arise on its own. It is a by-product of a silent communion. You don't become knowledgeable, but you are so full of understanding.

But this is a totally different kind of understanding. You have not made any effort; it has showered on you.

Any understanding that comes through your effort can be lost. Perhaps more effort and you may start seeing things in a different light. Perhaps less effort and you will lose the thread of understanding. So there is an understanding which should really only be called knowledgeability, that comes by effort; and there is an understanding which comes not by your effort, but when all efforts are forgotten.

February 12, 1987,   8 a.m.

Beloved Bhagwan,

Nearly eight years ago, during farewell darshan, I was called forward, and You asked me the question, "Anything to say to me?"
I nodded and felt something strong I wanted to say but I could not express a word. You said, "I have heard you."
Today I found out what I wanted to say: I love you.
I have heard myself.

Anand Govind, the most difficult thing is to hear yourself. Your mind is so full of others, there is so much noise, so much traffic of thoughts and feelings and emotions, that the still, small voice of your heart is drowned in it.

It took eight years for you to hear it. Still it is early. There are people who have not heard it even for eighty years; and most people die without hearing their own heart, without hearing that still, small voice.

I remember the moment when I asked you, "Have you anything to say to me?" because I felt in your eyes the stirring of your heart. But you could not hear it. You were certainly aware that there was something you wanted to say – but what it was, was very vague, nebulous.

Now it has become a condensed phenomenon, and your mind has also become more and more silent. You can hear the heart. Rejoice, and be grateful to existence, because you are fortunate, you are blessed. Most people are born with something to say, something to express, something to create, and their heart is continually knocking on the doors of their mind; but the mind is such a chaos, those knocks are not heard.

Once you have started hearing those knocks, it shows two things: your mind is becoming calm and quiet; and second, that you are becoming aware of the deeper things of life.

When I said to you, "I have heard you" – because I could see the tears almost in your eyes – that which was not apparent to you, to your mind, was visible in your eyes. Eyes say so much that language seems to be very poor in comparison. I heard exactly the same thing that you have now heard: I love you.

This is one of the most difficult phenomena: to hear the knock of love – because love does not make a noise; it does not make sounds while it reaches to your mind. It is an absolutely silent experience. You never become aware of the passage from the heart to the mind. It is a long journey.

Physically your heart and mind are not so distant –

a few inches only – but existentially your mind is one polarity, your heart another. And the distance is long. But love walks so silently – just the way spring comes: you cannot hear the footsteps, neither can you see the footprints. Suddenly it is there. Before you hear it, before you become aware of it, the trees have become aware: they have started dancing. Flowers have become aware: they have opened their hearts to the new messenger. Birds have become aware: they have started singing their best songs.

If you have heard . . . and I trust what you are saying, because without hearing it you would have said anything else, but not "I love you." It is a dangerous thing too. It is almost like walking on the razor's edge, because love ultimately means dissolving and melting and disappearing. It is not an ego trip; it is moving towards nothingness, nobodyness. It will not make you somebody special; it will make you absolutely ordinary, just like the trees and the bushes and the rivers and the mountains.

But be careful, because love is not a solid thing that you can possess. On the contrary, love is an energy. You can be possessed by it. And most of the people in the world have killed their love in the effort of possessing it. The moment you possess love, you have destroyed it, you have made it a thing. Then you can decorate your sitting room with a golden cage and a dead lovebird. If you want it to be alive, *you* have to disappear – you cannot exist together.

You have heard, "I love you"; soon the "I" will disappear, only love will remain, because with the "I" disappearing on the one hand, the "you" on the other hand also disappears. Hidden behind this message is still something more, and that is simply "love" – no "I", no "thou." But people are so cunning . . . you cannot imagine. One of my sannyasins, Zareen, asked Swami Ajit Saraswati, who has been in contact with me for almost

twenty years . . . . He was in the commune in America, and the day he departed from there, he promised me that he was simply going to spread my message.

But I have been here for so many days, and he has not been seen. Zareen was puzzled. She enquired of Ajit Saraswati when she met him, "Why are you not coming?" And this is how the cunning mind is: he said, "I love Bhagwan. Bhagwan is in my heart. There is no need to come to the ashram to see him."

Is this the language of love? It is the cunning mind which does not want to accept the truth, that Ajit Saraswati has proved to be a coward. He is afraid of the Hindu chauvinists, of which Poona is full. Coming to me is risky, dangerous. It would have been far more credible if he had said the truth: I am a coward, and I cannot come because I am afraid of the society.

But instead of saying this, he says, "I love Bhagwan so much. He is always in my heart" – that is why there is no need to come here. Then why does he go to his wife? – does he love her or not? Why does he go to his children? – does he love them or not? Why does he go to his friends? – is there any love, or not? Or am I the only exception?

Let him come one day – he will have to come – but I am not going to see him, because I love him so much. He is in my heart. Why should I see him? Even Zareen was shocked – the way he used the word "love." Beautiful words can be destroyed by the cunning mind.

You have heard rightly, because I remember having heard it eight years ago. Now I am saying that you will also one day hear only love: no "I," no "thou" – just an oceanic feeling of love overwhelming you, for all that lives, for the whole existence.

Unless love spreads its wings to the whole sky and covers all the stars, it remains imprisoned – an imprisoned splendor. Do not imprison your love, because that is your very spirit.

Beloved Bhagwan,

You once talked about past lives becoming an everyday experience when we are in Your mystery school. Here my days are so full and Your dance is so infectious that I don't care anymore about anything except dancing with You until my whole body is on fire. Am I losing my marbles?

Devageet, in the first place you never had any marbles. So you are absolutely safe; you cannot lose them.

And even if one has to lose his mind, one is losing the only barrier that divides him from existence. The moment mind is lost, you suddenly find yourself in tune and in harmony.

That is what is happening to you. While dancing, singing madly, you are becoming aware . . . of the songs of the birds, of the dance of the peacocks, of the flight of the eagles. And you are all one.

Charles Darwin was only partially right when he said man has come from the monkeys. But he has stumbled upon a fragment of truth. In my vision, man contains in himself all the animals and all the trees and all the birds. When he dances, the peacock dances in him; when he sings, the nightingale sings in him; when he runs, a deer runs in him. When he is struck with the beauty of a sunrise, he has become a tree. When he dances in the rain, he knows something that goes on happening in the deepest souls of all the trees. When he becomes full of light, all the stars that have been hidden in him have become manifest.

Man is not only one of the species of animals. Man is an immense synthesis of all that is living – alive, dancing, singing, joyful.

Mind is rubbish. The sooner you lose it, the better. Then nothing prevents you from talking to the trees, dancing in the wind, having a dialogue with the stars. Of course, the world will say you are mad; but at least I am here – the majority of one – who says you have come home, you have become sane.

Beloved Bhagwan,

The more I try to understand You, the more You baffle me. Every day You are becoming more and more mysterious. What is this unending mystery?

Anand Maitreya, you say, "The more I try to understand You, the more You baffle me." Stop trying to understand me. Just *be* with me. Trying to understand is creating the problem. Just be here now – no need to understand. I am not a problem, neither am I a hypothesis. I am a living presence. Don't try to understand me.

Otherwise, if you love me you will feel baffled; if you don't love me you will become my enemy. Those are the two possibilities of trying.

If the friend and the enemy both can just be silent with me, understanding will arise on its own. It is a by-product of a silent communion. You don't become knowledgeable, but you are so full of understanding.

knowledgeable, but you are so full of understanding. But this is a totally different kind of understanding. You have not made any effort; it has showered on you.

Any understanding that comes through your effort can be lost. Perhaps more effort and you may start seeing things in a different light. Perhaps less effort and you will lose the thread of understanding. So there is an understanding which should really only be called knowledgeability, that comes by effort; and there is an understanding which comes not by your effort, but when all efforts are forgotten.

Understanding is just like sleep. If you make efforts to go to sleep, it is very difficult to go to sleep. Your very efforts are disturbing. And there are so-called wise people advising others to do this mantra, do this chanting, take a shower or a hot bath – and all these efforts will make you more and more awake.

When people ask me what to do when sleep is not coming, I say, "Go for a long walk in the dark night, alone. Forget all about sleep. If it is not coming, it means it is not needed. And after a long walk in the forest, in your aloneness, you will become relaxed. Or if you cannot go for a long walk, then just close your eyes. But don't make any effort to sleep; just wait for it. Watch from which door it comes. And you will find yourself in the morning waking up saying, 'My God, when did sleep come and from which door?' "

When you are not making any effort, you become relaxed. Effort creates tensions, and you cannot attain to understanding through tensions. Relaxation is the door. Just relax in my presence and there will be no question of bafflement, of any puzzle, of any problem. You will understand, but it will not come as knowledge. It will come more and more like love, which you *know* and yet you know not.

Millions of people have loved, but nobody has been able to define it, because love cannot be translated into knowledge. It is very shy.

You say, "Every day You are becoming more and more mysterious." This is a good symptom. That means you are slowly, slowly coming closer and closer to me. The closer you come to me, the more mysterious you will find me.

And that moment will also come, Maitreya, when not only *I* will be mysterious; you will also be mysterious. And when two mysteries meet, they are not two. There is no demarcation line between two mysteries. Two mysteries always become one, just like two zeros always become one; two nothingnesses always become one.

You are asking, "What is this unending mystery?"
This is life.
This is love.
This is a deep laughter.

Beloved Bhagwan,

You are all the rivers reaching to the ocean, where the sky seems to disappear into the earth – that "there" which is here. At dawn I bathe in the warmth of Your compassionate love and understanding, and when dust settles, one can see the vast firmament reflected in Your eyes, where the distant echoes of unforgettable melodies can be heard in the silence of Your songs.
You are truth, You are love, You are beauty.
And yet all of this, for the one who finds it, is said to be but nothingness.
Beloved master, forgive me if, in the attempt to thank existence for all these blessings of Your presence here, I fall short of something intelligent to say and sound like a poet without poetry. I just don't know anymore. It is all so vast that this heart can only repeat on and on: Thank You.
Buddham Sharanam Gachchhami,
Sangam Sharanam Gachchhami,
Dhammam Sharanam Gachchhami.

Nivedano, don't feel that you fall short of something intelligent to say. All that is really intelligent, is impossible to say. And it is not just a coincidence that whatever you say sounds like poetry, although you are not a poet.

There are poets and there are poets. There are poets who compose poetry; they are composers. Their poetry is shallow. It is only a linguistic and grammatical game. They know the technique of how to create the fallacy of something being poetry. And there are poets who are not even aware of their poetry. They are not composers; but their hearts are so full of love and beauty and truth that whatever they say becomes poetry. It may have the form of prose; that does not matter.

You have to understand this: there are poems which have only the form of poetry, but they are really prose. And there are pieces of prose which have the form of prose, but are really poetry.

Poetry and prose are not a question of form; it is a question of content. Even silence can be poetry. Listen to this silence . . . this silence can defeat any Shakespeare, any Kalidas, any Milton. These birds are not composing poetry. Just the beautiful sun and the beautiful trees are making them explode into singing. They don't know the art of composing poetic pieces. Do you think peacocks go to a school to learn dancing – *kathak* – or cuckoos go to a school of music? What can a school of music teach a cuckoo? A cuckoo is already cuckoo enough.

Whatever your heart is pouring is poetry: "You are all the rivers reaching to the ocean, where the sky seems to disappear into the earth, that 'there' which is here. At dawn I bathe in the warmth of Your compassionate love and understanding, and when dust settles one can see the vast firmament reflected in Your eyes, where the distant echoes of unforgettable melodies can be heard in the silence of Your songs. You are truth, You are love, You are beauty. And yet all of this, for the one who finds it, is said to be but nothingness."

It is said to be but nothingness because anything less than nothing will not do justice to all the songs and the beauty and the truth that are born out of it. What is the womb of a woman, except nothingness? But out of that womb life arises. And where does life disappear after death? You burn the body. Life moves back into nothingness to rest.

"A little rest on the wind," says Almustafa to Almitra, "and another woman will bear me as a child."

Birth is from nothingness, and death takes you back into nothingness. Nothingness is a rest – the ultimate rest. And all that is beautiful in the world, created by man, has come out of nothingness.

When Picasso was asked . . . . He was going to the beach with his canvas and colors and brushes, to paint. One of his girlfriends was with him, and she asked, "What you are going to paint today?" He said, "I don't know." The girl was certainly puzzled. She said, "Then who knows?" He said, "That too I don't know."

The girl said, "Are you going to paint or not?" He said, "Why unnecessarily torture me? I will wait on the beach. If the painting comes out of nothing and wants to be born, I will be a womb to it. I am ready to be a mother to it, but I am not a painter in the sense of one who has a certain idea in the mind and then brings that idea to the painting."

It happened once: a man purchased one of the paintings of Picasso for one million dollars. Of course he wanted to be sure that it was an authentic original, that it was not somebody else's painting, a fake painting – and there are thousands of fake paintings in the world.

But the critic who was helping him to find the best painting in the museum told him, "Don't be worried, because at the time Picasso painted this painting, I was present with him. I am a friend of his. I was a guest in his house. And if you still don't believe me, you come with me to Picasso."

He took the man to Picasso. Picasso looked at the painting, and he said, "It is not original."

The critic could not believe it. He said, "What are you saying? You painted it in front of me."

Even Picasso's secretary said, "That critic is right. You have forgotten. It is *your* painting, your signature."

He said, "I have not forgotten anything. But this is not original, because I have painted the same painting before. That time it came from the beyond. I had no idea what I was painting – only as the painting went on growing did I become aware of it. And that original painting is in a certain museum, you can go and see; you will not find any difference between the two.

"This second painting I *had* to paint because somebody was there who was insisting on buying a painting, and I had no painting. And you cannot provoke the beyond according to your desires; it comes to you on its own. Sometimes months pass and I cannot paint a single thing. And sometimes for months I am painting and painting; the sky goes on pouring like rain.

"So, because the man was rich and I was in need of money and he wanted a painting, I remembered this painting and I painted it. So you are right that *I* painted it. But listen to me: this is only a copy, it is not original. I will not count it as an original Picasso. The original Picasso always comes from the beyond – Picasso is only a medium. In this painting Picasso was the technician, not the painter."

So all the beauty and truth and silence and unforgettable melodies that you hear . . . trust me, they are coming out of nothingness. I don't speak. I am just a hearer amongst you.

"Beloved master, forgive me if, in the attempt to thank existence for all these blessings of Your presence here, I fall short of something intelligent to say, and sound like a poet without poetry." Don't feel sorry – feel blessed that you cannot say anything intelligent, intellectual. On the contrary, your heart comes in and creates poetry.

You know perfectly well you are not a poet by profession; but poetry is not the monopoly of the professionals. The greatest poetry is born not from the professionals, but from those amateur wanderers who don't know what they are doing.

The moment a person becomes an expert, professional, he does not look at the beyond. He simply goes on painting, or creating poetry, or music, or a sculpture through his own mind. It is man-made. And unless something is coming from beyond the man, from beyond the mind –something that is transcendental –it is not poetry.

Don't feel sorry; instead rejoice – that you wanted to say something intelligent, but instead you are talking like a poet without knowing what poetry is. No poet knows what poetry is. Professors of poetry know what poetry is, but they never create a single poem. It is a very strange world, where experts are superficial and where amateurs touch the very depth of existence or the very height of the Himalayas.

"I just don't know anymore." That's great! Ignorance is a cousin-sister of innocence. There is not much difference: ignorance is asleep, innocence is awake. The moment you understand that you don't know anymore, you are coming very close to the innocent heart. Just a little more awareness and you will be awake.

"It is all so vast that this heart can only repeat on and on: Thank You." In fact, every heart in its every beat is doing the same to existence. You have not understood it, because you don't know the language of the heart. This is the beginning of understanding the language of the heart. Each beat is nothing but a thank-you.

One Zen master used to wake up every morning and call loudly, "Bokuju, are you still here?" – that was his own name. And his disciples were very much ashamed: "If somebody hears, they will think you are mad. Why do you do it?"

He said, "In the night, when I go to sleep, I say, 'Bokuju, one does not know whether tomorrow morning you will be able to see the sunrise again . . . the song of the birds, the vast sky, the dance of life.' So when I wake up, the first thing, I want to do is to make certain that Bokuju is still here." So he used to call, "Bokuju, are you still here?" – and then he would say, "Yes, sir!" Then only would he get out of bed.

His disciples said, "This is absolutely insane." He said, "It may be, in your eyes, but not in my eyes – because I am not Bokuju. Bokuju is the name of my body and my personality. After a deep sleep I want to know whether the body is still there or not; otherwise, who is going to get up? And when I hear 'Yes, sir!' then I say, 'That's perfectly good: one day more to live, one day more to sing, one day more to love, one day more to dance.' "

You are right. Because of the poverty of language, of the poverty of philosophy, of the poverty of religion, one cannot do anything better than what for thousands of years . . . . One does not know who said it first:
Buddham Sharanam Gachchhami – I go to the feet of the awakened one.
Sangam Sharanam Gachchhami – I go to the feet of the commune of the awakened one.
Dhammam Sharanam Gachchhami – I go to the ultimate truth of the awakened one.

This is the only prayer possible, because this is nothing but thankfulness, gratitude.

Okay, Vimal?

Yes, Bhagwan.

God Has No Hands

The hand of the master is the hand of the greatest friend you can find; and the hand of the master is the hand of God, because God does not have his own hands – he uses the hands of those who have realized him.

God has no hands; the ordinary friend has no godliness; the master has both. He has a love that transcends any friendship, and his hand is no more his own; his hand belongs to God. It is beautiful that the master's hand is accepted. One would have thought that God's hand would have been accepted. But God does not have any hands; God is only an experience.

Being close to the master, you are close to your greatest lover, your greatest friend; and you are also close to the ultimate truth, which has been known down the ages as God. I call it "godliness," because God gives a wrong idea, as if he is a person. He is only a presence.

The master, perhaps, is the most significant link between this world and that, between the known and the unknowable, between the visible and the invisible. And being close to the master means nothing but being consumed in his fire.

A moment comes . . . you disappear, with all your problems and all your dark nights, and only that which is twenty-four carat gold in you remains.

February 12, 1987,   7 p.m.

Beloved Bhagwan,

You seem to me the only person in the world who never disappoints me, never abandons me, never lies to me, never frustrates me. The love, joy, bliss and ecstasy I sometimes feel inside myself when I feel close to You, feels like the only real thing in the world.

Why is it that I've always to be so frustrated with the outside world before I am ready to look inside?

Anand Tarika, it is easy with me not to be disappointed, not to be frustrated, for the simple reason that you never expect anything from me. The whole problem is: the moment you start expecting, you are bound to be disappointed, frustrated.

With me, your love is not that of expectation, not that of any demand. Whatever I have, I give you – not because you expect it, but because I am so overburdened with it. It is so abundant in me that I have to give – it does not matter to whom; whoever is ready to receive, I am available.

It is not something in me that does not disappoint you; it is something in you that does not expect anything from me. The day you do not expect anything from the world, there will be no frustration for you.

Being with a master, you have to learn just a simple lesson: why you are so ecstatic, why you are so happy. Your happiness, your ecstasy, is not dependent on me; I am no more than an excuse. It is your own. Just behave with the outside world in the same way as you behave with me, and you will be surprised: the same people, the same situations which have been very frustrating,

disappointing, are no more so. On the contrary, they become a tremendous source of nourishment.

It all depends on you – not on me.

That is a fallacy, and if you go to your so-called priests, preachers, they will all say you are happy because of them – because of Jesus Christ, because of Gautam Buddha, because of the great tradition you belong to. They go on poisoning you. It is very fulfilling to their egos that so many people are happy because of them. The reality is – you are not happy because of anybody else.

At least I can say to you that you are not ecstatic because of me. You are ecstatic because you don't have any expectations from me. Learn the lesson, and use it in the outside world, in your other relationships. Don't expect, don't demand. Give as much as you can, and never even think of your reward.

Even your greatest saints are not in the purest state of consciousness; they are hoping and expecting that for all their austerities, for all their so-called virtues, they will be immensely rewarded in the other world.

I want you to remember it: all these saints are going

to be very disappointed in the other world. Here, they suffer in order to be fulfilled in the other world; and in the other world they will suffer because the mind that demands, the mind that expects, can never be blissful – either in this world or in any other world.

You say, "You seem to be the only person in the world who never disappoints me." I may be the only person in the world with whom you don't have any expectations. Just try . . . and you will find many people who will not disappoint you. The seeds of disappointment are in your expectations. There may be a few people even here who may be disappointed in me, if they are carrying in their unconscious some desire, some longing that should be fulfilled.

I am not going to fulfill anybody's expectations.
I am not here to fulfill *your* expectations.
Neither are you here to fulfill my expectations.
I have to be myself, and you have to be yourself.
We create bridges of expectations, not knowing that expectation can never become a bridge – it always becomes a wall. The more you expect, the more frustrated you are.

Don't expect anything, and suddenly you find a tremendous contentment arising within your own self. This is the essential core of religion.

But even a man like Jesus was expecting on the cross that God was going to do some miracle, and the miracle was not happening. Naturally, he must have felt very disappointed in the God for whom he was sacrificing his whole life. And he shouted at the sky, "Father, have you forsaken me?" This is the language of expectation and demand. Then, even God is going to disappoint you.

But he must have been a man of sharp intelligence. He must have understood that he was carrying a wrong desire. You cannot demand anything from existence. You can only give. Existence returns a thousandfold, but not according to your expectation. He must have seen that there has been, in his unconscious, a demand. He dropped the demand at the last moment. At the very last moment he looked again at the sky and said,

"Father, thy will be done, not mine." And a great serenity and silence descended upon the man, even though he was suffering on the cross.

In a certain way, everybody is suffering. The only difference is that in the case of Jesus the cross was made by other people, and he was crucified. In your case, you are the cross, you are the crucifier, and you are the crucified. Except you, everything else is irrelevant. If you want to get out of your miseries, your frustrations – just drop expecting. Who told you that you have a right to expect? But we are all carrying subtle expectations in every relationship, and then small things become frustrations.

You are saying, "You never abandon me." I cannot, because it is not that I have imprisoned you – it is not in my hands either to imprison you or to make you free. You are here of your own accord, and you can leave at any moment. Within you is the whole source of your being here, or going away. I have never abandoned anyone, for the simple reason that I don't dominate anybody.

Nobody is my possession.

People have to abandon each other because the possession becomes too heavy; the burden becomes intolerable. It is almost like – you can say, "You never divorce me." Even if I want to divorce you, no court is going to accept my application because I've never married you. Who am I divorcing? Divorce necessarily has to be preceded by marriage, and vice versa: marriage necessarily brings divorce in. Whether you are courageous enough to go through the whole process or remain in limbo, it is going to be a suffering.

You say, "You never lie to me." Why should I lie to you? I don't have any business with you. I am not asking you to give anything; on the contrary, I am simply asking you to receive something. I am not a beggar. In all your relationships, you are all beggars – everybody wants to get something from the other.

I say emphatically: I am an emperor. I don't ask you to give me anything. I am available; if you want to take something from me, I will be grateful to you.

Remember, you need not even be grateful to me, because that too becomes a deep expectation.

Even if you are waiting for somebody to say, "Thank you" to you, you are bound to feel frustrated. I don't want any gratitude. On the contrary, I am grateful to you because you were so generous in receiving. You have heard of the generosity of giving; you have not heard of the generosity of receiving.

Tarika, the love, joy, bliss and ecstasy you sometimes feel inside yourself when you feel close to me, "feels like the only real thing in the world." It is. The purity of love is the only real thing in the world – uncontaminated, unpolluted by any desires. ~~When love is pure, you are in paradise. Your paradise is within you. Just let your love be absolutely pure.~~

Being close to me is simply a taste of the only real thing in the world. It is not the whole thing, but even the taste is so fulfilling. Just think: the moment you become just a flame of love, you will know reality in its wholeness.

Beloved Bhagwan,

You have caught eternity in Your net of silence and You shower us with the diamonds of Your clarity. Enlightenment and bliss seem to be so close, buddhahood just a step away, when You speak to us. So why do I behave like a grumpy gorilla when I am with my girlfriend?

Devageet, ~~being with a girlfriend, everybody behaves like a gorilla. Otherwise, the girlfriends feel very much frustrated. The more you behave like a gorilla, the more they feel satisfied.~~ Just watch: ~~your behaving like a gorilla is such a joy, no girlfriend is going to miss it. If you behave very gentlemanly, the girlfriend is going to be very frustrated.~~

But enlightenment is still one step away from the gorilla. It makes no difference where you are, enlightenment is always at a constant distance of one step. Just get out of the gorilla and you are enlightened.

Sometimes it is easier to get out of the gorilla – because who wants to be a gorilla? It is more difficult if you are President Ronald Reagan or a prime minister of a country or the richest man in the world. It is more difficult for you to get out of that role – these are all roles played on the stage of life's drama.

~~Enlightenment becomes easier when you are playing a role which you don't like;~~ you hate it from your very guts – ~~but because of the girlfriend, you have~~ to play the role. The girlfriend is also trying to play her role – but two gorillas in one bed will be very difficult to contain; so man has managed that the girl should be ladylike, with closed eyes, lying almost dead, so he can jump like a gorilla all over the bed.

But you don't like the role. It would be good for you to have a camera fixed up to film you when you behave like a gorilla. And later on, seeing it, you will feel so ashamed: What are you doing? What kind of idiot are you? It is good that people put the light off. And every society in the past has been against people making love in the open, on the sea beach, or in the park. Every society in the past has been very much against it, for the simple reason that anybody behaving like a gorilla on the sea beach reminds every man on the beach that, "this is what I am also doing. Just, I do it in the darkness of the night."

But, Devageet, the step from being a gorilla to enlightenment is just a single step of ~~becoming aware of what you are doing,~~ and slipping out of your act just the way a snake slips out of its old skin. Jump out of the bed and become a buddha. Tonight, try it! Just in the middle of being a gorilla, immediately jump out of the bed, sit in a lotus posture and become a buddha! And I promise you, your girlfriend will be even more blissful and more happy: "At last some sense has happened to you." And you will find it a surprising fact that the distance is so close. You can become in your sleep a gorilla; you can become in your sleep a president; you can become in your sleep the richest man – but these are all dreams.

In fact, when you become a gorilla in your sleep, it becomes a nightmare. All love affairs turn into nightmares. And to get up from the nightmare also seems very difficult, but people only try to get up when their dreams start turning into nightmares. If the dream goes on, sweet, beautiful – who wants to get up?

It is good that you have recognized one thing – that you behave like a gorilla. This is a great understanding. Now, tonight, take the first step of becoming enlightened; and tomorrow morning everybody will see that Devageet – who used to be a gorilla – has become enlightened. Miracles still happen.

Beloved Bhagwan,

Problems seem to disappear into thin air. They keep trying to come, but cannot take root; and if for a few moments one settles, it soon looks ridiculous, so fades away. Does the light you share with us dispel even the dark night of the soul? What is the dark night of the soul? Is it really true?

Prem Shunyo, problems are never solved. They remain in different forms; you go on solving them, and they go on appearing in different forms. That is the way of philosophy where every question that was asked at the very beginning of human thinking, is still asked. Millions of solutions have been proposed, but the problem is as fresh and as pertinent as ever.

All the philosophers of the world have not even been able to make a dent in the problem – because they have moved in a wrong way. Problems are not to be solved; problems need to be dissolved, and that is a totally different path – the path of the mystics. They don't solve the problems, they simply create devices in which problems disappear into thin air.

One great philosopher came to Gautam Buddha. He was known all over the country for his great commentaries on the *Vedas* and the *Upanishads* and the *Gita*. He had thousands of followers. He had brought his most scholarly followers with him. Still, the number was big enough – five hundred scholars followed him. They were going to challenge Gautam Buddha; and the man had challenged many, many scholars, professors, learned people – and he had defeated them. This was a routine thing in India – that scholars used to move from town to town, challenging; and if anybody who accepted their challenge was defeated, he had to become their follower; or if the scholar was defeated, he had to become *their* follower with all his followers. The country had remained for almost five thousand years in a very strange philosophical atmosphere.

This man came to Gautam Buddha and said, "I have come here to challenge you. I want to know what is your definition of truth, and from there we can begin our discussion. I have brought with me my five hundred most scholarly followers. If you win we will all become your disciples, but if you are defeated, then this is the condition: you, with all your disciples, will have to become my disciple."

Gautam Buddha said, "There is no problem in it. Before we begin the discussion, I want to ask one question. It is not part of the discussion; it is just to be acquainted with each other. Have you asked this question of other scholars and so-called wise people?"

He said, "Yes, I have asked thousands of people. Many of them are my followers, because I defeated them."

Gautam Buddha said, "What have you gained? Have you come to know the truth by discussing it? Have you come to know the truth by defeating these people? One thing is certain: that you are logically more clever, sharper, than these other people. But it does not prove that you know what truth is – and even if you defeat me, you will not know what truth is. Do you want to know the truth, or simply to waste your life in defeating people?"

The man had never been faced with such a question. He said, "I really want to know the truth."

"Then," Buddha said, "discussion is not going to help; because the truth that I know cannot be brought into words – and you don't know the truth. Otherwise, what was the need to travel thousands of miles to come to me?

"I suggest one thing: you just sit by my side. For two years you have to remain silent – no question, no speaking, and relax so totally that slowly, slowly even your thoughts disappear. When two years are over, I will remind you that now we can enter into the discussion: you can ask your question."

At that very time, Mahakashyapa, who was sitting under a tree, started laughing loudly. The man said, "Is this man mad?"

Buddha said, "He used to be, but now he is not."

The man said, "Then why suddenly . . . for no reason . . . ? He is sitting alone, and laughing so loudly . . . what has happened?"

Buddha said, "You yourself can ask."

And he asked Mahakashyapa. Mahakashyapa said, "If you really want to ask the question, ask *now*. This man is a great deceiver. This is the way he deceived me. After two years, when all thoughts have disappeared and the inner silence has blossomed, you will not ask anything – and he will not answer, of course. He has not answered me. But I cannot blame him – because I cannot ask the question. I know the answer – but he has not answered me. He is tricky.

"So I laugh: again, another idiot is going to fall into the trap. I have suffered . . . . Two years of silence . . . everything disappears. Who cares about questions? Such well-being, such ecstasy, such joy arises. Who bothers about conquering in a discussion . . . defeating somebody? One has found the greatest treasure, and the greatest kingdom, within oneself. But it is up to you. Right now he will not answer. And after two years you will not ask."

Buddha said, "It is up to you. If you are really in search of the truth, then sit silently by my side. Thousands of people will come and go . . . . Your whole effort for two years is only to be silent, and more silent."

And the man became silent. He forgot even to count the days. When two years had passed, he was not aware. It was Gautam Buddha himself who reminded him: "I know that you have forgotten the calendar. Two years have passed. This is the day two years ago that you came. Do you have any question?"

The man had tears of joy in his eyes, and he said, "You have answered everything, although I have not questioned. This is a strange game that you played – you have not discussed with me, and yet I am defeated. You have not uttered a single word – and you are victorious. But the most mysterious thing is that in *your* victory is *my* victory – because in this two years' silence not only have thoughts disappeared; even the idea of myself, the idea of the ego, has dissolved."

This is the way of the mystic: where problems dissolve, disappear into thin air. They are never answered.

Shunyo, you are right when you say, "It seems that problems are disappearing into thin air. They keep trying to come, but cannot take root." They are just old customers; out of old habit they go on coming back. But because you are no longer interested in them – you don't give them any juice anymore – they cannot take root in you. They come from one side, and they get out from another side.

"And if for a moment one settles, it soon looks ridiculous, so fades away." Except silence, everything will look ridiculous . . . because only in silence do you become part of the immensity of reality.

Any idea, howsoever beautiful, divides you from reality, cuts you away from the whole. And that is the misery of man . . . just as if a tree has been cut from its roots, soon it will start dying; it cannot live without roots.

Sometimes you may not be so alert and some idea may settle for a moment; but the moment your awareness returns, it looks so ridiculous. You need not throw it away – the very understanding that it is ridiculous is enough to kill it.

"Does the light You share with us dispel even the dark night of the soul?" What do you think, Shunyo? My light cannot dispel the darkness that surrounds you on the outside – otherwise you will not have the chance to enjoy the electric failures. It is so beautiful when once in a while the electricity fails and you all are waiting in silence . . . a great peace that passeth understanding envelops you.

Certainly, my light cannot dispel the outside darkness. To dispel the outside darkness, you need an outside light. My light is of the inner; it can only dispel your inner darkness.

So even when the light fails, and you are sitting in darkness, you are connected with me by far more subtle rays of light, which are not visible to the eyes; but your heart feels them, dances with them. So many people suddenly become one . . . or even better: so many people suddenly disappear. There is only silence. I think that the electric failures must be managed by existence itself to give you some glimpses of the inner light.

You are asking, "What is the dark night of the soul? Is it really true?" First, the dark night of the soul is a state of your being where you are cut off from the whole – because the source of light and life and laughter . . . all comes from the source that is beyond you. You are not the source of your own life.

And there are moments when you are cut off completely. Because of your jealousy, you are surrounded by a poisonous cloud, and you are cut off from the whole – because of your anger, because of your violent rage. And there are so many things which cut you off from the whole.

Anything that cuts you off from the whole creates the dark night of the soul. So it can be said that to be separate from the whole is to be in darkness; and to be one with the whole is to be in light. And it is an existential phenomenon – it is real.

There are very few significant words uttered in the world: amongst those few words are three small sentences from the *Upanishads*. Those sentences can become a bridge to the divine. Nobody knows who uttered those sentences first. Perhaps thousands of mystics may have uttered them again and again – not repeating, but on their own – and slowly, slowly they became condensed.

Those three sentences are: Lead me from darkness to light; lead me from death to deathlessness . . . . They appear as if they are a prayer, but they are not a prayer because the *Upanishads* don't have a god. They are invocations to existence itself.

Lead me from the unreal to the real.
Lead me from darkness to light. And,
Lead me from death to deathlessness.

In these three small sentences is contained the whole message of the East, a message that can never be out of date – which will always remain significant, meaningful, in every age, in every time. I cannot conceive of any time, any age in the future when these three statements will have become out of date. When all your scriptures may have become out of date, these three statements will still remain significant.

In Sanskrit they are very beautiful, because Sanskrit

is a very poetic language – *asto ma sat gamaya:* from the false to the real; *mrityorma amratam gamaya:* from death to deathlessness . . . . Just within three words a sentence is complete.

In fact, all the three sentences are three aspects of one reality. And there is no question of any belief; there is no question of becoming part of an organized religion – and whatever is said is the very longing of every human soul. Can you find a human soul which is not longing for light, not longing for eternal life, not longing for ultimate truth?

Being close to a master there is a possibility that you may catch his health and his wholeness. People think that only sicknesses can be contagious; that is a half truth. Why can't wholeness, well- being, blissfulness, ecstasy, be contagious? You just have to be open, available, fearless. Then truth can enter you and can wake up your own truth, which is fast asleep. Then light can enter you and enkindle your own flame. Then something of the eternal can touch you and destroy your fear of death, and can open your eyes about your own being as part of eternity.

Just the other day I was telling you about the Sufi story: The man is drowning and he refuses the hand of the friend, and he refuses the hand of God – but he accepts the hand of the master. There are so many implications in this story. The hand of the master is the hand of the greatest friend you can find; and the hand of the master is the hand of God, because God does not have his own hands – he uses the hands of those who have realized him.

God has no hands; the ordinary friend has no godliness; the master has both. He has a love that transcends any friendship, and his hand is no more his own; his hand belongs to God. It is beautiful that the master's hand is accepted. One would have thought that God's hand would have been accepted. But God does not have any hands; God is only an experience.

Being close to the master, you are close to your greatest lover, your greatest friend; and you are also close to the ultimate truth, which has been known down the ages as God. I call it "godliness," because God gives a wrong idea, as if he is a person. He is only a presence.

The master, perhaps, is the most significant link between this world and that; between the known and the unknowable; between the visible and the invisible. And being close to the master means nothing but being consumed in his fire.

A moment comes . . . you disappear, with all your problems and all your dark nights, and only that which is twenty-four carat gold in you remains.

Beloved Bhagwan,

Where am I?

My God! Om Saraswati, you are not. You are nowhere. You have never been – and you will never be. Om Saraswati is just a name given to a nameless reality for utilitarian purposes. Otherwise, you are just a presence.

Every child is born as a presence, with no name, with no address. And becoming a sannyasin is a second birth, far deeper and far greater than the first. In the first, at least you are a body. You may not have a name, you may not have an address; but you have an abode – in the body.

The moment you become a sannyasin, you have

dropped the idea of being a body, too. Now you are just pure consciousness – either everywhere or nowhere. Both the words mean the same. You can choose. You can choose to be everywhere, or you can choose to be nowhere. In either case, you are not limited anymore; you don't have any boundary, you cannot be caught hold of.

It is a very special question . . . because people have been asking thousands of times: Who am I? Om Saraswati is a rare genius – he is asking, "Where am I?"

Nowhere. Or, if you cannot read such a big word – 'nowhere' – then cut it in two: 'now,' 'here.' To me, both are acceptable. But remember that your inner being is without any limits – even the sky is not the limit. So everything can be in you – the faraway stars can be within you – but you are not within any cage, however big, however beautiful, however valuable.

Realization of this truth – that I am 'everywhere,' or 'nowhere,' or 'now,' 'here' – I call enlightenment. And I am giving you three choices; three choices have never been given by any mystic before. My own choice is 'now,' 'here.' But I am not addicted to any certain opinion. 'Nowhere' will do. But if a negative statement like 'nowhere' makes you afraid, then 'everywhere' will do.

Hence, drop finding where you are; start looking for who you are. The where is not important; the who is important – and if you know who you are, you will know where you are.

In my humble opinion, you will find it *now, here*.

Beloved Bhagwan,

During my whole life, I always thought that I loved somebody. Now, being here for the first time with You, I ask myself: Have I ever really been in love? Am I even *able* to love? Am I able to love You? Or has life brought me to a point where happiness in love does not happen anymore?

Anand Tosha, the basic fallacy that you are carrying within you is that you always loved somebody. This is one of the most significant things about all human beings; their love is always *for* somebody, it is addressed – and the moment you address your love, you destroy it. It is as if you are saying, "I will breathe only for you – and when you are not there, then how can I breathe?"

Love should be like breathing. It should be just a quality in you – wherever you are, with whomsoever you are, or even if you are alone, love goes on overflowing from you. It is not a question of being in love with someone – it is a question of being love.

People are frustrated in their love experiences, not because something is wrong with love . . . they narrow down love to such a point that the ocean of love cannot remain there. You cannot contain the ocean – it is not a small stream; love is your whole being – love is your godliness. One should think in terms of whether one is loving or not. The question of the object of love does not arise. With your wife, you love your wife; with your children, you love your children; with your servants, you love your servants; with your friends, you love your friends; with the trees, you love the trees; with the ocean, you love the ocean.

You *are* love.

Love is not dependent on the object, but is a radiation of your subjectivity – a radiation of your soul. And the vaster the radiation, the greater is your soul. The wider spread are the wings of your love, the bigger is the sky of your being.

Anand Tosha, you have lived under a common fallacy of all human beings. Now you are asking, "Am I able to love You?" – again, the same fallacy.

Just ask: Am I able to become love?

When you are in my presence, you need not think of loving *me;* otherwise, you have not come out of your ordinary fallacies. Here, you have to learn . . . just being loving. Of course your love will reach me too; it will reach others too. It will be a vibe surrounding you, spreading all over, and if so many people are simply broadcasting their love, their song, their ecstasy, the whole place becomes a temple. There is no other way of making a temple. Then the whole area is filled with a new kind of energy, and nobody is at a loss – because on you is showering the love of so many people: on each single person, so many people's love is showering.

Drop that fallacy. And because of that fallacy, another question arises in you: " . . . or has life brought me to the point where happiness in love does not happen anymore?" Life is nothing but an opportunity for love to blossom. If you are alive, the opportunity is there – even to the last breath. You may have missed your whole life: just the last breath, the last moment on the earth, if you can be love, you have not missed anything – because a single moment of love is equal to the whole eternity of love.

Okay, Vimal?

Yes, Bhagwan.

The Mind Has No Reverse Gear

A master finds a way through all your defenses to the very core of your being. And the whole work of the master is to wake you up. But man's unconsciousness is such that he can even dream that he is awake and continue to sleep. Your mind is so rooted in doubt, suspicion, distrust, that even if I really come to your place, the first idea in your mind will be: is it true? Doubts grow in the mind just like leaves grow on the trees. You have to put a full stop to your doubting mind, and immediately your trusting heart takes charge.

These are the qualities: mind is doubt, the heart is trust. Mind is imagination, thinking, hallucination. Heart is only love. And you can see the whole world through the mind, except yourself – because you are behind the mind, and the mind has no reverse gear. You just cannot go backwards. Hence, the mind has to be completely dropped; only then does your heart, for the first time, start functioning in its totality.

February 13, 1987,   8 a.m.

Beloved Bhagwan,

Last night I woke as a mosquito screamed in my ear. I looked at him and he had Your face.
I said, "My God!" and You replied, "That's right!" I said, "I must be dreaming."
You said, "That's what I keep telling you."
I said, "Bhagwan, this is going too far."
You said, "That's true. With me, you only start the journey
when you go too far."
And then You flew right through my mosquito net, laughing at my flimsy defenses.
On the other side You stopped, looked at me again, and said,
"I'm going to bug you until you wake up."
And then You were gone. Bhagwan, did it really happen?

Devageet, it really did happen. Don't mistrust your dream. This is the situation: all your defenses are nothing but mosquito nets – and you can keep out of your mosquito nets only mosquitoes who are not masters.

A master finds a way through all your defenses to the very core of your being. And the whole work of the master is to wake you up. But man's unconsciousness is such that he can even dream that he is awake and continue to sleep.

Your mind is so rooted in doubt, suspicion, distrust, that even if I really come to your place, the first idea in your mind will be: is it true? Doubts grow in the mind just like leaves grow on the trees. You have to put a full stop to your doubting mind, and immediately your trusting heart takes charge.

These are the qualities: mind is doubt, the heart is trust. Mind is imagination, thinking, hallucination. Heart is only love. And you can see the whole world through the mind, except yourself – because you are behind the mind, and the mind has no reverse gear. You just cannot go backwards. Hence, the mind has to be completely dropped; only then does your heart, for the first time, start functioning in its totality.

I am reminded of a great king, Prasenjita, who had come to see Gautam Buddha. As he was coming, he found in his garden a very beautiful lotus flower. He thought, "It will be a good present to put at the feet of Gautam Buddha."

But his wife said, "It is better you bring out from

your treasures . . . . You have the best diamond in the country – a flower is just momentary. And love for Buddha and respect for Buddha are like a diamond that is forever."

So he said, "I will take both."

And one of the most significant things happened. When Prasenjita offered the flower to Gautam Buddha, he said, "Drop it!"

There were ten thousand sannyasins present, in absolute silence, because it was a great meeting – a meeting between a great emperor and their master. And they could not understand why Buddha said, "Drop it!"

Prasenjita thought, "Perhaps my wife was right. A flower is, after all, just for a moment." So he dropped the flower, and with the other hand he offered the best diamond of the country, thinking that it should be accepted now.

Buddha smiled and again said, "Drop it!" This was too much; but because Buddha was saying 'drop it' – it was his most precious diamond – still, because of Buddha and ten thousand people watching, he dropped it on the ground. Then he was standing with empty hands, and Buddha said a third time, "Will you listen to me or not? Drop it!"

He looked at his hands. He had nothing to drop. The flower is dropped, the diamond is dropped. One of Buddha's very intimate disciples, Mahakashyapa, said, "Prasenjita, you have not understood what he is saying. He is not concerned with the flower, he is not concerned with the diamond. He is concerned with you. Drop yourself."

Unless you drop yourself, nothing is dropped. And the moment you drop yourself, the ego, the idea of "I," all the doors of existence open to you.

Devageet, drop the mind and start functioning from the heart. And whenever there is a question of choice, the heart has to be chosen. The mind is very rational; the heart knows nothing of reason. But I am saying choose the heart, because the heart is just in between the mind and your being. Without passing through the heart you cannot reach to your own center.

So your dream brings a message to you, that you cannot protect yourself with any kind of defenses. It is better to drop all defenses; all defenses belong to the mind. The heart is open; it has no defenses. And that's why it has the great opportunity of becoming a door to your very soul.

Beloved Bhagwan,

This morning, again, as so often before, the questions were so much my questions that I applied Your beautiful answers to myself. Why do I not ask them myself?

Deva Gita, first I will answer for all, although the question is yours, and second I will answer you.

I would like to answer all . . . that there are many who are in the same situation. They have questions, but they do not ask. The wrong reason is that they are afraid to expose themselves.

Your question is not just a question, it is accepting ignorance. It is opening your wounds, which you have covered very cleverly, not only from the eyes of others, but from yourself too. You have almost forgotten them. They have faded far away as dreams, but they are still there – covered or uncovered. In fact, covered they are more dangerous, because you cannot allow them to heal. They need the wind, they need the sun, they need to be open to existence. Without that opening there is no healing. But nobody wants to accept a simple fact: I am ignorant. I don't know.

Your question brings your ignorance to the surface. If this is the reason why you are not asking, this is a wrong reason. But there is a possibility of a right reason too.

As far as Gita is concerned, she has been with me for a long time, and perhaps this is the first time she has asked. Her reason for not asking is that whether she asks it or not, I am always giving the answer while I am answering somebody else's question. And slowly, slowly a great trust has arisen in her that there is no need to ask. If an answer is needed, it will be given. To whom it is given does not matter. If it is relevant to *your* question, you have received the answer.

Hence, the desire to ask has disappeared. You have been able to understand a very significant factor: that before you ask the question, the master knows the question. Whether you ask it or not does not make much difference. He will answer it in some way or other.

Secondly, listening to all the questions asked by other people, you have also become aware that the real thing is not the answer. The real thing is dissolving the question. For the answer you have to depend on somebody else; but for dissolving the question, dropping the question, you are absolutely independent.

Why go on carrying questions? Drop them – because they are wounds in your soul.

And remember, by dropping the questions you will not become ignorant, neither will you become knowledgeable. You will become innocent, just a pillar of silence – with no thoughts stirring your peace, disturbing your being, with no ripples on your consciousness. And this is the answer to all the questions. Questions can be millions, but the answer is one, and that answer is to be questionless.

Those who have been listening to me for years – there are many who have never asked, for the simple reason that I am not answering questions, I am destroying questions. That kind of work you can do yourself. Because you are not courageous enough to destroy them, you need my help. Just a little courage . . . drop the questions, and then you *are* the answer. Your innocence is the answer. The answer does not come in words. It comes as ecstasy, as peace, as serenity, as centering, as maturity.

And that is the difference between a teacher and a master. The teacher answers your question; the master destroys it. The teacher makes you more knowledgeable; the master helps you to become a child again – full of wonder and innocence. That is happening to you, and this is the greatest thing in existence that can happen to a person: being reborn in this very life as innocence.

Beloved Bhagwan,

Last night I read this quote from Krishnamurti:
"Analysis cannot lead to understanding or insight – observation and not analysis!"
The first years running groups here in Poona, it was mainly problem-oriented. It felt like a big cleanup.
In Rancho Rajneesh somehow I knew therapy was really finished,
yet I did not know how to bring meditation into the group room.
I was still focusing on the dark side and too scared to really move into the unknown.
Being here now, for the first time I get a glimpse that through meditation, observing, and simplifying,
everything that is in the way slowly dissolves by allowing the lightness to shine within. And without
doing anything, suddenly the click happens. Everything is light and playful, and with it comes an
incredible feeling of preciousness and gratitude that we can all be here with You at this time.

Prem Turiya, J. Krishnamurti is right. Analysis cannot lead to understanding or insight.

First, analysis is something like . . . you break a mirror into a thousand pieces, but each small piece of mirror reflects you exactly – as the whole mirror used to reflect you. Instead of one reflection, now you have one thousand reflections.

So I would like to say to you that J. Krishnamurti is not only right . . . he is only half right. Analysis cannot lead to understanding or insight; on the contrary, analysis will lead you to thousands of reflections of the same problem. In the place where there was one problem, now there are a thousand problems. You have broken the glass. You will be more puzzled than you have been ever before.

And secondly, the analysis is being done by somebody else. And analysis is not a science; it is just a hunch. The same problem . . . you go and be analyzed by Sigmund Freud and the conclusion of his analysis is not going to be the same as it would have been if you had gone to Carl Gustav Jung or to Alfred Adler or to Assagioli. And now there are thousands of schools, each pretending that they have found the fundamental truth. They have all found different pieces of the mirror.

Analysis simply breaks the mirror into parts. Analysis is perfect as far as objects are concerned.

Dissection, analysis – that's the only way to find out the truth about the objects that surround you. But you are not an object.

And I have not used the metaphor of the mirror without any reason. Your consciousness is a mirror. It reflects the whole world, just as your eyes are mirrors and they reflect the world. The eyes carry the impressions inside, and your consciousness reflects whatever the eyes bring to it. Your consciousness is your deeper eyesight. No eye specialist will suggest that to understand the eyes one has to dissect them into pieces. That will be destroying them.

In Jaipur, in India, there is a palace made by the same man who created the city of Jaipur, Maharaja Jai Singh. Perhaps Jaipur is the only city in India which is planned. And Jai Singh's whole idea was to create a city which is far more beautiful than Paris. He was almost succeeding, but he died in the middle of the process – only half the city was made.

But still, it shows signs that if he had lived he would have defeated Paris, certainly. It has a beauty of its own kind: very broad roads, which no old city can have, neither Paris, nor London, nor New York – very straight roads that you can see . . . they go for miles; and on both sides of the road all the houses are made of the same red stone – no two houses are different. It gives a very different feeling, as if the whole city is one house.

And while Jai Singh was alive, only one color, the color of the red stone, could be used to paint anything in the city. It seems that Jaipur is the only city which can be called, amongst cities, a sannyasin. On both sides of the road, on the pavement . . . for miles all the pavements are similar; but they are all covered, so even in hot summer or in the rains, you need not take an umbrella with you – there is no need.

Simple, very simple architecture, but absolutely the same all over the city. It was unfortunate that he died – and his successors were worried that he had been putting too much money into the city. The royal treasury was almost empty. But Jai Singh was a very proud man. He had asked loans from all over the world from great banks, and he was going to complete the city. Inside Jai Singh's palace there is a small temple. That is the only place which he has not made similar to the whole city, because it is a temple, and a temple of God should be different from the abodes of man. It is made of small pieces of mirror.

It happened once that in the evening, when the priest closed the door, he forgot to look inside for a dog that had entered. All the worshipers were gone, but the dog could not get out. He was very much puzzled, because he saw so many dogs all around, reflected in thousands of mirrors.

The priest locked the temple and went home. The dog barked, fought, hit his own head against the walls, thinking that he is fighting with other dogs. And naturally, when he barked, the other dog reflected in the mirror also barked. When he approached him, that dog also approached. But he was alone – surrounded by thousands of dogs. Still he fought, and in the morning was found dead.

The gardener said, "The whole night he was fighting inside, but we don't have the key. The key is with the priest. And we knew what was happening: he was surrounded by reflections and he was taking those reflections for reality."

Analysis does not bring any transformation or understanding. It simply analyzes your mind, which is nothing but a reflector. Instead of one problem you find a thousand problems; as your analysis grows, more and more problems come up.

There are people who have been in psychoanalysis for fifteen years continuously, but there is not a single person in the whole world who is completely psychoanalyzed. In fact, there will never be any man in the world who is completely psychoanalyzed. You can go on and on, but mind is a reflector. Your analysis, rather than bringing understanding, only brings more problems.

It is not a coincidence that more psychoanalysts go mad than any other profession, more psychoanalysts commit suicide than any other profession. Almost all the psychoanalysts sooner or later go to other psychoanalysts to be psychoanalyzed – and these people think they are bringing understanding to humanity!

Krishnamurti is right, that analysis cannot lead to understanding or insight. You go to one psychoanalyst and he has a certain conception which he imposes upon your mind. It does not matter what your dream is, Sigmund Freud is going to reduce it to something sexual. In fact, he is obsessed with sexuality, he is sick. He is almost in the same position . . . .

I have heard: psychoanalysis was being done upon a man who was going insane. He was brought to the psychoanalyst's office. Just to figure out what kind of man he was, the psychoanalyst drew a line on a paper and asked the man . . . . But the man was keeping his eyes closed. He said, "Keep it away, no obscenity." The psychoanalyst said, "Obscenity? Does this line remind you of sex?" He said, "Yes, of what else can it remind me? And your mind is dirty. I have come here to be helped. Is this help?"

The psychoanalyst said, "Wait." He made a triangle, and the man turned his chair to the other side. He said, "This is too much. If you do anything more I will hit you. Forget all about analysis. You are mad – *you* need psychoanalysis. You have become even more obscene.

First it was a male genital, now it is a female vagina. You idiot! – you think you are a psychoanalyst?"

The psychoanalyst was completely at a loss. He said, "Forget all about these, just look out of the window." A camel was passing and he asked, "What does that camel remind you of?" He said, "Why are you torturing me? A camel always reminds me of sex and nothing else." The psychoanalyst said, "This is strange!"

He said, "Nothing is strange . . . because everything reminds me of sex. It is not a question of a camel, or an elephant, or a man, or a woman, or a tree – it does not matter. Everything reminds me of sex."

And this was the situation of Sigmund Freud himself, the founder of psychoanalysis. Whatever kind of dream you brought to him to be analyzed, or thoughts to be analyzed, he would manage to reduce it to repressed sexuality.

But if you go to Alfred Adler, sex will not be mentioned at all – the same dream, the same problem. Alfred Adler was obsessed with another idea: will-to-power. He will reduce everything, even sex . . . . You can bring him a purely sexual dream – no psychoanalysis is needed, no interpretation is needed, the dream is simply that you are making love to a woman – and still Alfred Adler will say this is will-to-power. This is will-to-power, because the man is on top and the woman is below him. That's what every man wants.

If you go to Carl Gustav Jung, he will not talk about will-to-power, he will not talk about sex, he will talk about your past lives – that this dream comes from some experience in your past life.

Psychoanalysis is not a science. These people were very clever intellectuals, argumentative, rational. They could manage to prove anything. And the poor patient has not come to discuss philosophy or to discuss the reasonability of the conclusion; he has come there to be cured. He does not bother what the conclusion is – "Just show me the cure."

But psychoanalysis has no cure. "Bring more and more dreams, and we will go on analyzing them." And finally, when the analysis is complete . . . . And no man has ever come to the point where psychoanalysis is complete. It can never be complete, because mind not something that remains the same.

You don't dream the same dream again. Every day you are dreaming new dreams, every day you are repressing new desires. Every day you are jealous of this person or that person; every day you are full of longing for power, for money, for prestige, or for saintliness, or for God – the laundry list of your mind is infinite. It begins, but it never ends. And you are in the hands of the other person who goes on imposing his ideas on you.

So all that psychoanalysis does is . . . after a few years of psychoanalysis, you also become a psychoanalyst; you start analyzing other people. You are not cured; your sickness is still there, but now it is covered with a certain expertise. In three or four years you yourself have become an expert.

You will be surprised to know that Sigmund Freud, the founder of psychoanalysis, never allowed himself to be psychoanalyzed – for the simple reason that he was afraid to expose his dreams and inner world, because they were not different from anybody else's. Perhaps they were worse. A man who, the whole day, from morning till evening, is reducing everything to sex – you can imagine in the night he cannot dream of anything else.

Your night is nothing but a by-product of your day. Hence, so many times his friends, his disciples, asked him, "It will be a great experience for us all if you lie down on the couch and start relating your dreams, and we can analyze them." He never agreed. His non-agreement shows his fear.

How can psychoanalysis bring understanding if even the founder is full of garbage and is afraid of anybody coming to know this garbage? His whole profession . . . and he established a great profession. Jews are clever as far as establishing firms is concerned. They don't do small business. One Jew was Jesus, who created the firm of Christianity. Another Jew was Karl

Marx, who founded an equal establishment: communism. Another Jew was Sigmund Freud, who established psychoanalysis. Now psychoanalysts are the highest paid people in the world – and they do nothing.

~~Observation can bring understanding, but analysis cannot.~~ In analysis you become dependent on the other person. People become addicts of particular analysts; they *have* to go there. Just as there are alcoholics and there are drug addicts, there are analysis addicts. After two or three days they start feeling fidgety: analysis is needed. Somebody has to listen to all their crap. And of course when somebody listens to your crap for one hour continuously, you have to pay for it! ~~Observation~~ is a totally different phenomenon – what I call ~~witnessing, awareness.~~

It does not make you dependent on the other; it is your own growth of ~~being alert.~~ And the miracle is that ~~as your observation becomes more and more clear, your dreams start disappearing~~ – just as the morning comes close, stars start disappearing. When the sun has risen all the stars have disappeared from the sky. ~~When your sun of observation and witnessing arises within you, all dreams and all problems simply disappear, leaving the whole sky absolutely clean.~~

Turiya, you say, "The first years running groups here in Poona, it was mainly problem- oriented." It had to be, because the people who were coming were not coming to know themselves – they were simply coming to get rid of their problems, of their anxieties, of their anguish, of their despair. "It felt like a big cleanup." It was exactly that.

"In Rancho Rajneesh somehow I knew therapy was really finished . . . ." In the commune I had hundreds of different therapeutic schools working, but *I* was working to destroy every therapy. The therapists were working to destroy your problems, and I was trying to destroy therapies and the therapists! – because a therapy can be only a temporary relief, and the therapist can be only a very superficial help.

You say, "I did not know how to bring meditation into the group room. I was still focusing on the dark side and too scared to really move into the unknown. Being here now, for the first time I get a glimpse that through meditation, observing, and simplifying, everything that is in the way slowly dissolves. By allowing the lightness to shine within, and without doing anything, suddenly the click happens. Everything is light and playful and with it comes an incredible feeling of preciousness and gratitude that we can all be here with You at this time."

Now the people who are with me are not here to solve any problems, they are here to know themselves.

You can go on solving problems for lives together. There is no scarcity of problems. The moment you open your eyes, problems start arising. Your mind has been conditioned in such a way that very stupid things can become problems: somebody steps out of bed with the wrong foot and the whole day everything goes wrong, and he goes on saying, "I stepped out of bed wrongly." Now, for the bed, whether your right foot comes out first or your left foot comes out first does not matter. But superstitions . . . .

You go for a morning walk and you meet a man with only one eye – finished, your whole day is finished. Now nothing can be right. Strange . . . what does that poor fellow have to do with your whole day? But a superstition, centuries old . . . .

I had a small boy in my neighborhood with only one eye. Whomsoever I wanted to torture . . . early in the morning I would take the boy and just give him chocolates, and he was ready. I would watch from far away: "You just stand in front of the door. Let the fool open the door . . . ." And the moment he would open the door and see the one-eyed boy, he would say, "My God! Again? But why do you come here in the morning?"

One day he became so angry that he wanted to beat him. I had to come from my hiding place, and I said, "You cannot beat him. It is a public road, and it is his right to stand here every morning. We used to come once in a while; now we will come every day. It is up to you to open your door or not to open your door."

He said, "But if I don't open my door, how will I go

to my shop?"

I said, "That is *your* problem, not our problem. But this boy is going to stand here."

He said, "This is strange. But why this boy . . . ? Can't you take him to somebody else? Just . . . my neighbor is a competitor in my business, and I am getting defeated continually because of this boy."

I said, "It is up to you. *Baksheesh!* – if you give one rupee to this boy, he will stand at the other gate."

He said, "One rupee?" In those days one rupee was very valuable, but he said, "I will give."

I said, "Remember, if the other man gives two rupees, then this boy will still be standing here. It is a sheer question of business."

He said, "I am going to report to the police. I can . . . ." I said, "You can go. Even the police inspector is afraid of this boy. You can get him to write the report, but he will not call him into his office. Everybody is

afraid – even the teachers are afraid. And this boy is so precious . . . so whoever creates any trouble in the city, I take this boy. Nothing has to be done – he simply stands there in front of the door."

Problems are all around you. So even if you somehow get finished with one problem, another problem arises. And you cannot prevent problems arising. Problems will continue to arise till you come to a deep understanding of witnessing. That is the only golden key, discovered by centuries of inward search in the East: that there is no need to solve any problem. You simply observe it, and the very observation is enough; the problem evaporates.

Now the people who are here are not here to solve their problems. They are here to dissolve themselves. They are here to know the very secret of their life. For that, no therapy is needed. For that, only meditation – and *only* meditation – is the way.

Beloved Bhagwan,

When You come into the auditorium, Your beauty, Your grace and fragrance, are so overwhelming and beyond any words that I can find. Inside I feel such an intense fire and longing to be free, unbound to the mind, the body, the heart.
I realize that this same intensity also creates a lot of tensions
and is coming from a place of not trusting that this freedom, this liberation, will ever happen to me. Could You please comment?

Turiya, it is most human and natural. It is not arising out of distrust; on the contrary, it is arising out of a deep trust because you love me, you trust me, you feel me in thousands of ways in your heart. Naturally, a longing arises out of this trust; a longing: when will the same fragrance, the same freshness, the same insight, the same understanding, the same light, happen to me? And it is simply human frailty. One feels: Perhaps it is too much and I am not capable of it.

Perhaps it is too far and I may not be able to go on a pilgrimage in the unknown, alone, on my own.

This is absolutely natural, nothing to be condemned. And rather than thinking that it is arising out of distrust, distrust in yourself . . . . No, it is arising out of trust in me. I have become to you such a certainty that there is no question that space of this tremendous freedom , liberation, glory and grandeur exists.

You have seen the sunlit peaks in me and naturally

you feel yourself weak: The peak is too high, too far away; so immensely beautiful – but is it possible for me to reach to the peak from my dark valley? This is a human question. You are afraid: I can walk only one step at a time, and the distance seems to be infinite.

In China they have the right proverb for you: The journey of a thousand miles begins with one step. And nobody is given the right to take two steps together. Everybody is equal as far as steps are concerned. You can step one by one, and a journey of ten thousand miles can be completed just by small steps.

If you look too much at your small step and the faraway sunlit peak, you are bound to feel: Perhaps this is not for me. But I say unto you: it is for everybody.

Just as love and trust have arisen in you about me, wait a little more. You will find that same trust and the same love arising within you for yourself too. The master is only a catalytic agent. He triggers a process in you. All that is needed is a little patience, just a little patience. Wait with gratitude and start the journey.

If *I* can reach to the sunlit peak, then every human being is capable of reaching it; because I am not special, I am just one amongst you. There was a day when I was in the dark valley and I was also trembling, seeing the unknown, far-away peaks. But I thought: At the most I may not reach. Anyway I am in the valley – even if I don't reach to the peak, even if I reach only halfway, what is the harm? In the next life perhaps I may be able to complete the journey. But there is no point in wasting time, just sitting in the darkness of the valley and always remaining afraid.

I started the pilgrimage – not with the certainty that I *will* reach, but with the certainty that at least I can get out of the darkness of the valley – and once I was out of the darkness of the valley, suddenly my steps became bolder, my heart became more certain. And it was not only me who was moving to the peak – it will be very difficult for you to understand – I saw that in every movement, the peak was also moving towards me.

Another Arabic proverb: When you move one step towards God, he moves one thousand steps towards you. These small proverbs contain the essence of centuries of wisdom. When you see the peak also moving towards you, suddenly you grow wings. Now there is no need to walk – you can fly. Such lightness comes to your being; all fear, all weakness, all human frailty, disappear. Suddenly you understand it is not only you who need the peak – the peak also needs you. It was not only you who were waiting for the peak – the peak was also
waiting for you. In your meeting, the whole existence is going to celebrate.

Okay, Vimal?

Yes, Bhagwan.

Arguing With The Ocean

A moment comes when you start talking with the trees, playing with the stones, arguing with the ocean . . . because your very idea of being separate has disappeared. Now this whole existence is one organic unity.

And it is not that when you talk to a tree it does not respond to you; if you are crazy enough, there is a dialogue. Perhaps one time you have to speak from your side; another time you have to speak from the tree's side – because the tree cannot speak, but you can understand what it wants to say.

Just remember the basic criteria – that your happiness, your blissfulness should go on growing; your intelligence, your clarity should go on growing; your love should go on becoming more and more pure . . . and your understanding should start giving you insight into your past lives and into your future lives. You should become part of eternity – spread from the very beginning to the very end. Naturally, people around you will think you are crazy. But I say to you: to me you have become for the first time sane.

Man, in his ordinariness, is insane.

Every thing that he goes on doing – you can watch . . . and you will find that it is out of insanity. Your craziness is not the ordinary insanity of humanity; it is the craziness of all the mystics, of all the poets, of all the creators. It is the craziness that happens only to the blessed ones.

February 13, 1987,   7 p.m.

Beloved Bhagwan,

Paltudas says, "Every art takes place in its own time, so why get impatient? No matter how much you water it, the tree comes into fruition in its own time."
Bhagwan, please say something about impatience on the spiritual path. Is impatience an essential part of human growth? Please comment.

I t is true that everything takes place in its own time – but it is only half true. Paltudas says, "Every art takes place in its own time, so why get impatient? No matter how much you water it, the tree comes into fruition in its own time." But that does not mean that you need not water the tree; that does not mean that you have not to sow the seeds. The seeds have also to be sown in time – only then will the fruits come in their own time.

What Paltudas is saying is only half of the whole thing. From the seed to the fruit is a long journey, and great patience is needed on the part of the gardener. But the patience must not become laziness, because the difference is very delicate and very fine. The patience should remain, in its heart of hearts, very impatient – knowing perfectly well that when the spring comes, flowers will come. That does not mean you have to forget longing, desiring, for the spring to come; praying, waiting, for the spring to come. Wait – but your waiting should not be a dullness on your part.

The guest will come – and one never knows when the guest will come; but wait like a lover, with doors open, eyes fixed on the road . . . as if the next moment is going to be the meeting with the guest, with the friend.

On the spiritual path, things which ordinarily appear contradictory become complementary. Be impatiently patient, or be patiently impatient; but both have to be together. If you choose one, there is danger. Patience alone is going to become laziness; impatience alone is going to become unnecessary anguish, anxiety. They both are needed, balanced; so impatience keeps you longing, waiting, and patience keeps you from becoming tense, from creating anxiety. Both have their parts to fulfill on the spiritual path.

And it is not only so about this contradiction; about many other contradictions the same is true. One has to be both together, in deep harmony. What do you think this is about – the gardener? Paltudas has forgotten completely that the real question is about the seed, not about the gardener, because the gardener is going to remain the same; there is going to be no growth, spiritual or unspiritual. The growth is going to happen to the seed, and if the seed is too patient it will die; it will lose the very longing to live, the zest for living. Long months have to pass before the rains will come

If it becomes too patient, it will die before even being born. It needs a certain impatience on the part of the seed – a tremendous desire to grow, to blossom, to come to fruition. But even if there is tremendous desire and longing for growth, it will happen in its own time. Your longing cannot arrange that the spring comes a little sooner, but it can keep you awake – so that when the spring comes, you are not fast asleep and dead.

The seed has to continue to dream, desire . . . has to remain discontent as it is, because this is not its destiny, it is only a potential – otherwise it is empty. Everything is going to happen in the future, so it has to be alert, hopeful, aware of the unknown, listening to the footsteps of the spring coming. And on the other hand it has to be patient, because there is nothing it can do to bring the rains or to bring the spring – they will come in their own time.

So if the seed can keep a balance between patience and impatience, it will remain alive, and it will also not go mad. Too much impatience can make you insane, and too much patience can make you one of the living dead. Both are needed in the right proportions: a deep harmony between the contradictions, so they are transformed into complementaries.

On the spiritual path a deep harmony is needed with every step – a little imbalance and you will be lost. And that's what your religions have been teaching you: they have been teaching you imbalance, not balance. They have been telling you to choose between two contradictions.

I say unto you: Never choose.

Remain choiceless. Both are yours. Use them – and use them in such a way that they both create a beautiful music in your heart. It looks very strange to say, but nothing can be done about the mysteries of life.

I can only say – even if I appear to be very contradictory – be patiently impatient, or be impatiently patient – but be both.

Beloved Bhagwan,

A few years ago I asked You a question, with great fear and trembling: "Bhagwan, is it inevitable that I will go crazy?" And now, beloved Bhagwan, at last it has finally happened: I *have* gone crazy. Thank You, Bhagwan, thank You.

Anand Vimal, that's great! Rejoice in your craziness! . . . because in this world, where the whole of humanity is insane, to become sane looks as if you have gone crazy.

Some criteria have to be remembered: if your craziness brings you more joy, more intelligence, more silence, more peacefulness, more understanding; if your craziness dispels darkness from your life – darkness of jealousies, anger, rage, violence, destructiveness; if your craziness becomes a light unto yourself . . . then all the buddhas in the world were crazy. And it is better to be in the good, crazy company of Gautam Buddha, Lao Tzu, Kabir, Nanak, Mahavira, than to be in the so-called mob, millions of people who all think that they are not crazy.

One has to be very clear-cut: if Gautam Buddha is right, then the whole world is crazy; and if the whole world is right, then of course Gautam Buddha is crazy.

One thing is certain, that buddhas are in a very small minority; so if it is a question of voting, they are going to be defeated–any crazy man, any madam, can defeat them. But fortunately, the idea has not yet come into people's minds that enlightenment has to be decided by voting. If two persons stand as candidates for enlightenment, and whoever gets more votes becomes enlightened, then one thing is certain – the really enlightened ones will never be known to the world, because it is impossible to conceive that a Gautam Buddha is going to compete for enlightenment. The very idea of competition is irrelevant to the consciousness of a buddha.

So you have to remember – people will call you crazy; don't be offended. If you are still offended, then something in you is still sane, something in you still belongs to the masses; you are not fully crazy.

Don't be offended; rather, gratefully accept it, that you are blessed to be crazy. It is a very strange fact that only sane people can accept that they are crazy. No madman in the whole history of man has ever accepted that he is mad. You can go to any madhouse, and you will not find a single madman who thinks he is mad.

One of Kahlil Gibran's friends became mad, and Gibran went to see him in the madhouse. The friend was sitting on a bench on the lawn. Kahlil Gibran was feeling very compassionate. The madman laughed; he said, "Don't feel compassionate." Kahlil Gibran could not understand why the man was so angry about his compassion.

The friend said, "I am feeling compassion for all those people who are outside the wall. The whole world is mad. Only a very few people who are not mad have been kept in the madhouse, just for security reasons. Who allowed you in? We are not mad, and we don't need your compassion."

I have visited many mad asylums, but I have never found a single man who would accept that he was mad; because to accept that you are mad means that you are sane enough even to see your own madness.

The question is asked by Vimal – and just nearby is sitting Narendra. His father had a strange disease: six months he used to be mad and six months he used to be sane – a great balance of enjoying both worlds.

Whenever he was sane he was always sick, always grumpy. He would lose weight, and he would fall victim to all kinds of infection; all his resistance to disease would be lost. And in the six months when he was mad, he was the healthiest person you could find – no disease, no infection – and he was always happy.

The family was in trouble. Whenever he was happy the family was in trouble, because his happiness was a certain indication that he was mad. If he was not going to the doctors, if he was enjoying his health – he was mad.

While he was insane, he would get up early in the morning, four o'clock, and wake up the whole neighborhood saying, "What are you doing? Just go for a morning walk, go to the river, enjoy swimming. What are you doing here in bed?"

The whole neighborhood was tortured . . . but he enjoyed it. He would purchase fruits and sweets and say, "You can come to my shop and get your money." Naturally – Narendra was very small, his other brothers were even smaller – even the smallest children were watching him, that he does not steal the money. But whether they watched or not, he would go on distributing fruits and sweets to people and saying to them, "Rejoice! Why are you sitting so sad?" Naturally, they had to pay money to all kinds of people.

It was a very strange situation. Children steal money, and fathers, grandfathers, prevent them. In Narendra's house, the situation was just the opposite: the father used to steal money, and the small children would shout for the mother: "He is taking money again!"

And by the time the mother was there, he was gone – gone to the market to purchase sweets, fruits, or anything whatsoever, wholesale! He was not concerned with small things – just wholesale purchase and distributing. And everybody loved it, but everybody was tortured, also.

Once it happened that he escaped while he was insane. He had just gone to the station, and the train was there, so he sat in the train. One thing just led to another . . . and he reached Agra.

In India there is a sweet; its name is such that it can create trouble, and it created trouble for him. He was feeling hungry, so he went to a shop and he asked what it was, and the man said, *Khaja.* Khaja in Hindi means two things: it is the name of that sweet, and it also means, "Eat it" . . . so he ate it.

The man could not believe it. He said, "What are you doing?" He said, "What you said."

He was dragged to the court because, "This man seems to be strange. First he asked the name, and when I said 'khaja,' he started eating it!"

Even the magistrate laughed. He said, "The word has both meanings. But this man seems to be insane – because he seems so happy, so healthy." Even in the court he was enjoying everything – no fear, no sign of fear. He was sent to a madhouse for six months, and he asked happily, "Only six months?"

He was sent to Lahore – in those days Lahore was part of India – and just by coincidence . . . . There was some cleaning stuff for bathrooms; after four months in the Lahore madhouse he drank the whole drum of that cleaning stuff and it gave him vomits and motions. For fifteen days he could not eat anything . . . but it cleaned his whole system – so he became sane!

And then began a great period of difficulty. He went to the superintendent and said, "Just because of drinking that stuff, for fifteen days I could not eat anything, and my whole system has been cleaned. I have become sane."

The superintendent said, "Don't bother me, because every mad person thinks he is sane."

He tried his best to convince him, but the superintendent said, "This is the whole business here every day – every madman thinks he is sane."

He was telling me that those two months were really very troublesome. Those first four months were perfectly beautiful: "Somebody was pulling my leg, or somebody was cutting my hair – it was all okay. Who cares? – somebody was sitting on my chest . . . so what?

"But when I became sane, and the same things continued – now I could not tolerate it if somebody was sitting on my chest, somebody was cutting my hair, somebody has cut half my mustache . . . . "

They were all mad people. Amongst those mad people he was the only one who was sane. No mad person ever accepts that he is mad. The moment he accepts he is mad, sanity has started coming.

Anand Vimal, your accepting that finally great craziness has happened to you, is a moment of rejoicing for all those who have either already become crazy or are on the path of becoming crazy . . . .

There are all types of people here at different stages of craziness. But don't be satisfied. Rejoice! – but remember that there are still crazier states. A moment comes when you start talking with the trees, playing with the stones, arguing with the ocean . . . because your very idea of being separate has disappeared. Now this whole existence is one organic unity.

And it is not that when you talk to a tree it does not respond to you; if you are crazy enough, there is a dialogue. Perhaps one time you have to speak from your side; another time you have to speak from the tree's side – because the tree cannot speak, but you can understand what it wants to say.

Just remember the basic criteria – that your happiness, your blissfulness should go on growing; your intelligence, your clarity should go on growing; your love should go on becoming more and more pure . . . and your understanding should start giving you insight into your past lives and into your future lives. You should become part of eternity – spread from the very beginning to the very end. Naturally, people around you will think you are crazy. But I say to you: To me you have become for the first time sane.

Man, in his ordinariness, is insane.

Every thing that he goes on doing – you can watch . . . and you will find that it is out of insanity. Your craziness is not the ordinary insanity of humanity; it is the craziness of all the mystics, of all the poets, of all the creators. It is the craziness that happens only to the blessed ones.

Beloved Bhagwan,

Floating in the sea of love that surrounds you, I feel I am expanding and expanding . . . . A deep wound in me is healing. I cannot really express what is happening. It is as if after a furious thunderstorm the sky is clearing, giving view to a breathtaking dawn of something inexpressibly beautiful, which has been covered under heavy, choking layers of pain, anguish and self-deception.

Tears of gratitude towards You, my Master, fill my eyes. To me You are not only the master of love, but You are also a master fire-worker. Will You please keep my fuse burning till the final explosion – or is it an implosion – happens?

I don't know what more to ask, and yet to me it is the most important question of my life.

Premda, it is certainly one of the most important questions – not only of your life, but of everybody's life.

But the thing that you are searching for cannot be expressed by the word "explosion"; it can only be expressed by the word "*im*plosion." Reality is not somewhere outside you, you *are* it. So if all your energy starts moving inwards – just as if a lotus is closing its petals – you will find what has been the greatest search and exploration of all human beings down the centuries. And this is the only experience which will always remain in the future too – the search.

Existence can be divided into three categories: the known, the unknown, and the unknowable. Science believes only in two categories: the known and the unknown. Between the known and the unknown there is not much difference – only a difference of degree – because what is known today was unknown yesterday; and what is unknown today may become known tomorrow. So the difference is not qualitative, but only quantitative.

And because science accepts only two categories, it feels certain that our world of the known is becoming greater, and our world of the unknown is shrinking into a smaller thing. Every day a chunk of the unknown becomes known. It can be expected that one day there will be only one category – the known. The whole unknown will have disappeared into the known. That is

not a great future; that is very dangerous.

If a point comes some day when everything becomes known, existence will be demystified. Then love will be just hormones, chemistry. There will be no possibility of any poetry, there will be no possibility of any beauty – it will be only make-up. There will be no possibility of anything that in any way indicates the mysterious, the miraculous.

All mystery will be gone, all miracles will be gone, and man will come to a dead-end street, where life will not have any more challenges – no adventure, nothing to explore, nowhere to go. It is not inconceivable that the people who have been always exploring, accepting challenges from the unknown, may want to commit suicide, because now there is nothing that interests them.

But there is no need to fall into a sad or pessimistic attitude, because science has not covered the whole of existence in its two categories. The most important category has remained out of it – and that is the category of the unknowable, that is the world of religion.

In science, the known goes on becoming bigger and bigger, and the unknown goes on becoming smaller and smaller. In the religious search, just the opposite happens – because science means going outwards and religion means going inwards; it is implosion.

As you go deeper into yourself, the unknowable

becomes more and more unknowable, the mystery deepens, the miraculous expands. You are engulfed in a wonderland where everything is beautiful – where everything can be experienced but cannot be converted into knowledge.

Premda, you are asking that I should continue to burn you to the point where the implosion happens. As far as *I* am concerned, I promise you. As far as you are concerned, you have to remember not to escape – because it is a question of fire, and you are entering into the fire.

For the fire, there is no problem in promising you. Any flame can promise the moth, "Darling, come on!" The problem is with the moth – that as it comes closer to the flame, it becomes hotter and hotter and hotter . . . and there is every desire to escape, not to go nearer – because it seems it is going to consume you.

Remember my promise – and you have also promised to yourself that you will not escape; even if death happens, you will still go on. Death is *going* to happen – because your whole personality has to die; but the innermost being is not part of your personality.

Your ego has to die. In the death of your ego is the resurrection of your soul. The moment you die, God is born. Death is the price to be paid.

So I will keep my promise. You have not to forget your promise – given to yourself, not to me. It is totally *your* exploration; you are going inside yourself. I will keep on pushing you. I will keep on blocking all the ways by which you can escape. I will go on breaking all the bridges that you have crossed, so that you cannot return. But remember your promise: that whatever happens, unless you have reached your innermost being, you will not stop.

You will never reach your innermost being. Just before entering your innermost being, you will disappear – and in your place you will find a totally new face, with which you have never been acquainted. This is your original face. When the personality dies, your individuality is discovered. When all masks fall, you discover your original face.

It is one of the most important questions, not only of Premda, but of everyone who wants to travel in search of his own soul, in search of his own home.

Beloved Bhagwan,

Who is this guy Devageet? Why do You encourage all his meaningless questions? I can't stand another question from this stupid guy. Stop him, Bhagwan, for God's sake, before he drives us all as crazy as he is.

Devageet, I was also wondering . . . who is this guy Devageet?

You are asking me, "Why do You encourage all his meaningless questions?" Because they are everybody else's questions too. Devageet is simple, innocent . . . therefore he never bothers about what others will think of his questions. He simply asks them. Hence, I am going to encourage him.

And it is true when you say, "I can't stand another question from this stupid guy." You may not be able to stand – then try to *under*stand, because this crazy guy is asking very significant questions.

You are asking me, "Stop him, Bhagwan." No, absolutely no, because he is bringing up everybody else's meaningless gibberish – which they themselves are not courageous enough to put forth, to expose. He is the mouthpiece of you all – this stupid guy, Devageet.

And you are asking. "For God's sake, before he

drives us all as crazy as he is." That is the time I am waiting for. The moment I see everybody is driven crazy, my job is done; then I can say to you, Goodbye.

Everybody is so sane, he needs to be hammered continuously so that his insanity, which is hiding inside, comes out. It is like pus, which people are covering; and they think that by covering them, their wounds will be healed. No, the pus has to be taken out, and the wound has to be left open to the sun, to the wind – then only is there a possibility of its being healed.

And Devageet is doing you all a great service. Just last evening I suggested to him that in the middle of the night, when he becomes a gorilla with his girlfriend, "Just suddenly jump out of the bed, sit in a lotus posture and become a buddha." And he did it! He is a very innocent fellow. His girlfriend has reported to me:

Beloved Bhagwan,

Now my love is totally ruined. My gorilla has turned into a lotus flower. Are You trying to get me enlightened too?

His girlfriend is Prem Nityamo. It will take a little longer time for you. Now you start becoming the gorilla – because everything has to be done in the proper way.

When Devageet becomes a buddha, you disturb him: become a gorilla, and do anything that comes into your mind. Don't bother what it is, because nobody expects anything sensible from gorillas. And I know that your boyfriend, who has become a buddha, a lotus flower . . . now it is a question of self-respect and integrity. You can dance like a gorilla, you can do anything you want to him, but he will remain a buddha.

Watching him being a buddha, perhaps you may also jump on the other side of the bed and sit in a lotus posture. It will be something unprecedented in the whole history of man – in one bedroom, two buddhas . . . . That close it has never come. Mahavira and Gautam Buddha stayed once in one caravanserai, but not in the same room. But this is my deepest dream: that in every bedroom there should be two Gautam Buddhas. Only then we can have a sane world.

So, it is good: Devageet has turned into a lotus flower. It is a challenge to you. You also become a lotus flower – and forget the old, traditional idea that two buddhas cannot be in love with each other. In fact, only two buddhas can be in love with each other. Others are only playing the game of love, but deep down it is hate, possessiveness, domination. Only two buddhas can love without any politics, without any effort to be superior to the other, without torturing each other. They can share their love, because now they have got it.

Otherwise, in every bedroom there are two beggars, and each is insisting, "Give me love." And both are beggars; nobody has love. How can he give love to you? He himself is asking, "Give me love." Every husband feels the wife is not giving him love; every wife feels the husband is not giving her love; every friend feels the other friend is not giving him love. It is always a question of giving: the other is not giving. But nobody bothers to ask how the other can give. The other has not got it.

Only two buddhas, two enlightened beings, can give. They don't beg, they don't ask, "Give us . . . ." They simply ask, "Be available to us. We are so overburdened with love; such an abundance of love is arising in us that we will be grateful if you can receive it." They become like rain clouds wandering in the sky, full of rain, asking the earth, "Accept us."

Love, in ordinary life, is only a word. Only a man of deep meditation starts giving content to the word "love," and it is full of flowers when one becomes totally awakened. Two awakened persons will be sharing, dancing, singing, loving – and there is no possibility of any quarrel; the quarrel arises only because you want to get more and give less. The moment you are fully conscious, the situation is reversed: you want to give more and get less, because you don't have any space. You are too full, your heart is overflowing – it has become a fountain.

So, Nityamo, you need not be worried, just jump onto the other side of the bed. But start from being a gorilla. First, the gorilla has to be released – that is, all your repressions that make you the gorilla. To let the gorilla out of your being is the deepest cleansing, the deepest catharsis. And only when all the animality has gone out of you . . . buddhahood is not far away – just one step.

Buddhahood is your birthright, and the gorilla is only your conditioning. Your society goes on telling you to repress – and soon the repressed part of your being becomes so big that you are sitting on a volcano. It can erupt any moment; before it erupts, it is better to release it.

So first be a gorilla – with intensity and totality. And Devageet will help, because he has passed through the stage of being a gorilla. He will understand, he will have compassion, he will support. In this world there is only one who can be called your real friend: one who brings your enlightenment – not as a potential, but transforms it into an actuality. Actualization of your potential is what enlightenment is all about.

But before you can reach to that peak, you will have to get rid of much rubbish and luggage that you have been carrying for lives together. I have managed my meditations in such a way that first the gorilla has to be catharted out. That's what happens in Dynamic Meditation: you allow your gorilla to be released, with no inhibitions. And because of that Dynamic Meditation I have been condemned all over the world.

Keep the gorilla in and everybody is happy with you – but if the gorilla is in, you can never be at peace. I say to you: Let it out. It evaporates in the air, and what is left behind is pure space.

That pure space has many names: jina, buddha, enlightenment, samadhi, paramahansa – different aspects, but they indicate only one thing, that now inside you Charles Darwin has disappeared. Now Charles Darwin cannot find any trace of any gorilla or chimpanzee in you, not even the footprints; because the inner sky is just like the outer sky – when the bird flies, it leaves no footprints. When your gorilla goes out, in the sky of your inner world no footprints are left.

And the silence that descends, and the serenity that blossoms, and the blissfulness that becomes your fragrance, and the coolness which is not of this world – this is your true heritage. Unless you claim it, you have lived in vain. Only those few people are blessed who have claimed their inheritance, and they have found in themselves the greatest of treasures.

Outside you can, at the most, find a few reflections of beauty – in a sunset, in a full moon. But *inside*, every moment is full of beauty and full of joy; every moment is full of song and full of dance; every moment is ecstatic.

Being part of this ecstasy is being part of the unknowable, the miraculous, the ultimate mystery of existence.

Okay, Vimal?

Yes, Bhagwan.

A More Human Technology

It is not the fault of modern technology; the fault is that we have not been very clear what we want from modern technology and what we don't want. The scientist has been discovering almost in a blind way, and whatever he discovers we start using – without thinking of the aftereffects.

Going back is impossible and idiotic, the only way is forward. We need a better technology – better than modern technology, which can avoid plastic garbage and disturbance in the ecology. The scientist has to be very alert that whatever he is doing should become an intrinsic part of the organic whole; technology should not go against the whole. And it is possible, because technology does not lead you somewhere in particular; it is you who go on discovering things in a blind way.... We need a superior technology, a more enlightened technology. There, I part from Mahatma Gandhi, who goes backwards – where there is nothing but death. I go forwards. Technology is in our hands; we are not in the hands of technology. We can drop all those parts which are dangerous, poisonous, and we can discover substitutes which enhance the ecology, which enhance the life of man, which enhance his outer and inner richness and bring a balance into the world.

February 14, 1987,   8 a.m.

Beloved Bhagwan,

By using modern technology, I feel we are hurting this vibrating,
juicy earth with the dead garbage
of plastic, radioactivity, bad air and so on.
Please would You comment.

Dhyan Tara, it is one of the most complicated questions . . . . It is true that, "by using modern technology we are hurting this vibrating, juicy earth with the dead garbage of plastic, radioactivity, bad air and so on."

This question has two possible answers. One is that of Mahatma Gandhi: "Go back . . . to the point where all modern technology is dropped" – which superficially looks right. If modern technology is creating an ecological crisis on the earth, disturbing the balance of nature, then it is a very simplistic solution to drop modern technology and go back.

But you have to understand that in Gautam Buddha's time, just twenty-five centuries ago, this country only had twenty million people. The earth was enough to support them. Today, this country alone has nine hundred million people. If you want to go back to the days of Gautam Buddha, you will have to kill or allow to die such a large part of the population. And when only twenty million people are saved, and the remainder of the nine hundred million people are lying dead all around you – do you think those twenty million will be able to live either?

And the population goes on increasing . . . . By the end of this century, the population of India may have increased by half again. That means it would be one billion, three-hundred million people – from nearly nine-hundred to thirteen-hundred million people.

That is why I have been disagreeing with Mahatma Gandhi on every point. He talks about nonviolence – but this is not nonviolence; nothing can be more violent a step than this. No war has destroyed so many people as will be destroyed without any war. And it is impossible to live amongst dead bodies piled all around you. There will be nobody to take them to the funeral or to take them to the graveyard. So many people dying at such a rate is going to kill the remaining twenty million people too; their rotting bodies will create thousands of diseases, infections.

Mahatma Gandhi used to think that we should stop technology at the point where the spinning wheel was invented. The spinning wheel was invented somewhere around ten thousand years ago or even earlier. The people were so few and the earth was so big . . . the earth was giving so much that those people could not even absorb it all; most of it was going to waste.

So this is one solution, which came to Mahatma Gandhi from Leo Tolstoy – he was also against modern technology. But I cannot support it, because it means no railway trains, no hospitals, no surgery, no medicine, no post offices, no telegraphs, no telegrams, no telexes, no electricity; and all these have become part of your life. You cannot conceive of yourself without electricity!

There was just one failure of electricity in America. For three days people were in such a panic, because the elevators were not working and to go by the stairs in a high-rise building – perhaps one hundred stories, one hundred and twenty stories – just coming down and going up was enough to finish anybody. People became aware for the first time, in those three days in New York, that now there is no possibility of dropping technology.

I have another alternative. It is not the fault of modern technology; the fault is that we have not been very clear what we want from modern technology and what we don't want. The scientist has been discovering almost in a blind way, and whatever he discovers we start using – without thinking of the aftereffects.

Going back is impossible and idiotic, the only way is forward. We need a better technology – better than modern technology, which can avoid plastic garbage and disturbance in the ecology. The scientist has to be very alert that whatever he is doing should become an intrinsic part of the organic whole; technology should not go against the whole. And it is possible, because technology does not lead you somewhere in particular; it is you who go on discovering things in a blind way.

Now that it is clear that whatever we have discovered up to now, much of it is a disturbance in the harmony – is finally going to destroy life on the earth – still, scientists go on piling up nuclear weapons. They don't have the guts to say to the politicians, "It is enough. We are not slaves. We cannot create anything that is going to destroy life."

All the scientists of the world have to come to a consensus: they have to make a world academy of sciences, which decides what should be discovered and what should not be discovered. If something wrong is discovered, it should be undiscovered immediately.

We need a superior technology, a more enlightened technology. There, I part from Mahatma Gandhi, who goes backwards – where there is nothing but death. I go forwards. Technology is in our hands; we are not in the hands of technology. We can drop all those parts which are dangerous, poisonous, and we can discover substitutes which enhance the ecology, which enhance the life of man, which enhance his outer and inner richness and bring a balance into the world.

But I don't see anybody in the whole world preaching for a more sophisticated, more enlightened technology. Sometimes I wonder: millions of people, thousands of great scientists – are they all blind? Can't they see what they are doing is cutting their own roots?

And if technology can manage to do miracles – it has managed on the path of destructiveness, it can also manage miracles on the path of creativeness. All that has been discovered, if it is a disturbance to nature, should be dropped. But I don't see that electricity is a danger to nature; I don't see that railway lines or airplanes are disturbing the ecology; I don't see that innocent telegrams, post offices, have to be destroyed. That will be moving to the other extreme.

That is how the human mind works: it works like the pendulum of a clock, from one end to the other end. It never stops in the middle. I want human consciousness to stop exactly in the middle, so that it can see both sides. Certainly, destructiveness cannot be supported; and the energy that goes into creating destructive things has to be converted into creativity.

But Mahatma Gandhi is not the way. His ideology will prove more dangerous than modern technology has proved. Modern technology may still take hundreds of years to destroy everything. If we follow Mahatma Gandhi, within a day everything that we have achieved in thousands of years will be destroyed.

You could not have cold and hot water in your bathrooms – that depends on modern technology. It is true that it has polluted the air, but that is our fault, not the fault of modern technology. If we had insisted that petrol should be refined to such a point that it did not pollute the air, and that there should be devices which went on every car, to purify the air of whatever damage the petrol was doing, so the balance remained the same . . . but it was, in a way, natural. You know something only when it has happened.

Nobody was aware that going to the moon was creating dangerous holes in the protective shield around the earth. There is a subtle, invisible layer of ozone twenty miles above the earth, all around it. This ozone layer has been protective. It does not allow all the rays of the sun to enter; it allows only the rays which are helpful for life, for trees, for human beings – and the destructive rays are turned back. But nobody was aware of it, so nobody can be blamed for it.

When our first rockets went beyond the twenty-mile thick atmosphere, they created holes in the ozone layer; and from those holes, the protective layers disappeared. Now the all the rays of the sun can enter through those holes, and they have brought many diseases which have not been known before.

But now we can make arrangements if we want to go to the moon. In the first place, it is lunatic; only people who are in some way mad want to go to the moon. For what? – there is neither water nor greenery nor air to breathe. What is the point of it all? Perhaps military experts may be the only ones who are deeply interested in acquiring the moon – because then the moon can be made a base for throwing nuclear weapons at the Soviet Union, if America gets hold of the moon, or if the Soviet Union gets hold of the moon, it becomes their territory.

But even if you want to go to the moon, you should be careful not to create these holes; and if you are creating them, you should immediately make arrangements that they are covered again, so destructive rays from the sun cannot reach the earth.

One thing has to be remembered, Tara: man can only go forward; there is no way backward. And there is no point, either. It is just people's imagination that in the past, when there was no technology, everything was beautiful and good. That is absolutely wrong. I will give you a few examples.

Hindus brag very much that in the golden old days, people were so rich that locks were never used on the doors. Yes, it is mentioned in the scriptures that locks were not used. But it does not say that people were so rich and there was no stealing around – hence, locks were not used. My conclusion is just the opposite: locks were not invented yet, so how could they use them? Secondly, people were very poor; there was nothing to lock up.

And if somebody says that people were rich and there were no locks and there was no stealing, then they should look again into all the scriptures of the past. Gautam Buddha, every day for forty-two years continually, was teaching that stealing is evil. I wonder whom he was teaching? If there was no stealing happening – even locks were not needed – then he must have been mad, talking to people who have never stolen and who were not going to steal, they were themselves so rich. Then why did he go on, every day?

And it was not only Gautam Buddha; Mahavira went on doing the same, and other scriptures and other masters of the past all insisted that stealing was a sin. That is enough proof that there were thieves all around. So the only possible way to explain why locks were not used is mine: because locks were not invented yet.

Locks are also part of technology. If you go to an aboriginal society living in the forest they don't use locks, because they cannot create locks and they are not rich enough even to purchase locks from the cities. And for what? – because they don't have anything in their houses. If they can get one meal a day, that is a great blessing from God. Most of them don't get even one meal a day.

Technology should not be looked at only negatively. In India, just before this century, nine children used to die out of ten. Today the situation has reversed: only one child dies out of ten, because of the advancement of medicine. The clothes you are wearing . . . soon it will be impossible to provide cotton clothes for everybody – and there is no need either: better clothes can be produced by technology. Just as a symbol of my philosophy, I never use anything that is cotton. My clothes are pure productions of technology – one hundred percent polyester.

Technology can create better houses, lighter houses and more beautiful; there is no need to use heavy material, costly material. Technology is bound to create better food, more proportionate, giving you all the vitamins that are needed and giving you a better taste, too – now plants are not so scientific. Any flavor can be given to your food. There is no need for people to eat meat just for taste, because any food can be given the flavor of meat.

Technology has a better side also; but if you drop all modern technology, you will be falling into the dark ages, and it will be the greatest violence on the earth, preached by the man who thought that his philosophy was nonviolent.

But something has to be done. Up to now, technology has been just groping. Now we can give it a direction; and we can drop all those things which are destructive of ecology, harmony, nature, life.

I am all for technology – but a better technology, a more human technology.

Beloved Bhagwan,

Is it possible to be married and to be free at the same time?

Dharma Priya, it is difficult but not impossible. Just a little understanding is needed.

A few basic truths have to be recognized. One is that nobody is born for another. The second is that nobody is here to fulfill your ideals of how he should be. The third is that you are master of your own love, and you can give as much as you want – but you cannot demand love from the other person, because nobody is a slave.

If these simple facts are understood, then it does not matter whether you are married or unmarried, you can be together – allowing space to each other, never interfering in each other's individuality.

In fact, marriage is an out-of-date institution. In the first place, to live in any institution is not good. Any institution is destructive. Marriage has destroyed almost all possibilities of happiness for millions of people – and all for useless things. In the first place, marriage, the very ritual of marriage, is bogus.

I used to work in a university. One of my colleagues, a professor of psychology, was continuously tortured by his wife. It is very difficult to find a couple who are not tortured; and strangely enough, the wife tortures the man. It has a long history behind it – because man has reduced the woman to a slave, she is taking every opportunity to take revenge. It is all unconscious.

That woman was really a monster – she used to beat the poor fellow. One day he came to me and he said, "You are the only person whom I can tell and trust that you will not say anything to anybody else."

I said, "I promise."

He said, "My wife beats me."

I said, "This is not a secret!"

In some way or other, every wife beats the husband. It may not be physical, but to beat psychologically is more dangerous and more harmful. But the woman cannot be held responsible for it; for centuries she has been tortured, killed, beaten, buried alive –and all that has accumulated in her unconscious. The nearest man is the husband, so any excuse and she starts creating trouble. The husbands don't want the neighbors to know, and wives know the weakness, so screaming is one of their methods – throwing things, shouting – so the whole neighborhood knows. And the husband has to compromise immediately, because it is a question of his respectability.

So I told the professor, "Don't you be worried – they all come to me and say the same thing. The moment somebody says, 'Please don't tell it to anybody,' I know what the secret is. I can tell even before they have told me."

He said, "But I want to get out of this prison – I have lived in it enough. It is a twenty-four hour torture."

So I said, "There is no problem in it."

He said, "No problem? But I am married to her!"

I said, "Marriage is just a children's game. How did you get married?"

He said, "A priest was chanting mantras, the fire was burning . . . ." The fire is thought to be the divine, the presence of the divine. So if you take an oath in front of fire, then you cannot go against it. And he said, "I walked in a circle seven times, and the priest tied my clothes to my wife's sari. We took the oath, he chanted, and we moved seven times around the fire."

I said, "Clockwise or . . . ?"

He said, "It is always clockwise."

I said, "Then there is no problem – bring your wife, I am the priest – because whatever the priest was chanting, you did not understand . . . ."

He said, "No."

I said, "So that's perfectly okay. I will chant something that you will not know – nor will I. I will go on inventing as I chant, and you can move seven times anti-clockwise around the fire – and then I will cut the knot that has been tied by the priest, so the marriage is finished."

He said, "My God! – but who is going to bring my wife here? You suggest a very simple solution, but you don't know my wife."

I said, "I know her – because she came even before you did! She also wants to get rid of this continuous quarreling – she is not living a joyous life. Either you can both be joyous or you can both be miserable; it is not possible that one remains joyous and the other remains miserable. So I will convince her – she is almost ready – you just go and tell her that I have sent you. So get into your marriage clothes . . . ."

He said, "Marriage clothes?"

I said, "Yes. The whole ritual has to be done in the reverse order."

The man never came back. I had to go to his house many times. I would knock, and he would plead, "Forgive me for telling you. When I came home I got such a beating that I forgot all the beatings that had happened before! In this life there is no way out; and now I understand why Hindus have invented future lives!"

But I said to him, "Do you know that on a particular day every year Hindu wives fast and pray to God in the temple that they should get the same husband in the next life?"

He said, "That's true – but I never thought about it. So how to avoid it?"

I said, "Simply fast on the same day. Go to the temple and pray – silently so your wife cannot hear. She is praying that she should get the same husband; you simply say, 'One life is enough. My wife is great – give her to somebody else now!' "

He said, "That's good – that I can do."

You are asking, Priya: "Is it possible to be married and to be free?"

If you take marriage non-seriously, then you can be free. If you take it seriously, then freedom is impossible. Take marriage just as a game – it is a game. Have a little sense of humor, that it is a role you are playing on the stage of life; but it is not something that belongs to existence or has any reality – it is a fiction.

But people are so stupid that they even start taking fiction for reality. I have seen people reading fiction with tears in their eyes, because in the fiction things are going so tragically. It is a very good device in the movies that they put the lights off, so everybody can enjoy the movie, laugh, cry, be sad, be happy. If there was light it would be a little difficult – what will others think? And they know perfectly well that the screen is empty – there is nobody, it is just a projected picture. But they forget it completely.

And the same has happened with our lives. Many things which are simply to be taken humorously, we take so seriously – and from that seriousness begins our problem.

In the first place, why should you get married? You love someone, live with someone – it is part of your basic rights. You can live with someone, you can love someone.

Marriage is not something that happens in heaven, it happens here, through the crafty priests. But if you want to join the game with society and don't want to stand alone and aloof, you make it clear to your wife or to your husband that this marriage is just a game: "Never take it seriously. I will remain as independent as I was before marriage, and you will remain as independent as you were before marriage. Neither I am going to interfere in your life, nor are you going to interfere in my life; we will live as two friends together, sharing our joys, sharing our freedom – but not becoming a burden on each other.

"And any moment we feel that the spring has passed, the honeymoon is over, we will be sincere enough not to go on pretending, but to say to each other that we loved much – and we will remain grateful to each other forever, and the days of love will haunt us in our memories, in our dreams, as golden – but the spring is over. Our paths have come to a point, where although it is sad, we have to part, because now, living together is not a sign of love.

If I love you, I will leave you the moment I see my love has become a misery to you. If you love me, you will leave me the moment you see that your love is creating an imprisonment for me."

Love is the highest value in life.

It should not be reduced to stupid rituals.

And love and freedom go together – you cannot choose one and leave the other. A man who knows freedom is full of love; and a man who knows love is always willing to give freedom. If you cannot give freedom to the person you love, to whom can you give freedom? Giving freedom is nothing but trusting.

Freedom is an expression of love.

So whether you are married or not, remember, all marriages are fake – just social conveniences. Their purpose is not to imprison you and bind you to each other; their purpose is to help you to grow with each other. But growth needs freedom; and in the past, all the cultures have forgotten that without freedom, love dies.

You see a bird on the wing in the sun, in the sky, and it looks so beautiful. Attracted by its beauty, you can catch the bird and put it in a golden cage. Do you think it is the same bird? Superficially, yes, it is the same bird who was flying in the sky; but deep down it is not the same bird – because where is its sky, where is its freedom?

This golden cage may be valuable to you; it is not valuable to the bird. For the bird, to be free in the sky is the only valuable thing in life. And the same is true about human beings.

Beloved Bhagwan,

Drinking You during discourse in the morning or darshan in the evening, it feels like I am drinking from a fresh mountain well. But after drinking this crystal-clear water to quench my thirst, I find myself drunk, as if the water had been champagne. And as if that was not enough I find myself addicted to it. Is it okay to be drunk? Is it okay to be addicted?

Anand Neerjo, have you not heard that Jesus used to transform water into wine? Now you know how water becomes wine. It is not a miracle. You *are* drinking champagne – but keep it secret. The police commissioner of Poona should not know about it: that all these people are drinking champagne and getting addicted and drunk.

As far as *I* am concerned, if your love can transform water into champagne, it is absolutely the right thing to happen. And to be addicted to love is to be addicted to God. To be addicted to love is to forget yourself and your ego and disappear into the whole, without leaving a trace behind. It is perfectly okay.

If my words make you drunk, then drink them as much as you can; be a drunkard, because this champagne is going to transform you totally. And no government can prohibit *this* champagne, because it is a miracle that is happening within you. And words changing into champagne must be coming from a source which is totally drunk. *I* am a drunkard, and my whole mission is to make as many drunkards in the world as possible – because only people who are drunk with the divine know what beauty is, what truth is, what ecstasy is.

Okay, Vimal?

Yes, Bhagwan.

I Am A River
Continuously Flowing

So many came in these twenty-five years, and it was natural that many would turn away at a certain point: whenever their philosophy felt offended, their mind felt that they would have to change their way of thinking.

Rather than choosing me, they had chosen themselves – and moved away. With you it is a totally different thing. In these twenty-five years, there have been many springs.

And I am not a static person; I am just like a river – continuously flowing. If you can come with me, good; if you cannot come with me, that too is good. But I cannot change my flow just to adjust to people; I have never adjusted to anybody. I don't know any compromise. So only those people who have loved me so much that if there was a question of choosing between me and themselves, they would choose me – only those people have remained with me for these twenty-five years.

You have seen so many changes, and you have become seasoned. Now you can be without any fear. Changes will be coming.

As long as I am breathing, I will go on moving. And those who have learned to move with me have also learned the joy and the dance of movement. They are going with me towards the ultimate ocean.

February 14, 1987,   7 p.m.

Beloved Bhagwan,

Twenty-five years have passed since we saw You, knew You, and dissolved in You.
There have been others also. There has been no "turning back" either, in our thoughts.
We have seen many people making sudden turnabouts, even after reaching to heights – even Ajit Saraswati.
What is this phenomenon?
Bhagwan, please explain.

Sohan and Manikbabu, the phenomenon you are asking about is very simple. In fact, the simplest things in life are the most difficult to understand – one almost always misses the obvious.

It is true: twenty-five years have passed, and you both have not wavered for a single moment since the day you saw me. You have become part of me, and I have become part of you. Many more have come in these twenty-five years, and many have dropped out – even a person like Ajit Saraswati. He is your friend; hence, you have mentioned his name.

The simple phenomenon that I want you to understand is, how you approach me. It can either be the approach of love, or it can be the approach of logic. Love knows no turning back; logic cannot be relied upon. You have been in love with me; hence, there was no question of turning back. Love knows no doubt – it trusts, and trusts absolutely.

But people like Ajit Saraswati have not approached me in the same way. Their approach has been of the head, of the intellect. They were convinced that what I was saying was exactly what they believed. *I* was secondary; *they* were primary. They were comparing continuously: my being right was dependent on whether it fitted in with their own intellectual garbage. Any moment, if I said something that did not fit with their ideas – immediately there were doubts.

They did not love me, they only loved their own thoughts. And what thoughts do they have? Everything is just borrowed from here, from there – and it is impossible for me to go on saying things which suit the philosophy of everybody who comes to me.

Neither of you was related to me in any intellectual way. That is the worst kind of relationship – it is always on the point of breaking up.

You did not love me because I was saying things which were according to your knowledge, according to your philosophy, according to your religion. You loved me first, and once you love, then it is not a question of my statements fitting in with your statements.

Love is such a fire that it burns all the garbage that

you have been thinking of as tremendously valuable. All that remains is pure gold. Except through love, in existence there is no way to find pure gold.

You both are fortunate – you have never discussed any question with me. I have been staying with you for many years – others have been coming to your house with questions, with their doubts, with their arguments – but you have never asked anything. Only at night when everybody else was gone, you both used to sit by my side on the balcony of your house, in deep silence, facing the sky and the stars.

Our meeting has been of a totally different quality. It was not a mind-to-mind relationship; it was a heart-to-heart melting. I have never felt that you are separate from me; not even for a single moment could I have conceived that you could turn away – away from me. That point we crossed on the first day.

The first day, when we met, everything became absolutely decisive for the future. It was not that tomorrow one does not know whether you will be with me or not – I could have said on the very first day that not only in this life, but in coming lives too, you will be with me. When love is pure, when there are no conditions to it, when there are no causes for it, when it is uncaused . . . there is no way of turning back.

But as far as Ajit Saraswati is concerned, I was never certain, even for a single moment – because he was continuously thinking that he knows. Perhaps he is not capable and articulate enough to say it, but whatever *I* am saying is *his* knowledge; as long as he found that they were running parallel and together, he was with me. Although he thought that he was in love with me, his love was unconscious, only a thought. Your love is a reality.

Whenever you have a headache, you don't say, "I think I have a headache." There is no question of thinking; you simply say, "I have a headache." If a person says, "Perhaps I have a headache . . . " he himself is not certain about his own headache.

Ajit Saraswati, and people like him, thought that they loved me, but they simply loved their own thoughts – and they found echoes of their own thoughts in me, but more clear. Perhaps I was a mirror – they saw their faces in the mirror and they enjoyed that: "How beautiful is the mirror!" They were only saying that about their own faces, reflections. They were not even aware that they were standing before a mirror.

So many came in these twenty-five years, and it was natural that many would turn away at a certain point: whenever their philosophy felt offended, their mind felt that they would have to change their way of thinking. Rather than choosing me, they had chosen themselves – and moved away. With you it is a totally different thing.

In these twenty-five years, there have been many springs. And I am not a static person; I am just like a river – continuously flowing. If you can come with me, good; if you cannot come with me, that too is good. But I cannot change my flow just to adjust to people; I have never adjusted to anybody. I don't know any compromise. So only those people who have loved me so much that if there was a question of choosing between me and themselves, they would choose me – only those people have remained with me for these twenty-five years.

You have seen so many changes, and you have become seasoned. Now you can be without any fear. Changes will be coming. As long as I am breathing, I will go on moving. And those who have learned to move with me have also learned the joy and the dance of movement. They are going with me towards the ultimate ocean.

When my river meets the ocean, I am absolutely certain that Sohan and Manik will still be with me.

Beloved Bhagwan,

Seven years ago I took sannyas from You and I found myself totally melted and tuned in with You.
But for some time I have felt that something has remained unmelted in me and at times I am
overpowered by that, despite myself. I am not able to digest what You say.
Bhagwan, I am even guilty of having doubted You.
Please forgive me, as I don't know what to do during these moments.

Krishna Chaitanya, I remember the evening seven years ago when you and your wife became sannyasins.

You say, "Seven years ago I took sannyas from You and I found myself totally melted." I cannot agree with that, because I remember perfectly: your wife was certainly totally melted, but not you. You were half-hearted, still wondering deep down whether what you are doing is right or wrong. You may have forgotten it . . . I have not forgotten it – I have a god-damned memory!

This is only your retrospective imagination, that you totally melted and tuned in with me. If it had happened, then the remaining question was not possible. It was a very superficial phenomenon. You are also an intellectual. You took the step into sannyas after long consideration – and you were also afraid of the society around you.

I remember perfectly well: before I came to Poona in 1974, I lived in Bombay for four years, in Woodlands. You were living in the same building, but in four years you never came to see me. And thousands of people were coming and going – it was not that you were not aware; but you were afraid of society . . . . When I came to Poona, it was easy for you to come to me – because in Poona nobody knew you.

Is it not strange that for four years I was living in the same building and you never came to see me, when hundreds of people were coming every day? And when I left Bombay and came to Poona, soon you appeared here – not only appeared, but you were ready to take sannyas.

Once in a while I saw you and your wife, Krishna Chetana, in great mass gatherings in Bombay, where I was speaking on *Shrimad Bhagavadgita.* You used to stand in the line, where I would come down from the stage and go towards the car. I touched your hand . . . your wife's hand . . . and many people were standing there – even *that* I remember: that your hands were always cold; your wife's hands were always warm. Without that warmth, melting into me is not possible.

It seems perhaps you came here because of Krishna Chetana, your wife; and also perhaps because in those days I was speaking on Hindu scriptures, and they were very gratifying to your mind, your conditioning, your upbringing. But my river has been changing many times, many turns, passing through valleys and mountains – and always moving into new territory.

So I have been watching your face many times here. When Krishna Chetana had tears in her eyes, you had only doubts. When she was crying with joy, ecstasy, your mind was full of questions, doubts . . . . And it is not as you say, that "for some time I have felt that something has remained unmelted in me." It has been so from the very beginning – and you *knew* it; perhaps not very clearly, perhaps it was just an unconscious feeling. Now you may have become more alert about it.

And the reason why you may have become more alert about it is that there has been a five-, six- year gap, while I have not been here. In these five, six years, hundreds of people from India reached the commune in America – even people for whom it was absolutely impossible to reach; they had to sell their houses, their land, everything. But they wanted to see me at least once before they die.

I waited for five years, and many times I thought: Krishna Chaitanya, Krishna Chetana . . . they are rich enough; they can afford to come to America very easily – there is no problem – they can be here at each festival time at least. But I did not receive even a single letter from you.

Now that I am back . . . many things which you cannot see when you are close, you become aware of when there is distance. You were left alone for these six years; that's why you are now feeling that something has remained unmelted. It is not "something," it is almost everything that has remained unmelted.

You are saying, "And at times I am overpowered by that, despite myself." Just think of it: if it is just a small part – "something" – how you can be overpowered by it, in spite of yourself? It must be something very big. It must be something more powerful than yourself – otherwise how can you be overcome by it? It is better to be very clear about it: that your sannyas has been very superficial. It is good to be alert and aware of its superficiality. Then the possibility opens of going deeper into it. Remaining unaware of it is dangerous.

You are saying, "I am not able to digest what You say." You are perfectly able to digest what I say, because your digestion system is perfectly okay. The problem is somewhere else: you do not want to digest it. It goes against your upbringing, it goes against your tradition, it goes against your orthodox mind. You can digest very well if I appreciate Krishna – but if I criticize him, then you cannot digest it. For digestion, it makes no difference: if it can digest appreciation, it can digest criticism.

And if the relationship between me and you is that of love, it does not matter whether I am appreciating Krishna or criticizing Krishna. What matters is that *I* am appreciating, *I* am criticizing. Nobody has appreciated Krishna the way I have appreciated, and nobody has criticized him either, the way I have criticized – because I am not looking only at one aspect. My effort is to give you life's contradictions and make you aware that life is not a non-contradictory, consistent phenomenon. It is basically contradictory.

Wherever there is a height like Krishna, there are bound to be on both sides deep dark valleys. And it will be unjust and unfair only to talk about the heights, or only to talk about the valleys. Both these things have been done. Those who are enemies talk only about the valleys: Jainas have criticized Krishna and thrown him into the seventh hell. They have only looked at the valley part, the dark part; they have never looked at the sunlit peaks. And there are people – Shankaracharya Ramanujacharya, Nimbaraka, and thousands of others who are followers of Krishna – who have only looked at the sunlit peaks, the heights. They have never bothered to see that the peak cannot exist without the valleys.

My whole approach is totally different from anybody else's: I want to present Krishna, or Christ, or Mahavira, or Buddha, in their totality. I am neither their friend nor their enemy – I am just trying to make you understand that even the greatest amongst you have their darker parts.

So if you find a dark part within yourself, don't condemn it. And even the people who had such dark valleys around them managed to reach to the highest peak of consciousness. So if you are surrounded by darkness, don't be worried: the dawn is not far away. It is just in the womb of darkness that the dawn grows. And as the darkness becomes darker, the morning comes closer.

I am not concerned with Krishna, not concerned with Christ, I am concerned with *you*. And these are just my excuses to give you a deep understanding that life is a harmony between contradictions – that the lowest is not separate from the highest, that the saint is not separate from the sinner. That's why I had to do both things: to appreciate and to criticize.

Whenever I was appreciating something that satisfied your ego, you felt you were melting with me, that you were in tune with me. And whenever I said something that went against your conditioning, immediately you were overwhelmed by doubt – "in spite of yourself." What do you mean by it? Were you fighting with the doubt?

When you say, "At times I am overpowered by that . . . something that has remained unmelted, despite myself," are you separate from it? You ~~are~~ it. You ~~are your doubt, and you are your trust; you are your love~~, and ~~you are your logic~~.

You are saying, "I am not able to digest what you say." Just watch what it is that you cannot digest, and *why* you cannot digest it. Do you want to digest it? – or don't you want to digest it? It will be a great spiritual insight for you to watch something that seems to be indigestible: Why? And I am here – you can ask as many questions as possible about that indigestible thing, and I will hammer it on your head, every day. So either you digest it or you disappear – but don't leave anything undigested in yourself; that becomes poisonous. Why have you not been asking about it? It is just the fear that shows doubt – but nothing is wrong with doubt.

Why should you ask, "Bhagwan, I am even guilty of having doubted You?" From where have you got this idea? That's what I am saying: you are continuously carrying your orthodox mind. My whole effort is to help you to be completely be free of guilt.

There is nothing wrong if you doubt something – openly expose it. Perhaps it needs to be explained to you from a different angle – but don't say, "Please forgive me." Who am I to forgive you? I am not angry at you. It is your *right* to doubt, it is your *right* to question, it is your *right* to be a sannyasin or not to be a sannyasin. In either case, my blessings are with you. There is no question of me forgiving anybody – because you cannot hurt me; hence, the question of forgiving you does not arise.

And you should not feel guilty about your doubts. You should only feel ashamed that you have not brought your doubts here. Every morning, every evening, I am talking to you. People are asking . . . . Why are you keeping your doubts within yourself? And whenever I have looked at your face, I have seen all those doubts in your eyes, in your face; I have never seen those doubts in your wife's face or her eyes.

This time when you came to see me in Bombay, your daughter was also with you. For six years I had not seen her. She has grown – but I feel a little sorry for her, because she has not grown like her mother; she is growing like you. I could see the same kind of expression in her eyes and on her face.

It happens naturally: ~~girls fall in love with their fathers~~, just as ~~boys fall in love with their mother~~s. So without your knowing, you must be sowing seeds of doubt in her also. Don't do that – because doubt never brings anybody any joy; it never brings any blessing in life; it never brings any ecstasy – ~~particularly to a woman, whose heart should grow, whose love should grow~~. It seems she has stopped the growth of her heart, her love, and she is following you, in your footsteps. And perhaps you are happy that your daughter is following you – but you are unconscious that you are destroying her.

~~It is not logic that brings life's blessings to people – it is love~~. Let her become more like her mother. Krishna Chetana is certainly *immensely* blessed. And if you have been here, perhaps you should be grateful to your wife; most probably it is she who has brought you close to me. She is a rare woman. There are hundreds of women here, but she is still a rare woman: so full of love that I don't think she has ever doubted, or has ever thought about doubting.

You are asking, "Please forgive me, as I don't know what to do during these moments." It is not a question of certain moments – it is a question of your very approach: you will have to change your very approach.

First, there is no need to feel guilty.

Second, when a doubt arises, there is no need to suppress it – otherwise, one day it will become too much and it will overwhelm you.

A doubt is like pus. Don't force it inside the body – bring it out. These meetings are therapeutic. These are not philosophical meetings; these are meetings where you can bring your doubts out and dissolve them.

Not that I am going to give you the answer – I am simply going to destroy your question, and your answer will grow within yourself.

Everybody is born with the answer: you can call it the soul, you can call it God, you can call it the truth. Everybody is born with the truth – it just has to be uncovered . . .from so many layers that the parents and the society and the educational system go on putting on you.

So, Krishna Chaitanya, from now onwards don't go on hiding and keeping your doubts to yourself. Don't be afraid: nobody here feels that if you bring your doubts out, you are committing a sin. This is not a church. This is not a gathering of believers – it is a gathering of lovers.

If a doubt is there, nothing is wrong in it. Bring it out. Keeping it inside is dangerous; it may become a cancer. Bring it out – I will try my best to destroy it. And once your doubts are destroyed – not replaced by belief – that's my whole process . . . . I am not trying to replace your doubts with new beliefs. I am not trying to take your old beliefs out and put new beliefs in. I am simply trying to take all beliefs out, and leave you alone, silent, in immense peace.

And in that peace, the seed of your soul starts growing. And one day you will find the mythological lotus blossoming in you, with all its fragrance.

Beloved Bhagwan,

Your whole message is for us to find that silent center at the core of our being. You have told us millions of times to meditate, to enquire within and search for our own incontrovertible truth. I hear You calling, calling me to awaken. These last discourses have been so crystal clear and utterly beautiful. Please tell me why I am so slow in getting out of my sleep?

Devageet, everybody has his own pace; and there is no need to force yourself to wake up sooner than it was going to happen naturally. There is no harm in waking up a little later.

I am reminded of a beautiful story: A man was a nuisance to all his neighbors because he was continually arguing against God, against heaven, against hell. He was an atheist, out-and-out. Even the king of the territory heard about him. He was invited to the court of the king, and even the wise people of the court could not manage to convince that man.

In fact, to convince an atheist is an almost impossible job. Unless you can find a man like me, the atheist is going to destroy all your arguments – because you are arguing for a hypothetical God. You cannot produce any evidence, you cannot produce any eyewitnesses, and you cannot produce any argument which is authentic. All arguments about God have been broken and been thrown away by atheists for centuries.

But the king said, "Just give me one more chance: I know about a man . . . only he can do something in this matter." And he gave him the address of the man and told him to go to the next village, where he lived. "By the side of a river, in a temple, you will find him. His name is Eknath. That is the only man . . . . If he can change you . . . otherwise, you are an impossible job."

But the man was very happy: it was a great challenge. So he went to the other village. It was somewhere around nine o'clock in the morning. He said, "By this time he must have finished his worship, bath; this is the right time to reach there." And when he he could not believe his eyes: Eknath was fast asleep – not only fast asleep, but he was putting his feet on the statue of God. He was using the statue as a good resting place for his feet.

The atheist, for the first time in his life, said, "My God! Even *I* cannot put my feet on the statue of God, although I am an atheist and I don't believe in God. But who knows – in the end it may turn out that God is, so I cannot do such a thing. This man is a sannyasin – supposed to be awake early in the morning, five o'clock, before the sun rises. It is nine o'clock and he is fast asleep – and he is going to convince me about God? He has not taken his bath, he has not worshiped, and I don't think he is going to worship – he is putting his feet on the statue of God."

Afraid – this man seems to be dangerous – he sat still in the temple, waiting for whenever he wakes up. About half an hour afterwards, Eknath woke up. He did not even ask God, "Forgive me, in my sleep I have touched you with my feet"; he did not even look back.

The man said, "You are a sannyasin? Is it not written in the scriptures that a sannyasin should wake up in the morning before the sunrise?"

Eknath said, "Yes, it is written. And my interpretation of it is: whenever a sannyasin wakes up, the sun should rise. Who is this sun? If he does not care about me, why should I care about him?"

The man said, "Strange . . . but you were putting your feet on God's feet, God's head . . . ?"

He said, "Where else can I put my feet? – because the scriptures say, 'God is everywhere.' Do you mean to say that I cannot put my feet anywhere?"

The man said, "Just don't get angry! . . . but your argument makes sense: ~~if God is everywhere, then whenever, wherever you put your feet, it is always on God's head.~~"

"So what is the problem? And this is such a good rest for my feet. Some idiots think that this is God. God is everywhere – so how can he be just in this stone, manufactured by the hand of man? You cannot befool me."

The man said, "Forgive me for interfering in your life so early in the morning, but I have come from the other village, sent by the king himself. And I am puzzled – what to say to you, because I used to be an atheist" . . . *used* to be, because this man seems to be a greater atheist than he had ever seen before.

Eknath said, "It is perfectly good; you can be an atheist, nothing is wrong in it. God does not mind it at all – just believe me. And now get lost!"

The man said, "But that king has put me in a strange situation. I came to be convinced about God."

Eknath said, "Convinced about God? What business do you have with God?"

He said, "No, I don't have any business."

"Then," he said, "why bother about useless things? Find something useful. Now I am going, because it is time for my food."

The atheist said, "Are you not going to take a bath in the river?"

He said, "Who cares about the river! It is always there. I can take a bath at any time – in the middle of the night, in the afternoon – what is the hurry? It is always flowing there. But if I don't reach in time to a house where they have promised to give me food today, that will be difficult – so I will take a bath after my food."

The man said, "But we have never heard of sannyasins taking food without a bath, without worship."

He said, "You must be talking about old-fashioned sannyasins. I am a contemporary man . . . and just don't waste my time: you can take the bath and worship God – meanwhile I am coming with my food."

And somebody had promised him . . . so he brought the food. He was sitting just in front of the temple, and a dog came and took one of his chappattis and ran away. And the man was watching; Eknath ran behind the dog: "You idiot, wait!"

He said, "My God, is he going to take that chappatti back?"

So he also followed, and Eknath managed to get hold of the dog, and he told the dog, "I have told you many times that if you want a chappatti, just wait there

– but I will not allow you to eat a chappatti without butter." So he took the chappatti back, put the butter on it, gave the chappatti back, and said to the dog, "Ram!" – which is the name of God in India – "now you can eat it, but always behave."

The man watched this whole scene: to the dog he is saying "God" and he will not allow the dog to eat the chappatti without butter . . . a very strange and unique man. Perhaps the king is right: that if this man cannot convince you of God, then nobody else can.

He touched the feet of Eknath. He said, "Just forgive me . . . . I was going under a great misunderstanding about you. It was not just a rationalization to put your feet on the statue of God. In the dog also you see God, and you won't allow the dog . . . half a mile you have run – and I have run – just to put butter on the chappatti!"

Eknath said, "It doesn't look right that I should eat with butter and God should eat without butter. And I have told him – but he is a very idiot God. This happens almost every day: as I open my food, he is hiding somewhere. You must have read in your scriptures that God is everywhere; this is the God who is everywhere, omnipresent.

"But I am also a stubborn man. This was only a half mile; one day it took ten miles. But unless I buttered the chappatti, I would not let him eat it. It doesn't look right. One has to be courteous."

The man said, "Of course. I have seen your courtesy from the very morning. But I don't have any argument with you; I am going home as a theist, because I have seen the first theist in my life – all other theists were simply just using words, not knowing anything about God. *You* certainly know something – every gesture is indicative of it. It can be misunderstood; I myself have misunderstood it before – but now I can see."

Eknath said, "Forget all this. Come on, join me; I have got enough food for both me and you, because I knew you must be waiting there."

The man said, "But I have to take a bath."

Eknath said, "Forget all about the bath. I have told you, the river is flowing the whole day. You can take a bath anytime; there is no prohibition."

He said, "But . . . although I am – I *used* to be – an atheist, just let me go in the temple to touch the feet . . . ."

Eknath said, "If you go into the temple . . . you will not find a worse man than me. First, eat; and then do whatsoever nonsense you want to do. I am feeling hungry, I cannot wait. But you are my guest – this temple is my house. Since I started living here, everybody has stopped coming in. This has been my whole life's experience: wherever I want, I enter in any temple – and soon worshipers disappear; because I do all kinds of things in the temple . . . you have not seen much. You just come, take your food."

Devageet, there is no hurry. Whether you wake up slowly, or whether you wake up quickly, there is eternity. How slow can you be? Try . . . . You cannot be eternally slow: that eternity passes by, and you are still in your bed. You will have to come out of the bed, and you will have to come out of your sleep.

Hence, don't feel any guilt, that "I am very slow in understanding." Don't compare with others. Just follow your natural course; slow or fast – but be natural. And existence loves those who are natural.

Jesus has forgotten completely one blessing: blessed are those who are natural. And my people are blessed people. No competition . . . everybody is going at his own pace. Somebody is resting under a tree, somebody is having a nap, somebody is fast asleep and snoring . . . . This is a beautiful variety. Never on the spiritual path has there been such variety.

Beloved Bhagwan,

Outward expression, declaring to the world the joy I feel, certainly has its limitations, its point of frustration. But falling inside, it looks limitless, endless – a vast cool cave – and nobody is there. What concerns me is: if I wander in, in the silence and stillness, will You be there?

Deva Surabhi, I rarely promise – but if you are absolutely certain that you will go on digging deeper and deeper to the very ultimate center of your being, I promise you I will be there to welcome you. Because the center is one . . . we are different only on the periphery.

Just think of a circle and a center: from the center towards the circle many lines can go. On the periphery those lines are very distant; as they move towards the center they come closer, and closer, and closer, and closer. And those who have reached the center are all ready to welcome you.

Not only will I be there, you will also find all those people whom I have been talking about. Just reach to the center, so I can introduce you to Chuang Tzu, to Lao Tzu, to Kabir, to Gautam Buddha, to Eknath, to Hotei, to Tilopa, Naropa . . . unique people; every one a unique flower, with a fragrance of his own.

And it is not only a promise to Surabhi, it is a promise to you all: the day you reach the center, you will find me there ahead of you. I am already there, just waiting for you. Don't get lost on the way: reach to the very end.

Okay, Vimal?

Yes, Bhagwan.

Freedom Opens The Door Of Responsibility

Freedom will create in you an authentic individual, with great challenges and responsibilities, dangers, risks.

But a life without dangers and without risks is not life; then the safest place is the grave, where no disease happens – no hepatitis, no AIDS, no homosexuality, no crime, no rape, no murder – *nothing* happens.

You are absolutely secure . . . and you cannot even die. One death is enough; after that there is no question of death. But do you want to choose a grave? Those who have chosen fear have chosen a psychological grave. My effort here is to bring you out of all kinds of graves. Jesus has brought only one man out of the grave, and that was Lazarus.

I am trying to bring thousands of people out of greater graves – which are psychological – and give them the opportunity to be free, and to be responsible; to take the risk, to accept the adventure. Climbing in the mountains *is* dangerous, but unless you accept the danger, you will never reach to the peaks of your being.

February 15, 1987,   8 a.m.

Beloved Bhagwan,

What is the difference between waiting for the ship to come in, and being passive and fatalistic?

Satyam Svarup, the difference between waiting for the ship to come, and being passive and fatalistic is immense, although very delicate.

The fatalistic mind does not believe in the individual's own freedom, does not believe in the individual's own longing and search. Its belief system is that everything is predetermined; the individual is just a puppet in the hands of existence.

Fatalism destroys your individuality, your integrity, your pride, your self-respect. It destroys everything, that is valuable in man. The fatalist is bound to be passive, because what is going to happen is not his desire, is not his longing – at the most it is just his acceptance. Whatever happens, he will accept it; he is, dull, unintelligent.

But waiting for the ship is a totally different phenomenon; waiting for the ship does not mean fatalism. The coming of the ship is not predetermined – it depends on the intensity of your longing: it depends on your love, on your heart, on your being afire.

You are arrowed towards the ship – but still it is not impatience. You trust your own longing, not fate. You trust your own dreams; you trust yourself. It brings more integrity to your individuality, more centeredness, more rootedness. And you are patient, because you know your longing is total, and existence is fair. It cannot defeat you, it cannot leave you aside in darkness, because you have longed, you have loved, you have desired, you have searched – although there is no impatience.

Impatience also shows that you are not trusting your dreams, you are not trusting your totality of longing. Patience simply means: I will wait, whatever time it takes for the spring to come – but I will not wait patiently; I will wait with a heart throbbing, desiring, waiting . . . each moment, day in, day out. Waiting for the ship is a very total action on your part – because the action is total, your trust is total.

But all the mystics of the world have been teaching you to wait patiently, and the masses of the world have turned waiting with patience into a passive and fatalistic attitude. They are indifferent: there is no longing, there is no desire, no dream, no vision. If it comes, it is okay; if it does not come, it does not matter.

The whole world has fallen into a deep spiritual sickness of fatalism. It has stopped people from growing; it has stopped people from searching. It has stopped people . . . even when the ship has arrived, they are fast asleep and unconscious.

Unless you have seen the ship in your vision with

total clarity, you will not be able to recognize it when it comes. How are you going to recognize that your ship has come ? You can recognize it only because a thousand-and-one times in your dreams it has been there – slowly, slowly becoming more and more clear.

It is as if you have seen it thousands of times, so when it comes – even when it is far away, surrounded by mist – you recognize it, you know it. This is the way it has been coming into your dreams. And when you see it coming closer, and the mariners and the captain standing on the deck, you are absolutely certain: these people belong to the land from where you come – because you have dreamt about the land, you have dreamt about these people. If the ship comes without your active desire and active longing, you may miss it. It may come and it may go, and you may not be able to recognize that it is *your* ship, that it has come for you, to take you back to the original source.

Beloved Bhagwan,

I really love that image of You being like the sun rising in the morning, and us, Your disciples, being like the birds and trees and flowers starting to sing and dance in the warmth and light.
It looks to me like there is one difference in the analogy: the actual sun doesn't have a mischievous sense of humor, and the actual birds and trees and flowers aren't giggling – or are they?

In the whole of existence it is only man who can giggle and laugh. Laughter is part of the highest consciousness achieved by man.

You are right: the sun rises, but there is no laughter; the birds sing, but there is no giggling. They are far lower as far as consciousness is concerned. Your saints also don't laugh; in your churches also there is no giggling. It is not an improvement for consciousness, but a going downwards, backwards.

Seriousness is a disease.

Only the sick mind is serious.

The youthful, the young, laugh, dance, sing, giggle. But with the serious mind, man loses that beautiful foam that comes on the ocean waves. Although it is just foam, without that foam those waves will look naked. That foam makes almost a crown to the waves. With the white foam, tidal waves coming towards the shore remind one of Himalayan peaks, where snow has never melted – eternal snow. And the whiteness of the foam gives a beauty, a life, a certain dance to the wave.

I am against all those religions which make you serious – and almost all the religions do make you serious. They destroy all possibilities of laughter: laughter seems to be profane. But I say unto you: Laughter is the most sacred phenomenon on the earth – because it is the highest peak of consciousness.

It is not only the religions, but almost all kinds of serious people – whether they are religious or not – are serious because the society gives respectability to seriousness.

If you meet Jesus with the cross . . . long British face – I sometimes wonder why he was born in Judea. Britain was the right place for him; he is British, out-and-out. He never laughed. And then that serious cross . . . and not only *he* has to carry it, he is telling his disciples that everybody should carry his cross on his shoulders. Why should everybody carry his cross on his shoulders? – why not a guitar? My people are going to carry guitars on their shoulders.

But for thousands of years seriousness has been so much respected that a few countries have completely forgotten how to laugh. It is said that when you tell a joke to an Englishman, he laughs twice: first he laughs so that nobody sees that he has not understood the joke, and then secondly he laughs in the middle of the night, when he gets it.

If you tell the same joke to a German, he laughs only once – just for etiquette's sake; because everybody is laughing, he has to make the effort. Deep down he cannot understand why people are laughing. But he never gets it, so the second time is out of the question. If you tell the same joke to a Jew, rather than laughing he will say, "Wait, don't waste time! It is an old joke, and moreover, you are telling it all wrong."

~~People behave differently, because they have been conditioned differently.~~ I have been searching for a joke that is purely Indian, but I have not been able to find one, all jokes are imported. It is good that there is no taxation on imported jokes; otherwise, in India there would be no jokes at all.

The Indians have been too serious about things, about God, about the ultimate. You cannot conceive of Gautam Buddha laughing, or Shankaracharya laughing, or Mahavira laughing – that is impossible. I have always wondered about it . . . because some of the first statues in the world were made of Gautam Buddha; those are the most ancient statues.

And why have they chosen cold marble to make the statues of Buddha? Buddha *is* cold. ~~Laughter brings warmth; seriousness slowly, slowly becomes coldness – inhumanly cold.~~ And the white marble represents his face exactly – because he never showed any emotions on his face; nobody ever saw tears in his eyes, a smile on his lips. Even while he was alive, he was just a marble statue.

India has been very serious for centuries, and that is one of the causes of its degradation. ~~Silence is beautiful~~ – but ~~silence does not mean seriousness.~~ ~~Silence can be full of smiles~~; in fact, ~~authentic silence~~ is bound to ~~be full of smiles, joy.~~ People who have been experiencing ecstasy – even they have not burst into laughter.

This is contrary to my own experience, and it is contrary to the existential law.

The first thing that happens to the enlightened person is a deep belly laughter – for the sheer stupidity that he has been searching for something which is within himself. He has been carrying it for centuries within himself, and he never looked there; and he looked all over the world – carrying within himself the treasure which was available within a minute.

Just close your eyes . . . be silent . . . and it is there.

I cannot conceive that anybody finding it within himself should not have laughed – but the stories of hundreds of awakened people don't mention it. Perhaps they laughed, but they did not allow the laughter to reach out; they controlled it.

Just because the whole tradition says that the higher you go into consciousness, the more serious you become . . . . But I know from my own experience – and logically it is relevant – that if you have your glasses and are looking all around for them, and then suddenly you become aware that they are sitting on your nose, it is impossible not to giggle, not to laugh.

The spiritual experience is no different from that: It is just sitting on your nose – and you are searching for it all over the world. You are missing it because you are searching all over the world. Just sit down, forget the world, and it is there. Who is searching? . . .

~~The seeker is the sought.~~
~~The hunter is the hunted.~~
~~The observer is the observed.~~

But ~~because you never look withinwards~~ . . . and ~~you cannot find it anywhere outside~~ – neither on the Himalayan peaks nor on the moon – naturally, failure after failure will make you serious, sad, as if you are not adequate enough, capable enough to find it. The truth is: you are not finding it because it is not outside you.

So ~~*all* paths are wrong.~~ Wherever you go you will find failure and nothing else. ~~Drop going, stop~~

searching, be calm and quiet. First one should look into oneself. If you cannot find it there, then it seems logical that you should move further away. But anyone who has ever looked withinwards has always found it there.

And in this finding, there is going to be a great laugh at yourself, because existence has played really a great joke.

There is an old story: When God created the world he used to live in the world, in the marketplace. But his life was becoming more and more a torture, because people were continuously coming with complaints: somebody's wife is sick, somebody's child has died, somebody is not getting employment – all kinds, all sorts of complaints and complaints. And people were not even concerned whether it was day or night: twenty-four hours a day he was listening to the complaints and, naturally, losing his marbles.

Finally he asked his advisers. They said, "The only way is . . . . In the first place, it was wrong for you to create the world; in the second place, it was wrong for you to live in the world. Now escape; otherwise these people are going to kill you."

But he said, "Where to escape to?"

Somebody suggested, "Go to Everest!"

He said, "You don't know the future. I know past, present, future: soon a guy – Edmund Hillary – will reach there. And once he sees me, soon the same trouble will start: buses, roads, airports, restaurants, hotels all around . . . because people will be coming there to complain about their problems and troubles. The same thing will start."

Somebody said, "Then it is better you go to the moon."

He said, "You don't understand: there is not a single place in the whole world where man is not going to reach some day or other."

One old adviser, who rarely used to speak, whispered in the ear of God, "I know about one place where man will never reach: you just get inside him. He will look everywhere – but he will not look within himself."

And God said, "That seems to be sensible." And since then he has been living within you.

Now I have told you the secret, it is up to you: if you want to go and meet him, go within! But don't complain . . . . In fact, he will be very happy to see you, because he has not seen very many people in thousands of years – only once in a while.

And the people who have reached him have reached by becoming silent, alert, conscious. They don't complain – they giggle, they laugh. And I say to you: God joins in the laughter with you.

But it has to be an experience; otherwise it will be only a belief – and I don't want to create any belief system. I am simply telling you my own experience; you can make it your own experience too.

You say that fear and freedom, like ambition and love, cannot co-exist. But it is existence that brings into being fear and love of freedom, together.
Please comment.

Anand Maitreya, it is true that it is existence itself which brings fear and love of freedom together – and I have been telling you they cannot exist together. They cannot.

Existence gives you an alternative: to choose, so that your freedom is not interfered with. You can choose fear, or you can choose freedom. Freedom is not being imposed by nature on you, neither is fear imposed. Nature gives you alternatives. Now it is your own choice, out of your own intelligence that you have to choose.

You cannot choose both together – that is what I mean when I say they cannot exist together. Existence makes them both available, but you have to choose one. Most people have chosen fear. Out of fear they have created all kinds of gods, theologies, religions; out of fear they are being dominated by stupid politicians; out of fear they have been exploited for thousands of years; out of fear comes their whole spiritual slavery. But there must be some reason why they choose fear and why they don't choose freedom. Very few people have chosen freedom.

There is something which has to be understood: freedom brings responsibility. The moment you choose to be free, you are responsible for every one of your acts. You are responsible for your whole life; you are responsible for your misery or your blissfulness; you are responsible for remaining asleep or becoming awake.

Freedom opens the door of responsibility. Fear takes away all responsibilities – you are just a slave. The responsibility is in the hands of somebody else, who dominates you. He will provide you with food, he will provide you with clothes, he will provide you with a shelter – you need not worry about it. If he wants a slave, he has to provide all these things.

Fear is a kind of security, safety – somebody else has taken the responsibility and the burden of responsibility – and this is the reason why millions of people have chosen fear. But the moment they choose fear, they also lose many things: not only responsibility – they lose their very souls. They are no longer themselves. They lose all possibility of growth – they are in the hands of somebody else. If your growth is going to be beneficial to those hands, the growth will be allowed; but if your growth, your intelligence, is going to be a disturbance, then your roots will be cut.

In Japan they have a strange kind of plant – three hundred years, four hundred years old, but only five or six inches tall. Many families of gardeners have taken care of those plants for centuries. You can see they are old, very old; every branch shows their age – but why have they remained only six inches high? They would have grown one hundred feet, one hundred and fifty feet high; they would have had such foliage that thousands of people could have sat under their shadow – and you can take them in your hand.

The strategy is simple and very symbolic for man too. They think it is an art; I think it is a crime. The method for keeping those trees growing old, yet not growing upwards – remaining small, pygmies – is that when they are four, five inches tall, they put them into earthen pots without bottoms. Whenever their roots grow, they go on cutting the roots – and if the roots cannot grow, the tree cannot grow.

There is a certain balance between the roots and

the tree: the higher the tree goes, the deeper the roots go. You cannot have a one-hundred-foot-tall tree with six-inch-long roots – it will fall. By cutting the roots, they don't allow the tree to grow. People come from far away to see those plants; and those families brag about them – this tree is four hundred years old. And it looks so old . . . but it is very strange that it has remained only six inches high.

The same is true about man. The moment you allow somebody else to take responsibility for you, he starts cutting your roots – because a slave has to remain weak, has to remain retarded in the mind, otherwise he will be dangerous. If he is strong, intelligent, he may revolt. To avoid revolt, to avoid any kind of revolution, the slave has to be kept at the minimum of his growth, not at the maximum. So they don't allow you to grow upwards as an individual; they don't allow you to become intelligent.

For example, in India, one fourth of the society consists of the sudras. They are untouchables; you cannot touch them – or if by chance you touch each other, you have to take a shower immediately and change your clothes. They are dirty people; they do all kinds of dirty jobs for the society. They should be respected – because a society can exist without painters, without poets, without singers, without mystics. It is beautiful to have them all, but a society can exist without them. But a society cannot exist without all those people who are doing all kinds of dirty jobs: cleaning your toilets, cleaning your streets. They are not allowed to live in the city; they have to live outside the city. They are the poorest of the poor in the world. They are not allowed any education; they are not allowed even to listen to religious scriptures; the question of their entry into the temple of God is impossible.

These are ways of cutting roots: no education, no possibility of moving from one profession to another; they look as if they are living without the walls of a prison, but the subtle bars of the prison are there. There is no movement in Hindu society: the sudra,

whatever he can do, can never become a saint; however virtuous, however pure he may be, he cannot be accepted into the higher classes of society. And he cannot move from the profession that has been his for thousands of years, that his forefathers have been doing. He has to do the same kind of job.

You have taken their freedom, you have taken their responsibility. Yes, they are given food, they are given clothes, they are given small huts – and that is all. They have a certain security; but because of this small security, they have lost their spirituality.

Existence always gives alternatives in every dimension, because existence does not want anything to be imposed on its children. You have to choose.

I have been talking to these sudras, untouchables. At first they could not believe that anybody from a higher caste would come into their small village outside the city; but when I started visiting them, slowly, slowly they became accustomed to it – that this man seems to be strange.

And I told them, "Your slavery, your oppression, your exploitation, is because you are clinging to such small securities. When society cannot give you your individuality and your freedom, that society is not yours. Leave it! Declare that you do not belong to such an ugly society! Who is preventing you?

"And stop doing all these dirty jobs. Let the brahmins and the higher castes clean the toilets, and then they will know that just sitting and reading the scriptures is not virtue; it is not purity."

Brahmins have not done anything except be parasites on society; but they are the most respected people, because they are educated, they are well-versed in religious scriptures. Just to be born into a brahmin family is enough; no other quality is needed: people will touch your feet. Just being a brahmin by birth, you have all the qualifications to be worshiped. And this has continued for at least five thousand years.

Talking to the sudras, I became aware they have become so accustomed to a certain security that they have forgotten the alternative of freedom. And whenever I tried to convince them, sooner or later the question was asked, "What about responsibilities? If we are free, then we will be responsible. Right now we are not responsible for anything. We live safe and secure, although in utter humiliation" – but to that they have become accustomed and immune.

Anand Maitreya, existence gives you fear, existence gives you freedom. You cannot have both together.

Freedom will create in you an authentic individual, with great challenges and responsibilities, dangers, risks. But a life without dangers and without risks is not life, then the safest place is the grave, where no disease happens – no hepatitis, no AIDS, no homosexuality, no crime, no rape, no murder – *nothing* happens. You are absolutely secure . . . and you cannot even die. One death is enough; after that there is no question of death. But do you want to choose a grave? Those who have chosen fear have chosen a psychological grave.

My effort here is to bring you out of all kinds of graves. Jesus has brought only one man out of the grave, and that was Lazarus. I am trying to bring thousands of people out of greater graves – which are psychological – and give them the opportunity to be free, and to be responsible; to take the risk, to accept the adventure. Climbing in the mountains *is* dangerous, but unless you accept the danger, you will never reach to the peaks of your being. Freedom brings you to the highest peaks of enlightenment.

Beloved Bhagwan,

Seven years ago You gave me the name "Patience" and said,
"For one who can wait infinitely, things happen immediately."
Oh, my Master, it seems I've lost track of what I'm waiting for, or where I've been, or where I'm going.
A stranger to myself, the journey grows ever stranger; yet just the waiting, more and more is enough.
I feel pregnant with a soft throbbing in my heart, miracle of miracles to be here with You again.
Is this the beginning of patience, or am I fooling myself again?

Sudhiro, I repeat it again to you: for one who can wait infinitely, things happen immediately.
In these seven years you have been searching here and there. You could not trust what I said to you: "Wait, and wait infinitely; allow existence to happen to you, and all miracles are possible within you."

You have come back to me; now let this be the beginning of patience. Don't wander unnecessarily here and there. You cannot find truth; it is not an object that you have to go somewhere and find. It is your subjectivity; it is your interiority. By being patient, silently waiting, you suddenly come across yourself.

And the first taste of oneself is so tremendous that one cannot go back; one wants to go deeper and deeper into oneself. But it is a different kind of pilgrimage: you have not to do anything, you have just to be silent, allow things to settle on their own.

You are not fooling yourself – but if you don't understand the message, there is every possibility you can start fooling yourself again. To be foolish does not need much intelligence; but to be patient, waiting, needs great intelligence.

Have you ever thought why sick people in hospitals are called "patients"? There is some meaning in it, because all the medical people in the world have found that medicines can only help, it is really the relaxed sick person who heals himself – by being patient.

What is true about the body is even more true about the soul. Be patient. There is no place to go. Yes, there is a space within you in which you have to get more and more drowned. People don't go inwards because they are afraid of drowning – it *is* an overwhelming experience.

Once I was sitting by the side of the Ganges in Allahabad, and a man jumped into the river and started shouting, "Help me! Save me!" I am not a savior, so I looked all around to see if some savior could be found – otherwise this idiot was going to spoil my clothes also. But there was nobody – so finally I had to jump.

He was a heavy man, a big man, but somehow I pulled him out. He said, "What kind of man are you? Why did you pull me out?"

I said, "This is strange. You were shouting, 'Help! Help! Save me.'"

He said, "That was out of fear. Really I was committing suicide!"

I said, "Then forgive me. I had no idea that a man who is committing suicide would shout for help – but I can understand that before jumping it is one thing; and when you really start drowning a fear arises . . . . You forget all the troubles because of which you were committing suicide: a new trouble has arisen which is far bigger." So I said, "I will never do such a thing again." And I pushed the man back into the river!

He said, "What are you doing!"

I said, "Now you commit suicide. I will sit by the side and wait."

And he started shouting, "Help me! What kind of strange man are you? Help me!"

I said, "Now help yourself."

But another man came meanwhile, jumped, and took him out. I said, "What are you doing? I did this – and he was very angry." But this time he was not angry; he had understood that he had not the courage to drown. I said, "What is the matter? You are very silent. Last time you were very angry."

He said, "I have understood one thing: that I will have to find some other way of committing suicide. This drowning in the river is not for me."

I said, "I can help you."

He said, "You are *really* a strange man. First you pulled me out, and then you pushed me back . . . and now you want to help me some other way."

I said, "I know many ways . . . ."

He said, "I don't want to listen. I am going home."

I said, "That is up to you. You can go home, and if you want I can accompany you. On the way I can tell you many methods to commit suicide."

"But" he said, "I don't *want* to commit suicide."

But I followed him. He would stop and he would say, "Will you leave me or not?"

I said, "I am not going to leave you till we come to your home."

He said, "This is something. If I want to commit suicide, or if I don't want to commit suicide – it is *my* problem. You have made it *your* problem."

I said, "I am just trying to be helpful – just to be of some service at the last moment of your life."

He said, "But I am going to live!"

I said, "That you can decide later on. First, understand all the methods – simple methods." And then we passed a railway line and I told him, "This is also a good method. And it happens so quickly that even if you shout 'Help' . . . this and that . . . it will not disturb . . . ."

He said, "But many times trains are very late."

I said, "That is true. You should always come with a tiffin carrier, so if the train is late you can have a good lunch and lie down again."

He said, "This I have never heard – that anybody committing suicide first enjoys lunch and then lies down . . . . And moreover it is going to rain; there are so many clouds."

I said, "Don't be worried about that. Don't you have an umbrella? . . . so while the train is coming, you keep the umbrella up. That will help you in two ways: you will not see the train coming, and your clothes will not be destroyed by the rain."

He said, "I pray to you, just leave me! I don't want to show you my house, because you seem to be a very strange person – you may start coming there." He said, "Really we have passed my house. I did not enter . . . I am going to meet a friend."

I said, "You can go anywhere. This is my address . . . whenever you need any suggestions about suicide. This is my expertise – to help people commit suicide."

He threw my card away. He said, "Keep your card. I am never going to commit suicide. I will never need you."

When you go inwards, you will feel afraid. You become alone – nobody is with you; and your center is almost a magnet – it pulls you. A fear can take grip of your mind: Where are you going? Will you be able to return? Many people become afraid of meditation.

They just touch a superficial level and run away. But unless you gather courage and allow existence to dissolve you . . . .

It is a dissolution. You will not be the way you used to be anymore – but you will be vast, as vast as existence itself.

So you are not going to be the loser – but that you will find only later on. When you have lost yourself, then you will find the treasure: it is not a question of your search – it is a question of your disappearance. Your absence becomes the presence of God.

Okay, Vimal?

Yes, Bhagwan.

Rebellion Is A Style Of Life

The rebel lives individually – not as a cog in the wheel, but as an organic unity. His life is not decided by anybody else, but by his own intelligence. The very fragrance of his life is that of freedom – not only that he lives in freedom, he allows everybody else also to live in freedom. He does not allow anybody to interfere in his life; neither does he interfere in anybody else's life. To him, life is so sacred – and freedom is the ultimate value – that he can sacrifice everything for it: respectability, status, even life itself.

Freedom, to him, is what God used to be to the so-called religious people in the past.

Freedom is his God.

Men have lived down the ages like sheep, as part of a crowd, following its traditions, conventions – following the old scriptures and old disciplines. But that way of life was anti-individual; if you are a Christian you cannot be an individual; if you are a Hindu you cannot be an individual.

A rebel is one who lives totally according to his own light, and risks everything else for his ultimate value of freedom.

February 15, 1987,   7 p.m.

Beloved Bhagwan,

What is Your notion of rebellion and of a rebel?

Giulia, my notion about the rebel and rebellion is very simple: a man who does not live like a robot conditioned by the past.

Religion, society, culture . . . anything that is of yesterday does not in any way interfere in his way of life, in his style of life.

He lives individually – not as a cog in the wheel, but as an organic unity. His life is not decided by anybody else, but by his own intelligence. The very fragrance of his life is that of freedom – not only that he lives in freedom, he allows everybody else also to live in freedom. He does not allow anybody to interfere in his life; neither does he interfere in anybody else's life. To him, life is so sacred – and freedom is the ultimate value – that he can sacrifice everything for it: respectability, status, even life itself.

Freedom, to him, is what God used to be to the so-called religious people in the past.

Freedom is his God.

Men have lived down the ages like sheep, as part of a crowd, following its traditions, conventions – following the old scriptures and old disciplines. But that way of life was anti-individual; if you are a Christian you cannot be an individual; if you are a Hindu you cannot be an individual.

A rebel is one who lives totally according to his own light, and risks everything else for his ultimate value of freedom.

The rebel is the contemporary person. The mobs are not contemporary.

Hindus believe in scriptures which are five or ten thousand years old. Such is also the case with other religions too; the dead are dominating the living.

The rebel rebels against the dead, takes his life in his own hands. He is not afraid of being alone; on the contrary, he enjoys his aloneness as one of the most precious treasures. The crowd gives you security, safety – at the cost of your soul. It enslaves you. It gives you guidelines on how to live: what to do, what not to do.

All over the world, every religion has given something like the ten commandments – and these were given by people who had no idea how the future is going to be, how man's consciousness in the future is going to be. It is as if a small child were to write your whole life's story, not knowing at all what youth means, not knowing at all what old age means, not knowing at all what death is.

All the religions are primitive, crude – and they have been shaping your life. Naturally the whole world is full of misery: you are not allowed to be yourself.

Every culture wants you to be just a carbon copy, never your original face.

The rebel is one who lives according to his own light, moves according to his own intelligence. He creates his path by walking on it, he does not follow the crowd on the superhighway.

His life is dangerous – but a life that is not dangerous is not life at all. He accepts the challenge of the unknown. He does not meet the unknown that is coming in the future, prepared by the past. That creates the whole anguish of humanity; the past prepares you, and the future is never going to be the past. Your yesterday is never going to be your tomorrow.

But up to now this is how man has lived: your yesterdays prepare you for your tomorrows. The very preparation becomes a hindrance. You cannot breathe freely, you cannot love freely, you cannot dance freely – the past has crippled you in every possible way. The burden of the past is so heavy that everybody is crushed under it.

The rebel simply says goodbye to the past.

It is a constant process; hence, to be a rebel means to be continuously in rebellion – because each moment is going to become past; every day is going to become past. It is not that the past is already in the graveyard – you are moving through it every moment. Hence, the rebel has to learn a new art: the art of dying to each moment that has passed, so that he can live freely in the new moment that has come.

A rebel is a continuous process of rebellion; he is not static. And that is where I make a distinction between the revolutionary and the rebel.

The revolutionary is also conditioned by the past. He may not be conditioned by Jesus Christ or Gautam Buddha, but he is conditioned by Karl Marx or Mao Tse-tung or Joseph Stalin or Adolf Hitler or Benito Mussolini . . . it does not matter who conditions him. The revolutionary has his own holy bible – *Das Kapital;* his holy land – the Soviet Union; his own mecca – in the

Kremlin . . . and just like any other religious person, he is not living according to his own consciousness. He is living according to a conscience created by others.

Hence, the revolutionary is nothing but a reactionary. He may be against a certain society, but he is always for another society. He may be against one culture, but he is immediately ready for another culture. He only goes on moving from one prison into another prison – from Christianity to communism; from one religion to another religion – from Hinduism to Christianity. He changes his prisons.

The rebel simply moves out of the past and never allows the past to dominate him. It is a constant, continuous process. The whole life of the rebel is a fire that burns. To the very last breath he is fresh, he is young. He will not respond to any situation according to his past experience; he will respond to every situation according to his present consciousness.

To be a rebel, to me, is the only way to be religious, and the so-called religions are not religions at all. They have destroyed humanity completely, enslaved human beings, chained their souls; so on the surface it seems that you are free, but deep inside you, religions have created a certain conscience which goes on dominating you.

It is almost like one great scientist, Delgado . . . . He has found that in the human brain there are seven hundred centers. Those centers are connected with your whole body, the whole system. There is a center for your sex, there is a center for your intelligence, and for everything in your life. If at a particular center an electrode is implanted in the brain, a very strange phenomenon happens. He displayed it for the first time in Spain.

He put an electrode in the brain of the strongest bull – a remote control was in his pocket – and he stood in a field, waved a red flag, and the bull rushed madly towards him.

That was the most dangerous bull in the whole of Spain, and thousands of people had gathered to see. They were looking at the phenomenon . . . their breathing stopped – their eyes were not blinking . . . . The bull was approaching closer and closer, and they were afraid that Delgado was going to be dead within a second. But he had in his pocket this small remote controller . . . . Just when the bull was one foot away, he pushed a button in his pocket – nobody saw it – and the bull stopped as if suddenly frozen, like a statue.

Since then, Delgado has experimented on many animals, and on man too; and his conclusion is that what he is doing with electrodes, religions have been doing by conditioning. From its very childhood you condition a child; you go on repeating, repeating a certain idea which becomes settled near his center of intelligence, and it goes on goading the center to do something or not to do something.

Delgado's experiment can prove dangerous to humanity. It can be used by the politicians. Just when the child is born, in the hospitals, a small electrode needs to be pushed into his skull near the intelligence center, and a central controlling system will take care that nobody becomes a revolutionary, nobody becomes a rebel.

You will be surprised to know that inside your skull there is no sensitivity, so you will never be aware whether you have something implanted in your head or not. And a remote controller can manage . . . from Moscow even the whole Soviet Union can be managed. Religions have been doing the same in a crude manner.

A rebel is one who throws away the whole past because he wants to live his own life according to his own longings, according to his own nature – not according to some Gautam Buddha, or according to some Jesus Christ, or Moses.

The rebel is the only hope for the future of humanity.

The rebel will destroy all religions, all nations, all races – because they are all rotten, past, hindering the progress of human evolution. They are not allowing anybody to come to his full flowering: they don't want human beings on the earth – they want sheep.

Jesus continuously says, "I am your shepherd, and you are my sheep . . . . " And I have always wondered that not even a single man stood up and said, "What kind of nonsense are you talking? If we are sheep, then you are also a sheep; and if you are a shepherd, then we are also shepherds."

Not only his contemporaries . . . but for two thousand years *no* Christian has raised the question that it is such an insult to humanity, such a great humiliation to call human beings sheep and to call himself the shepherd, the savior.

"I have come to save you" . . . and he could not save himself. And still almost half of humanity is hoping that he will be coming back to save them. You cannot save yourself; the only begotten son of God, Jesus Christ, is needed. And he had promised to his people, "I will be coming soon, in your own lifetime" . . . and two thousand years have passed – many lifetimes have passed – and there seems to be no sign, no indication . . . .

But all the religions have done the same in different ways. Krishna says in the *Gita* that whenever there will be misery, whenever there will be anguish, whenever there will be need, "I will be coming again and again." Five thousand years have passed, and he has not been seen even once – never mind "again and again."

These people, howsoever beautiful their statements may be, were not respectful to humanity. A rebel respects you, respects life, has a deep reverence for everything that grows, thrives, breathes. He does not put himself above you, holier than you, higher than you; he is just one amongst you. Only one thing he can claim: that he is more courageous than you are. He cannot save you – only your courage can save you. He cannot lead you – only your own guts can lead you to the fulfillment of your life.

Rebellion is a style of life. To me, it is the only religion which is authentic. Because if you live according to your own light you may go astray many times, and you may fall many times; but each fall, each going astray will make you wiser, more intelligent, more understanding, more human. There is no other way of learning than by making mistakes. Just don't make the same mistake again.

There is no God, except your own consciousness.

There is no need for any pope, or for Ayatollah Khomeini, or for any shankaracharya, to be mediators between you and God. These are the greatest criminals in the world, because they are exploiting your helplessness.

Just a few days ago, the pope declared a new sin: that one should not confess directly to God; you have to confess through the priest. Confessing directly to God, communicating directly with God, is a new sin. Strange . . . you can see clearly that this is not religion, this is business – because if people start confessing directly to God, then who is going to confess to the priest and pay the fine? The priest becomes useless, the pope becomes useless.

All the priests are pretending that they are mediators between you and the ultimate source of life. They know nothing of the ultimate source of life. Only you are capable of knowing your source of life. But your source of life is also the ultimate source of life – because we are not separate. No man is an island; we are a vast continent underneath. Perhaps on the surface you look like an island – and there are many islands – but deep down in the ocean, you meet. You are part of one earth, one continent. The same is true about consciousness. But one has to be free from churches, from temples, from mosques, from synagogues. One has to be just oneself, and take the challenge of life wherever it leads. You are the only guide.

You are your own master.

Beloved Bhagwan,

Do You think Your teaching is a radical one?

Giulia, I do not have any teaching. My life is that of a rebel. I do not have a doctrine, a philosophy, a theology to teach you. I have only my own experience of rebellion to share, to infect you with rebelliousness. And when you are a rebel you will not be a copy of me; you will be a unique phenomenon in yourself.

All Buddhists are trying to be carbon copies of Gautam Buddha. He has a teaching: If you follow this certain discipline, you will become just like me. All Christians are carbon copies – the original is Jesus Christ.

I don't have any teaching, any doctrine, any discipline to give to you. My whole effort is to wake you up. It is not a teaching – it is just cold water thrown into your eyes. And when you wake up you will not find that you are like me – a carbon copy of me. You will be just yourself – neither Christian, nor Hindu, nor Mohammedan . . . a unique flower. There are not two persons alike – how can there be so many Christians? How can there be so many Buddhists? And the whole of history is a proof of what I am saying.

For twenty-five centuries, millions of people in the East have tried the discipline and the teaching of Gautam Buddha – but not a single one has been able to become a Gautam Buddha. Nature does not allow two persons to be the same. Nature is not an assembly line where cars are produced . . . so you can see hundreds and thousands of Fords coming off the assembly line – the same, exactly the same. Nature is very creative, very innovative. It always creates a new man. It has created millions and millions of people, but never two people the same. You cannot find even two leaves on a tree just exactly the same, or two pebbles on the seashore just exactly the same. Each has his own individuality.

I don't have a teaching; but whatever I have experienced, it is a living phenomenon I share with you – not words, not theories, not hypotheses. I can give you as much closeness as you need; just as when you bring an unlit candle close to a candle which is burning there is a point where suddenly the fire jumps from the lit candle to the unlit candle. The lit candle loses nothing, and there has not been a transfer of any teaching, but a transfer of fire.

Giulia, I would like to say that I don't have any teaching, but I have great fire in my heart, and whoever comes close to me becomes aflame.

These people here are not my followers. They are just friends who are sharing in an experience which can burn all that is false in them, and can purify that which is their essential individuality, their authentic potential. This is an alchemical school, a school of mystery. I am not a teacher; I don't have any ideas, concepts . . . but I have a life to share, I have a love to share, and to those who are ready, I am ready to give all that I have – and in no way will they be enslaved.

The closer they come to me, the more they understand me, the more they will be themselves: that is the miracle.

I don't believe that walking on water is a miracle – it is sheer stupidity. The real miracle is to wake you up, to bring the message of freedom to you – freedom from all fetters. And I do not replace your imprisonment with new fetters and new chains; I simply leave you in the open sky. I fly with you a little while so that you can gather courage: there is no need to be afraid – you also have wings, just like I have wings. You have not used them; you have never been told that you *have* wings. So this is a place where I make every effort that you become aware of your wings, encourage you, push you into the infinite sky which belongs to you. This is a totally different place – it is not a church, it is not a temple, not a synagogue. I am not your savior, and I am not the messenger of any God. A messenger is just a postman and nothing else.

I don't have a message to give to you, but I have a fire to impart to you. And if this fire is not radical, then nothing else can be radical in the whole world.

Beloved Bhagwan,

In which way do You think Your presence in a political party would help people who act politically in this party?

I hate politics. I am not a politician, and I am never going to be a politician.

An invitation has come from the Italian Radical party that they would like me to be their president. I have informed them: I cannot be a member of your party, but I can be a friend – and if you need guidance in bringing more rebellion to your country I can be immensely helpful.

I am particularly interested in Italy because of this pope: until the Vatican is destroyed completely, humanity will not know what freedom is. The pope is not the representative of God, he is the representative of the whole idea of how to enslave people.

Italy has been destroyed by the Catholic religion. Otherwise, in its golden days, when Rome was at its highest peak of glory, it was one of the most beautiful countries in the world – for the simple reason that it was pagan. It had no religion; it believed in life, it believed in love, it was earthbound. Those were the most beautiful days Italy has seen. The whole country was full of Zorbas.

But the trouble started because Judea, where Jesus Christ was born, was under the Roman Empire; and Jesus Christ was crucified on the demand of the Jews, but under the control of Pontius Pilate, the Roman governor of Judea.

It is a strange story of deep human psychology. Pontius Pilate never wanted to crucify Jesus, because he could see there was nothing wrong in that man. At the most he was a little crazy, was talking about things which were harmless . . . . Anybody can say, "I am the only begotten son of God" – what harm is there? He has not harmed anybody.

But the Jews – and particularly the chief priest and the rabbis were very much against him, because they thought that God is their monopoly; and this carpenter's son, who is uneducated, uncultured . . . is destroying their very concept of God, and he is pretending to be the long-awaited messiah of the Jews. They could not tolerate it.

Pontius Pilate behaved politically, as politicians are supposed to. Knowing perfectly well Jesus Christ is innocent . . . just some screw is loose in his head, that's all, but that is not a crime – you cannot be crucified because some screw is loose or tight. You can go to a workshop and get the screw put in the right position – but crucifixion is not the way.

Hence, a very symbolic act, which Christians have never discussed – but Sigmund Freud was very much interested in that act . . . . Jesus was crucified to satisfy the Jews. Judea was their country and if Jesus was not crucified there was every possibility that the Jews might rebel against the empire. The empire could not take such a risk just to save one innocent man . . . .

When Pontius Pilate ordered the crucifixion and went inside, the first thing he did – he was seen doing – was to wash his hands, without any soap or water, but he was washing his hands. This washing of the hands has been taken very seriously by Sigmund Freud, himself a Jew: unconsciously Pontius Pilate was trying to say that "I am not responsible for it. I wash my hands completely of it. This is the Jews and their doing. I am not guilty of it." But the idea of guilt had arisen.

Slowly, slowly the followers of Jesus started moving into the Roman Empire; and the feeling of guilt grew, because it was under the Roman Empire that Jesus had been crucified. Many Romans started feeling guilty that they were also part of it; just to save the empire they had crucified an innocent man, a man of God.

This was a turning point in the history of Rome, and it ended finally with the whole pagan, earthbound, pragmatic philosophy of Rome disappearing under a dark cloud of Catholic, Christian ideology. Rome lost its glory because of Christianity – because Christianity teaches: Blessed are the poor, blessed are the meek, blessed are those who are standing last in the queue – because they shall inherit the kingdom of God.

The Roman Empire disappeared. Every empire disappears after a certain height. In this world nothing remains permanent, everything is in a flux. And Christian missionaries were roaming around in Italy preaching this ideology of poverty, meekness . . . that you are born a sinner, that unless Jesus saves you, you will fall into the darkness of hell for eternity.

Out of fear, out of helplessness, Italy became a victim of Christianity. It had killed Jesus Christ. But man's psychology takes strange turns; the crucifixion of Jesus finally became the crucifixion of the pagan, and the crucifixion of Rome and all its glory.

Italy will remain a neglected country. Only in the proverb now its glory has remained. "All roads lead to Rome" – no more. Once it was true; now half the roads lead to Washington and half the roads lead to Moscow – not a single road goes to Rome. Destroy the Vatican and make at least one road.

I can help the Radical party of Italy to bring the beautiful pagan approach to life again, because deep in the soul of Italy that pagan is still present; and that is why I love the Italians tremendously. I see a certain hope that things are not always going to remain the same. The pagan will assert again, it is time. And that is why I have accepted that if you want me to be a friend, a guide, I am available – because I am immensely interested in the repressed pagan of the Italians.

It is difficult in India, because for ten thousand years at least, the pagan has not been heard about. It may have died . . . . But I have so many sannyasins in Italy, and whenever they come I can see that their Christianity is superficial; their paganism is a reality – and I am interested in their pagan.

Italy can come to its glory again, but not as a Catholic country. Catholic . . . the very word shows the degradation of the Italian mind, Italian soul. Its beauty was in its paganism, in its love for existence, in its love for songs and dances, in its love for the body.

To me, the pagan is the beginning of real spirituality; it is not the end. Zorba is the beginning and Buddha is the end. The beginning I have to find in Italy, and the end I have to find in India. And once we can create a synthesis between the pagan and the awakened, the enlightened being, we have the whole man.

You can call that my philosophy: the philosophy of the whole man. Nothing has to be denied; everything has to be absorbed in a beautiful orchestra, in a beautiful symphony.

Beloved Bhagwan,

You said that Italians are the most pagan among the European people.
Do You think the Catholic religion destroys the pagan soul less than other religions?

Giulia, the Catholic religion destroys the most. But the Italian soul is so deep-rooted in the pagan philosophy and the pagan approach to life, that in spite of the Catholic religion it has still remained pagan.

The Catholic religion has not been able to reach to the very center of the Italian people, it has touched just their surface; and this I am saying out of my own experience.

The Italian is Christian only skin deep; just one layer has to be peeled and the pagan will be there, still throbbing, alive, dancing, full of juice. It is a miracle that the Catholic religion has not been able to destroy the soul of Italy – and in that there is great hope.

I would like the radical people in Italy to destroy that thin layer of Catholicism as quickly as possible, because once that layer is destroyed, all the radical changes that they want will become absolutely easy. With the Catholic layer, no radical change is easy; it is going to be very difficult – so it is better first to destroy that layer.

The Catholic religion is such a poor religion; it has no arguments. Italy has enough intelligentsia. It is simply unbelievable that with so many intellectuals, so many geniuses in every dimension, they still go on tolerating this pope – and that too a Polack! I sometimes wonder whom you are going to choose next, a buffalo or a donkey? – because you have fallen to the bottom.

Who has ever heard of any Polack who has been intelligent?

Italy is still deep down the same – just a thin layer has to be removed. And I have seen this happening here. To change the Italian into a living, dancing, joyous human being is so easy; but to do the same with an Indian is so difficult. You go on digging and you go on digging . . . the water has disappeared completely; there is no juice anywhere.

I wanted to go to Italy because I feel a deep spiritual affinity between myself and the Italian soul; but for almost one year the pope has been preventing my entry into Italy. Not only are these people retarded, they are cowards too.

This is my open challenge to the pope: I am ready; alone I will come to the Vatican, amongst *your* people, and I am ready to discuss each single point of your religion. With a single condition: if you win, I will become a Catholic; if I win, I become the pope, and the Vatican becomes the capital of the sannyasins of the whole world.

But he is such a coward that the government goes on saying, "We are giving you a visa for three weeks only." They are afraid because the pope is absolutely against my entry into Italy. In just three weeks these priests are afraid that I may destroy their tradition, their culture, their religion, their morality, that I will corrupt the whole country – in just three weeks. And they have not been able to corrupt the country in two thousand years; that shows their weakness, their impotence.

When he was here, I was the only man who welcomed him; I was the only man who opposed the people who were preventing his entry, who were not allowing him to move from one city to another. I condemned them, and I said, "This is stupid. Welcome him. He is a guest. Invite him to an open discussion. You need not be worried about it" – because all the basic foundations of the Catholic religion are so poor, indefensible.

The virgin birth of Jesus Christ . . . there is no way to prove it; it is so unscientific. The concept of God as a trinity: God the Father, the Son, and the Holy Ghost . . . and this "holy ghost" made the poor girl Mary, Jesus' mother, pregnant – without any license – and still he is holy? Then what is unholy? And in this trinity there is no place for any woman? A strange family, three men. It is just to humiliate womankind. Even Jesus' mother – although they put up her statues, they worship her statues – she is not part of their ultimate trinity. Their ultimate trinity is a gay group – and I have every suspicion that the disease AIDS has come from the trinity. Everything has arisen from God – why not AIDS?

I know so many Italians that I feel perfectly at ease that they will be able to understand me: that this is not religion – this is simply mythology; there is no science for inner transformation in it. It cannot create an awakened, enlightened human being. Its whole structure is based on belief, and a true religion is always based on doubt, not on belief.

Doubt until you come to a point when doubt becomes impossible; that means you have arrived at the truth, indubitable. Only truth cannot be doubted. So one has to search within oneself for a place, a space, a quality, which even if he wants to doubt, he cannot doubt – it is so absolutely certain, so categorically ultimate.

Christianity is one of the lowest pseudo-religions of the world. All religions are pseudo; but in those pseudo-religions are also categories.

Beloved Bhagwan,

Old Abraham is on his deathbed. He says, "Isaac, my son, are you here?" "Yes," Isaac says.
"And you Rachel, are you here?" "Yes, father." "And you Sarah, my beloved wife, are you here?"
"Oh yes, my Abraham!" And with his last sigh, Abraham whispers, "And who is tending shop then?"
Beloved master, why can't I stop thinking of business when the moment comes to let go?

Satyam Svarup, perhaps you are also a Jew. Maybe not in this life, but in some past life. But to be a Jew is such a disease that it goes on and on from one life to another life. So don't be worried; because I am an experienced hand at killing many Jews. I will kill you, too.

While you are meditating and the business goes on in your mind, let it go on. You just remain a witness, as if you are seeing a movie. The movie is there on the screen; so is your mind, with all its thoughts of business and other things – just a screen. You remain a witness.

In the beginning you will forget again and again and get involved in the business things. But the moment you remember, never repent, never feel guilty. Just the moment you remember, again settle down to be a witness. It is only a question of some waiting; soon you will see gaps happening on the screen. For a few seconds there is no thought moving on the screen, and those moments will be of such serenity, such silence, such joy, such beauty, such ecstasy . . . .

That experience will help you to become a stronger witness – because now witnessing is not just an empty exercise; it is now helping you to discover treasures within yourself. All your business will fall away . . . soon you will find the mind is empty. But this emptiness is not negative; this emptiness is the most positive thing in existence. It is so full of blissfulness – as if thousands of flowers have suddenly blossomed, as if spring has come to you.

To me, the coming of this spring is the goal of the search for which you have all gathered here. And the fullness in this emptiness is multidimensional. It is not only the fragrance of many flowers; it is also as if many suns have arisen around you . . . so much light, so much music – and your heart is for the first time in a mad dance.

So don't be worried about the Jew. Everybody's mind is a Jew. So I am not using the word in a racial sense – because mind always means business; and we have to go beyond the mind; we have to go beyond the mundane and trivial thoughts. We have to come to a point where everything becomes still, silent, serene. From there begins the world of the mysterious, of the divine.

I call it the beginning of godliness – not of God, because that gives a wrong conception, as if God is a person. God is not a person, he is not like a flower; he is more like a fragrance. God is a quality. And when you experience godliness your life is fulfilled, contented. Then you have not been here unnecessarily.

Okay, Vimal?

Yes, Bhagwan!

All Buddhas Are Gamblers

Everybody wants to love – but only to a certain extent. Beyond that, fear grips you . . . because love is so overwhelming it seems if you go deeper into it there is no possibility of turning back. It is so overwhelming that it is going to evaporate your ego, your personality – which you have cultivated with such care; for which you have wasted your whole life.

People say they would like to experience ecstasy – but they don't understand the fact that you cannot experience ecstasy.

Only when you disappear is ecstasy there – and very few people in the long, long history of humanity have been able to gamble. All Gautam Buddhas are gamblers, because they are gambling for something unknown, and staking something which is known to them.

The ordinary wisdom of humanity says that half a loaf in your hand is better than the whole loaf far away. But the wisdom of those who have really known says: Risk everything for the unknown and for the unknowable – because you don't know how much fragrance, and how much joy, and how much life is available to you. Only one step has to be taken, and that is to get ready to be drowned in it, to disappear in it.

February 16, 1987,   8 a.m.

Beloved Bhagwan,

Why, when truth and lies meet, does trouble arise?

Waduda, man almost *lives* in lies, because they are comfortable, convenient. You don't have to make much effort to find a lie. The whole of society is ready to give you all kinds of lies – but truth is an individual search.

Lies are a social invention.

So whenever truth is discovered, there is trouble. You have lived all your life in lies – beautiful lies – and suddenly you find your whole life collapsing.

To choose truth, first you have to make an immense effort to find it. Second, when you find it, you suddenly also find that the whole of society is against you – the whole world is against you.

If you want to live according to your own truth, you have to face the whole world: your job may be lost, your wife may divorce you, your parents may abandon you; your priests will condemn you, your politicians will be against you. Suddenly you find yourself in an immense world, absolutely alone. You have to depend on this society in a thousand and one ways, and this society wants you to live acccording to its lies – hence the trouble.

But it is only on the outside that finding the truth creates great turmoil in your life. As far as your inner world is concerned, when you find the truth, for the first time you are at home, at ease, relaxed, strong – so strong that you alone are enough to face the whole world. Those troubles are trivial. What you find with the truth is such a treasure, that once you have known it you cannot exchange it for lies.

So it is true that there is trouble. But it is only half true: it is only on the outside – and that too because you have not become accustomed to truth yourself. Once you see its strength, its power – then the whole world seems to be impotent. You can fight it, you can make your way, you can live your life according to your own light, and for you there is no trouble. For others there may be trouble.

This I am saying to you on my own authority: for me there is no trouble . . . and the whole world is in trouble. It is none of their business to get into trouble; *I* should be in trouble.

But the truth has such great strength, such tremendous power of its own, that there is no need to be worried about it. Why are other people worried? Why are they creating trouble? They are worried and creating trouble because your truth makes them aware of their own lies; and that they don't want. To know one's own lies and go on living them is the most torturous experience; they would like to remove you.

You have become a stranger, an outsider. You don't believe in their God, you don't believe in their heaven and hell; you don't believe in all kinds of superstitions which they think are of great value. But before your truth, their lies start disappearing like darkness.

You have found the light: now the whole darkness of the world cannot do any harm to the light. Just a small flame of light is more powerful than all the darkness of the universe.

But certainly those who are living in darkness and have become accustomed to it, have molded their lives according to it, will find it too much of a revolution. And people don't want to change – because every change means learning to live again: each change is a new birth. They had become comfortable; they were living with the crowd with all its superstitions; they were respectable, honored. Your truth certainly makes them aware that their whole life has been just a castle made of sand; just a little breeze of truth and it will collapse. To save their own sandcastles they will create every kind of trouble for you.

But the man of truth is able to accept all the troubles, because what he has got inside himself is so blissful, is so great, is so immortal . . . who cares about small troubles? The job may be lost, the wife may escape, the parents may disinherit . . . all that is of no meaning compared to what you have got within you.

Those people don't know what you have got within you – so there is trouble. But it is not for you. Only in the beginning will you feel suddenly taken out of the comfort of society, the coziness of the crowd. But as you become more and more aware of your inner warmth, you don't need any crowd. You alone are enough. Truth is such a nourishment, such an ultimate achievement, that now you can lose your life very easily – sacrifice it, because you have found something greater than life; you have found the very source of life, from where all life arises.

So don't be worried about trouble. It is because of trouble that millions of people never think about truth. They feel it is better to go on following the crowd of sheep and never declare their lion's roar.

Beloved Bhagwan,

Being here with You . . . thirsting and drinking and dancing . . . waiting . . . feeling . . . being . . . I lose the distance, the bridge, and it becomes almost an effort to come back to the daily flow of life . . . . Yet it all happens easily. And Bhagwan, even the gratefulness melts in the soft flow of silence. It feels so new, so unspoken . . . so good . . . . Is this the fragrance of what You call an open secret?

Kavisho, this dance, this song, this ecstacy, this fragrance, is certainly what I call an open secret. But there is much more: it is only the beginning; and I can take you only to the beginning; from there you have to go deeper into yourself, absolutely alone.

But that aloneness is not lonely because you are surrounded with such beauty, such joy, such blissfulness, that you will never feel that you are lonely. Alone you are, but not lonely. And this aloneness also becomes a great joy, because it is freedom: freedom from the crowd, from the mob, from the church, from religions, from politics – from everything that has been part of your life before. You have discovered yourself.

I call it an open secret because it is available to

everybody – and yet everybody is unaware of it. It is so close that you have just to move your hand a little deeper inside yourself, and you will find it.

Yet people go on searching in the scriptures of ancient days, in philosophies . . . and what they find is mere words. Those words don't bring you a dance; those words bring you a kind of death. Those words don't bring you fragrance, but only the stink of the old scriptures – rotten. They can give you beautiful systems, but all without any foundation.

I call it an open secret because it has always been known that the kingdom of God is within you. Still nobody searches for it there. Perhaps you are afraid to find God. Perhaps you are afraid to be ecstatic, afraid to be blissful, afraid to be loving – because these are dangerous ways of life. But because they are dangerous they have a thrill: your heart beats faster, your life-flame burns brighter; each of your moments becomes more total and more intense.

So I call it open because it is known to everybody; and still I call it a secret, because nobody tries to find it. Those words are contradictory: "the open secret." But this is the whole history of human consciousness: you may not be conscious of the fact that you are afraid of things which you long for.

For example, everybody wants to love – but only to a certain extent. Beyond that, fear grips you . . . because love is so overwhelming it seems if you go deeper into it there is no possibility of turning back. It is so overwhelming that it is going to evaporate your ego, your personality – which you have cultivated with such care; for which you have wasted your whole life.

People say they would like to experience ecstasy – but they don't understand the fact that you cannot experience ecstasy. Only when you disappear is ecstasy there – and very few people in the long, long history of humanity have been able to gamble. All Gautam Buddhas are gamblers, because they are gambling for something unknown, and staking something which is known to them.

The ordinary wisdom of humanity says that half a loaf in your hand is better than the whole loaf far away. But the wisdom of those who have really known says: Risk everything for the unknown and for the unknowable – because you don't know how much fragrance, and how much joy, and how much life is available to you. Only one step has to be taken, and that is to get ready to be drowned in it, to disappear in it.

And, Kavisho, I can see it happening to you. You are moving towards it . . . a little hesitant. I see sometimes you are just on the boundary of it and then you stop. Don't stop. You don't have anything to lose. Your personality has given you nothing but misery; your ego has given you nothing but pain; your mind has given you nothing but empty thoughts. So there is nothing to lose. Perhaps you may lose your bondage, your chains, your handcuffs, but they are not worth preserving – they are not your ornaments.

Put everything at stake.

I have been watching you, and I see you coming to a point very close to the open secret . . . and you stop or pull back. It is a natural fear, perhaps it is too much, and too sudden. But remember, nobody can be ready for it beforehand. Everybody has to go into it without any preparedness, and everybody has to take the jump one day, without thinking. You can think later on as much as you want.

The proverb goes: Think before acting. I would like to say to you: Act first, and then think whatever you want to think. You are absolutely free to think . . . .

As one comes closer to the open secret, the mind creates a fear. Perhaps you may go mad. Wait . . . to go more into it seems to be dangerous; you may lose your sanity. But what kind of sanity do you have? What flowers has it given to you? And what juice has it given to your life? And what light has it given to your eyes?

So don't think when you come to the boundary: Where does the world of the open secret begin? Gather courage and jump.

In my childhood, just by the side of my village was a beautiful river, and this was my joy: to find the highest spots from which to jump into the river. And seeing me enjoying it so much, many of my friends would go with me, and they would see that I have jumped and I am still alive, and swimming in the river. They would make every effort . . . .

Most of them were Hindus, and Hindus have a certain small book, *Hanuman Chalisa.* You have seen the monkey god and his statues – it is in praise of the monkey god. It is thought that if you repeat the *Hanuman Chalisa,* you become strong like the monkey god, who even carried a mountain in his hands.

I was surprised: they would repeat the *Hanuman Chalisa* and they would gather courage and rush violently – and just on the brink they will stop, as if an invisible wall is there. I would say, "What happened?"

They said, "This is too deep . . . and unnecessarily one may get fractures or one may even die."

But I said, "You have seen me jumping . . . ."

They said, "We always think of you as an exception."

I said, "That's strange. I have the same kind of body: why should I be an exception?"

This is what we have done with Buddha, Mahavira, Adinatha, Patanjali, Kabir: we have put them in a separate category. They are special people; we are ordinary people. But they were also ordinary before they took the jump. It is the jump that has made them extraordinary; not that they were extraordinary – hence they could jump. The reality is just vice-versa.

And slowly, slowly I persuaded those people . . . . A few of them jumped, and they said, "Really there is no problem. But it looked so fearsome . . . almost like death. But you are so persistent that we started feeling that we must be very cowardly, afraid, that we don't have any life in us. So we thought that at the most, death can happen – and who bothers once death has happened? There is no problem . . . we will not be here."

But once they jumped . . . then they started jumping from even higher peaks. The railway bridge was the highest on the bank, and a policeman used to stand there twenty-four hours a day with his machine gun,

because that place was used for committing suicide. After examinations, when people failed, they would commit suicide; somebody would go bankrupt and he would commit suicide.

When we had jumped from all the other heights, I went to the policeman and I said, "I am not committing suicide, so don't stop me. If you stop me, I *will* commit suicide!"

He said, "This is strange. Then what are you doing, if you are not committing suicide?"

I said, "I am simply enjoying the jump. This is the highest place . . . and I have brought my friends with me. You can see."

He said, "But remember, nobody should know. And I am worried – you may not be jumping to commit suicide, but suicide may happen. Even though I have been here for years, I could not think of jumping."

I said, "If you start by thinking . . . nobody can jump. This is the whole secret: we don't think first; first we jump, and then we think."

He said, "Then what is the use of thinking? When you have jumped, you have jumped."

So I told him, "You need not bother. And you need not use your machine gun – that may kill unnecessarily."

He became curious and he allowed me to jump. I jumped while the others were reciting the *Hanuman Chalisa* and trembling, because this was the highest place. It was summertime, and the river had become shallower and the height had become greater. But when I jumped and the policeman looked and saw that I was perfectly happy, and I waved to him, he said, "My God! Then what happens to those people who commit suicide?" And he asked my other friends, "What are you doing?"

They said, "We are reciting the *Hanuman Chalisa!* First we will invoke the *Hanuman Chalisa* . . . because that guy is mad. We don't follow him; we have our own ritual: first we will do the *Hanuman Chalisa* and pray to God to save us." And then one by one they jumped. And you will be surprised: when the last boy had jumped and the policeman saw that we were all alive, he put his gun away, recited the *Hanuman Chalisa*, and jumped. And he said, "This is strange, nobody died. And I have seen people dying . . . ."

I said, " . . . because they wanted to die. To us, it is a challenge of life; to them it was not."

The open secret is a subtle boundary. Everybody comes close to it and feels that if he goes one step further, madness is going to happen. I have seen Kavisho getting almost to the brink . . . and then holding herself back. Avirbhava goes to the brink immediately; then she tries to stop me. She shows me this . . . and no more. She closes her eyes . . . she wants to make me afraid by opening her big eyes – but I can also open my big eyes.

One day she was at such a brink: she became so much afraid now the moment has come, that she put her head between her legs and her hands under her legs – just to avoid me. She sometimes starts crying . . . . But I don't care at all; I go on doing my thing! Just to avoid me, sometimes she sits on this side; when she gathers courage, she sits on that side.

Yes, Kavisho, this is the open secret. Today, try to go into it. I am here; don't be worried. I have gone more deeply into it than anyone else: no madness happens, no insanity happens, no death happens. Just once you have to go into it, and then you are absolutely relaxed. Then you can move into it and out of it just like you move in and out of your house: you never wonder whether to go out or not, whether to go in or not.

Your inner being is your greater life. ~~Death can happen outside, but not inside. Even when people die, they die only on the outside; the inside is immortality.~~

And ~~madness happens through thinking; madness has never happened through non-thinking. So when the moment comes and the mind is empty,~~ and ~~all thoughts have disappeared and you see a deep tunnel into yourself, don't turn back.~~ Slowly, slowly people go: inch by inch people go. Gather courage! Don't experience God in installments: don't be American.

Beloved Bhagwan,

You said a few days ago that the really innovative man comes two hundred years ahead of his time. You also said that time is elastic. Haven't You chosen to come precisely now, before these chaotic times the world is facing, so men will be more receptive to a radical change? And is the ever-faster-growing communication technology not making in this respect the world smaller for Your message to spread? Will it really take two hundred years for mankind to open up to Your vision?

Govindo, we are living in a very special time. There are not two hundred years available. If man does not understand my message now, there will be no man after two hundred years to understand. Two hundred years is very long; even twenty years . . . .

Mankind has never been at such a critical moment as it is today. There have been wars – thousands of wars – but they were not going to destroy all life. In the ancient days, wars were almost like football games.

The greatest war in India, Mahabharat, happened somewhere around five thousand years ago, and it gives the idea – because that is the only war in India which has been described in such minute detail. Just one family – two brothers: one brother who was sick, had five sons; the other brother was blind, but he had one hundred sons. He must have had many women – to manage one hundred sons from one woman is almost impossible.

Now the question was: who was going to succeed? The five brothers were very intelligent, courageous, trained in many martial arts. One of them was a great archer; another was a great wrestler; the eldest was a very intelligent man. But the hundred brothers were all what you would call "bad guys" – so everybody wanted the kingdom to go to the five brothers and not to these hundred rascals; even without power they were harassing the people so much. But they were not ready to agree so easily, so the final decision had to be made by war – whoever wins . . . .

Now it was a family war, and they invited all their friends, all their relatives – and they were all interrelated. The grandfather, although he loved those five, had chosen to be with the one hundred, for the simple reason that those five were the sons of a sick man, and a sick man could not rule, because of his sickness. So the kingdom had gone into the hands of the brother with one hundred sons, and to give the kingdom back to the other party would be unfair; although he loved those five and he hated those hundred – still, he was fighting with them.

In the evening, as the sun was setting, the war would stop, and people would go into each other's camp. The whole day they were killing each other, and at night they were playing cards, and they were gossiping about the events of the day. That was a totally different kind of war. Man was directly involved, and only soldiers had to fight, not civilians. Thousands of wars of that kind we have survived.

But now we are in a very exceptional time. A nuclear war simply means total destruction – a global suicide. Nobody is going to be defeated; nobody is going to be victorious: all are going to be dead. And not only man – birds, animals, trees, all that is living on the earth will be dead.

And both the great powers – America and the Soviet Union – go on piling up more and more nuclear weapons. The Soviet Union has proved more sensible. Seeing the fact that right now we have so many nuclear weapons that every man can be killed seven times – although there is no need to kill any man seven times, once is always enough – the Soviet Union has proved far more intelligent than Ronald Reagan. First they tried hard to negotiate that we should stop this piling up of nuclear weapons – it is pointless now, wasting money on it – but Reagan is not willing. So, of their own accord, the Soviet Union for many months has not created any nuclear weapons. They have stopped, but America goes on piling up . . . .

The danger is so great that if man can survive this century, it will be a great miracle. So there is not that much time, Govindo. For the first time the future is very short. It always used to be eternal; now it is at the most twenty years.

So in the lifetime of each of you, the decisive moment is going to come: either man commits suicide or, seeing that this is an absolute absurdity, man changes his consciousness. It often happens that under pressure people change – and there will never be again a greater pressure than is present today. It is most probable that man will go through a transformation. In that sense my message is exactly at the right time: that nations should disappear, because it is nations who fight; religions should disappear, because it is religions who fight. The idea of races – of superiority and inferiority – should disappear, because that has been one of the causes of wars.

It is a time either to destroy the whole earth or to destroy all these arbitrary conceptions of nation, race, religion, and make the whole earth one humanity.

But I do not agree on one point with you. You say, "Have not You chosen to come precisely now, before these chaotic times the world is facing?"

I have not chosen anything. Perhaps existence has chosen me to be a vehicle to give you the message – but I have not chosen. I have disappeared long ago . . . and existence can speak through you only when you are not.

It is hoping against hope – but I still hope that the danger of global death will be the shock which awakens humanity. If man survives after this century, it will be a new man and a new humanity. One thing is certain:

Either man has to die or man has to change.

I cannot think that man will choose to die. The longing for life is so great . . . just to think that the earth has become dead – no trees, no humanity, no birds, no animals, no sea animals . . . . It is such a great crisis, because in the whole universe – it is only an assumption of the scientists that there may be life on fifty thousand planets, but there is no absolute evidence. It is just a mathematical and logical conclusion, but there is no scientific proof.

As far as we know, only this earth is green, only this earth has flowers, only this earth has love; only this earth has produced people like Gautam Buddha; only this earth has birds which sing, people who dance, people who love. This is the only place in the whole universe where people search and seek for truth. To destroy it – for no particular reason at all – is such utter stupidity that I don't think that the third world war is going to happen.

And if the third world war does not happen, that will mean a great change, a tidal change in human consciousness. We will see a new man, who is not Christian, not Hindu, who is not a Jew, who is not a Chinese, who is not an American. If all these trees can exist without being Christians and without being Hindus; if all these birds can exist without any boundaries of nations . . . and when a bird passes the boundary of India and enters into Pakistan, he does not need any entry visa, does not need even any passport . . . .

Except for mankind, the earth is one. And it is only a question of raising human consciousness . . . . Nations can disappear, religions can disappear, discriminations can disappear; and with that, much crap will disappear. Politicians will not be of any use; priests will not be of any use; churches and temples and mosques will not be of any use. There are millions of people who don't have homes, and God – who is just a lie – has millions of houses for himself.

We have lived in an insane way, and now it is a choice between insanity and sanity. If insanity wins, there will be no life at all. If sanity wins, life will become for the first time free from all superstitions, all boundaries, all divisions – one humanity, one earth; freedom of expression, freedom of movement, freedom to choose where you want to live.

It is our earth.

Beloved Bhagwan,

Inside of me there is such tension that it is killing my heart. I have known it for years, and always I have avoided looking into it. I feel it when I sit in front of You, and it prevents me from melting in You. In this Buddhafield I use it to stay aloof and distant, arrogant and judgmental of others. The woman I love, I care not for her freedom; but only when I have power over her do I relax. In my work I seek success and praise, and forget the gratitude for the opportunity given to me. Bhagwan, I am afraid that one day I'll wake up just to realize that it is too late, that I have failed You, missed this unique chance You are giving to us, to me. Yes, my beloved sweet Master, I have no other question – just this tremendous need to expose myself at Your feet, asking for Your divine words of guidance and light. There is so much pain, Bhagwan, and so much love, too.

Prashantam, your whole problem is a will-to-power.

In your work you want to be powerful. You are a therapist; in your therapy groups you want to be powerful. Even in your love, you want to be powerful over the woman you love. Reduced to a single point, will-to-power is your problem, is your tension.

It is good that you exposed it, because any wound exposed starts healing. If you understand it – that will-to-power is your problem – then there is nothing to be worried about. Then you have to look into it – why will-to-power arises in the first place. It arises out of an inferiority complex. You must be always comparing yourself with others: somebody is superior and I am inferior.

This has been the teaching over the centuries: that there are superior people and there are inferior people; and the whole teaching is a lie. There are only unique individuals – nobody is superior, nobody is inferior. I am not saying that everybody is equal. So let me emphasize the fact:

I don't believe in equality, I believe in uniqueness.

Equality is a very poor idea, a very dull idea. "Everybody is equal" gives a feeling of flatness. No, the marigold and the rose and the lotus are not equal; neither are the peacocks and the cuckoos equal – but they are all unique.

People have lived with the idea that either all are equal or they are unequal. I give you a new concept: Equality, inequality – both are two sides of the same coin. Throw that coin away completely. Everybody has a unique personality of his own; he is neither superior nor is he inferior.

You have not been meditating. This has been one of the calamities that has happened to all the therapists. Because in their therapy groups they become mini-gurus, they start thinking that there is no need for them to meditate. They start solving other people's problems, and forget that their own problems are waiting to be solved. So start meditating; start becoming aware that you are an unique individual, just as others are. And once this idea of uniqueness settles in you, you will drop your judgmental attitude. What is there to judge? – people are unique.

The idea of judgment was part of the old philosophy which said that somebody is superior, somebody is inferior; somebody is a saint, somebody is a sinner. Then there was certainly a question of judgment: to call somebody a saint, you have judged; to call somebody a sinner, you have judged. And this judgment is not going to be only about others; it will be about you, too.

When you see a saint, you will judge yourself: "I am far inferior." And feeling inferior, one wants to become powerful, to prove to oneself and to the world that "I am not inferior." With the idea of uniqueness all judgments disappear.

I am reminded of a very famous butcher. His fame was that for twenty years continually, he was cutting up animals for the king of China – but he never changed his weapons. Even after twenty years' use, the weapons were as fresh, as new, as they were on the first day. The king has become old, the butcher has become old . . . .

One day the king was walking in the garden. He came around to the butcher's place and saw his weapons so fresh, so new, and he asked "How do you manage? You have not changed your weapons; you have not even polished them."

The butcher said, "There is no need – because when I am cutting the animal, it is a meditation for me. I am a disciple of a master, and I asked the master, 'Should I leave my profession of being a butcher?' He said, 'Why? Somebody else will have to do it, and nobody can do it better than you; so you continue.'

"I was shocked that a master who teaches nonviolence is not stopping me from being a butcher. On the contrary, he is saying, 'You are rare and unique; you continue – but make it a meditation. Before killing the animal, say to him, 'Brother! . . . ' While killing him, be full of reverence. Don't kill out of cruelty; be graceful.'

"And because of his teachings – gracefulness, meditativeness, and a reverence for life – the animal who is being butchered does not struggle, does not fight, does not try to escape. He allows my weapons without any friction. That's why the weapons have remained as new, as fresh, as shiny as they were on the first day. I am killing certainly, but with a heart, with love."

There were other butchers in the palace, and they could not believe how he could manage. And they saw that first he would hug the animal, kiss the animal, talk to the animal, say to him, "Even if I don't kill you, somebody else will kill you. It is better I should kill you, because I can kill you with deep reverence, compassion, love, so it is not a fight between you and

me. Allow it, so that you are not hurt. Don't try to escape."

This simple butcher became a great master later on. He used to say to people, "I don't know anything much. All I know is that if you love even an animal, he understands, and he is ready – because you love him – even to die at your hands, joyfully."

He had asked his master, "Don't you judge me, that I am doing something sinful?"

The master said, "Those who judge don't understand life. Somebody has to be a butcher; somebody has to chop the wood, somebody has to be a thief – because people go on gathering money."

The thief is nothing but a practical socialist.

A deep understanding will bring you a non-judgmental approach; then nobody is a sinner and nobody is a saint. Then the whole point is: if you are a sinner, be as totally and intensely a sinner as possible – because what ultimately counts is totality and intensity. If you are a saint, don't be half-hearted; be totally and be intensely, because that's what counts ultimately: not *what* you were doing, but *how* you were doing it – meditatively, silently.

Prashantam, you need not be afraid that a day may come when you will realize that it is too late. It is never too late. Even if you realize at the last breath of your life – that's enough. A single moment of understanding is far weightier than a whole life of misunderstanding; a single moment of understanding erases a whole life of misunderstanding – so it is never too late.

And don't be worried that you may feel one day that you have failed me. You cannot fail me – nobody can because I don't have any expectations of you. I accept you as you are, and I will always accept you as you are. I have no judgments, so how you can fail me? But this is what for centuries you have been conditioned for: the father says to the son, "Don't fail me"; the master says to the disciple, "Don't fail me." They have expectations that you should be a certain way; that you should be successful.

Whatever you can do, do it totally, do it intensely,

But you cannot fail me, because I don't have any expectations; you cannot frustrate me. I have worked on so many people for years, and then our ways separated. I don't say to them that they betrayed me, I simply say that our ways separated – because there is no question of betrayal. I have never asked for loyalty, so how can I say they betrayed me? Life just brought us to a point where we could not be together.

My heart is still full of blessings for all those who have gone their own way. Wherever they are, my blessings will follow them like a shadow.

Okay, Vimal?

Yes, Bhagwan.

God Is The Ocean You Are In

God is the ocean you are in, because God is another name for life. You are breathing God in and out every moment. It is God who is beating in your heart. It is God who is flowing in your blood. It is God who is your marrow, your bones, your intelligence, your very consciousness. But because the fish is born in the ocean – it is so close – she thinks: This is only water.

This is only air that you are breathing in and out. And people are searching just like the fish, and they will never find – unless they stop searching and just start looking at what they are, what their consciousness is, what their life is. And they will be surprised that there was no need to go anywhere. All that they were searching for they were surrounded by on the outside, and they were filled by it in their innermost being.

The whole existence is God. It is the religions which have created the fallacy that God created the world – so they have given you an idea that the world and God are two, so that you will have to search for the creator. I want you to destroy that duality completely. God is not the creator, but the creation itself. He is in the trees and he is in the rivers and he is in the moon and he is in the sun and he is in you.

Except God, there is nothing else.

February 16, 1987, 7 p.m.

Beloved Bhagwan,

When You say that You want us to raise the consciousness of the world, it puzzles me. I feel I need all my energy to get my own feet off the ground.
And I am in a way totally forgetting "that world," and glad to be able to let go and disappear in this buddhafield of drunken bliss, dance and silence.
So what is it that we need to do in order to fulfill this vision?

Prem Turiya, all that is needed from you to raise the consciousness of humanity, is just to raise your consciousness to its fullest peak. You don't have to do anything else. So there is no puzzle at all – the puzzle is created by your mind; because mind always separates, divides: you, and the world. And then the problem arises: if you have to put energy into raising the consciousness of the world, what about yourself? Your own consciousness is still not on the wing.

But as far as I am concerned – and it should be remembered by all, it is not only Turiya's question – you are the world. There is no division. The moment you are raising your consciousness higher, you are raising the world's consciousness higher. If you can become enlightened, you have done everything that was possible, within your capacity, to raise the world's consciousness. No extra effort is needed. In fact, every extra effort will be a hindrance. You should concentrate totally on your own being and its blossoming.

There is a secret law of life: just as water tries to be on one level, consciousness also tries in the same way to be on one level. If one person's consciousness reaches a high peak, soon many people will find explosions happening within them. It is also a well-known fact that if you are awakened, your very awakening triggers processes around you.

It is not by your action, not by any doing – but just by being awake suddenly all around you, sleep starts disappearing. Just as when you bring light into a dark room, you don't ask, when we have brought the light into the dark room, now, how are we going to dispel the darkness? Do you think some extra effort will be needed? Just the light itself will dispel the darkness.

Become a light unto yourself, and you have done all that was possible within the capacity of a human being to raise the whole world's consciousness.

It is perfectly right: be totally drunk, be totally blissful, be totally silent, and dance so intensely that the dancer disappears and only dance remains – and your very dance . . . with such intensity and such totality, will make thousands of hearts suddenly dance. They may never know who is the source; they may never know who has triggered the process . . . you may never know how many people you have transformed. But that is unimportant; your drunkenness will become the drunkenness of many; your dance will drown many into the same blissfulness; your song will be sung on many lips, and your silence will resound in thousands of hearts. You just change yourself.

I repeat again: you are the world.

Beloved Bhagwan,

When I hear You talk about past lives I get scared. I have never had any remembrance, just a vague feeling, and somewhere I know that I don't want to know . . . unless it's a remembrance of You. And about future lives, I get so sad – just the idea of starting all over again, the family, the school, the fight for survival, and, above all, You won't be there.
How will I remember You, how will I not forget this tremendous gift that You are?
I would like this moment to stretch into eternity . . . and forget about anything else.
Is there any great magical surgery possible? I want to heal . . . .

Kavisho, I am *exactly* doing the magical surgery you are asking about. Do you think my work consists only of communicating words, concepts, and philosophies to you? You are lying down on my surgical table.

There is no need for you to remember the past. Whenever I have talked about the past, it is just to make you aware that you have missed many opportunities before. Make it a point that you don't miss now.

Thousands of lives have passed, and you have been moving in a wheel, in a routine. This time, come out of the circle. And if you can come out of the circle this time, there will be no future life for you – eternity will be yours.

And that's what you are asking me: Is there any possibility to stretch this moment into eternity? This is the opportunity: this silence, this dance, this blissfulness can help you to come out of the vicious circle, and you will never enter another womb again. You will remain here – not embodied, but just as pure consciousness, spread all over existence.

My whole effort is to persuade you to take a jump from being a dewdrop and become the ocean. And the surgery is not very difficult; it is one of the simplest things possible: just get out of your mind. Become a witness to the mind; watch all its traffic pass by. Don't be part of the traffic; stand by the side of the road – because you are not the mind.

Once this statement becomes your experience – that you are not the mind – then there is no question of being born into another stupid routine. It is the mind and the identity with the mind which is the cause of continuously moving in a circle. Disidentify. You are neither the body nor the mind. You are simply the pure watcher.

It is a simple method – the simplest possible method for the greatest experience – the most shortcut way. Whenever you have time – lying down on your bed, no special posture is needed, or standing under your shower – just remain a watcher: of the body, of the freshness of the water, of the coolness, and of the thoughts that are passing in the mind. Just by watching, mind disappears.

One day, you suddenly find an absolute silence

123

within you – no traffic . . . the road is empty. The surgery is complete. You will not be born again in another body, although you will remain as part of eternal life.

And don't be worried – I will be there. I am already there just calling you all to the sunlit peaks of consciousness from your dark valleys. Start climbing.

You can miss me only in one way, and that is: if you choose your mind, then you cannot choose me. If you choose me, you will have to drop your mind.

In the eternity of life, we all will be meeting – of course, without our old photographs, without our old faces. But nobody loses his individuality of consciousness even in the universal. He becomes part of the universal, and yet that universality does not destroy his individuality but enhances it. So not only me, but all the souls that have moved into time and gone beyond time, are still here now.

There is a beautiful story in the life of Mahavira. The followers of Mahavira have not been able to explain the mystery of the story. The story is certainly not historical; it is a parable, poetry, an indirect way of saying the truth. It says that Mahavira never spoke. The historical fact is that for forty years, he spoke continuously. But the story is that Mahavira never spoke. He was always silent, and in the audience there were three categories: one was of those who had left their bodies and had not entered in bodies again. They were all around – only visible to Mahavira, not visible to anybody else.

In the second category were human beings – seekers and searchers who had come to him, pulled by his great magnetic, charismatic personality.

And there was a third group, of his most intimate disciples – eleven disciples. They were also human beings, but they have to be put into a separate category because they had come to such communion with the master that they could understand his silence.

He never spoke – but those eleven disciples, called *ganadharas*, spoke to the people who could not understand silence. They said to people what Mahavira had communicated to them in his silence.

And there were two pieces of evidence whether they had heard rightly or not. One was that all the eleven had their own disciples: there were eleven branches of the disciples; if they all spoke the same message, that was one evidence that nobody had heard wrongly, that nobody was trying to make up the message himself.

And the second piece of evidence was that whenever those *ganadharas*, those eleven disciples spoke, the unembodied souls showered flowers, because they were able to understand the silence directly. And they were rejoicing because if these eleven people had not been there, Mahavira's message would have been lost. Those unembodied people could not communicate with human beings. The flowers were showered on the eleven *ganadharas* as a proof to all human beings that souls – which had become enlightened before – were still supporting and giving evidence that what these people were saying was exactly what had arisen out of Mahavira's silence.

It is very difficult to give historical proofs for it. But my own experience is that it may have some basis in reality, because I have come to know a few disciples of my own who can understand when I am not speaking. And whatever they understand is exactly what I wanted to convey, but kept it within myself. Here, also, many of you not only understand my words, but also my silences.

The day the electricity went off many times, I received many letters saying that it was such a great experience to sit silently for those few moments. In any other gathering in the world that would have been a disturbance; but in this gathering it was a tremendous experience – people loved those gaps. Perhaps those electricity failures were managed; but those people must have come to know that we enjoyed it – and since that day, those electricity failures have stopped.

Kavisho, do not think of the past and do not think of the future. I am here with you and I know your heart. You are here with me, and there is no need to fear that you will miss the opportunity. You are coming closer and closer to the fulfillment – to the ultimate contentment. You are going to be one of my most blessed disciples.

Beloved Bhagwan,

I would like so much to find beautiful questions, beautiful words, but nothing comes. In this moment, I realize that one of my deepest desires is just to hear you utter my name.

Prem Anutosha, you have got a very beautiful name. It means "love" and "total contentment." ~~Love is total contentment. The greatest misery in life is that one's love remains unfulfilled~~. That unfulfillment is not only of love – it is the unfulfillment of one's very soul.

You wanted to hear your name from my lips . . . I have fulfilled your desire. I would like that this name does not remain just a name – it becomes your reality too.

The name is beautiful but the reality is going to be a million times more beautiful.

Beloved Bhagwan,

The latest news from public health officials and private AIDS physicians is that Catholic priests are now a high risk group for AIDS, in view of the high incidence of homosexuality among these priests. Catholic priests seem to be about ten times more likely to be homosexual than the rest of the population – and most of them are actively homosexual.
Beloved Bhagwan, I am worried about Your going to the Vatican.

Prem Amrito, it is your duty to be worried. He is my personal physician, and if I go to the Vatican, he will have to go with me.

But it is not going to happen. The pope is such a coward that he will not allow the Italian government . . . for one year he has been preventing it; and the message has come from a personal friend of the prime minister of Italy that it is the pope who is absolutely stubborn that on no condition should I be allowed entry into Italy.

Now another difficulty has arisen: my personal physician does not want me to go to the Vatican.

The Catholic situation is getting worse and worse. They are certainly a high-risk group, Catholic priests, where ten times more homosexuals exist than anywhere else; and ten times is not the actual figure, because they are hiding it in every way.

Many Catholic priests have died of AIDS, but the Catholic Church declares that they have died of this disease, they have died of that disease. The church does not want to accept that they have died of AIDS.

It is from the medical profession that things started leaking out, because the medical profession became afraid that it was dangerous. A priest, particularly a

125

Catholic priest, comes in personal contact, in private contact, in confessionals. Those confessionals are private . . . .

And the disease is not just ten times . . . ten times is now accepted. They were denying for years that there was any homosexuality; now they accept that there is ten times more homosexuality than in any other profession. And how many of these Catholic priests are suffering from AIDS? The church is silent – and these are the servants of the people.

In America, two priests were found to be suffering from AIDS. Immediately they were transferred to faraway cities. They were not thrown out of the church for fear that they would expose it. They blackmailed the church: "If you throw us out, we will expose the fact that we are suffering from AIDS – and not only us, but many more of our colleagues."

So they were transferred to other churches, to spread the disease to other cities. And when those cities became aware, then it became a problem, because they insisted that these people should be relieved and they should not be given another church. But the problem was that if they were released, they would expose it. So they were promoted and sent into monasteries with all their salaries, all their benefits. The whole church management seems to be so stupid: the monasteries are full of homosexuals, and sending these two priests to be hidden in the monastery is a danger for all the priests and all the monks in the monastery.

In one monastery in Europe, half of the monastery is homosexual – and there are almost fifteen hundred monks. Now there is such a conflict, because it is not a small number – seven hundred and fifty are confirmed homosexuals. They have divided the monastery into two parts, and one part is a homosexual part. They have chosen their own high priest, and they have declared homosexuality not to be against the Catholic religion.

Now, you cannot throw out seven hundred and fifty monks. They will expose you before the whole world. And in all the monasteries this is happening, because

the pope goes on insisting every day . . . .

Anando has brought the latest data on Catholic monks: Every day the pope is asking the governments of the world to condemn homosexuality as a very fundamental sin, a crime – at least ten years in jail. Why has he suddenly become so interested that homosexuals should be sent to jail, and that all the governments should make it a crime, a major crime? Man's retardedness is such that nobody bothers that homosexuality is only a symptom. And one can see that even in the twentieth century we cannot understand simple logic. The pope on the one hand says, "Condemn homosexuality as a crime; and praise celibacy from all the pulpits in every temple of every religion, as the only cure." The fact is: Celibacy is the cause of homosexuality.

Why are Protestant priests not suffering so much from homosexuality? Why are Jewish rabbis not suffering from homosexuality? Why only Catholics? And soon you will find the same situation in Hindu monasteries, in Jaina monasteries, in Buddhist monasteries – wherever celibacy is the rule, homosexuality is bound to come in.

And every effort is being made to throw the responsibility onto somebody else. Nobody has the courage to say the simple thing: Celibacy is the cause. Let celibacy be the crime! Ten years of jail for anybody who wants to be celibate . . . and homosexuality will disappear. Let all the nuns and monks be married; if not married, then let nunneries and monasteries become one, mixed – and homosexuality will disappear.

But nobody wants to see celibacy as the cause, because it is their fundamental, religious discipline. So they are completely blind.

Just the other day I had another report: in Africa, where AIDS has perhaps spread to the greatest area – and the report was from there – that a scientist who was working to find out why AIDS has become so widespread in Africa, has discovered that it has come from monkeys. He found that eating the meat of the monkeys creates AIDS.

But he should know that his own conditioning is still working: from where did the poor monkey get AIDS, that his meat is full of the virus? ~~In Africa~~ it is a common thing that ~~in deep jungles people make love to female monkeys~~. It must be man who has created AIDS in monkeys – and now the poor monkeys are blamed for creating AIDS. But this is stupid, because if in Africa monkeys are creating AIDS because people eat them . . . Catholic monks in Europe and America don't eat monkeys – so this cannot be the real cause.

All the religions, for thousands of years, have insisted that ~~celibacy is something spiritual. It has nothing of spirituality in~~ it. But it could have been tolerated: if somebody wants to remain celibate, it is his freedom; but if he becomes homosexual, it is not his freedom – he is entering into the life of another person. Still it could have been tolerated, because it is a question only of two persons – and if they both are consenting . . . .

But now the problem has become of tremendous importance. It is creating a disease for which there is no cure, and a disease which has strange ways of infecting people. You may not come into sexual contact with any AIDS patient – still you can get it. Anything coming out of the body of the person carries the virus – even tears. If some child is crying, it is better to let him cry. Don't wash his tears with your hands – because many children are born with AIDS, if their mother or father was suffering from AIDS.

And AIDS takes a long time to mature – up to eight or ten years. Once it has matured, then it takes two years for the person to die. Within two years he is bound to die. But during these eight years he can go on producing children – and those children will all be born with AIDS.

Sooner or later even kissing has to be stopped, because saliva carries the virus. Only the Eskimos are right – they have never kissed in the whole of their history. When they saw Christian missionaries kissing for the first time, they could not believe it: "How dirty these people are – mixing each other's saliva, playing with each other's tongues – French kissing!" The Eskimos could see the ugliness of it, the dirtiness of it. They have never kissed each other; instead of kissing, they have a far more hygienic way of showing love: they rub noses. It is far more hygienic, clean – except for the few days when you have a cold; at that time it can be dangerous. When your nose is flowing, nobody wants to make love to your nose.

Amrito, I have said that I would like to go to the Vatican, but the Vatican is not ready to welcome me. And this is not the first time I have said it – I have said it many times, particularly to all the newspapers and news media that come from Italy. Yesterday I had to say it because there was a woman news reporter, Julia, and those were her questions.

The Pope has no religious understanding or philosophical depth. Christianity itself is such a poor religion that it has not been influential over the intellectuals in any country. For example, in India, now there is a large minority of Christians – they are the third greatest religion in India. But all the people who have become Christians are beggars, aboriginals, orphans, prostitutes, widows – who as Hindus cannot be married again, but can be married again as Christians.

And these people have not become Christians because they are convinced of Christianity's superiority over their own religion.

Taoism, Buddhism, Jainism are far higher in their analysis of human consciousness, in finding ways and means to help humanity to come back home. Christianity has nothing comparable to it; and whatever they have can be easily destroyed by argument – and the pope understands that; all Christians understand that. I have come in contact with many bishops, and I have seen their embarrassment – because they cannot support any of their fundamentals.

So, Amrito, there is no need to fear – neither will they allow me there, nor will you allow me to go. But once in a while, just allow me to hammer the pope

Beloved Bhagwan,

"Excuse me," said an ocean fish, "you are older than I, so can you tell me,
where do you find this thing they call the ocean?"
"The ocean," said the older fish, "is the thing you are in now."
"Oh, this? But this is water. What I am seeking is the ocean," said the disappointed fish
as he swam away to search elsewhere.

Anand Katyayani, this is an old parable. But this is one of the beauties of parables – that they never become old, they always remain relevant . . . because the parable is about you – not about the fish, not about the ocean.

Everybody is searching for truth; everybody is searching for God; everybody is searching for the miraculous, the mysterious source of life. And the situation is the same: the younger fish is asking the older fish, "Where is this thing they call the ocean? I hear so much about it."

And the older fish said, "You are in it."

And naturally, the younger fish said, "But this is water and I am searching for the ocean." She was so disappointed that she said, "It is better to go away somewhere else to find the truth – what the ocean is."

God is the ocean you are in, because God is another name for life. You are breathing God in and out every moment. It is God who is beating in your heart. It is God who is flowing in your blood. It is God who is your marrow, your bones, your intelligence, your very consciousness. But because the fish is born in the ocean – it is so close – she thinks, this is only water.

This is only air that you are breathing in and out. And people are searching just like the fish, and they will never find – unless they stop searching and just start looking at what they are, what their consciousness is, what their life is. And they will be surprised that there was no need to go anywhere. All that they were

searching for they were surrounded by on the outside, and they were filled by it in their innermost being.

The whole existence is God. It is the religions which have created the fallacy that God created the world – so they have given you an idea that the world and God are two, so that you will have to search for the creator.

I want you to destroy that duality completely. God is not the creator, but the creation itself. He is in the trees and he is in the rivers and he is in the moon and he is in the sun and he is in you.

Except God, there is nothing else.

The seeker is the sought, the hunter is the hunted, the observer is the observed. And the moment you realize this, such a deep relaxation comes, such a peace descends deep in you that you have never dreamt of before. Such clarity comes to your eyes that everywhere you start seeing immense beauty, immeasurable beauty, tremendous goodness. In the smallest things of life you start feeling the heartbeat of the universe.

This is our temple, and this is our God, and we are part of it. The worshiper is not separate from the worshiped.

To understand this organic unity is the true religion.

Okay, Vimal?

Yes, Bhagwan.

The Golden Key

This life – what we understand as life – is in the hands of death, and there is no way of protection. But I know a golden key, which is to find in yourself a deeper layer of life, deeper than this life and deeper than this death. That deepest layer is eternal. There is no need to protect it; it is protected by the whole of existence itself. There is a lock, and that is your mind, which prevents your going in. And there is a key: I call it meditation. Before meditation, the mind disappears. Not that the lock is opened . . . but the lock simply disappears, and you enter into your kingdom of eternity. And only then does one feel secure.

Even if death comes, and it is *bound* to come, you will be watching it: you will not be dying. Your body will be dying, your mind will be dying, but before death you have already abandoned them. You have gone deeper than both the superficial layers.

Except through meditation, nobody has come to know about eternity, about immortality, about the timelessness of our being. Therefore to me religion simply means meditation. Anything else is superfluous, nonessential.

February 17, 1987,   8 a.m.

Beloved Bhagwan,

For quite some time now I have been looking into why and how I protect myself, and who I'm protecting myself from. I find it expresses itself through arrogance, and the safety of only wanting to stay on the side of the giver. I feel like a rocket which is all prepared to be launched: all the systems have been cleared but one lock is still on – the lock of protection.
Bhagwan, would You show me the key to unlock protection – or is there no lock?

David, man is born with death in his heart. As he grows, death also grows. Life and death are almost like two wings. The day life has reached to its peak, death also reaches its peak; hence the unknown fear, and the desire to be protected.

But there is only one way to unlock – only one key. This desire to be protected can disappear only when you understand that the life that you have known is not the eternal life. The dewdrop has to die; there is no way of protecting it.

But in the death of the dewdrop is a new beginning. It is not an end; it is the beginning of the very ocean. The dewdrop becomes the ocean. Then all fears – of insecurity, of death, of disease, of old age – they all disappear together.

But man goes on doing just the opposite. Seeing that there is a desire to be protected, he tries to find all kinds of protection – in money, in power, in respectability. But the longing is simply the same: somehow I should be so powerful and so secure that the fear of the unknown, of death, can be forgotten.

But there is no way to forget it. You can get busy with thousands of things, but it is always there like an undercurrent – because it is a natural phenomenon. Death is not something that is going to come from outside.

I have always loved an old parable: A king was very much afraid of death. He had conquered many lands, he was a great warrior, he was adequately safe, secure – there was no need to be afraid. But the problem is: death does not come from outside – it grows within you. You bring it with your birth.

But nobody told him this; on the contrary, his advisers told him, "You should make a palace in which there should be no windows, no doors – just one door, and on that door there should be seven-fold security. One guard – but who can trust? – then another guard to guard the first guard, and so on. Seven lines of guards . . . you will be absolutely protected."

He made the palace. The idea looked logical; but all that is logical is not realistic – logic is not equivalent to life. The palace was made. The king was very happy, the guarding system was so secure. There was only one door; no enemy could enter from anywhere.

One of his friends, another king, heard about the palace and came to see it. He was immensely impressed. It was a piece of art inside, was made all of marble, and everything for the king's pleasure was there: beautiful fountains, waterfalls – but everything was inside the palace. The friend said, "I would like a palace just like this in my own kingdom. It feels so secure."

As he was leaving, the host king came out, and the friend thanked him again. As he was getting into his golden chariot he said, "I am immensely grateful, because you have made something which is really secure. Just help me with your architects and the stonecutters; I want to make exactly the same palace in my kingdom."

Just then a beggar sitting in the street started laughing. Both the kings felt embarrassed, and the host asked the beggar, "Why are you laughing?"

He said, "Once I used to be a king myself, but just to find security I became a beggar. Since I have become a beggar, nobody is interested in killing me. I sleep in the street without any fear. I have one suggestion to make to you – and I am older than both of you, and my kingdom was far bigger than your kingdoms.

"My suggestion is that there is a flaw in your palace. I have been sitting here and watching – but nobody has bothered about the flaw."

The king said, "What flaw?"

The beggar said, "There is one door. The best security will be for you to get in and let your stonecutters close the door. Instead of a door there should be a beautiful marble wall. Then nobody can enter there.

"Even these seven lines of guards can conspire – it is not inconceivable – to acquire the whole kingdom. You are in the hands of these seven men. If they join together, they can kill you and divide your whole kingdom. And it is such a simple thing that it is bound to come into their minds. You think you are secure –

you are more insecure than ever; you are just in the hands of seven people."

The king said, "Your idea is right – but what is the point of living if there is no door to come out?"

And the beggar laughed again. He said, "You need not come out. Death can enter without a door – because in fact it does not enter from the outside; it is sitting within you, just like a seed."

You may not be very conscious, David, nobody is very conscious – that you are dying every day, inch by inch. And one day the process is complete. Death is not an incident, but a process: it has the same length as your life. If you are going to live seventy or eighty years, your death also has eighty years to live with you.

This life – what we understand as life – is in the hands of death, and there is no way of protection. But I know a golden key, which is to find in yourself a deeper layer of life, deeper than this life and deeper than this death. That deepest layer is eternal. There is no need to protect it; it is protected by the whole of existence itself. There is a lock, and that is your mind, which prevents your going in. And there is a key: I call it meditation.

Before meditation, the mind disappears. Not that the lock is opened . . . but the lock simply disappears, and you enter into your kingdom of eternity. And only then does one feel secure.

Even if death comes, and it is *bound* to come, you will be watching it; you will not be dying. Your body will be dying, your mind will be dying, but before death you have already abandoned them. You have gone deeper than both the superficial layers.

Except through meditation, nobody has come to know about eternity, about immortality, about the timelessness of our being. Therefore to me religion simply means meditation. Anything else is superfluous, nonessential.

This is the miracle of meditation: that it does not divide people. There is no Christian meditation, there is no Hindu meditation, there is no Mohammedan meditation, and there is no Jewish meditation.

Meditation is a science. All that is nonessential in religions divides people; and the non-essential becomes so big, so heavy, that the small key of meditation is lost or forgotten. People feel offended with me, annoyed with me, irritated, because I want them not to be Hindus, not to be Christians, not to be Jainas – but only to be meditators . . . because meditation is the only essential religion that can join you to your real self.

The word "religion" has to be understood. It means "bringing together." You have gone far away from yourself.

To bring you back together with your reality is the only religion there is.

Beloved Bhagwan,

Every day I come out of Your discourse, having been sitting with You, listening to Your voice and dancing to Your music. Coming out of the gate the world looks so fresh, the green so deep and shiny, the play of the sun with the shadow so rich, and the people soft and open. Beloved Master, what's the magic You use in cleaning my eyes? Is it this or is nature rejoicing too in the presence of such a beautiful Master and showing its most celebrative and beautiful side to us? Is this Your buddhafield flowing through everybody and everything present here?

Anand Premartha, it is both. Sitting here in silence, being showered by my silence, my serenity, everything in you becomes fresh, young. Silence is such a shower of the soul.

Listening to the music – not only listening, but participating, almost dancing with joy – you forget your ordinary worries and the world, the tensions and anxieties; those are the layers of dust on your eyes.

And just being with me here, something that is not visible to the eyes transpires between me and you. Some energy, which can only be called divine, passes from heart to heart. I can see that there are moments when you all disappear, and only one consciousness remains. You forget your individuality, your separateness. And this is such a rejuvenation, such a refreshment, such a rebirth, that when you go out – things are the same – but the green looks greener; the people look softer and more loving. The song of the birds, although meaningless, starts having a significance of its own. All your senses are at their maximum sensitivity. The light passing through the trees fills you with wonder. The wind passing through the trees whispers unknown secrets to you.

So on the one hand you are ready, available, fresh, rested, relaxed, and silent; and on the other hand you are part of existence. Existence rejoices with you. It is not only that your eyes are fresh and your mind is silent, that the trees are greener – that is only one part of the story.

The other part is that because of your silence, because of your dance, because of your music, they really are greener – just for you, a special gift.

It is said that whenever Gautam Buddha passed by any path, even if it was not the time for the trees to blossom, they blossomed. Buddhists have not been able to explain it; no scientific explanation is possible. Only a mystic can understand it; only a meditator can understand what it means – that trees which were without leaves immediately started growing leaves and foliage, preparing a little shadow for the tired Buddha to rest under.

That is what you are experiencing: existence certainly rejoices when you are blissful. Existence is almost an echo of your being. If you are in anxiety, everything around you becomes tense; and if you are silent, everything around you becomes a silent music, a silent dance.

Remember that you are not separate from existence; so when you are happy, all these trees are also happy. Happiness is contagious. When you are dancing, these trees are also moving in rhythm with you.

When you are full of love whoever meets you – he may be a very primitive, crude man, but your love is more powerful than any crudeness, any primitiveness . . . with you, suddenly he feels he is becoming soft.

You have known this experience in many other ways. There are people with whom you become sad. They have not done anything to you and they have not said anything to you, but their sadness is so heavy and so powerful. We are continuously broadcasting our hearts all around us.

If a sad man passes by, his sadness is going to touch your heart too, unless your joyfulness is bigger than his sadness; then he will be touched. And you know about people with whom you suddenly become joyous for no reason at all, just being with them it feels as if a certain joy, a certain happiness has entered into you.

But listening to me is nothing but a meditation. This is my simplest device, in which you have not to do anything at all. I tell you to meditate, but I cannot leave it to you. You may think, "Yes, I will meditate," and you go on postponing. That is why every morning and evening I speak to you. It does not matter what I say. I am not an orator, neither am I a preacher, nor am I giving you a doctrine or a philosophy. This is a device: because you want to listen to me, you are bound to be silent. Without your knowing, you are falling deeper and deeper into your being.

So when you go out, you have not gone out of a lecture hall. This Chuang Tzu hall is not a lecture hall, it is a place – a temple – of meditation. That's why I always go on leaving gaps for you: in those gaps there is every possibility you may touch your innermost core.

So don't say after "listening" to me, say after "meditating" with me, when you go out all your senses are more sensitive. And the whole of existence rejoices because you have a totally different fragrance, a different presence. You carry something of me with you every day.

Slowly, slowly you will be able to sit by yourself alone, doing nothing, sitting silently. And in that silence, you will know all the mysteries of existence.

This is one of the mysteries: that everything is interconnected. Your joy is felt by the trees – your sadness too. Your silence is experienced by the birds – your dance, your music too.

Beloved Bhagwan,

Many times in my meditation I asked You not to show me directly the tremendous tragedy that is happening on earth today, as I know I could never tolerate such suffering. Yet I'm sensing this all the time, even with my buffers. I know You are the light for this whole planet, and knowing this carries such a responsibility. I would be so grateful to hear You speak to me on helping, knowing I can't help, and the angst of feeling helpless – and also of relaxing when feeling such a state of urgency.

Prem Kaveesha, I can understand your anguish about the whole of humanity, about this planet earth; because every day we are coming closer and closer to a disaster.

It is because the disaster is coming very close; even with your buffers you cannot forget it – and it hurts. And it hurts more because you feel you cannot help; you cannot do anything. It is simply beyond the capacity of any individual to prevent this calamity, this disaster, this global suicide that seems to be almost certain. But I have a way of my own.

You feel helpless because you think in terms of helping other people to understand, and that is an impossible job. The world is so big, and ~~people are so full of violence~~ that it seems the calamity is not coming from outside, but it is the accumulated violence in people themselves that is going to explode this earth.

But don't think in terms of helping. Then you will not feel helpless and you will not feel tense. *I* don't feel helpless, *I* don't feel tense, *I* don't feel any anguish – and I am more aware of it than you can be – because my approach is not of helping anybody, but just for you to raise your own consciousness to the highest peak possible . . . of which you are perfectly capable.

If we can create only two hundred enlightened people in the world, the world can be saved.

Kaveesha was born in a Jewish family, hence she will understand a beautiful story. In the *Old Testament* it is mentioned that there were two cities, Sodom and Gomorrah, and both became sexually perverted. In Gomorrah, homosexuality was so prevalent, and in Sodom people had fallen even lower in their perversion: they were making love to animals. Hence, the English word "sodomy" – it comes from the city of Sodom. And God decided to destroy those two cities completely.

He destroyed those two cities completely – and it is very strange that those two cities had the same population as Hiroshima and Nagasaki. Hiroshima and Nagasaki were destroyed by man, but the *Old Testament* story is that God destroyed those two sexually perverted cities. What I am going to tell you is a Hassidic story based on the *Old Testament* version of the destruction by God of two sexually perverted cities.

Judaism has blossomed in its totality in Hassidism. Hassidism is a rebellious, and essentially religious, phenomenon. All the religions have given to the world something beautiful – although those religions were against that something beautiful – except Christianity.

Mohammedanism has given Sufism, although Mohammedans have killed Sufis. Buddhism has given Zen, although Buddhists don't accept Zen as an authentic teaching of Gautam Buddham. Hinduism has given Tantra, but Hindus are very much against Tantra – and that is their very truth. It is a very strange thing . . . and the same is the situation with Judaism.

Hassidism is a small, rebellious phenomenon within the world of Judaism. The man who founded Hassidism was Baal Shemtov. He also relates the story and you can see the beauty and the difference.

Somebody asked him, "What do you think about Sodom and Gomorrah?"

And Baal Shem said, "That story is not written in its completion. I will tell you the whole story." And he said, "When God declared that he was going to destroy these two cities, one Hassid, a mystic, approached God and asked him, 'If in these cities there are one hundred people who have experienced you, what will you do with these one hundred people? Are you going to destroy them too, with the whole cities?'

"For a moment God was silent and then he said, 'No. If there were one hundred awakened souls in these two cities, because of those one hundred people these two cities would be saved; I would not destroy them.'

"The Hassid mystic said, 'If there were only fifty, not a hundred? Will you destroy these cities, and those fifty awakened people?'

"Now God saw that he had been caught by the mystic. He said, 'No, I cannot destroy fifty awakened people.' And the Hassid said, 'I want you to know that there is only one man who is awakened; six months he lives in Sodom and six months he lives in Gomorrah. What do you say about it? – Will you destroy the cities?'

"God said, 'You are a very cunning fellow. Who is this man?' He said of course, 'I am.'

"And God could not deny him because it is not a question of quantity, it is a question of quality: one awakened person or one hundred awakened persons. The awakened person cannot be destroyed by existence, because the awakened person is the longest dream of existence itself, the deepest longing of existence itself – to reach to the stars." And Baal Shem said that Sodom and Gomorrah were never destroyed.

Jews are angry about Baal Shem, that he is just inventing this story; the whole story is written in the *Old Testament*. The Jews don't accept the Hassids as authentic Jews. In the same way, everywhere the really religious person will be condemned by the so-called religious.

Whether Baal Shem invented the story or whether he was telling the true story, I am with him. In the first place a God who believes in destruction is not a God. A God who cannot transform people from their perversions is not a God. Baal Shem is not only saving those two cities, he is also saving God's godliness: his compassion, his love, his understanding.

Kaveesha, forget all about the world. You become the one Hassid, the one mystic. And if we can create around the world just two hundred enlightened people . . . . That number is also exactly like Baal Shem's Hassid. When he started talking with God, negotiating, it was only a question of two cities. The world has become big and it is a question of the whole world – so I am starting negotiating with two hundred. But I want to tell you that even two enlightened people will be enough, and the world will be saved; because existence cannot destroy its own ultimate flowering.

So you forget about the world; otherwise it will create unnecessary anxiety and will destroy your own awakening, which is the only possibility to save the world.

Anybody who wants to help the world should forget about the world and concentrate upon himself. Raise your consciousness to such a height that existence has to think a second time whether to destroy this world or to save it.

The masses as they are don't matter; existence will not care about them. In fact, existence would like this whole humanity – this rotten humanity – to be destroyed, so that evolution can start from scratch again. Something has gone wrong . . . .

But if there are a few enlightened people, they are far weightier than billions and billions of people on the earth. Existence cannot destroy the world – not only because of those few people who are enlightened; but because of their enlightenment, the unconscious masses also become valuable, because it is from these unconscious masses that those Himalayan peaks have arisen. They were also unconscious yesterday, today they are conscious. And existence is very patient: if it sees that unconscious people can become fully conscious, then this great mass of people, which is absolutely unconscious, also has a possibility.

I depend on the individuals, not on the collectivity. The collectivity is so rotten that it will be an act of compassion to destroy it. But we have to prove that out of this unconscious, almost dead humanity, a few lotuses can blossom. Then, just given time, perhaps more lotuses will be coming. Some may be just buds, some may be just in the seed; but even if there is one man who is enlightened, with him the whole of humanity becomes valuable, because that man shows the hope that every man is capable of the same miracle.

So, Kaveesha, forget about helping. You cannot help; nobody can help. But you can become a mystic, a Hassid, and you can argue with God, that "I am here; are you going to destroy me? And these people who are somnambulists, walking in their sleep – I was also one of them. That is my yesterday. These people should be given their tomorrows. There is every possibility that every human being can become a Gautam Buddha."

This is the only way to save this beautiful planet earth.

Beloved Bhagwan,

I've been with You for twelve years, listening to You answering thousands of questions. The questions all sound very similar, yet Your answers with each of them are so new, so fresh, so crystal clear. Even though You have said everything that is possible to be expressed through words, I hear everything as if it is for the first time, as if I have never heard it ever before. Even though words repeat, it never feels like repetition. It is like floating in a cool, clear, mountain lake, that I come out of totally fresh, clean and clear. Bhagwan, You are such a wonderful mystery to me, always catching me by surprise and in awe and wonder.

Prem Turiya, you have heard many people, you have read many people; but hearing me or reading me is a totally different experience, for the simple reason that I am not a speaker, an orator, a lecturer.

Your questions may be the same, but my answers cannot be the same for two reasons. First, I have forgotten your questions and my answers – I cannot repeat, I am not a gramophone record. Secondly, your questions may be the same, but the questioners are different – and I answer the questioner, not the question.

Naturally, words will be repeated. Somebody has counted that I have answered fifteen thousand questions, and I am not a learned man; my vocabulary is very limited. But because I am not answering the question, even though the words may be the same, the answer has a different nuance every time. Not that I am making an effort not to repeat myself . . . I don't remember at all, I have never read any of my books.

Each time when I am answering you, I am never prepared for it. I don't know myself what is going to be my next sentence. It is not ordinary speaking; it is a communion, not only communication. I have nothing to communicate. I am not trying to convince you about something – because if I am trying to convince you, then the only way is to repeat the same thing again and again and again so it becomes a conditioning in your mind.

My words are not important. What is important

is your silent listening. ~~What is important is that my words are not coming from the mind, but from my deepest silence. Although they cannot contain silence, when they come from the deepest silence something of that silence surrounds them.~~ They cannot contain it, but something of the silence surrounds them. It is as if you have taken a bath in a lake; you cannot contain the lake, but when you come out of it, something of the lake – the freshness, the coolness – comes with you. The lake is left behind, but some quality of the lake is carried with you.

You are listening in silence; I am speaking in silence. My words reach to you with some freshness, with some fragrance; and because you are silent, that fragrance, that silence, deepens your silence – makes it fragrant.

It is very difficult for intellectuals to understand what is happening. It is a very non-intellectual, heart-to-heart communion. Words are only excuses.

I would love to sit silently with you, but then *you* cannot be silent. If I am silent, then your mind will go on: yakkety-yak, yakkety-yak. Just to save you from trouble, I have to speak, and because I am speaking, your mind becomes engaged in listening. It forgets its own yakkety-yak, or postpones it.

It is certainly a miracle. And these are authentic miracles, not miracles like Jesus walking on the water.

I have heard a story: Two rabbis and one bishop were very great friends. All three had gone fishing on the same lake where Jesus used to walk – Lake Galilee.

The bishop was an American; those two rabbis were local Jews. Talking about Jesus, one rabbi said, "You Christians make too much of small things. Here, everybody knows how to walk on water."

The bishop said, "Everybody . . . ? You can walk on water?"

The rabbi said, "Of course," and he stepped over the side of the boat and walked on water.

The bishop could not believe his eyes . . . . He is a Jew, he does not even believe in Christ! These are the people who crucified Jesus. This is absolutely unfair of God – that even rabbis should be allowed to do miracles.

The first rabbi came back. The bishop asked the second rabbi, "Can you also walk?"

He said, "Everybody can walk. You have unnecessarily made too much fuss about Jesus – that he walked on water. In Israel, everybody walks on water."

The bishop said, "This is a new thing; I have never heard of it. Just show me that you can also walk on water." And the second rabbi stepped out of the boat and walked on water. The bishop looked with unblinking eyes – he even forgot to breathe.

And the second rabbi came back, and both of them said, "Now, you are a follower of Jesus; you can try. Do you trust Jesus?"

The bishop said, "Absolutely."

Then they said, "You can try."

So the bishop stepped out on his side – this was the other side of the boat – and started drowning. One rabbi said, "What do you think, should we tell that American idiot where the stones are?"

Local people know where the rocks are. These are not miracles. The real miracle happens almost invisibly. Your being silent here . . . just listening to the birds: tweet, tweet, toot, toot – it is a miracle.

Okay, Vimal?

Yes, Bhagwan.

God The Father –
Just Another Teddy Bear

Whenever I see people who are fixated – and there are rarely people who are not – I always remember small children on railway stations, at airports, carrying their teddy bears – dirty, smelly, greasy, almost looking like Italians, as if they are stuffed with spaghetti. But they are clinging to them, they cannot sleep without them. Wherever they go, they carry their teddy bears.

You also have your teddy bears, but they are not visible. It is okay for small children but one should get out of this kind of childish psychology; one should become more mature.

No Catholic can be mature, no other religious person can be mature, because there is always the teddy bear above – God. They cannot live without a false hypothesis, a lie, but that lie helps – it gives you a certain solace. To seek solace or consolation is to remain retarded. Come out of this retardedness and become mature.

February 17, 1987,   7 p.m.

Beloved Bhagwan,

When my father died ten years ago, he was my last reason for living. After this strong experience, I
have felt more alone every day. When I met You it was like meeting my father again.
But now, with You, I feel more and more alone.
Beloved Bhagwan, what can I do? Is aloneness my way?

Prem Matwala, aloneness is not only your way to truth, it is everybody's way. It is the only way. Your whole approach from the very beginning has been wrong. First, life is a reason unto itself. The moment you make something else a reason for living, you have moved on a wrong path.

You are saying, "When my father died ten years ago, he was my last reason for living." This is a very wrong approach, a wrong way of looking at things. Everybody's father is going to die sooner or later. Your father's father must have died . . . and still *he* lived.

You have not lived on your own, you have always needed somebody else to be your reason for living. That reason can disappear at any moment: the father will die, the mother will die, the wife can go with somebody else, the business can go bankrupt. If you make anything other than your own being a reason for living, you are insulting yourself, you are humiliating yourself – and this kind of humiliation is being supported; your father must have supported it.

Every father wants, and every mother wants their children to live for them. It is a strange demand: if it is

to be fulfilled, then nobody can live in this world, you have to live for your father, and your father has to live for *his* father, but nobody can live for himself, and unless you live for yourself you cannot find any joy, any bliss. You have degraded your life; you have lost your dignity, your self-respect.

Your father had to live for himself and had to die for himself. You could not die for your father; how can you live for your father? And it is not insulting to your father that you have to live for yourself.

If parents were really understanding, they would help their children not to be dependent on them, not to get any kind of fixation – father fixation, mother fixation, all fixations are of a pathological mind. Only freedom, and living for oneself totally, is the sign of spiritual health.

Then you met me and you started the same old story again. Your father died and you had to live alone every day. Could you not find a friend? Could you not find a woman to love? Could you not create your own life, devoted to music or poetry or dance or painting? The father is not going to be with you forever . . . . And then, meeting me, you shifted your father fixation onto me – without even asking my permission. You had a gap and you thought you had found a father.

It is not coincidental that the religions call God "the father." These are the ideas of psychologically sick people. Christians call their priests "father." These religions which call God "father" and religions which call their priests "father" – rather than helping you to come out of your pathology, your sickness – help you to be more sick, to be more pathological. Their whole business depends on your sickness.

You should have at least asked me whether I was willing to be your father. That very day I would have tried to persuade you to change your direction. Life is enough unto itself. One does not live for somebody else. Even if you love somebody else, you love because of yourself, because you feel joyous. The other is only an excuse. If you enjoy friendship, it is your enjoyment; the friends are only helping you to fulfill your own longing.

Then life has a health, and only the healthy person, the psychologically healthy person, can discover his spiritual being. The sick person cannot move, he is so much involved with his pathological desires – which are going to remain unfulfilled, which are going to remain like wounds. Otherwise, the death of your father would have helped you immensely to become aware not to depend on anyone else again.

But you did not use your intelligence at all. It was your dependence on your father that created the sadness, the misery. Now the father is gone; the first step of any intelligent person should be that this should not be allowed to happen again. One has to learn to be alone.

That does not mean that you have to cut yourself off from friends, from family, from people, from society – no. The art of living alone does not mean renouncing the world, the art of being alone simply means that you are not dependent on anybody else. You enjoy people, you love people, you share everything with people, but you are capable of being alone, and yet blissful. That

is the path of meditation.

Accidentally you arrived here, and you committed the same mistake again: you replaced your dead father with me. You started looking at me as if I am your father. But I am nobody's father . . . I am not even married!

It is very strange that God, who is not even married, is called "father"; priests, who are not even married, who don't have any children, are called "father." But they are called "father" because some day or other, everybody is going to miss his father; then they will be the replacement. They are substitute fathers, but they are also mortal, so they can die any day. Even the pope can pop off at any moment. So the religions have created an eternal father – at least God will remain with you always; and all the religions define God as everywhere present – omnipresent; all powerful – omnipotent; all knowing – omniscient.

I have heard about a nun who used to take her bath in a closed bathroom with her clothes on. The other nuns became aware that this seemed to be some kind of insanity. They asked the nun, "What is the matter? Why don't you take your clothes off and take a good shower?"

She said, "How can I do it? Because God is present everywhere." Even in the bathroom, with closed doors, you are not alone. God seems to be a kind of Peeping Tom, so whenever you close the door of the bathroom, look all around – he must be hiding in some corner and watching what is going on.

The nun was logically right because, if the hypothesis of God's omnipresence is true, then certainly he cannot leave the bathroom just because a lady is taking a bath – he is not that much of a gentleman. Even if he was outside, if the lady is taking a bath he would enter the bathroom; that nun was doing absolutely the logical thing.

But this God is created just to help those people who are always in need of some father figure who is protecting them, who is their security, who is their bank balance. Without him, they will be left alone in this vast existence. You carried the idea even here. But I cannot support your pathology. I am here to destroy all kinds of psychological sicknesses, to give you a spiritual well-being.

The first principle is: freedom from everybody: father or mother, husband or wife. And remember, I repeat again, freedom does not mean that you have to renounce. In fact, the people who renounce are not free: they renounce out of fear, they are afraid that if they don't escape from home, they cannot be free. But if they cannot be free in the home, they cannot be free even in the Himalayas. They may be sitting alone in the Himalayas, but they will be thinking about their wife, about their children, about their father, about their mother, about their friends. The whole crowd will be there.

You have to learn the art of meditation. The whole art consists of a simple fact: move within inwards, because there is no society, no father, no mother; you are alone – absolutely alone. Move inwards and find your being; and suddenly your loneliness will go through a transformation; your loneliness will become aloneness. Loneliness is sick, aloneness is beautiful, immensely beautiful.

You say, Matwala: "Now, with You, I feel more and more alone." That's my whole business, to make people feel more and more alone. But remember, feeling alone is not loneliness. The distinction is subtle, but has to be clearly understood: when you are feeling lonely, you are missing someone; when you missed your father, you were feeling lonely. If you are not missing anyone but you have found yourself, then you will be alone but not lonely.

And to be alone is so beautiful. All fetters have been dropped, all relationships have disappeared, nothing pollutes your consciousness. You are like a cedar of Lebanon standing alone, high in the sky; the higher you go, the more and more alone you will become.

So if being here, you feel more and more alone, it is perfectly good. But I know you have used a wrong word, you wanted to say, "more and more lonely." If

you were feeling alone, you would also have felt a tremendous joy arising in you – the joy that only freedom can bring, a blissfulness that comes to you from your own inner core. And because you are knowing yourself, you know there is no death; hence, there is no need of any security, no need of any protection.

Out of this aloneness arises love – you will be surprised when you hear it – because only a man who is full of joy can be loving. Only a man who is so overflowing with bliss can share, can give it to someone as a present. Love is nothing but sharing your joy – but first you have to find your center of being.

Matwala, you are asking, "What can I do? Is aloneness my way?"

It is certainly your way too, but it is everybody's way. It is the only way. But remember to distinguish between loneliness and aloneness: loneliness is a sickness and has to be destroyed; aloneness is a tremendous revolution – freedom from all, no dependence on anything, no fixation. You are enough unto yourself; nothing else is needed.

I am reminded of Alexander the Great meeting Diogenes. Diogenes used to live naked. Outside India, perhaps he is the only one who can be compared with Mahavira.

In India, there have been many great masters who have lived naked, but the West knows only one man, Diogenes. And they have been ignoring him, ignoring his philosophy. But he was such a rare man that even Alexander the Great wanted to meet him, because he had heard so many beautiful stories about the man.

He had heard that he carried a lantern in the daylight, a lighted lantern. And whenever he is asked, "What kind of nonsense is this? First, you are naked; second, in full daylight you are carrying a lighted lantern?" Diogenes used to say, "I am naked because clothes were a dependence. I had to ask somebody, and that I don't like. And it took me only a few years to become seasoned, just like animals. Now I don't feel the summer, I don't feel the rain, I don't feel the winter;

on the contrary, I enjoy the changes of the seasons. And I carry the lighted lantern because I am searching for an authentic man. I want to see everybody's face to see whether there is a mask or not."

And people used to ask him, "Have you found anybody with his original face?"

He said, "Not yet."

Alexander had heard that in the beginning, he used to carry a begging bowl – just like Gautam Buddha. One day he was going to the river because he was feeling thirsty – immensely thirsty. It was a hot summer day, and as he was reaching close to the river, a dog came running by, passed him, jumped into the river and started drinking the water.

Diogenes thought, "This is great! No begging bowl, nothing. He was behind me and he jumps ahead of me. If a dog can manage without a begging bowl, it is beneath my dignity to carry a begging bowl." First he threw the begging bowl into the river, and then he jumped in, just like the dog, and drank the water. He said, "It was such a joy."

Such stories Alexander had heard about him. So when he was coming to India, and he heard, on the way that Diogenes was very close by, he was living there by the side of a river, Alexander stopped and said, "I would like to see the man. I don't want to miss this opportunity, I have heard so much about him."

It was morning, a winter morning, and the sun was rising. Diogenes was lying on the beach of the river, taking a sunbath. He did not even get up when Alexander reached there. Alexander said, "I have heard much about you and I have loved all those small anecdotes about your life. I wanted to see you, and just seeing you, I can understand that you are a beautiful man."

He had such a beautiful body, almost like a statue, and was so joyous that Alexander said, "I would like to give some present to you. You just ask – anything! Don't feel embarrassed. Whatever you ask for – even if you ask for my whole empire – I will give it to you."

Diogenes laughed. He said, "That is not the thing that I am feeling embarrassed about. I am going to ask something else . . . that's why I am feeling embarrassed."

Alexander said, "You just say it."

He said, "Just stand a little to the side, because you are blocking the sun and I am taking my sunbath, and this is not my meeting time." And he closed his eyes.

That's the only thing he asked from the man who was the world conqueror. Alexander must have felt a poor beggar in comparison to Diogenes. He did not care at all about his empire, and yet he was feeling embarrassed to ask such a small thing: "Just stand to the side. I am taking my sunbath."

These people have known the beauty of aloneness. They are unburdened by anything. I am not telling you that you have to be naked, that you have to throw away all your possessions. Once in a while, one Diogenes is good – but I am certainly telling you, you should not be possessive. Possessions don't matter; you should not be possessive. You can use all that is made available to you by existence – but don't become attached to it.

I have been condemned all over the world because of my ninety-three Rolls Royces – but nobody has bothered to notice that I have not looked back: what happened to those ninety-three Rolls Royces? You can have the whole world in your hands; the real issue is: don't be attached. I have never looked back.

A few sannyasins have even purchased those Rolls Royces thinking that if I need them, they can present them again to me. They have written letters to me, they have phoned me: "We have got one of the cars and we are not using it. We are keeping it; if you want it back . . . ."

I said, "What is gone, is gone. You use it; you enjoy it. Just remember that your master never looked back at anything."

The real thing is not that you don't possess anything – just don't be possessive. Enjoy everything of the world – it is for you; but enjoy it the way you enjoy the moment – don't possess it. Don't be like those two drunkards who were lying down on a full moon night by the side of a tree, enjoying the full moon. One of them said, "Sometimes I think I should purchase the moon." The other said, "Forget all about it because I am not going to sell it." Just enjoy it – why bother about purchasing and selling?

Your aloneness is a deep, inner experience. It is the experience of your own consciousness. There is not even a shadow of misery or pain. It is pure bliss, it is absolute benediction, as if God is showering on you. Only when you are alone God showers on you – only then.

So, Matwala, remember it is the only way to bliss, to freedom, to truth, to godliness, to eternal life. Don't be addicted to anything and don't be fixated psychologically – by your father, by your mother, by your friend.

Whenever I see people who are fixated – and there are rarely people who are not – I always remember small children on railway stations, at airports, carrying their teddy bears – dirty, smelly, greasy, almost looking like Italians, as if they are stuffed with spaghetti. But they are clinging to them, they cannot sleep without them. Wherever they go, they carry their teddy bears.

You also have your teddy bears, but they are not visible. It is okay for small children but one should get out of this kind of childish psychology; one should become more mature.

No Catholic can be mature, no other religious person can be mature, because there is always the teddy bear above – God. They cannot live without a false hypothesis, a lie, but that lie helps – it gives you a certain solace. To seek solace or consolation is to remain retarded. Come out of this retardedness and become mature.

Beloved Bhagwan,

There is a growing awareness of when I am not "myself." In meditation, and being in Your presence, in the good moments, there is no "myself." Beloved Master, what do You mean when You say, "Be yourself?"

Prem Purna, it is one of the greatest statements made by Socrates: "Know thyself." But I have always thought it is incomplete. Unless another statement is added to it, it will not be complete, and that statement is: "Be thyself."

To *know* thyself, first you have to *be* thyself, otherwise, how can you know?

The second thing: as you enter into the inner world of mystery, of being oneself, of knowing oneself, you will come to a point where you become aware that the word 'self' is confusing – confusing in the sense that it has two meanings. Its true meaning is your soul, and its pseudo meaning is your ego. And that's what is creating your problem: whenever we use the word 'yourself', usually we mean your ego, your I-ness.

When Socrates says, "Know thyself," or when I say, "Be thyself," we are not using the word 'self' in the sense of ego. We are using the word 'self' in the real sense of soul – your consciousness. That will explain to you why you are puzzled.

You are puzzled because you are accustomed to the linguistic meaning of the word, but not to the existential experience of it. The 'self' as ego will be absent when the 'self' as soul becomes present to you. Those two meanings are very dangerous. Either you can be an ego or you can be a soul, and the word 'self' has been used for both. If you want to know yourself, you have to be absent as an ego, as an entity separate from existence. You have to become pure presence.

The ego is your personality, the ego is your person, and the soul is your presence; it is not a person.

So when you are here with me, you feel as if you are not: In meditation, and being in Your presence, in the good moments there is no "myself." That's absolutely true. That is the right space, when you can know yourself – when you are not and there is only a certain "am-ness;" no "I," but only an existential "isness" – no boundaries to it, just an oceanic feeling.

So there is no contradiction. In your good moments you find you are not. Now, wait a little more: go deeper into this state of not being yourself, and you will discover the immense depth of your "isness," of your being.

One Taoist master, Hui Hi, used to say to his disciples: "When you come to meet me, leave yourself out." And he was not one of the so-called saints you have become accustomed to hearing about. He used to keep a big staff; if a disciple entered in with his ego, he would get a good hit.

So the disciples used to be very afraid to enter into the room of the master, unless their meditation was complete, unless they were absolutely clear that now they could leave themselves outside where they left their shoes, and could enter . . . . And whenever some disciple entered without his 'self' with him, the master hugged him with immense love.

Prem Purna, you have already done half the process – that in good moments, in blissful moments, sitting here, listening to me, or meditating, you don't find yourself. Just wait a little more. When every trace of yourself has disappeared and you are just pure space, being will arise in you as a great peak arises suddenly out of the ocean.

It happens once in a while that a sudden island arises out of the ocean – it was not there one moment before and now it is there. You will be surprised to know that the greatest mountains in the world, the Himalayas, are the youngest mountains. In the oldest Hindu book, *Rig Veda*, there is no mention of the Himalayas. It is very strange, because it was written so close to the Himalayas. They have mentioned rivers – even one river, the Saraswati, which has disappeared since then – but they have not mentioned the Himalayas. The Himalayas are very new, very young, very fresh, are still growing. Each year they go on growing one foot higher.

The oldest mountain in the world is the Vindhyachal. My village, where I was born, is very close to the Vindhyachal. It is so old, that just like an old man, it cannot stand erect; just like an old man, it has bent down.

A beautiful story has arisen out of its situation. One great enlightened master, Agastya, was going towards the south. And Vindhya bent down to touch the feet of Agastya, and the master said, "Vindhya, remain in this position – because it will be easier for me to pass over you in this position. When you are standing erect – I am old . . . it will be very difficult for me. And soon I will be returning. My disciples have been inviting me continually, and now, seeing that death is very close, I should fulfill their desire. So I am going to see them, and I will be coming back soon – so don't stand back up in your erect position."

Agastya died in the south, he never came back; and Vindhya is still waiting, bent over, for the master to come back. It must have been thousands of years ago when the master went to the south . . . .

The story must have arisen because of the situation of Vindhyachal. Vindhya is the oldest mountain in the world; it came out of the ocean in the very early days of this planet. And Himalaya is the latest, the youngest – almost a child in comparison to Vindhyachal.

If you can remain in a space of being no-self, no-ego, in a state of egolessness, then there is the possibility of a sudden rising up of the Himalayan peak of your own being. You will be, for the first time, your reality; and at the same time you will know what it is. It is immortality, it is eternity. It is there from the very beginning – and it is going to remain there to the very end.

Beloved Bhagwan,

I thought you would like this – from Walt Whitman's *Passage to India*.

Sail forth – steer for deep waters only,
Reckless, O Soul, exploring I with thee, and thou with me,
For we are bound where mariner has not yet dared to go,
And we will risk the ship, ourselves and all.
O my brave Soul!
O farther, farther sail!
O daring joy, but safe! Are they not all the seas of God?
O farther, farther, farther sail!

Prem Turiya, Walt Whitman is perhaps the only man in the whole history of America who comes very close to being a mystic. Otherwise, the American mind is very superficial. It is bound to be very superficial because it is only three hundred years old. It is a child's mind which is curious about everything: it goes on questioning this and that and even before you have answered it, it has moved to another question. It is not much interested in the answer; it is just curious, it wants to know everything simultaneously. It goes from one religion to another religion, from one master to another master. It goes on searching for answers at the farthest end of the world – but everything remains almost like a fashion.

The psychologists have found that in America, everything lasts not more than three years. That is the usual limit for any fashion – a certain toothpaste, a certain soap, a certain shampoo, a certain hair conditioner, a certain guru – they all come into the same marketplace.

Now you don't hear anything about The Beatles. Just twenty years ago, they were on top; now, nobody even cares who they are. What happened to those poor fellows? Now you hear about the Talking Heads; the same is going to happen to them. During these twenty years, many musicians and many dancers, many singers, have risen to the heights and disappeared.

It has been calculated that in America, every person changes his job every three years, changes his wife every three years, changes his town every three years. Three years seems to be long enough: something new is needed.

Walt Whitman seems to be a rare individual to have been born in America. He should have been born somewhere in the East – and he was immensely interested in the East.

This small piece that Turiya has sent is from his long poem, *Passage to India*.

Sail forth – steer for deep waters only,
Reckless, O Soul, exploring I with thee,
and thou with me,
For we are bound where mariner
has not yet dared to go,
And we will risk the ship, ourselves and all.

He is saying that a spiritual seeker needs to be aware that he is going into unknown waters where no mariner has ever dared to go. And the risk is not small because the challenge is "Steer for deep waters only" . . . leave the shallow waters for shallow minds. Those who want to know their own depths have to steer into deeper waters.

Sail forth – steer for deep waters only,

Reckless O soul, exploring I with thee,
and thou with me,
For we are bound where mariner
has not yet dared to go . . .
Our goal is where no one has ever dared to go.
"And we will risk the ship" – if the worst comes to the worst, we are ready to "risk the ship, ourselves and all." But we are determined to explore the unknowable. It is a tremendously beautiful passage for every seeker of truth, every searcher for the ultimate mystery of existence: shallow waters won't do.

People want everything without risking anything, and because of this, there are so many exploiters. They tell you, "Just go to church every Sunday and you need not worry. Believe in Jesus Christ, and on the day of judgment, he will sort out those who believe in him. They will enter into paradise; and those who are not chosen by Jesus will fall into hell for eternity."

A very cheap, very shallow solution: just believe in Jesus Christ. Hindus say the same: "Just believe in Krishna. Just go on repeating, 'Hare Krishna, Hare Rama.' "

The other day, I saw in a news cutting, that the head of the Hare Krishna, Hare Rama movement in Europe had escaped with all the money back to America – he was American, just his name was Indian. He had left all his followers starving in France. The American mind is so dollar-oriented that when it comes to a question of choosing between a dollar and God, he will choose the dollar – because God is going to be there forever. First use the dollar, then we will see about God. And, in fact, without the dollar how can you enter into the kingdom of God? . . . some *baksheesh* will be needed.

And what are you going to choose? If you choose God – unnecessary trouble. You cannot live twenty-four hours a day with God, because the very idea of God is judgmental. God will be continuously judging you: you are doing wrong, you are doing wrong . . . this is a sin . . . I will throw you into hell. I don't think any man can remain sane and live for twenty- four hours with the so-called God. It is good that nobody has up

to now had the misfortune to have such an experience.

Walt Whitman is one of the people who is not understood in America at all – and yet, he is the only one America can be proud of.

O my brave soul!
O farther, farther sail!
O daring joy, but safe! Are they not all the seas of God?
Don't be worried about safety. Is not this whole existence one? Are you and existence separate? Don't you belong to the same source, the same God? All these seas are of God, so you are safe. Don't be worried, you can "Risk the ship, ourselves and all," — and yet, you are safe in the hands of existence.

O farther, farther, farther sail!
Go as far as possible. Don't leave any place unexplored.

He is not saying these words about the outside world; he is saying these worlds are within you. When he is saying, "farther and farther," don't misunderstand him. His meaning in the whole poem – this is only a passage, a part – is to go into the inner and risk everything – "the ship, ourselves and all."

And there is no need to be worried about security, about safety, because all this is part of one whole. To see this whole existence – outside and inside – as one, is an immense insight; only very rarely does a poet rise to such heights.

He had something of the mystic in him. Although he was born in America, he had something of the East in him; hence, this *Passage to India*. India has been for centuries the symbol of the inner journey. It is not just a political entity – it is a spiritual phenomenon. As far back as we know, people have been coming to India from all over the world in search of themselves. Something is in the very climate, something is in the very vibe, that helps.

I have seen it – going around the world I was watching – and it was a very puzzling experience. And those who are here and who have also been in the commune in America, all feel it. So many letters have come to me: "it is strange . . . we were in the commune in America, all feel it. So many letters have come to me: "it is strange . . . we were in the commune for five years, but we never felt the same joy, the same song, the same dance, that we are feeling here." And I was also seeing the fact that because there has been no spiritual inheritance, the air is empty, dry. It does not have the juice that nourishes the soul.

And then I went around the world and I could see the difference. Perhaps, because for thousands of years the eastern genius has been consistently in search of the soul, it has created a certain atmosphere. If you meditate in the East, it seems as if everything helps: the trees, the earth, the air. If you are meditating in America, you have to meditate alone – there is no help coming from anywhere.

In Spain, in Portugal, there was every possibility to create another commune, but I saw the same thing would happen. The whole effort of five years in America was simply destroyed by the fanatic Christians – who don't understand anything of religion – and the fascist politicians.

In fact, they were afraid of the commune. It became their basic concern: the attorney general declared, "To destroy this commune is our priority," and the commune was not doing any harm to anybody.

But I can understand: deep down the commune was vibrating on a different wavelength; it was not part of America, and it could never be part of America. Its vibe was so strong that there was no way to defeat it – because America knows nothing about spirituality; it has never gone deeper than the skin.

And moving around the world my experience was the same. The East has fallen politically, economically, but it still carries a shadow of its golden flights. And those who are in search of themselves will find here, in this poor third-world country, immense nourishment for their souls.

Scientifically, technologically, it is not advanced; and poverty is growing every day more and more. But still, in spite of all this, it remains the richest land in the world as far as the spiritual search is concerned.

Okay, Vimal?

Yes, Bhagwan.

The Present Is The Only Time You Have

It is the miserable man who plans for the future, because his present is so miserable that he wants to avoid it, he does not want to see it. He thinks about tomorrows: good days are going to come. He is utterly impotent to transform this moment into a good moment. A long habit of transferring everything to the future, postponing, living for the future, will take your whole life out of your hands. There is no other way.

You are asking, "Is it really possible to be in the here-now all the time?"

This is the *only* possibility. You cannot be anywhere else. You try: try to be in the tomorrow. Nobody has succeeded up to now – you cannot be in the coming minute. Do you think you can jump and reach into the future, jump out of today and reach into tomorrow? Even if you are planning for tomorrow, that too is being done here-now; even if you are worrying about the future, that too is being done here-now. You cannot be anywhere else; whatever you do, existence allows only this space of here and now.

February 18, 1987,   8 a.m.

Beloved Bhagwan,

Is it possible to die consciously without being enlightened?

Nirah, existence follows certain laws – and there are no exceptions. If one wants to die consciously, the only way is to be enlightened. Death is such a great surgery: your soul is being taken apart from the body and mind, with which it has been involved for seventy or eighty years. Even for a small operation you need anesthesia; and this is the greatest operation in existence.

Unconsciousness is nothing but nature's way of giving you anesthesia. Unless you are completely unidentified with body and mind, you cannot die consciously – and a death which is not conscious is a great opportunity missed.

Enlightenment is an absolute necessity.

Enlightenment only means that your whole being is conscious: there are no dark corners left inside you. Dying in such consciousness the body, the mind, the brain can be taken away from you, because you know now – not just as a theory, but as your authentic experience – that you have always been separate. The involvement with the body was broken the day you became enlightened.

In the ancient scriptures of the Buddhists, enlightenment is called the "great death" – not that you are going to die, but the death is great because you will be able to see it happening, you will be a witness. Now you are no longer attached to the body, no clinging, and you have become aware of your immortality.

You can die consciously only when you know that you are immortal, that you belong to eternity, not to time; that deep within you is the beginning of existence and the end of existence – if there is any beginning or if there is any end. In fact there is no beginning and no end; you have always been here, and you will always be here.

A conscious death is one of the miracles of life, because after that you will not be born again in any form – as a man, as a bird, as a tree. You will remain in the eternal consciousness of the universe, spread all over the ocean. Hence, it has been called the "great death." But there are no exceptions. Existence follows absolutely definite laws, and this is a law of the highest order, because it concerns your consciousness, your life, your death.

Beloved Bhagwan,

I sit here feeling the stillness of the universe, listening to a bird's sweet song – and I wonder. Then I listen again to Your vision for mankind now, and I wonder that perhaps I am Your hands and Your feet – that perhaps I should be out there. I wonder whether this frail bud is yet ready enough, that maybe it needs a little more sweet dew and sun fire . . . .

Jivan Mary, you are saying, "I sit here feeling the stillness of the universe, listening to a bird's sweet song – and I wonder. Then I listen again to Your vision for mankind now, and I wonder that perhaps I am Your hands and Your feet." You *are*.

Every sannyasin is my hands, my eyes, my soul.

I am not giving you a teaching, I am giving you myself.

But that does not mean that you have to go somewhere else. To transform human consciousness you have just to go on rising higher and higher in your own consciousness – you don't have to go anywhere. You are saying, "Perhaps I should be out there." There is no "out there"; everything is "in here." Don't waste a single moment in unnecessary worry. To me, if you are saved, the whole of humanity is saved.

It is not a question of going out into the world and trying to raise people's consciousness – it is more of a possibility that the crowd of sleepy people is too much, and you may start feeling sleepy yourself. Unless you are enlightened, it is dangerous to try to transform people. Right now, you are the whole world. Just be total in this silence, be intense in this ecstasy, and you are working for the whole of humanity – because you are part of it. If you become enlightened, that is the beginning of humanity becoming enlightened.

There is a beautiful story about Mulla Nasruddin. He used to steal fruits and sweets in the market, if he got an opportunity. One fruit seller had a dog specially for Mulla Nasruddin. The dog was very intelligent. The shopkeeper told the dog, "I am going for my lunch; you have to take care of the shop. Sit here, and remember that man, Mulla Nasruddin. If he comes here, watch his every action." The poor dog nodded his head.

The man went to take his lunch at home, and that was the time . . . Mulla Nasruddin was waiting somewhere close by. He had heard what the dog was told; he sat in front of the shop, closed his eyes, and pretended to fall asleep. Seeing him asleep – sleep is contagious – the poor dog also closed his eyes and fell asleep. And then the Mulla took away whatever he wanted from the shop.

When the shopkeeper came back, he saw the dog asleep, and he saw that things were missing. He woke up the dog and said, "What is the matter with you? I told you to watch his every action."

Mulla Nasruddin by that time had put all the fruits in his house, and had come back to see what had transpired between the dog and the shopkeeper. He was standing just by the side of the shop.

The dog felt very miserable; tears came to his eyes. Mulla Nasruddin, out of compassion, came out and said to the shopkeeper, "This is too much. Your dog followed your instructions exactly. Sleep is also an activity – and when I fell asleep, the poor dog could not resist the temptation to fall asleep. Don't be angry at him.

"And when I was asleep, he thought, 'Now he cannot steal' – nobody has ever heard of sleeping people stealing fruits in the marketplace. But after all, he is a dog; he could not make a distinction between pretended and real sleep.

"Don't be angry at him. Next time you instruct him, tell him clearly, 'If somebody sleeps in front of the shop, that is the moment to remain very awake – because if you fall asleep that man is going to steal.'"

And he said, "Don't you worry, I will find some other way to steal."

The time is not yet right and ripe for going into the world. One day, I myself will tell you to go into the world, when I see that now the mob psychology cannot affect you; that your awareness will remain the same; that your silence will remain the same; that your ecstasy may even grow deeper.

Jivan Mary, you are right in saying, "I wonder whether this frail bud is yet ready enough, that maybe it needs a little more sweet dew and sun fire . . . ." It needs not "a little sun fire" – it needs much; not "a little dew" – it needs much.

But you are on the path, and to be on the path is almost half the pilgrimage.

The bud will soon become a flower, dancing in the wind and in the sun and in the rain. Then, whether you go or not, your fragrance will be reaching out there into the world – and that fragrance will trigger more people.

My own experience is that when you try directly to make somebody more aware, he starts defending himself. Rather than becoming more aware, he becomes more closed. It is a kind of attack on his territory – and it is an attack; you are destroying all his past, his lifestyle, his way of thinking. You are destroying his very mind – although you are destroying it to bring his reality to the surface. Your destruction is not for destruction's sake; it is in the service of the greatest creation in the world.

My experience is that it is far easier indirectly. For example, when I am answering Jivan Mary, others are listening more openly, because it is not their question; so they are not defending themselves in any way. When I am answering somebody else's question, it is possible that you will be benefited more than the questioner himself – because the questioner becomes in a certain way tense; it is his question, he is involved in it. Others are relaxed; it is not their problem – although it is

everybody's problem. Jivan Mary is just an excuse; she has asked it on behalf of all of you who are present here, and all of my sannyasins who are not present here will also listen to it.

Everybody feels that when joy comes, they want to share it; when awareness arises in them, they want to make others aware.

One of the great German philosophers, Immanuel Kant, was very particular about time – almost obsessed with it; it was an insane kind of thing. Once he was going to the university. It had just rained, the road was muddy and one of his shoes got stuck in the mud. But he was so particular about reaching his classroom exactly on time, that he went there with one shoe on one of his feet, and the other shoe left in the mud. "When I return I will pick it up; if I try to pick it up now I will be a few minutes late."

It was said that people used to set their clocks and watches when they saw Immanuel Kant going for a morning walk. It might be raining, it might be snowing, it might be any season – but his time was fixed. When he reached the university, all the professors did one thing and that was to set their watches to the right time.

He was a lifelong bachelor, dependent on a servant – much too dependent. Kant was giving him double the salary he would get anywhere else. But the servant had also become aware that Kant could not live without him. Kant would get rid of any new servant within a day – his demands about time and absolute punctuality were so difficult for new people to maintain.

The old servant never used to say, "Sir, it is lunchtime." He used to come and say, "Sir, it is one o'clock"; or at dinnertime, "Sir, it is nine o'clock"; or at sleeping time, he would come and say, "Now it is ten o'clock." He was told the time.

One day a guest was visiting, and Kant was so involved in a complicated philosophical discussion that he forgot to look at his watch. The servant came, interrupted, and said, "Sir, it is ten o'clock." Kant jumped – shoes, hat, and all – into his bed, and covered himself with the blanket. The guest could not believe what was happening. He asked the servant, who said, "It is time for him to go to sleep."

The guest said, "But he could at least have said 'good night' to me." The servant said, "He does not waste a single moment. You have seen the shoes and hat . . . he has not even changed them, because that would take time."

He used to get up at three o'clock in the morning; and that was the most difficult thing, where every servant failed. Just this one servant, who had been with him almost his whole life . . . . Once in a while he wanted more money, and if he did not get it, he would go away – knowing perfectly well that tomorrow he would be called back. New servants would be hired, because Kant was also tired of the man – he was always asking for more money, a bigger salary – but no other servant was even remotely a substitute.

The real problem was at three o'clock, early in the morning . . . . Kant used to explain to his servants, "At three o'clock, whatever happens, you have to pull me out of bed. I will fight you – I may beat you. *You* have to beat *me*. You have to wrestle with me, whatever happens, because I am asleep and I want to sleep at that moment. But that is my regular life; at three o'clock I have to get up."

Naturally, no new servant could beat the master. But the old servant was really good. He would hit him hard, pull him out of bed by his legs – and Kant is shouting, abusing him, but he would not listen. There were times when the servant would slap him: "Wake up! It is three o'clock. Don't create any nuisance and noise, because there are neighbors too, and they don't want to get up at three o'clock."

He almost had to wrestle with him. It was an everyday routine – three o'clock, a wrestling match. Kant would go on slipping under his blanket, and the servant would go on pulling him out.

The world may be attracted by the idea of awakening, but sleep has its own soothing calmness. So when you are talking with people about awareness, they may listen to it – they may even think that they will give it a try – but to remain unconscious is very consoling. And ~~when you are surrounded by millions of sleeping people, their sleep is going to affect you, unless you have come to the highest peak of awareness – from where there is no turning back.~~

Jivan Mary, I can see your frail bud, and I can see your immense longing to help people; but that can be done here and now, not there and then. You become more and more seasoned. When I see that you are in a position where no mob unconsciousness can crawl into you, I would like you to go into the world.

But you can help people from here; and you can help people from here more than you would be able to help people there, because here you are not alone. With you there are hundreds of my people – my whole garden, in different stages of growth. They are all a support to you; they are all a tremendous nourishment to you. You will not find these trees anywhere else, because these trees have been absorbing silence, peace, joy, ecstasy.

A few days ago the mayor of Poona came to my room. He could not restrain himself; he touched my feet. And when he was going out, he told Neelam, "I have never been in such a silent room, so cool, so fresh – it is *really* a temple. I am overwhelmed by the atmosphere of the room."

Anybody who comes here will be overwhelmed. These trees are no longer ordinary – they are sannyasins. The very air has a different vibe: even when you go away, your song, your dance, your joy go on vibrating here. This is how a temple is created. A temple is not made of bricks, is not made of statues; ~~a temple is made of a different vibe – the vibration of silence, peace, joy, and blissfulness.~~

Linger on a little more in this ~~buddhafield. When you are ripe, you will know it yourself.~~ Then there is no problem: either you can remain here and go on growing – your growth is going to be a tremendous help for the growth of humanity – or you can be somewhere else.

But here – because you are a commune, a *sangha* –

you are not alone; so many people are pouring their awareness, it becomes almost a pillar of fire.

I never go out of my room; I just come in the morning and in the evening to be with you. But remaining in my room, just sitting silently, I know I am doing everything that can be done to save humanity.

Beloved Bhagwan,

Is it really possible to be in the "now-here" all the time?
Most of my time seems to go in planning for,
or worrying about, the future.

Nitin, whether you know it or not, you cannot be anywhere else than here and now. Wherever you are it will be here and now.

You are given only one moment at a time – and you are wasting that moment in planning or worrying about the future; and the future never comes. What comes is always here, now: it is a series of 'nows' – one now, another now – but you are always living in the now.

There is no future – so how can you worry about the future?

It is because of this kind of worrying and planning for the future that a certain proverb exists in all the languages of the world: Man goes on desiring, planning, worrying about the future – and God goes on disappointing him.

There is no God to disappoint you. In your very planning, you are sowing the seeds of disappointment. In your very worrying about the future, you are wasting the present; and slowly, slowly it becomes your second nature to worry about the future. So when the future comes, it will come as the present; and because of your habit of worrying about the future, you will waste that moment also in worrying.

You will go on worrying about the future for your whole life. You will stop only when death comes and takes away all possibility of the future. You missed your whole life: you could have lived – but you only planned.

Live intensely and totally now, because the next moment will be born out of this moment; and if you have lived it totally and joyously, you can be absolutely certain that the next moment will bring more blessings, more joy.

I have heard: Three professors of philosophy were having a discussion at a railway station. The train was standing at the platform. There were a few minutes before it was due to leave, but they got so involved in their discussion that the train left without them – then they realized, and they ran . . . . In the last compartment, only two professors could enter; the third remained on the platform. The train had gone and he had tears in his eyes.

A porter was standing there. Seeing the scene, he said, "Why are you crying? At least two of your friends have got the train." He said, "That is the problem. They had come to see me off." They must also be crying, inside the train.

Existence also sometimes plays jokes on people.

Nitin, stop this habit of planning. Stop worrying about the future. If tomorrow comes, you will be there; and if you know how to live, if you know how to live joyously and dancingly, your tomorrow will also be full of dance and joy.

It is the miserable man who plans for the future, because his present is so miserable that he wants to avoid it, he does not want to see it. He thinks about tomorrows: good days are going to come. He is utterly impotent to transform this moment into a good moment. A long habit of transferring everything to the future, postponing, living for the future, will take your whole life out of your hands. There is no other way.

You are asking, "Is it really possible to be in the here-now all the time?" This is the *only* possibility. You cannot be anywhere else. You try: try to be in the tomorrow. Nobody has succeeded up to now – you cannot be in the coming minute. Do you think you can jump and reach into the future, jump out of today and reach into tomorrow? Even if you are planning for tomorrow, that too is being done here-now; even if you are worrying about the future, that too is being done here-now. You cannot be anywhere else; whatever you do, existence allows only this space of here and now.

I can say to you that I am living here and now. I also have tried somehow to get into the future – but there is no way. You cannot go back into the past, you cannot go ahead of time into the future. In your hands is always the present; in fact, the present is the only time you have.

And 'now' is such a meaningful word, because that is your whole life – a 'now' stretched from your birth to your death. But it is always now . . . and here is the only space. You cannot be anywhere else than here; wherever you are, that place will become here.

Just be clear about it, otherwise life goes on slipping through your hands like water. Soon you will have empty hands; and meeting death with empty hands is an utter failure. Meet your death full of joy, silence and serenity. Meet death with your hands full of ecstasy.

In that ecstasy, death itself dies. You never die . . . your here-now continues forever and forever.

Beloved Bhagwan,

Sitting in the discourse, closing my eyes, I find myself all alone with Your voice and the song of the birds, touching the space where all is one. It is an experience of silence, clarity and eternal peace. Even sleep, war or destruction appear as divine expressions of life. Returning to the world of forms, I see persons, conflicts, dualities everywhere. Existence becomes a question mark, and I am afraid this planet can be destroyed, and all its beauty disappear. Deep down, I sense that I am both and both are one. Beloved Master, is awareness a boat crossing to the other shore, and love a bridge to come back – uniting the banks of the river of life?

Dhyanand, what you are saying is absolutely true, "Awareness is a boat crossing to the other shore, and love a bridge to come back – uniting the banks of the river of life."

It is a very significant statement. Your so-called saints have gone only halfway. They may have attained a certain crystallization, a certain awareness, but they are not capable of coming back to the old shore with a shower of love. A saint who is without love is only half grown.

A lover who knows nothing of awareness is also living half-heartedly. Your saints are repressing their love; your lovers are repressing their awareness. I want you to be both together – awareness *and* love. Then only is the circle of life complete.

Zorba is love, Buddha is awareness. And when you

are Zorba the Buddha, you have attained the greatest height that is possible in existence.

But unfortunately, man has lived for centuries divided. Zorbas think they are against Buddhas, and Buddhas think they are against Zorbas. And because of this idea of antagonism, the Zorba is repressing his Buddha: he is beautiful in his love, in his song, in his dance – but his awareness is nil. The Buddha has repressed his Zorba: his awareness is very clear, but very dry. There is no juice in it, it is like a desert, where no roses blossom, where no greenery can be seen.

A Buddha without a Zorba is only a desert.

I am being condemned by both sides: the communists, the socialists, and other types and brands of materialists condemn me because I am talking about spiritual growth, awareness, enlightenment. According to them, man is only the body, and should live as a body. And I am condemned by the other side, the Buddhists, because I am bringing materialism into their spirituality; I am polluting their pure spirituality.

The ambassador of Sri Lanka in America wrote me a letter: "You call your restaurants, discos, *Zorba the Buddha*. It will hurt the feelings of the Buddhists all over the world – so I would like you to consider it and change that name. Zorba should not be joined with Buddha."

I wrote him a letter: "It is not only a question of my restaurants being called *Zorba the Buddha* – I am creating living human beings who *are* Zorba the Buddha. My whole life's effort, my whole dedication is to bring Zorba and Buddha hand in hand, dancing in a disco."

Both are deprived: the Zorba lives an unconscious life, the Buddha lives a life without love. The meeting of both will create the whole man – and the whole man is the only holy man.

Beloved Bhagwan,

Please talk to us about the coolness of love.

Dhyan Amiyo, you have become too accustomed to hot dogs! Passion is hot, but passion is not love. Passion is an effort to use the other for your own biological and sexual needs. And the man who has renounced passion becomes cold – ice cold, almost dead.

Love is just in between these two extremes, hot dogs and cold saints. In your restaurant you should start selling hot dogs and cold saints – they are the two extremes. Just between the two is the coolness of love.

Love is not cold and love is not hot; it is a cool breeze, a fresh breeze, an early morning breeze. When it comes to you, you feel almost young again, fresh again, as if suddenly you have taken a shower.

Passion uses the other; that's why passion is a continual fight – because so-called passionate lovers are both trying to use the other. Love does not use the other, it gives its own heart to the other. It is not a desire to get something, but a longing to share something. One is full of peace and silence and joy, and wants to share it with those who are close. They may be friends, they may be husbands, wives, children, father, mother – anybody.

Love has an immense coolness about it. But very few people have attained to the coolness of love. Either they are hot and passionate, or when they become tired and bored with this heat, they turn to the opposite – they become an ice-cold saint, frozen.

Mind has a way of moving like a pendulum, from one extreme to the other. That's how the clock runs, by the pendulum moving from one extreme to the other. If the pendulum stops in the middle, it will be the coolness of love; and if the pendulum stops in the middle, the clock will also stop.

I can say it in another way: in the moments of cool love, you feel time has stopped; there is no movement – everything has stopped. It is so silent that there is not even a ripple on the lake of your consciousness.

My longing is to fill this whole world with cool love; and through cool love we can give birth to a new man, to a new humanity – which are urgently needed. And I hope that man has enough intelligence not to choose death, that he will choose a different style of life – without conflict, without wars, full of the peace which passeth understanding. I hope man will not prove so retarded as to destroy himself. The greatest thing that can happen to save humanity is the coolness of love – friendliness. Passion burns you up, and in the same way, the frozen saint is already dead.

Love keeps you alive, and coolness keeps you young and fresh. Man can have such a beautiful planet and such a beautiful humanity. Just a little understanding is needed, and I think that understanding is arising, slowly but constantly.

If you can understand me, then everybody else in the world can also understand me. Maybe it will take a little more time for them, but there has never before been a time when understanding was needed so much. It is no small matter, because now understanding is equivalent to life.

Okay, Vimal?

Yes, Bhagwan

The Child Is Still Within You

In this temple you are allowed to be yourself without any inhibitions. I would like this to happen all over the world. This is only the beginning.

Here, start living moment to moment totally and intensely, joyfully and playfully – and you will see that nothing goes out of control; that your intelligence becomes sharper; that you become younger; that your love becomes deeper.

And when you go out into the world, wherever you go, spread life, playfulness, joy, as far away as possible – to every nook and corner of the earth.

If the whole world starts laughing and enjoying and playing, there will be a great revolution. War is created by serious people; murder is committed by serious people; suicide is committed by serious people – madhouses are full of serious people. Just watch what harm seriousness has been doing to human beings and you will jump out of your seriousness, and you will allow your child, which is waiting within you, to play and to sing and to dance.

February 18, 1987,   7 p.m.

Beloved Bhagwan,

Would You please talk about playfulness? I ask because there is a beautiful small boy within me whom I have neglected for a long time. This small boy is playful, curious and ecstatic – but most of the time I do not allow him to lose control. Please comment.

Anand Gogo, playfulness is one of the most repressed parts of human beings. All societies, cultures, civilizations, have been against playfulness because the playful person is never serious. And unless a person is serious, he cannot be dominated, he cannot be made ambitious, he cannot be made to desire power, money, prestige.

The child never dies in anyone. It is not that the child dies when you grow, the child remains. Everything that you have been is still within you, and will remain within you until your very last breath.

But society is always afraid of nonserious people. Nonserious people will not be ambitious for money, or political power; they would rather enjoy existence. But enjoying existence cannot bring you prestige, cannot make you powerful, cannot fulfill your ego; and the whole world of man revolves around the idea of the ego. Playfulness is against your ego – you can try it and see. Just play with children, and you will find your ego is disappearing, you will find that you have become a child again. It is not only true about you, it is true about everyone.

Because the child within you has been repressed, you will repress your children. Nobody allows their children to dance and to sing and to shout and to jump. For trivial reasons – perhaps something may get broken, perhaps they may get their clothes wet in the rain if they run out – for these small things a great spiritual quality, playfulness, is completely destroyed.

The obedient child is praised by his parents, by his teachers, by everybody; and the playful child is condemned. His playfulness may be absolutely harmless, but he is condemned because there is potentially a danger of rebellion. If the child goes on growing with full freedom to be playful, he will turn out to be a rebel. He will not be easily enslaved; he will not be easily put into armies to destroy people, or to be destroyed himself.

The rebellious child will turn out to be a rebellious youth. Then you cannot force marriage on him; then you cannot force him into a particular job; then the child cannot be forced to fulfill the unfulfilled desires and longings of the parents. The rebellious youth will go his own way. He will live his life according to his own innermost desires – not according to somebody else's ideals.

The rebel is basically natural. The obedient child is almost dead; hence the parents are very happy, because he is always under control.

Man is strangely sick: he wants to control people – in controlling people your ego is fulfilled, you are somebody special – and he himself also wants to be controlled, because by being controlled you are no longer responsible.

For all these reasons, playfulness is stifled, crushed from the very beginning.

You are asking, "There is a beautiful small boy within me, whom I have neglected for a long time. This small boy is playful, curious, and ecstatic – but most of the time I do not allow him to lose control." What is the fear? The fear is implanted by others: always remain in control, always remain disciplined, always respect those who are older than you. Always follow the priest, the parents, the teachers – they know what is right for you. Your nature is never allowed to have its say.

Slowly, slowly you start carrying a dead child within yourself. This dead child within you destroys your sense of humor: you cannot laugh with your total heart, you cannot play, you cannot enjoy the small things of life. You become so serious that your life, rather then expanding, starts shrinking.

I have always wondered why Christianity has become the world's greatest religion. Again and again I have come to the conclusion that it is because of the cross and the crucified Jesus – so sad, so serious; naturally . . . you cannot expect Jesus to be smiling on the cross. And millions of people have found a similarity between themselves and Jesus on the cross.

Its seriousness, its sadness, has been the reason that Christianity has spread more than any other religion.

I would like our churches and temples, our mosques, our synagogues to become nonserious, more playful, full of laughter and joy. That would bring to humanity a more healthy, wholesome, integrated soul.

But you are here . . . . At least being my sannyasin you need not carry your cross on your shoulders. Drop the cross. I teach you to dance, to sing, to play.

Life should be, each moment, a precious creativity. What you create does not matter – it may be just sandcastles on the seashore – but whatever you do should come out of your playfulness and joy.

Your child should never be allowed to die. Nourish it, and don't be afraid that it will go out of control. Where can it go? And even if it goes out of control – so what?

What can you do out of control? You can dance like a madman, laugh like a madman; you can jump and jog like a madman . . . people may think you are mad, but that is their problem. If you are enjoying it, if your life is nourished by it, then it does not matter, even if it becomes a problem for the rest of the world.

In my college days I used to go for a morning walk very early, three o'clock, four o'clock in the morning. Just beside my house was a small street with bamboo groves, very dark . . . . And that was the best place, because it was very rare to meet anybody there . . . just one watchman from a rich man's house used to see me.

But one day – this is what perhaps you would call going out of control – I was jogging along the street and the idea came to me that it would be good if I jogged backwards. In India there is a superstition that ghosts walk backwards, but I had completely forgotten that, and anyway there was nobody on the street . . . so I started jogging backwards. I was enjoying it so much, and it was such a cool morning.

Then the milkman happened to see me . . . . People used to bring milk from small villages, and he had come a little earlier than usual, so he had never met me before. Carrying his buckets of milk, he suddenly saw me. I must have been under the shadow of the bamboos, and when he came close to the shadow where there was a small patch of moonlight, I suddenly came out, jogging backwards. He shouted, "My God!" dropped both his buckets, and ran away.

Still, I did not realize that he was afraid of me, I thought he was afraid of something else. So I took both his buckets, although the milk was gone . . . . I thought I should at least give him his buckets, so I ran after him.

Seeing me coming . . . I have never seen anybody run so fast! He could have been a world champion in any race. I was very surprised. I was shouting, "Wait!" and he looked back, and without saying anything . . . .

The whole scene was being watched by the gatekeeper of the rich man. He told me, "You will kill him."

I said, "I am simply going to return his buckets."

He said, "You leave the buckets with me; when the sun rises he will come. But don't do such things – sometimes you make me afraid too, but because I know . . . . For years I have been seeing you doing all kinds of strange things on this street, but sometimes I become afraid; I think: who knows whether it is really you or a ghost coming backwards towards me? Sometimes I close the gate and go inside; I keep my gun always loaded because of you!"

I said, "You should understand one thing, that if I am a ghost, your gun will be useless – you cannot kill a ghost with a bullet. So don't ever use it, because a ghost will not be affected by it; but if a real man is there, you may be arrested as a murderer."

He said, "That's true. That I never thought about, that ghosts . . . ." And right in front of me, he took out all the bullets. He said, "Sometimes the fear is so great . . . I may shoot some man and kill him."

I said, "Just look at me: first be certain whether I am a real man or a ghost. You are taking your bullets out, and it may be just a ghost who is persuading you!"

He said, "What . . . ?" And he started putting the bullets back in his gun.

I said, "You keep these two buckets." I remained for almost six months in that part of the city, and every day I asked the watchman, "Has that man come yet?"

He said, "He has not come. These two buckets are still waiting for him, and I think that now he will never come. Either he has gone forever, or he has become so afraid of this place that he never comes on this street. I have been watching and when my shift changes and the other watchman comes, I tell him that if somebody comes . . . and we keep these buckets in front of the gate, so he will recognize that his buckets are here. But six months have passed, and there is no sign of him."

I said, "This is a very strange thing."

He said, "There is nothing strange about it. You would have killed anybody, coming suddenly out of the darkness. Why were you going backwards? Jogging I know many people do, but doing it backwards . . . ."

I said, "I have been jogging, and I became bored always going forwards; just for a change I was trying it backwards. I never realized that just on that day that idiot was going to come – nobody ever comes on this street. That man must have spread a rumor – and rumors spread like wildfire. Even the landlord in whose house I was living heard that on this street . . . . He told me, "Stop going so early for your morning walk; go only when the sun has risen, because one man has seen a ghost."

I said, "Who told you?"

He said, "My wife told me, and the whole neighborhood knows; after eight o'clock in the evening the street becomes empty."

I told him, "You may not believe it, but there was no ghost. In fact, it was I who was jogging backwards . . . ."

He said, "Don't try to befool me."

I said, "You can come with me. At three o'clock in the morning there is nobody."

He said, "Why should I take the risk? But one thing is certain: if you don't stop going, then you will have to leave my house. You cannot live here."

I said, "This is very strange. Even if the street is full of ghosts, why should you insist that I leave your house? You cannot force me. I pay the rent . . . you have given me a receipt. And in the court you cannot say that it is because this man goes on a street where ghosts jog – I don't think any court is going to accept this reason."

He said, "Do you mean you will drive me to the courts? If you are so insistent, you can live in this house. I will sell it. I will leave this house."

"But," I said, "I am not a ghost."

He said, "That I know – but mixing with ghosts? Some day some ghost may follow you into the house –

-and I am a man with a wife and children. I don't want to take any risks."

Here, you don't need to be afraid: you can jog backwards, and even if you are a real ghost, nobody is going to take any notice of you. If you cannot allow your playfulness here, then you will not be able to allow it anywhere in the world. Allow it totally – let it go out of control; and once your child is really alive and dancing within you, it will change the very flavor of your life. It will give you a sense of humor, a beautiful laughter, and it will destroy all your headiness. It will make you a man of the heart.

The man who lives in his head does not live at all. Only the man who lives in his heart, and sings songs which are not understandable to the head, dances which are not in any way relevant to any context outside you . . . just out of your abundance, out of your affluence: you have so much energy that you would like to dance and sing and shout . . . so do it!

It will make you more alive; it will give you a chance to taste what life is all about. The serious man is dead before his death. Long before his death, he remains almost like a corpse.

Life is such a valuable opportunity, it should not be lost in seriousness. Keep seriousness for the grave. Let seriousness collapse into the grave; waiting for the last judgment day, be serious. But don't become a corpse before the grave.

I am reminded of Confucius. One of his disciples asked him a very typical question asked by thousands of people: "Will you say something to me about what happens after death?"

Confucius said, "All these thoughts about death you can contemplate in your grave after death. Right now, live!"

There is a time to live, and there is a time to die. Don't mix them, otherwise you will miss both. Right now, live totally and intensely; and when you die, then die totally. Don't die partially: that one eye dies, and one eye keeps looking around; one hand dies, and the other hand goes on searching for truth. When you die,

die totally . . . and contemplate what death is. But right now, don't waste time in contemplating things which are far away; live this moment. The child knows how to live intensely and totally, and without any fear that he will go out of control.

In this temple you are allowed to be yourself without any inhibitions. I would like this to happen all over the world. This is only the beginning. Here, start living moment to moment totally and intensely, joyfully and playfully – and you will see that nothing goes out of control; that your intelligence becomes sharper; that you become younger; that your love becomes deeper. And when you go out into the world, wherever you go, spread life, playfulness, joy, as far away as possible – to every nook and corner of the earth.

If the whole world starts laughing and enjoying and playing, there will be a great revolution. War is created by serious people; murder is committed by serious people; suicide is committed by serious people – madhouses are full of serious people. Just watch what harm seriousness has been doing to human beings and you will jump out of your seriousness, and you will allow your child, which is waiting within you, to play and to sing and to dance.

My whole religion consists of playfulness.

This existence is our home: these trees and stars are our brothers and sisters; these oceans and rivers and mountains are our friends. In this immensely friendly universe you are sitting like a stone buddha – I don't preach the stone buddha; I want you to be a dancing buddha.

The followers of Buddha will not like it, but I do not care what anybody thinks. I simply care about truth. If a truth does not know how to dance, it is crippled; if a buddha is not capable of laughter, something is missing; if a buddha cannot mix with children and play with them, he has come close to buddhahood, but he has not yet been totally awakened. Something is asleep.

In Japan there is a series of nine pictures and those pictures are tremendously significant. In the first picture a man has lost his bull. He is looking all around

– there are trees and thick forests...but no sign of the bull.

In the second, he finds the footprints of the bull.

In the third, it appears that the bull is hiding behind the trees; just the backside of the bull is visible.

In the fourth, he has nearly reached the bull, and you see the whole bull.

In the fifth, he has caught the bull by the horns.

In the sixth, he has struggled with the bull.

In the seventh, he has conquered the bull. He is sitting on the bull.

In the eighth, they are moving back towards home.

In the ninth, the bull is in his stall, and the man is playing on his flute.

These nine pictures are missing one – they came from China, and the Chinese pack has ten pictures. When they were brought to Japan, the tenth was dropped because it looked very outrageous – and the tenth is my buddha.

In the tenth picture, the bull is in the stall and the buddha is going with a bottle of wine towards the marketplace. The Japanese mind thought that this would be too much: what will people think of a buddha with a bottle of wine? This is outrageous to the ordinary religious mind, but to me it is the most important picture out of the whole series. Without it the series is incomplete.

When one has achieved buddhahood, then one should become just an ordinary human being. Going to the marketplace with a bottle of wine is symbolic: it simply means that now there is no need to sit in meditation, meditation is already in the heart; now there is no need to be serious. One has found what one wanted to find; now it is time to rejoice. That bottle of wine is a symbol of rejoicing – now it is time to celebrate!

And where can you celebrate except in the marketplace? For meditation you can go into the forest, into the mountains, but for celebration, you will have to go to the marketplace. Where are you going to find a disco . . . ?

Always remember the tenth picture. Don't stop at the ninth – the ninth is beautiful, but incomplete. One step more . . . just playing the flute is not enough. Get drunk! . . . and dance madly!

And, Gogo, you have such a beautiful name – whatever you do will fit with Gogo.

Beloved Bhagwan,

My first meeting with You, thirteen and a half years ago at Woodlands,
ended with my getting up from sitting at Your feet and walking,
not out of the door, but into Your closet!
It has been an uphill battle ever since.
Bhagwan, what's happening?

Rama Prem, it was not only you, it happened with many people; because in Woodlands, where I used to live, the door to my room and the door to my closet were exactly the same. For anybody who entered for the first time, it was natural – the chances were fifty-fifty, so almost fifty percent of the people used to go into the closet – and I enjoyed it very much! I used to have an electric remote control lock by my side for both doors. Once a person entered my closet, I would lock it.

Perhaps you are still inside the closet – that is why you are saying, "It has been an uphill task, a battle ever since." You have not come out yet, and I don't live in Woodlands any more.

It was really fun, because people would come out of the closet so embarrassed, so upset . . . . The closet was big enough, so they would move around inside, and there were so many robes . . . so they would go around the robes, and finally they would come out, very shocked. What had happened? – they had entered by the same door, or so they thought.

Then as they came out, they became aware that there was another door just beside it, exactly the same, painted the same color.

There was also a third door, which led to my bathroom. Once in a while – it did not happen to you, Rama Prem – somebody would come out of the closet door in a hurry, and – as the mind is, it goes to extremes – he would miss the middle one and go to the third door, which would take him into the bathroom. Those who entered the bathroom would take longer to come out, because from my bathroom opened another door, which led to my sauna.

Coming out of all those doors, they would feel so embarrassed that they would ask, "What happened to the door by which I came in?" And I would say, "Always remember the golden mean, the middle one."

And it is not only true about those doors: in your life also, never go to the extremes. Always find the middle one, the golden mean. At the extremes, truth is always a half-truth, only in the middle is it complete, is it whole. But now there is no problem. You think that your life has been an uphill battle ever since. We make our lives, we are the creators of our lives – it all depends on you. If you are trying to achieve something far away, if you are trying to achieve something which is not natural, then life becomes an uphill task. But if you are not trying to achieve anything unnatural, then life becomes a let-go, then you start flowing downwards with the stream of life.

Lao Tzu has called it the watercourse way, and I think that is the right concept for anyone who wants to live a relaxed, silent, peaceful and joyous existence.

Never try to go against the current – you cannot win. Nature is too big, you are too small. You will simply get tired – and the more tired you become, the more life will look gloomy, dark, meaningless . . . just let the river take you wherever it is going.

A man who has a goal to reach is bound to remain in anguish and anxiety. My approach is that the river of life itself is going towards the ocean; you just float with it. Wherever it takes you is your home. And while you are floating with the river, you can enjoy the sun, the trees on the bank, the birds and their song, the stars in the night, and the moon. The whole existence – all is available to you because your whole energy is open, is not engaged, is free.

Rama Prem, just follow the watercourse way. Be relaxed, and allow life to take you wherever it is going. Don't be bothered that it should reach some specific goal; it has no specific goal. Just go on dancing with the river, singing with the river. You have made it a battlefield, fighting with the river, and then you are in trouble. You will never win, and you will never be able to enjoy a single moment, because every particle of your energy has to be put into fighting. Don't fight life.

But all the religions have been teaching you to fight life, to be anti-life. And they have created a poor humanity, which has forgotten to laugh, forgotten to dance, forgotten to sing; a humanity which knows only one thing: to fight.

Stop fighting. Every river reaches the ocean – and without any map, without any guidebook, without any guru. It is in the very nature of the river that it goes on flowing, and because it is not going upwards, there is no struggle. It is going downwards, so wherever it finds a lower level, it moves in that direction – and the ocean is at the lowest point, so no river can miss the ocean. The ocean is your goal, the ocean is God.

If you allow yourself to be taken by life without fight, you will reach God – nothing can be a hindrance or a barrier to you. So if you feel that it has become a battle, nobody else is responsible except you. And it is in your hands to change your direction within a moment. Don't fight . . . and to be defeated by life is not a defeat; it is our life: to be defeated by it is our victory.

The moment you start understanding this strange statement – that to be defeated by life is our victory – you have found the very secret of all success, of all blessings.

Beloved Bhagwan,

The other day I heard You speaking about the jump we all will have to take from the known to the unknowable. Originally what I wanted to ask You was: What is holding my legs and keeping my wings from unfolding to really jump and fly? But this morning, when You left Chuang Tzu, at the door You turned towards me and something happened between You and me which went beyond mind and heart. I felt my body moving in a way I could never do deliberately.
For seconds everything stopped, I had no control of anything. It was like a delicious, fearless dying. For a long time afterwards I felt drunk, weak and strong at the same time. I don't know what really happened. Did I jump too short, or didn't I jump at all? The only certainty I have now is that I cannot jump.
Beloved Master, please comment.

Premda, I am aware that something happened to you. It was a jump, and it was not short. But it was a jump of consciousness – that is why you are puzzled. And when consciousness jumps, the body goes into strange postures, which you could not do deliberately even if you wanted to. The jump of consciousness was not deliberate. Here, whatsoever happens is never deliberate.

Anything deliberate is going to be very small, it is going to be smaller than you. Anything that happens without any deliberation on your part – you are just a watcher, and it happens . . . you are just standing by the side, only an observer, not a doer: then something greater than you is happening.

Later on you felt both weak and strong. That must have puzzled you – and will puzzle others – but it is an absolutely certain consequence, because something happened that was beyond your control. Your ego was not in control, hence the weakness. Your ego felt threatened; you had come too close to the point where the ego can simply fall apart.

And at the same time you felt strong. Your consciousness felt strong because for the first time, for a few moments, it was not controlled by the ego. For the first time, for a few moments, it had wings of its own, it was not in the chains and the bondage of the ego. So your soul felt strong and your ego felt weak.

It is a good sign. The beginning of the death of the ego, the beginning of the end of the ego, and the beginning of your entry into the world of consciousness.

But later on your ego must have taken up its old possession, its old domination over your consciousness; and then you wrote: "The only certainty I have now is that I cannot jump." That is not *your* certainty, that is the ego, which has taken the power back into its own hands. For a moment the consciousness had slipped out.

You need not deliberately try to jump, that will not happen, because who will deliberately try? It will be your ego. You don't have any access to your consciousness yet. It was just that as I turned back and

166

looked at you, you completely forgot about your ego – and jumped. ~~Forgetting one's ego is the only jump that can bring you back to yourself.~~ But ~~never try deliberately. Allow it to happen~~ just as it happened this morning, on its own. ~~Do not make any effort. When it happens, just be totally with it, don't hinder it, and don't feel weak.~~ The weakness is not yours, ~~the weakness is of the ego – the false self~~ that is pretending to be your real soul.

Your real soul has felt strong for the first time. Give it more chances. And slowly, slowly it will become capable of coming out of the bondage on its own. The ego cannot keep it; it is just a kind of hypnotic conditioning, because from the very childhood your ego has been supported by everybody. All the nourishment has been given to the ego, and your soul has been starving. You have forgotten all about your soul.

Being here with me, it is going to happen more and more. Now that it has happened once, the possibility will become greater and greater. It will happen suddenly, first in my presence and then even without my presence. Sitting silently in your room, you will find a tremendous strength arising in you. And at the same time something is dying – something that is not you; something that has always been pretending to be yourself. The pretender has to die, ~~the false has to disappear, so that the real can take its place~~.

And ~~once the real is in its own place, your whole life becomes authentic. Each act takes on a tremendous beauty and grace; each word comes out from the very deepest part of your being, full of fragrance~~ – fragrance that you cannot find anywhere else in the world.

Once, a Sufi mystic came to see me. One of my friends had made a beautiful marble hall for me to conduct meditation classes in and to use for my library. It was surrounded by a beautiful garden. The whole day it was empty; only in the evening would people come to meditate. The Sufi had come in the afternoon, and he wanted to see the meditation hall, so I took him there. I was puzzled – it was the first time I had ever

seen anybody doing that kind of thing . . . . He went around the hall, sniffing like a police dog, smelling this corner, that corner . . . and that hall was pure marble, nothing else; there was nothing in the hall.

I have always liked empty places. I was standing there, looking at him – an old man; he sniffed all around, and he was very joyous. And he said to me, "Whatever has been happening here is good, because I can smell the same smell which arises in me when I am in meditation."

He first gave me the idea that ~~meditation can be smelled~~. Perhaps for Sufis it is easier, because for centuries they have been using perfume, certain perfumes which are in some way similar, a far away echo of the inner fragrance. They are the only people in the world who have worked for hundreds of years in search – in the outside world – of a similar kind of smell.

That day I started thinking, perhaps if somebody starts searching for taste? . . . ~~Meditation may give you a new taste~~ – because there are scriptures which say that ~~meditators start having a sweet taste in their mouth~~. Perhaps all the five senses may have something to say about meditation.

~~Eyes~~ – it has always been known that they express your meditativeness; ~~the energy that jumps from one person to another jumps from your eyes to the other person's eyes. Eyes are the most sensitive part of your body; naturally they are capable of catching the subtlest vibration of light, of depth, of profundity, of love~~.

You all know that ~~when you are in love, your eyes are not the same. When a lover looks at his beloved his eyes are not the same~~ – although they are the same eyes, but ~~something inside those eyes changes, some new energy starts flowing through those eyes~~.

~~Meditation is a far greater phenomenon than love~~.

Premda, you jumped well, but ~~don't try to do it deliberately because you will fail~~. Just be grateful that it happened, and ~~wait with silent longing, not expecting but just available~~; if it happens, you will be tremendously grateful.

Don't demand it, because these are such delicate things that expectations, demands, can destroy them. Simply wait, with a longing heart, and it will happen again and again, and it will start happening without me – I am just an excuse. And then slowly, slowly it need not happen . . . the ego disappears, your soul is settled in its right place. It has been displaced by society, by a false substitute. The false must die for the truth, for the real to assert itself. The false was feeling weak, and the truth within you felt strong. Nourish that strength, and let that weak part of you starve, and let it die.

The death of the ego is the birth of God within you. It is your real birth. From that birth, a totally different kind of life, a life of celebration, starts.

Okay, Vimal?

Yes, Bhagwan.

You Are The Mirror

It is perfectly good to go deeper into your feelings. But remember one thing: the one who is going deeper, the one who is coming across inferiority, insecurity, jealousy, is separate from them. It cannot be one with them, otherwise how can it feel inferiority, insecurity, jealousy? You are the witness; so, as you go deeper, you will come across many things which you have suppressed; or perhaps for thousands of years your whole race has suppressed; or perhaps the whole of humanity has suppressed . . . . But you are as pure as a mirror.

When you are going deeper, the mirror reflects jealousy, but the mirror is not jealousy; the mirror reflects insecurity, but the mirror is not insecurity; the mirror reflects inferiority, but the mirror is not inferiority. The mirror is not identified with anything that it reflects – the mirror is just empty, silent, clean. You are the mirror.

In meditation you will come to recognize that you are the mirror. All other things are reflected in you, but the mirror does not become a buffalo, because a buffalo looks into the mirror.

February 19, 1987,   8 a.m.

Beloved Bhagwan,

When I look at the moments when I feel separate from You, from my love and the rest of existence, it is usually the shadows of comparison and jealousy; and when I go deeper I usually get in touch with a deep insecurity and the feeling of being inferior.
Would You please guide me on how I can lift these shadows and how to feel free of them?

Latifa, you are suffering from a disease called "Germany." It is out of this disease two world wars have happened. It was not the superiority of the race that was the cause of the wars, it was a deep feeling of inferiority. To cover it up, they tried hard to be superior.

Only the person who tries to be superior suffers, necessarily, from an inferiority complex. Only the nation that tries to be superior to others suffers as a whole nation from a deep inferiority complex.

It is one of the most surprising facts, that India has never invaded any country. In ten thousand years' history there has been no invasion, and the reason is, India has never suffered from an inferiority complex. Invaders came and conquered India. Small groups of very primitive people conquered a vast land without much difficulty, for a simple reason – because the Indian consciousness was not afraid even of slavery. Even slavery could not make it inferior; its superiority was something to do with its inner growth, its evolution of consciousness.

It is not for any other reason that for two thousand years India remained a slave country, either of this land or of that land; and they were all small groups, small tribes, which could have been crushed by this vast continent without any difficulty. It was not cowardice: it was simply – if you are not suffering from an inferiority complex, the desire to fight, the desire to prove that you are superior, is not there.

Why did it happen in Germany? – The reason is that Germany was populated by millions of Jews, who have been carrying the idea that they are the superior race, the chosen race of God. And they have qualities . . . they are more intelligent, they easily become rich . . . and the Germans always compared themselves with their neighbors who were Jews. They were rich, they were intelligent; they were getting forty percent of the Nobel prizes, and the rest of the world was getting sixty percent.

The three great men of this century who are dominating people's minds are all Jews: Karl Marx was a Jew, Sigmund Freud was a Jew, Albert Einstein was a Jew.

Being in the shadow of the Jews, the Germans

started feeling they were inferior. And once you start feeling inferior, you cannot remain with your inferiority; it is a constant pain, a constant remembrance that there are people who are superior to you. You have to prove somehow that you are superior to the Jews.

This was the reason why a madman like Adolf Hitler managed to make even great German intellectuals his followers – because he promised them that he would get rid of all the Jews. That was simply symbolic. Getting rid of the Jews, there would be nobody to remind them of their inferiority; and getting rid of the superior race chosen by God, they would certainly prove to the whole world that *they* are in fact the chosen race, the Nordic German Aryans.

Nobody has gone deeply into the psychology of these two world wars, but this is one of the fundamentals: the Germans were trying hard to get rid of their inferiority complex. All over the world people have puzzled, as to how Adolf Hitler convinced Germans that it was because of the Jews that they were defeated in the first world war. There seems to be no relationship at all.

It is so absurd an idea, that even a retarded person will understand that there is no real reason why Jews should be the cause . . . . They did not betray the country; they fought hand in hand with the Germans against the enemy; they produced all the destructive weapons; they gave their best scientists for the war, their sons as soldiers – why suddenly did Adolf Hitler start saying, "Jews are the cause of our defeat, and unless they are completely erased from Germany, Germany can never win?"

Looking at the surface there seems to be no relevance, no reasonableness; it is almost as if he had said, "We have been defeated in the first world war, because people are using toothpaste." Jews have exactly the same kind of relevance to the German defeat.

But looking deeper into the psychology, Adolf Hitler is right. Because of the Jews they always remained inferior. They never became aggressive – how can an inferior person be aggressive? They never believed in themselves – how can an inferior person believe in himself? They knew beforehand they would be defeated; they are inferior people. Adolf Hitler wanted to prove: "We are superior." And the only way to prove it was to kill six million Jews. He killed six million Jews and millions of people from other countries. That gave a tremendous boost to the German ego; now nobody could say, "We are inferior."

Latifa, it is not your individual problem; it is a problem Germany has carried for centuries. It has almost become part of the collective unconscious; but by killing the Jews or killing anybody else, you cannot get rid of it.

You can pretend to be superior; you can even believe you are superior. You can even prove to the outside world that you are superior; but deep down you know perfectly well you are not superior.

All these cover-ups are not going to help. So when you come to me and you start meditating, slowly slowly those covers disappear, because they are created by the mind; and then the deep-rooted conditioning of inferiority surfaces.

The only way to get rid of it is to just watch it – let it surface, don't suppress it. If you suppress it, you will have to live with it. Let it surface, and you remain simply a watcher: that this idea of inferiority is only a thought, and you are not the mind that thinks.

You are the being that watches.

Your being is neither superior nor inferior.

It simply is; it knows no comparison.

Jews have suffered unnecessarily because Moses gave them this idea that they were the chosen people of God. He had to; I can understand his helplessness. Jews were in Egypt, slaves, and Moses was trying to get them to revolt against the slavery.

Now people who have remained slaves for centuries cannot even conceive that they can revolt against their masters; the very idea is fearful. Those masters have been beating them, killing them – they have treated them like animals – for so long. The question before Moses was, "How to create some idea in the Jews, that they are capable of revolution?"

He invented a beautiful idea: that they were the chosen people of God; and people who were suffering in slavery, being beaten, killed, accepted the idea immediately. It was such a consolation. But nobody raised the question that if we are the chosen people of God, then why are we slaves? The idea was so contradictory; but it was so consoling that they gathered courage once they had accepted the idea. Moses had managed, first, to get them to accept the idea: "You are the chosen people of God;" then he told them, "Now revolution is very easy for you – nobody can prevent you."

Their inferiority was covered by being the "chosen people of God"; and now being the "chosen people of God" was used as a foundation for revolution against the Egyptians. It was good strategy at that point. The Jews revolted – they left the land of Egypt.

Then Moses gave them another idea, that "God has made a special land for you, Israel; so we are going towards Israel." I don't think he had any idea where they were going, because it took him and his people forty years of wandering in the desert, searching for the land "Israel." No country was ready to give them shelter. A small country which they started calling "Israel" was not anything special – a desert.

If this is what God creates for his own people then he seems to be a little crazy. But Moses had to say somewhere, "We have found!" . . . Three-fourths of his original people had died on the way, out of starvation, hunger – and God did not care at all . . . . His own people in search of the land he had created for them and that land was also very difficult. The people who reached Israel were almost third, fourth generation. Their forefathers had started from Egypt, and the third or fourth generation arrived.

The first generation gap was felt by Moses: these were not the people he had convinced to revolt. He was almost ancient, perhaps one hundred years old;

tired, tattered, he simply said, "This is the land" – to somehow settle his people. But the people were surprised, because the land was barren desert. Another age of difficulties began to produce out of that barren land; and Moses was so tired, and he had lost his old youthful inventiveness. He left the Jews in Israel saying, "You take care of the land. A few Jews, one tribe of the Jews, has got lost somewhere in the desert and I am going in search of it."

That tribe had reached Kashmir in India. And Moses reached Kashmir, but could not live long – perhaps a year or two years – and died in Kashmir. If he had brought his whole tribe to Kashmir, that would certainly have been something, showing them: "God has created it for you." Kashmir is so beautiful, perhaps the most beautiful part of the earth; and that's why one tribe that had wandered away by mistake, when they reached Kashmir thought: This must be Israel, and the others will also be coming here – so they settled there.

Now the people who are in Kashmir are all Mohammedans. They were converted forcibly by Mohammedans, from Jews to Mohammedans. But you can see their faces, their color, their noses – and you can be absolutely certain that they belong to the Jews. They are not . . . . Jews have a personality of their own, as every race has a personality of its own. Moses died in Kashmir.

Israel was such a barren place, there was no opportunity and no challenge for intelligence – and Jews have remained slaves for centuries. Hence, they have never known intelligence.

Mind is something like the land. If, for centuries, nothing has grown on the land, it becomes more and more powerful, and if you sow seeds in it, it will give you the best harvest possible, because its energy has never been used. First, Jews were slaves, their intelligence was never used, it remained a potential. Then, in Israel, there was no opportunity to use it – they started spreading all over Europe, wherever there was opportunity.

They proved to be superior to everybody, because

they had such great potential, unused for centuries. They became the richest race in the world. It was not that they were God's chosen people, that was pure inventiveness of a revolutionary mind – Moses should be described as the first revolutionary of the world.

In one context it was perfectly right; but times change, contexts change, the same thing that had helped the Jews to become richer, more intelligent than others, became a curse: because everybody hated them, everybody was jealous of them; jealous of their intelligence, jealous of their riches, jealous of their possessions.

Hitler easily convinced Germany, that "It is the Jews. Their very presence is causing our failure." And a man like Martin Heidegger, one of the Nobel prize winning philosophers of Germany, and perhaps the most difficult philosopher the world has ever known . . . . He has never written a book that is complete; he will start a book; the first volume will be published, but by that time – he has such a great intelligence – he will start doing something else.

It was not enough to complete the book – he is the only man whose every book is incomplete. He will just go up to a certain length, then suddenly he will come upon a greater idea . . . he will drop the old project, start on the new project. But even his incomplete books are proofs of tremendous genius.

Philosophers have been wondering what would have been the result if he had completed them, because he was moving in such new dimensions, never touched; where no mariner has ever reached – virgin lands, which no philosopher had ever bothered about. And his insight is so deep, that to understand him, you need a very high quality intelligence; otherwise you cannot understand what he is saying.

Even Martin Heidegger became a follower of Adolf Hitler, because of that German inferiority. And Adolf Hitler gave the promise, and he managed the promise – for almost five years he went on conquering, convincing the Germans that "certainly we are the chosen race of people; we were just not aware of it:

Adolf Hitler has made us aware of it." But then Germany was defeated again, and the whole covered up inferiority complex erupted.

Latifa, it is not just your problem, it is the problem of the whole German race; and the way out of it is not to get identified with it.

Nobody is superior.

Nobody is inferior.

Everybody is unique.

Because there are not two persons who are the same, you cannot compare marigolds with roses: they are two different flowers. You cannot compare two human beings with each other, they are two different flowers. But this is not a question of intellectual conviction, it is a question of being aware, and destroying the identification.

Don't try to be superior, just try to be yourself. You are not inferior, but, remember it: nobody else is inferior. You are not superior.

Aristotle has created a difficulty for human beings. He created one of the basic troubles in the human mind, because he knew only: either you are superior, or you are inferior. In everything it was either, or: either you are white or you are black; either you are a saint or you are a sinner.

He never bothered to look at the rainbow, and the whole span of all the colors between white and black. And each color has its own beauty, has its own dance, has its own place in existence, which no other color can take.

My approach is that each individual is unique; I want to destroy the very idea of comparison. You are yourself, I am myself; neither I am superior, nor I am inferior to you. Just, it happens I am this way; it happens you are that way. But this has to come out of your meditations. What I am saying is my meditation, you are not to believe in it – you have to go into the experience of it. And the day you will see – you are just yourself.

For example, Latifa, think of one thing: everybody in the third world war dies, except Latifa . . . . Will she still think herself to be inferior? Inferior to whom?

Will she feel herself to be superior? But superior to whom? There are only dead bodies all around; with dead bodies you cannot be inferior nor can you be superior.

And in truth, we are all alone, as alone as Latifa will be alone when the whole world is destroyed. Even at this moment everybody is alone, just himself. A simple awareness and acceptance of oneself as one is, is enough, and the whole problem will disappear. Otherwise, it will torture you, it will remain like a wound your whole life.

You say, "When I look at the moments when I feel separate from You, from my love and the rest of existence, it is usually the shadows of comparison and jealousy; and when I go deeper I usually get in touch with a deep insecurity, and the feeling of being inferior."

It is perfectly good to go deeper into your feelings. But remember one thing: the one who is going deeper, the one who is coming across inferiority, insecurity, jealousy, is separate from them. It cannot be one with them, otherwise how can it feel inferiority, insecurity, jealousy?

You are the witness; so, as you go deeper, you will come across many things which you have suppressed; or perhaps for thousands of years your whole race has suppressed; or perhaps the whole of humanity has suppressed . . . . But you are as pure as a mirror.

When you are going deeper, the mirror reflects jealousy, but the mirror is not jealousy; the mirror reflects insecurity, but the mirror is not insecurity; the mirror reflects inferiority, but the mirror is not inferiority. The mirror is not identified with anything that it reflects – the mirror is just empty, silent, clean. You are the mirror.

In meditation you will come to recognize that you are the mirror. All other things are reflected in you, but the mirror does not become a buffalo, because a buffalo looks into the mirror. When the buffalo is gone, the mirror is again empty, even while the buffalo was looking into the mirror, the mirror was empty. A small mirror cannot contain that big buffalo.

You may have observed small children, when they see a mirror for the first time. Very small children who are learning to crawl on all fours . . . just put a mirror in front of them, and they will be very much surprised, seeing another boy. They will look with wondering eyes, and it is absolutely certain, that they will go behind the mirror, to find the boy – where the boy is hiding. They may touch the mirror to see, and they will be surprised that the other boy is also touching; then the only way to find him is to go behind the mirror. Every child will go behind the mirror to look for the boy who is hiding there.

A mirror is just a reflecting phenomenon; so are you. Be a mirror, and then all these problems, whatever their names, will start disappearing – they are only reflections. You need not try to get rid of them. The very idea of getting free of them, or getting rid of them, still accepts that they are realities of your being.

The mirror does not care whether a buffalo is looking in it, or a donkey is looking in it. It does not matter; it does not change the quality of the mirror at all. The greatest genius may be looking into it, and the greatest idiot may be looking into it: the mirror remains the same. Reflections don't change its quality, its being.

You are a mirror.

Discover this mirror and don't be bothered about getting rid of jealousy, of insecurity, of inferiority. There are thousands of problems; if you start trying to get rid of them you will need many lives . . . . It was because of so many problems that the East believed in many lives, because one life is not enough. You don't have much time.

Half of your life, if you count, is wasted in sleeping, taking food, taking a bath, shaving twice a day . . . . Accumulated in seventy years it is going to be a big amount. Going to some stupid job, seeing the movies, playing football, fighting with your wife, worrying about a thousand and one things which will never happen, remembering all the old things which have happened – and now there is no point in remembering them. You just count, and you will be surprised if in seventy years you can get even seven minutes for meditation.

Naturally, the East had to invent that in one life the problems cannot be solved, you don't have time, you will need many lives. But nobody has gone deeper into it, that in one life you cannot solve problems, but you are going to create many problems. And the second life will be more burdened with problems: the first life's problems and the second life's problems – and for meditation, again those seven minutes. Looked at in that way, even if you have thousands of lives, you are not going to get rid of them. They will go on growing, they will go on becoming bigger, they will go on becoming thicker, you will be more in their clutches . . . . That is a whole wrong attitude.

I am not saying that there are not future lives. I am saying that the idea appealed to people just because they needed time. The idea is right, but it should not be accepted because you need time to solve your problems. Your problems can be solved this moment, there is no need to wait for tomorrow.

So from this moment, Latifa, you are a German mirror. I am not saying Indian mirror, because you cannot trust an Indian mirror – you cannot trust anything made in India. People make things in India, and write on them, "Made in USA."

Once a watch was presented to me in Bombay. I looked at the watch; it looked absolutely Indian craftsmanship, but on the back of the watch was written, "Made in USA." So I asked the man who had presented it to me, "Are you certain that this watch is made in USA?"

He laughed, and said, "USA means Ulhasnagar Sindhi Association, it is just a small place near Poona."

Sindhis are very clever people; they have made the name Ulhasnagar Sindhi Association . . . USA; made in USA.

I have come across things in which it is written . . . if you don't carefully note, you will see: "Made in Germany." But if you carefully look, it is not "Made in Germany," but "Made as Germany." They have changed the 'in' into 'as'. But "Made as Germany" – what does it mean? That's why I say, you are a German mirror. Just get more and more settled in your quality of mirroring, and all the diseases that you are talking about are bound to disappear within a second.

I believe in such miracles.

Beloved Bhagwan,

It seems that whenever I have experienced a feeling of well-being inside, it is always followed by a wave of self-condemnation. And the deeper and more intense the laughter and celebration becomes, the deeper and more intense the condemnation that follows in its wake. I feel as if I am being strangled by it. Will there ever be a point when it will disappear or will it remain a shadow of my enjoyment?

Surabhi, it is your conditioning against everything that is pleasant. Pleasure has been condemned so many times that you have forgotten that it is one of the great lies. You say, "It seems that whenever I have experienced a feeling of well-being inside, it is always followed by a wave of self- condemnation."

That wave of self-condemnation is coming to you from your conditioning, most probably the Christian or the Catholic conditioning. Just condemn anything – and when you start condemning things before children, they don't have the capacity to argue against it. They trust in their parents and if they see condemnation, they learn the art of condemning themselves.

But nature gives you moments of well-being, of pleasure; you cannot resist that either. You are sitting in two boats: one is made of your conditionings, and another is your natural boat that you have brought with you – your life. You cannot leave pleasures completely, but you can do one thing – and that's what everybody has done – be half-hearted.

When they are feeling something pleasant, they hold themselves back; they are in a strange position. That's why you feel as if you are being strangled by it . . . a tension. Your conditioning is saying, "Don't go that way," and your whole nature is going that way. Deep down you want to go that way because it is so pleasant, so beautiful. But your mind goes on saying, "Listen, don't go that way, it is sin, you will suffer for it. Just for a momentary pleasure you will be thrown into eternal hell. Think of it, wait."

So you are always wavering between pleasure and the anti-pleasure attitude. That gives you the feeling of being strangled.

There are a few people who have dropped all their conditionings and go on moving in their natural course of life. They are happy people, dancing and singing – enjoying. Religious people condemn them: these are the sinners; eat, drink, and be merry is their only religion. They will suffer much.

There are people, very few, who have dropped their natural desires completely, and have settled into their social conditioning. They don't feel any joy, their song of life is lost. They feel crippled; they cannot dance. They can do one thing only; all their energy which would have been divided into many dimensions has become concentrated only on one thing: condemn those who are still enjoying.

These people are called saints. Their only work from morning to evening is condemnation. Slowly, slowly condemnation becomes their only pleasure. The more they condemn, the more they feel themselves holier, superior, divine, spiritual; and the others become materialists. There is only one consolation for them, that after death they will be in paradise, enjoying everything that they are missing here. And all these people who are running after momentary pleasures will be suffering in hell for eternity.

Even teachers like Jesus have supported these ideas. Lazarus asked Jesus, "You say, 'Blessed are the poor, because theirs is the kingdom of God,' but how to believe you?" Here we are starving; the summer is hot and the rains have not come for two, three years. The wells have become dry; even water has become a difficulty."

Jesus says to Lazarus, "Don't be worried, Lazarus; soon you will see, after death you will be sitting in the lap of God. And this rich man, who is giving a feast today to other rich and powerful people of the city, will be hungry and thirsty in hell. And they will say from there, 'Lazarus, give us something to eat; we are thirsty too.' And this is going to be their eternal fate. Even if you want to give to them you cannot give – because nothing passes from heaven to hell. You will have all the pleasures, and they will have all the sufferings. So it is only a question of a few years. It is worth suffering for a few years, and then enjoying for the whole of eternity."

To console the poor . . . and the poor have always been in the majority, they are the real clients of all religions. The religions have to console them, and they found out – all the religions of the world – the same consolation, after death . . . .

The trouble is that nature is too powerful; conditionings cannot destroy it completely, they can only poison it. And this, Surabhi, is what you are suffering: poisoning by conditioning.

Whenever you feel a certain well-being it is followed by a wave of self-condemnation. What is wrong in feeling well-being? You are not harming anybody. Well-being is not something quantitative that you have taken, so others cannot feel it. You have not deprived anybody. In fact, by your well-being you may trigger other people's well-being.

To be with a man who is full of well-being, radiates a certain joy which is contagious. Why should you feel self-condemnation? You have not done anything wrong. Just see that your conditionings have to be dropped – and they can be dropped because they are not part of your nature, they have been forced upon you by society. They are arbitrary. And the deeper and more intense the laughter and celebration becomes, the deeper and more intense the condemnation that follows in its wake.

Your dancing, your celebrating, your singing is not harming anybody. It may heal somebody, but it cannot harm anybody. These birds are singing and they don't feel any condemnation. They don't go to the Catholic priest to confess every Sunday "Father, forgive me. I again sang this week. I could not resist – when the sun rises and flowers open their fragrance . . . . I try hard, but I am a helpless, small bird, not much strong, so I have been singing the whole week. Now, forgive me, and ask God to forgive me."

These trees don't go to the priest; they dance, they enjoy the sun, they enjoy the wind, they enjoy the rain – they enjoy you. They must be waiting for you every morning, every evening, because we are all connected with each other. They must be waiting: it is time, you must be coming. And when you sing and when you clap, do you think these trees mind it? They enjoy it.

Man is the only foolish animal in the world, and the priests have found your weakness. Your weakness is that your mind can be filled by any garbage, whether you want it or not. People are continually pouring garbage into each other's minds – you will not see people sitting silently.

I used to travel a lot and it was the most troublesome thing to have another passenger with me. I always chose to travel in an air-conditioned coupe, so at the most there would be one other passenger; mostly there was nobody. But even one passenger is enough. And I was traveling around the year continually; so many incidents . . . .

I would enter into the compartment and the man might start smiling – that means now he is approaching – and I would put my finger on my lips, and he would look at me very disappointed. But still he would ask, "Are you silent?" And then to watch his fidgetiness was such an entertainment. He would open his suitcase, close it, take one book, look into it, put it back, read the same newspaper that he has been reading the whole day, put it back again . . . and I am simply looking at him! And finally he would say, "You can remain silent, but don't stare at me, because I am feeling so nervous." Why should he feel nervous? He would go into the bathroom, come again, go back, come again – just to keep himself engaged. People cannot sit silently.

Once in a while it would happen – I had many devices for these people – as I entered and the person looked at me I would tell him, "This is my name, this is my father's name, this is my father's father's name. I have so many uncles, so many brothers, so many sisters."

He would say, "But I have not asked!"

I would say, "You will be asking, so it is better to finish quickly! . . . That all my uncles are married, one uncle has two children."

He would say, "But I have not even spoken a single word – why are you saying all these things?"

I would say, "I know that soon you will ask my name, my father's name, where I live, where I am going, what is my business. I am telling you on my own, so nothing is left. If something is left you just tell me, because I want to finish it within five minutes; and then for forty-eight hours I am going to be silent, and then don't ask anything."

So first he was shocked, but he understood that he was going to ask these things. That's what people are asking each other – where they live, what they do. What is your concern? How does it matter to you where I am going or from where I am coming? – and it is expected that I should ask you the same questions.

So I used to say to these people, "In five minutes I will say everything possible, in a summarized form; and five minutes I will give you – you can say in five minutes all the things that could be asked of you – and then for forty-eight hours we both are going to be silent."

People used to think that this man seems to be mad! And for forty-eight hours there was such a circus to see: he would call the waiter and he would eat too much, and I saw that he was eating again and again, and calling for coffee and some cold drink. I was simply looking at him, not doing anything.

Finally he would get so tense that he would call the conductor, "I want to change. You put me into some other compartment."

But I would tell the conductor, "I will remain with him."

The conductor would say, "But this is strange."

I would say, "No, we are companions. I have introduced myself, he has introduced himself. Now it is a forty-eight hour contract, so if you have two seats, only then change him."

Most probably he had not two seats empty, and even if he had, the man would decline: "I don't want to go – what is the point? If I have to live with this man for forty-eight hours in another compartment, then this compartment is good."

All the conductors knew me, so when I would go out they would say, "Don't torture him. That poor fellow looks so shocked, as if he is traveling with a ghost or something."

~~People are chitchatting continually; pouring all their rubbish into your head and inviting you to pour your rubbish in their heads. And that rubbish becomes part of your mind.~~

Otherwise, Surabhi, can't you see it simply, that your well-being does no harm to anybody? Why should you feel self-condemnation? ~~It is just the rubbish that your parents and your priests have forced into you.~~

Your singing, your laughter, your celebration – if it can do anything it will be something good. Why should you feel a condemnation coming just behind it? These are your dead priests; centuries of dead people who are enjoying themselves in their graves, resting, relaxing; and they have given you these ideas. Just a little awareness, and you will not find any content in your condemnation.

I can understand it if you are harming somebody, if you are being violent with somebody, if you are angry with somebody and a condemnation comes in – it is understandable, it is reasonable. You misbehaved and your consciousness is trying to say, "Do not do such a thing again."

But this cannot be true about celebration and singing and dancing and well-being – so just watch it. And when you feel condemnation coming in, dance more madly. ~~Transform the energy that is condemnation into more intense celebration. Make it clear to your conditioned mind that if it interferes with you, you are going to do the same thing more and more.~~

If after laughter you feel condemnation, then go on laughing for hours until that stupid condemnation feels tired, saying "This woman is not worth it, I should choose some other Catholic!"

You are asking me, "Will there ever be a point when it will disappear, or will it remain a shadow of my enjoyment?"

It depends on you. It can disappear this very moment; but if you choose, it can remain. It is your guest. Just throw the guest out with all his luggage and say goodbye to him forever!

Make it clear. Don't look back, "Go somewhere else – there are many Christians around; enter into somebody else's head. I am finished with you!"

Try it! Pack all the suitcases, everything, and throw them out of the window. It is your decision you have accepted the guest. Don't forget that ~~you are the host~~ and ~~the guest is only the guest~~, and ~~can remain only with your permission.~~ And such ugly guests, when I can give you beautiful guests . . . . Be a little choosy.

The guests that you have been carrying in your head up to now are your diseases; they are making you sick. They are not allowing you to laugh, they are not allowing you to dance, they are not allowing you to celebrate. What do they allow? Just to be serious and sad – miserable. Look at the point: when you are miserable, there will be no self-condemnation.

This is the conspiracy that has been made by the religions against each of you. To be miserable is perfectly okay, to be sad is perfectly okay; your religion has nothing to say about it. But to laugh, to enjoy, to be drunk with beauty, with bliss, with ecstasy – and immediately all your religions start condemning you.

The religions have virtually made the earth a hell. If you were left alone, without any interference from your religions, this very earth could have been a paradise. At least in this house of God you should remember you are in paradise; and here the discipline is different. If you are miserable, condemn it; if you are

celebrating, appreciate it – give a gift to yourself.

When you see somebody celebrating, appreciate it – just a rose flower will be enough; give a gift to him. Perhaps this way you will learn that celebration can be appreciated. There is no need to condemn it.

Surabhi, your problem is very simple, it is an arbitrary problem created by others. It is not your problem, it is not coming out of your natural being. So today, when there will be singing and dancing, remember, if this self-condemnation comes in, throw it out. And the way to throw it out is to jump and jog and enjoy! Kill it by your blissfulness.

It is killing your blissfulness. You have every right to kill it by your blissfulness – by your ecstasy.

Okay, Vimal?

Yes, Bhagwan!

The Secrets And Mysteries Of Existence Are Infinite

Don't ask for anything to be repeated in your life, because there are always higher things. Why waste your life with anything lower? Always ask for the higher, for the better. And of course, you don't know what is higher and what is greater; again you are just waiting for the unknown. Just as the unknown has given you a gift in the past, it will be giving you many, many gifts; but you have to have the same childlike innocent heart – waiting and longing, but not definite about what you are asking. Just trust in existence, and you will find better spaces. There is no scarcity of paradises – there are paradises beyond paradises – one has just to be innocent and not cling to anything. You are clinging to a certain experience, and that very clinging is becoming a barrier to prevent another experience from happening....

But you are preventing existence from giving you anything. You are asking for something which has already been given to you; and nature does not want to bore you by giving the same paradise, the same home every time. Just imagine how many times it would take for you to become bored with it. Because it has not happened again, you are carrying a golden memory of it. Drop that memory. Be grateful that existence gave it to you, and wait. The future is vast, and the secrets and the mysteries of existence are infinite.

February 19, 1987, 7 p.m.

Beloved Bhagwan,

Seven years ago I took sannyas. You spoke to me about the witness and about watching. When You finished, and before I could leave, You stopped me and said, "And you're a good man." Your love and Your grace have been with me these seven years, beloved Master. I am still in wonderment: what is a good man?

Veet Mano, I remember I have said to you, "You are a good man," because I have given you the name, Veet Mano. Veet Mano means going beyond the good man.

Morality is concerned with good qualities and bad qualities. A man is good – according to morality – who is honest, truthful, authentic, trustworthy. But morality is not religion; even an atheist can be a good man, because all these qualities of the good man do not include godliness.

I have told you, you are a good man; so the work for you is not just to be good, but to transcend the duality of good and bad. The religious man is not only a good man, he is much more. For the good man, goodness is all; for the religious man, goodness is just a byproduct. The religious man is one who knows himself, one who is conscious of his own being. And the moment you are conscious of your own being, goodness follows you like a shadow. Then there is no need of any effort to be good; goodness becomes your nature. Just as the trees are green, the religious man is good.

But the good man is not necessarily religious. His goodness is out of great effort, he is fighting with bad qualities – lying or stealing, untruthfulness, dishonesty, violence. They are in the good man but only repressed – they can erupt any moment.

The good man can change into a bad man very easily, without any effort – because all those bad qualities are there, only dormant, repressed with effort. If you remove the effort they will immediately erupt in your life. And your good qualities are only cultivated, not natural: you have tried hard to be honest, to be sincere, not to lie – but it has been an effort, it has been tiring.

The good man is always serious, because he is afraid of all the bad qualities he has repressed; and he is serious because deep down he desires to be honored for his goodness, to be rewarded. His longing is to be respectable. Your so-called saints are mostly just good men.

I have given you the name: transcend the good man – and there is only one way to transcend the good man, and that is by bringing more awareness to your being.

Awareness is not something to be cultivated; it is

already there, it has just to be awakened. When you are totally awakened, whatever you do is good, and whatever you do not do, is bad. The good man has to make immense efforts to do good and to avoid the bad. The bad is a constant temptation for him. It is a choice: every moment he has to choose the good, and not to choose the bad.

For example, a man like Mahatma Gandhi: he is a good man, he tried hard his whole life to be on the side of good. But even at the age of seventy he was having sexual dreams – and he was very much in anguish: "As far as my waking hours are concerned, I can keep myself completely free from sex. But what can I do in sleep? All that I repress in the day comes in the night."

It shows one thing: that it has not gone anywhere; it has been inside you, just waiting. The moment you relax, the moment you remove the effort – and asleep you have at least to relax and remove the effort to be good – all the bad qualities that you have been repressing will start becoming your dreams.

Your dreams are your repressed desires.

The good man is in continuous conflict. His life is not one of joy; he cannot laugh whole-heartedly, he cannot sing, he cannot dance. In everything he continually makes judgments. His mind is full of condemnation and judgment; and because he is himself trying hard to be good, he is judging others also by the same criteria. He cannot accept you as you are; he can accept you if you fulfill his demands of being good. And because he cannot accept people as they are, he condemns them. All your saints are full of condemnation of everybody: you are all sinners.

These are not the qualities of the authentic religious man. The religious man has no judgment, no condemnation. He knows one thing: that no act is good, no act is bad; awareness is good and unawareness is bad. You may even do something – in unawareness – which looks good to the whole world, to the religious man that is not good. And you may do something bad, and you will be condemned by everybody – except by the religious man. He cannot condemn you, because

you are unconscious. You need compassion, not judgment, not condemnation – you don't deserve hell, nobody deserves hell.

As your meditation deepens, your witnessing becomes great. That's what I was saying to you about witnessing and watching when you took sannyas seven years ago. I had forgotten to tell you, not to think that witnessing or watchfulness are nothing but good qualities. That's why, when you were leaving, I stopped you again and told you that you were already a good man.

So something more is implied in transcending the duality of good and bad. Coming to a point of absolute awareness, there is no question of choice – you simply do whatever is good. You do it innocently, just as your shadow follows you, with no effort. If you run, the shadow runs; if you stop, the shadow stops – but there is no effort on the part of the shadow.

The man of awareness cannot be thought synonymous with the good man. He is good, but in such a different way, from such a different angle. He is good not because he is trying to be good; he is good because he is aware – and in awareness bad, evil, all those condemnatory words disappear as darkness disappears in light.

Religions have decided to remain only moralities. They are ethical codes; they are useful for society, but not useful for you, not useful for the individual. They are conveniences created by society. Naturally, if everybody starts stealing, life will become impossible; if everybody starts lying, life will be become impossible; if everybody is dishonest, you cannot exist at all. So on the very lowest level morality is needed by society; it is a social utility, but it is not a religious revolution.

Don't be satisfied by just being good.

Remember, you have to come to a point where you need not even think about what is good and what is bad. Your very awareness, your very consciousness simply takes you towards that which is good – there is no repression. I would not call Mahatma Gandhi a religious man, only a good man – and he tried really hard to be good. I do not suspect his intentions, but he was obsessed with goodness.

A religious man is not obsessed with anything – he has no obsession. He is just relaxed, calm and quiet, silent and serene. Out of his silence whatever blossoms is good. It is always good – he lives in a choiceless awareness.

That is the meaning of your name, Veet Mano: Go beyond the ordinary concept of a good man. You will not be good, you will not be bad. You will be simply alert, conscious, aware, and then whatever follows is.

going to be good. In a different way I can say that in your total awareness you attain to the quality of godliness – and good is only a very small byproduct of godliness.

Religions have been teaching you to be good, so that one day you can find God. That is not possible; no good man has ever found godliness. I am teaching just the reverse: find godliness and good will come on its own accord. And when good comes on its own accord, it has a beauty, a grace, a simplicity, a humbleness. It does not ask for any reward here or hereafter. It is its own reward.

Beloved Bhagwan,

About four years ago I was in a space which I always remember as "paradise on earth."
It felt as if I'd arrived home. Being in such deep and sweet relaxation and love,
I felt as if I had fallen deep inside myself.
Beloved Bhagwan, why is it so difficult for me to let myself rejoice like that again?

Sadhan, the very memory is preventing you from getting back into the same space again. Remember one thing: in life, nothing repeats itself. And the moment you become addicted to a certain idea, a certain memory, you are living in the past – which is dead – and you are always comparing everything that is happening now with a past memory. You want it to happen again, but you have forgotten one thing. When it happened, you were not wanting it to happen; it happened without your wanting, without your desiring, without your even being aware that it was going to happen. Out of nowhere, suddenly it descended upon you.

You are no longer in that state. You are waiting for it, you are asking for it, you are demanding it – and nobody can make any demands on existence. The more you demand, the more miserable you will

become. Forget what has happened, because even better spaces are available. Never ask again for what has already happened, because it will be at the most a repetition – and a repetition can never give you the same joy.

I have a beautiful story about Mulla Nasruddin: He was chosen to be an adviser to the king. The first day, the king and Mulla Nasruddin were both sitting at the dining-table eating. The cook had made stuffed bhindis, and the king liked them very much.

When Mulla Nasruddin heard the king praising the cook, he started praising bhindis like anything. He said, "In the ancient scriptures it is said that the bhindi is the most life-giving vegetable. It keeps you young longer than anybody else, old age never comes – and you start forgetting that there are diseases. It is almost like nectar on the earth."

The cook heard this, so the next day also he made stuffed bhindis. The king ate them, but did not say anything. Mulla Nasruddin went on praising them again. This went on happening for seven days, and on the seventh day the king became so bored with stuffed bhindis that he threw the plate away and said to the cook, "Are you mad, or something? – stuffed bhindis, stuffed bhindis . . . ."

Mulla Nasruddin saw the scene had changed, so he said, "This cook seems to be an idiot. It is said by the ancient sages that you should not eat bhindis every day; it is dangerous to health. You will become old before your time, and death is not far away."

The king said, "Mulla Nasruddin, for seven days you have been praising bhindis, and now suddenly you have changed your mind. Your scriptures and quotations and ancient sages, have all changed."

Mulla Nasruddin said, "Master, I am your servant, I am not the servant of bhindis. Whatever is your opinion is my opinion – I don't know anything about bhindis. Because you praised them, how could I remain silent? Now that you are condemning them, I am condemning them. You give me my salary, not the bhindis. And as far as the ancient scriptures and ancient sages are concerned, I know nothing about them. Who cares about ancient sages and ancient scriptures? If they knew that bhindis are nectar, they would be alive right now.

"The bhindi cannot make anybody immortal, that much is certain. It is good that you stopped, because I was also dying – I was becoming a stuffed bhindi! Every day bhindis . . . I was becoming worried myself about how to stop this madman?"

The king said, "You are telling me I am mad?"

Mulla said, "You started praising . . . I am just your servant. Anything – howsoever beautiful, howsoever delicious – will create only boredom if repeated continuously." Sadhan, simply think about it: if the space that you think was paradise is repeated every day, it will become hell. Then you will be asking me how to get rid of this space.

Don't ask for anything to be repeated in your life, because there are always higher things. Why waste your life with anything lower? Always ask for the higher, for the better.

And of course, you don't know what is higher and what is greater; again you are just waiting for the unknown.

Just as the unknown has given you a gift in the past, it will be giving you many, many gifts; but you have to have the same childlike innocent heart – waiting and longing, but not definite about what you are asking.

Just trust in existence, and you will find better spaces. There is no scarcity of paradises – there are paradises beyond paradises – one has just to be innocent and not cling to anything. You are clinging to a certain experience, and that very clinging is becoming a barrier to prevent another experience from happening.

If something great has happened, which gave you the idea that you have come home, that this is paradise – then forget all about it. The future contains much more. The past is dead and the future is alive, and the whole future is not exhausted by your past. Be open and be available, and you will find greater spaces – more precious.

Once you have learned the art of waiting without demanding, just trusting, nature goes on giving more and more gifts. It has to give, because it has so much abundance. It cannot contain it within itself – it has to share.

But you are preventing existence from giving you anything. You are asking for something which has already been given to you; and nature does not want to bore you by giving the same paradise, the same home every time. Just imagine how many times it would take for you to become bored with it. Because it has not happened again, you are carrying a golden memory of it.

Drop that memory. Be grateful that existence gave it to you, and wait. The future is vast, and the secrets and the mysteries of existence are infinite.

Beloved Bhagwan,

This poem from *Gitanjali* by Rabindranath Tagore echoes in my heart:
I am here to sing thee songs.
In this hall of thine I have a corner seat.
In thy world I have no work to do:
My useless life can only break out in tunes without a purpose.
The song I came to sing remains unsung to this day.
I have spent my days in stringing and unstringing my instrument.
The time has not come true. The words have not been rightly set.
Only there is the agony of wishing, in my heart.
The blossom has not opened: only the wind is sighing by.

Milarepa, it is one of the destinies of those who are born with genius. A genius never finds that what he has created is enough. He is always discontented. He goes on creating more and more beautiful things, but nothing satisfies; he knows that he has much more to give. His heart has to pour out more songs, more paintings, more music. He is fully aware that whatever he does falls short of the target; his target is such a faraway star.

It is not just about Rabindranath Tagore – these words are true about any genius in any part of the world, in any time, in any age. These words are the very essence of the discontent – because the painter feels in his dreams that he can paint something unique that has never been done before. It is so clear in his dreams, but the moment he starts translating his dream onto the canvas, he starts feeling that what is happening on the canvas is only a far away echo.

Coleridge, one of the great poets of England, left forty thousand poems unfinished when he died. During his life again and again he was asked, "Why don't you complete them? It is such a beautiful poem – just two lines are missing and it will be complete."

He always said, "It reflected something that was hovering in my being; but when I brought it into words, it was not the same thing. To others it may appear very beautiful, because they don't have anything to compare it with. But to me . . . I know the real poem which is within me, still trying to find new words."

Rabindranath himself used to write each poem many times. His father was a very talented man, though not a genius; his grandfather was a very talented man, but also not a genius. Both tried to convince him, "You are mad. You go on destroying . . . . You go on making beautiful poems and then you destroy them. Why do you destroy them?"

Rabindranath said, "Because they are not authentic representations of my experience. I wanted to do something, and something else has happened. It may look beautiful to you, but to me it is a failure, and I don't want to leave any failure behind me. That's why I am going to destroy it."

Rabindranath's father has written, "He has destroyed such beautiful poems . . . we cannot conceive how they can be more beautiful. He seems to be mad . . . " And when he used to write poems he would close his doors and inform the whole house that for no reason at all should he be disturbed – not even for food. Sometimes days would pass – two days, three days – and the whole family would be worried . . . he was constantly writing and destroying. Until he came to a settlement where something of his inner vision had been caught in the net of words, he would not open the door.

In this book *Gitanjali* – 'gitanjali' means 'offering of songs,' it is an offering to God – Rabindranath says, "I don't have anything else. I can only offer my deepest, heartfelt dreams, that I have brought into the poems." Hence he gave the name *Gitanjali* – 'offering of songs.' These are the very few chosen poems which he has not destroyed. They are immensely beautiful. But he was not satisfied even with these poems, although he got a Nobel prize for this book.

The original was in Bengali, which is a very poetic language – just the opposite of the Marathi you will hear in Poona. If two or three Maharashtrians are having a conversation, you will think that soon there will be a fight. The words are harsh – the language seems to be very good for fighting, but for no other purpose. Bengali is just the opposite polarity. Even if two Bengalis are fighting, you will think they are having a very sweet conversation, the language is so sweet. The words of Marathi have corners; Bengali is very rounded – no corners. Even prose in Bengali sounds like poetry; it has a certain music in it which no other Indian language has.

Rabindranath wrote *Gitanjali* first in Bengali, and for ten years the world remained absolutely unaware of it. Then, just an accidental suggestion by a friend: "Why don't you translate it into English?" – and he tried.

He was dissatisfied with the original Bengali, but he was more dissatisfied with the translation. Because there are a few nuances to every language which are not translatable. Particularly a language like Bengali is almost impossible to translate word to word. You can translate, but the sweetness, the quality of music in each word . . . from where can you bring it? Still, he got the Nobel prize for the translation. His friend said, "Now you must be satisfied."

He said, "I am more dissatisfied than ever. This shows that humanity is not yet mature enough to understand poetry. These are my failures, these poems of *Gitanjali*. I have saved them after many, many efforts. I became tired, and felt that perhaps something that is in my heart cannot be brought into words. The best I could do I did, but in my own eyes it was a failure, at the best, a very good failure. It can deceive everybody else, but it cannot deceive me."

This is the experience of all great geniuses – in every direction, in every dimension. The Dutch painter Vincent van Gogh painted for one year continually only one painting – again and again and again. The effort was so arduous, and what he was painting was so difficult: he wanted to catch the sun in all its glory and beauty, with the songs of the birds . . . . Now, no painting can sing but you cannot argue with geniuses.

He was standing in the field the whole day, from morning till evening – just watching the sun in all its phases, with all the colors that the morning brings, or the evening brings. For one year he was continually painting and destroying, and one year with the hot sun on his head the whole day . . . he went mad. He was put in a madhouse by his younger brother. In the madhouse he continued to paint the sun, but nothing came closer to his vision.

He was one year in the madhouse. The world may call him mad, but I cannot – because the paintings that he did in the madhouse are so full of intelligence, so sane, that the painter cannot be insane. And when he was released from the madhouse, again he went into the field to start his painting of the sun. And the day it was completed, the day he felt a little satisfied, he committed suicide.

He wrote a short letter to his brother: "My work is done. All I wanted my whole life was to paint the sun in its full glory. I cannot say I have succeeded totally, but I can certainly say I have succeeded more than anybody else in the whole history of man."

Nobody has ever tried so much – almost two and a half years on just one subject. He said, "Now I don't have any desire to paint, therefore there is no need to exist. My existence has come to a point of fulfillment and contentment. I am dying, not because of discontent or failure, I am dying because I have been victorious, so now there is no point in living."

These words of Rabindranath are worth remembering: *"I am here to sing thee songs."* His whole life was devoted only to one thing: to create songs; to sing songs. India was under the British Empire and Mahatma Gandhi and other freedom fighters were telling Rabindranath, "This is not the time to write poems; this is the time to fight. Freedom is the only goal in these moments."

He said, "I can understand your feelings" – and his participation in the freedom movement would have been of immense importance, because he was a Nobel prize winner, an international figure. His books were translated to almost all the languages of the world. If he was also fighting for freedom it would have been immensely helpful, but he said, "I am here to sing songs. I understand you, and I love freedom, but that is not my heart's desire. Freedom or no freedom – I have searched within myself and I have found only one thing: that my destiny is to sing. If I do anything else, that will be going against my nature."

I have far more respect for Rabindranath than for Mahatma Gandhi, because he never went against his nature; he was one of the most relaxed men you can find – immensely happy in singing, in creating more songs, more plays.

He is talking to God.

In this hall of thine I have a corner seat.
In thy world I have no work to do:
My useless life can only
break out in tunes without a purpose.

Everybody was saying, "You are good for nothing. When the whole country is afire with the idea of freedom, you are one of the greatest sons of the country, and you are involved only in small things: singing, playing on instruments. You are utterly useless."

He accepts it: "I am useless . . . my life is useless; it can break out only in tunes without a purpose. I am so useless that even my songs don't have any purpose – just as the birds sing, just as the flowers blossom with no purpose at all. The song I came to sing remains unsung to this day."

This was written while he was getting old. But even on his deathbed his last words were, "The song that I came to sing has remained unsung. My whole life I tried to sing it in different ways, with different tunes, with different instruments. People have loved them, people have appreciated them – but deep down I have a wound: I have not been able to sing the song I came to sing."

And this is the experience of all great mystics, all great poets, all great painters. Greatness is bound to have this feeling. Only small things can be completed, and only small desires can be fulfilled. The greater the desire, the more profound the longing – you are always coming closer and closer to the goal, but you never arrive. The distance between you and the goal remains almost exactly the same as it was the day you started your pilgrimage.

The song I came to sing remains unsung to this day . . . then what have I been doing all my life? *I have spent my days in stringing and unstringing my instrument* . . . just trying to find the right instrument, the right tuning of the instrument – but it has not happened.

The time has not come true.
The words have not been rightly set.
Only there is the agony of wishing in my heart.
I am going with a deep wound and agony in my heart.
The blossom has not opened:
only the wind is sighing by.

These words are immensely important, because they don't describe only Rabindranath Tagore's inner experience, they also describe that of thousands more geniuses of the world.

A genius has so much to say and so much to share that there are neither words to contain it, nor are there people to receive it.

A Sufi mystic, Bayazid, was once asked by a stranger, "What is your business?" He was not aware that Bayazid was a mystic; and Sufis live just like ordinary people. Unless somebody introduces you from their inner circle, you will never come to know that this man is a Sufi. When asked what his business was, Bayazid said, "My business? I sell glasses in the city of the blind."

The man looked at him: "What is he saying? What will the blind do with glasses?"

Bayazid said, "That is not my problem; that is their problem. My problem is somehow to persuade them to purchase a pair; whether they can see through them or not, I don't know."

The man said, "You seem to be mad."

Bayazid said, "That's true."

But this will be said by all the mystics – that they are selling glasses in the city of the blind, or that they are singing songs in the city of the deaf, or that they are teaching dances in the city of the crippled. Naturally, on the one hand they have a great ecstasy, which they want to express; and on the other hand they have a deep agony – that whatever they want to express always remains inexpressible.

If you can understand this statement of Rabindranath, it will help you immensely to understand the anguish of all the mystics, of all the great poets. It will also help you to understand why many mystics have remained silent. Seeing that there is no way of succeeding, only very few mystics have spoken. They have spoken, not because they think they are able to express what they have experienced; they have spoken so that perhaps listening to them, something may be triggered in the hearts of the listeners – something may be touched. Not that their words are going to convey the truth, but their constant effort may awaken something within you which is asleep. If not their words perhaps their presence, perhaps their silence, perhaps the depth of their eyes or the grace that surrounds them . . . hoping against hope that among millions, at least there may be one person who may be turned on.

Hence, they are not disappointed if nobody listens to them. They are not disappointed if people desert them. They are not disappointed even if people betray them. All this is expected. The miracle is that a few people don't betray, that a few people go on with them in deep love and trust.

Their minds may not be able to understand the mystic, but their hearts have heard the call, the challenge.

In this hope I have been speaking for thirty years continually. Even if a few people are turned on to God, I will feel utterly fulfilled. I will not die with the same agony as Rabindranath Tagore.

Okay, Vimal?

Yes, Bhagwan.

Forget All About Enlightenment

For a few moments just put aside your concern with yourself, and then you will not take it back up again. Because *you are* the agony, and your absence is ecstasy. And the whole work here is somehow to persuade you not to be the ego, but just a silent presence with no sense of "I."

The distance is very small . . . I am not telling you to go for a thousand miles pilgrimage – just a few inches, from your head to your heart. And it is so easy, because you are going downwards: you simply stop clinging to the head, where the ego resides, and immediately you will find yourself slipping into a totally new wonderland which you can see happening here, but which is not happening to you.

To you, it cannot happen. It is happening to those who are no longer concerned with themselves, no longer concerned with attainment, no longer concerned with transformation, no longer concerned with enlightenment. This contradiction has to be understood: unless you forget all about enlightenment, it is not going to happen to you, because it is not an achievement. All achievements are of the ego: they are decorations of the ego, and the ego is interested in decorating itself with enlightenment, too.

February 20, 1987,   8 a.m.

Beloved Bhagwan,

I feel in my element when extroverted and in action. When I am quiet, and this busy bumble bee doesn't feel she has to be buzzing, it is very uncomfortable. Is the "doer" in me dying? Will it ever be able to relax in action and silence?

Shantam Lani, you have raised a significant question. It is meaningful for everybody to understand that modern research into the human mind divides humanity into two parts: the extrovert and the introvert.

The extroverts are the doers, explorers, adventurers – objective, love being in the world, alone, they feel completely lost. The introvert is just the opposite of the extrovert: he feels at ease and relaxed with himself when he is not doing anything – when his eyes are closed, when he is silently drowning into his own interiority.

This division is good as far as it goes, but it goes only to the limits of the mind. You have an extrovert mind, that is why you say, "I feel in my element when extroverted and in action. When I am quiet and when this busy bumble bee does not feel she has to be buzzing, it is very uncomfortable."

Meditation is a totally different dimension from the mind. The psychologists are very confused about it because they know nothing about meditation; they think the meditator is just another introvert – that is not true. The meditator is one who can be aware of his extrovert mind and also of his introvert mind – aloof, far away on the hills, watching all the games of the mind.

You are too much attached to the extrovert part of your mind – and anybody who is attached to half of the mind is going to be in trouble, because the other half is also there, neglected, repressed, ignored, humiliated. It will take its revenge. And there are many who are introverts. They think they are meditators, but they are not. They have just chosen another part of the mind and have become identified with it. The essential meditator is beyond mind – beyond extroversion and beyond introversion.

So you have to pull yourself out of your obsession with action, with extroversion, because that is being a kind of alcoholic – they call it "workaholic." If action is there, you are involved in it, and you can forget all about yourself: all your problems and all your anxieties are no longer there – at least not in your consciousness. They *are* still there; so whenever you find a moment when you are not doing anything – and you cannot continue to *do* for twenty-four hours a day; you have to relax too, you have to rest too – in those restful moments the repressed and neglected introverted mind tries to possess you.

And into the introverted mind you have thrown all kinds of garbage that you don't want to be identified with. Your extroverted mind is clean – you think that is you, and the introverted mind is not you, so you can go on throwing all kinds of rubbish into it, but it will surface. Whenever you are resting, it won't allow you to be at rest, it will make you fidgety.

My suggestion is, Lani, to get out of the extroverted mind – and don't get into the introverted mind. They are two sides of the same coin. Learn a new secret: the secret of the watcher, who is neither *doing* something, nor deliberately *not* doing something. The watcher is just a mirror – he is reflecting whatever is happening. Going beyond mind is the greatest health and the greatest well-being possible to humanity. That does not mean that you cannot use your mind; in fact, only then *can* you use your mind. Right now the mind is using you; you are a slave of the extroverted mind.

There are many who have gone to the monasteries, to the mountains. They are introverted people – and to them introversion appears like meditation. That is not meditation either – they have just chosen the other side of the coin, and whenever there is a chance, immediately the extroverted mind will start creating desires and passions and longings and all kinds of things – hallucinations.

In all the old Indian scriptures, the sages come to a point . . . . The story is told about many saints and many sages – and it is not just a story, it is a very significant psychological fact: when a saint comes to the peak of his consciousness, Indian mythology says that the throne of the god Indra, in heaven, starts quivering. He becomes afraid – because if this man succeeds in attaining the highest consciousness, he will become Indra, and Indra will become an ordinary god.

So his strategy is to send beautiful women from heaven to distract the sage, and once he is distracted, he is destroyed. He loses his consciousness; desires start arising, lust overwhelms him – sensuality, sexuality, all raise their heads.

There is no Indra, and there is nobody who is sending things to distract you – it is your own mind. When the introverted mind reaches to its peak, the extroverted mind immediately becomes revengeful – it is being defeated . . . . Immediately it creates hallucinations – and sitting in the caves of the Himalayas or in a monastery, it is very easy to hallucinate.

All those beautiful women don't exist; they are just figments of your extroverted mind, which is saying, "What are you doing sitting here when such beautiful women are dancing around you? As far as your saintliness is concerned, you can pick it up again; but who knows whether these women will be there or not . . . ?" This is your own mind playing games.

The extrovert is happy when in action, in a crowd, with people; but soon it becomes exhausted and tired, bored, and starts thinking of relaxing. That is the introverted mind poking its nose into your extroversion . . . and this game goes on and on. You are neither of them – but you become identified with them.

My suggestion is, Lani: this is the place where you can become unidentified with your mind. So when there is need to act, act – but let it not be your obsession, and when there is need to relax, relax – that should not be your obsession either. While acting, remain alert that you are not the mind, and while relaxing, also remember that you are not the mind.

You are the one who is watching.

Slowly, slowly the watching becomes more and more crystallized; it becomes your very being, and then you are free of the mind – and free to use it the way you want. But that will be a totally different quality: your action will not be something insane, doing because you have to do it – as if you are under a kind of possession, and the mind is forcing you to do something. So people are doing all kinds of things which are not needed.

Once the watcher is clear and separate from the mind, you have come into a new land, a new space – the space of witnessing – and this is your real soul. This which is neither active nor inactive, which only reflects, is you. This is the greatest mutation.

Those who die without this transformation have lived in vain, because if you can watch your mind in action, in inaction, you can also watch your body – healthy, sick – but you are separate. You can even watch death happening to your body and to your mind, because you are separate – you simply reflect whatsoever happens.

That is why a man who is really a meditator can die joyfully, because he is not dying; only the reflections in the mirror are disappearing. And I don't think you will come across a mirror that has tears in its eyes when some reflection disappears, or even a remembrance of the past, or a desire that the same face should be reflected in it again. No past, no future . . . the mirror is always in the present, whatever happens, it simply reflects.

There is a temple in China where, instead of a statue of Buddha, there is only a mirror. The whole temple is empty. The people who created the temple must have been great meditators: the mirror is to remind you of your inner being.

And then you are at ease in action, at ease in relaxation. In fact, you start using both – like the two wings of a bird. And once both your wings are functioning together, you have the freedom of the whole sky. It is your own: all the stars and the moon and the sun and all the directions . . . you are out of the prison.

So don't try to change the extrovert mind into an introvert mind. You have to get out from both the extrovert mind and the introvert mind. Just make a little effort: when you are active, watch that also. I can move my hand, and still I can watch it. And this is the miracle – when you can watch your action, your action becomes very graceful, very beautiful; if you can watch your body, your body starts radiating a certain grace, a certain aura.

You have seen the whole world through your eyes. If you can watch from within your eyes, your eyes will start having a depth which you have not even conceived of in your dreams. Real life is far more beautiful than any dream, far more inconceivable than any imagination.

But get out of the mind.

Mind is your prison.

And here you can do anything you want – but remember watchfulness. Walking, also go on watching that you are walking. It is not that you have to repeat these words inside you, "I am walking" . . . just the feeling that I am sitting, that I am doing something, that I am not doing something, is enough.

And soon your watcher will come out of all kinds of fetters. It is your imprisoned splendor.

Beloved Bhagwan,

The other day You told me that my gorilla had turned into a lotus flower – a buddha. I know that You were joking and meant that, like all Your sannyasins, I am a buddha but sleeping still. But Your saying it has triggered something. My gorilla really has stepped out of his hairy suit, and someone is standing pink as a peach and as new as the dawn looking at me, daring me to trust what is happening. Bhagwan, even Your jokes are nuclear – or am I being too simple?

Devageet, my jokes are not jokes; they are my method to catch hold of you unawares. When you are listening to the joke, you are more intent not to miss the punchline . . . and that is a great opportunity for me to do my operation.

Your gorilla is dead. It was not a hairy suit; it was something in your heart – but it has been taken out. You are free from it.

Sometimes simple things can bring to you great experiences – because existence makes no difference between the simple and the great. Jokes have never been used for spiritual growth. All kinds of methods have been used, but nobody has dared to use jokes as a method . . . afraid that the joke may make the whole thing very nonserious.

I can use the joke as a method because to me, to be serious is not to be spiritual – it is only being psychologically sick. To be playful, to be smiling, to be laughing . . . when you burst forth in laughter, your ego disappears. A joke kills the ego without any murder, without any bloodshed. Just in the laughter, you are suddenly fresh; all the dust that had gathered on you falls away.

I was wondering if the operation had been successful or not, because Devageet has been silent for a few days. Gorillas cannot remain silent so long; they cannot even sit in one place for a few moments. They are really very active people . . . but Devageet is free from his gorilla.

And buddhahood is not an attainment, it is only freedom from the gorilla, and nothing else. The animal in you disappears . . . and the God in you is discovered. It is difficult to believe, Devageet, but believe it or not, it has happened. I am responsible for killing the poor gorilla. Nothing was wrong in the gorilla, but it was preventing your buddhahood and its growth. The gorilla had to be removed.

With great love, I have taken it with a simple joke. Now you have to be a little alert, because the world is full of gorillas. I have taken one; another may enter in you. Many gorillas are searching for some place, some shelter, and you are a perfect shelter . . . and the post is vacant – so be alert! Keep the doors closed. Just write on the door: "Gorillas not allowed in anymore."

Something beautiful has happened to you. The spiritual explosion always happens as a very simple phenomenon. It is the egoist who has been trying to prove to the world that to be spiritual is something very great, arduous, an uphill task; it takes lives and lives to attain it. It is not so.

You are all born buddhas – covered with something which has to be removed, and which is not part of your nature. It is the society around you that wants you not to be a buddha. If you are a gorilla, it is perfectly okay; nobody is worried about you. A gorilla is not dangerous – at the most a good entertainment – but a buddha is really dangerous. His very presence is a fire with a magnetic force in it. It attracts people even to the point of being consumed by the fire.

The buddha is the most dangerous person in the world.

That is why the world either kills the buddhas or

worships them. These are synonymous: killing is a way of getting rid of them; worshiping is also a way of getting rid of them.

When you worship a buddha, you are saying, "You are born a buddha; we are poor human beings. At the most we can put two flowers at your feet. Just leave us alone . . . we have so many other things to do." This is also a very cultured way of creating distance. That is why, in every culture, either they have killed such people or they have said that they are incarnations of God. "It is easy for them. We are human beings, with all kinds of frailties, weaknesses; we cannot do it."

Just to create a distance, so many stories have been created – and I have been wondering continually why no psychologist has the guts to go into those stories and expose what is hidden behind them. For example, Gautam Buddha was born when his mother was standing under a tree. Now, no woman has ever given birth to a child standing. Perhaps this was some accident, a kind of abortion; but the story is that Buddha was also born standing. As he came out of the womb, he stood on the earth, and the first thing he did was to take seven steps – a newborn baby taking seven steps and then declaring, "I am the greatest buddha in the world" . . . .

Now, the people who were creating these stories were trying to create a distance between themselves and these awakened people. They were not ready to accept them being as human as they are, because then a great responsibility arises: if a human being can become a buddha, then what are *you* doing? Then it will be a great weight on the chest; it is better to put these buddhas as far away as possible.

If you go to a Jaina temple, you will see a strange thing: there are twenty-four Jaina *tirthankaras*, Jaina gods; all their ears are so big, the earlobes so long, that they are touching their shoulders. That is one of the signs that a man is a *tirthankara*. You cannot find anybody who has such long lobes unless he goes through plastic surgery or some kind of massage continuously – like milking a cow.

But why does this kind of thing happen? Just to make them different from you. Mahavira lived naked in the hot sun of Bihar, but he never perspired. He does not perspire. This is possible only if he has plastic in the place of skin: plastic does not perspire. A human being has to perspire, because every pore in his body is breathing. It is not only your nose that breathes – if all the pores of your body are covered with thick paint, and your nose is left open, you cannot live more than three hours.

Each pore has its own way of breathing – and if there are pores, perspiration is not something evil, it is simply a natural way of keeping you at the same temperature, it is a protection. When it is too hot and you perspire . . . do you understand what it means? It means your body is bringing water out of the skin, so the heat evaporates the water, and is destroyed in evaporating it, and your temperature remains the same. If you cannot perspire, your temperature will go so high . . . and you don't have a wide range: after only one hundred and ten degrees, you will be flat on the earth, dead.

Perspiration keeps you continuously at the normal temperature: ninety-eight degrees. That is why when you are feeling cold you start shivering. Do you think it is the cold that is making you shiver? It is your body mechanism: by shivering, you create heat. Your teeth start chattering – that way you create heat. Any movement, and heat is created, and that heat is protective. Because Mahavira does not perspire, he need not take a bath. He never used to take a bath – there was no need. That was for ordinary human beings – to take a bath, to clean themselves; Mahavira was always clean.

Are these people talking about a real living being or about a marble statue? But they had to invent all these fictitious ideas to create as much distance as possible between you and those who have attained, so you can feel at ease, without any tension, that whatever you are, you cannot go beyond it.

But I say unto you: All these stories are fictitious. I

can say it with absolute certainty that if Mahavira lived, he *must* have perspired; only dead people don't perspire. If Buddha was not just a fiction but a reality, then he could not have stood up as soon as he was born and taken seven steps and declared, "I am the greatest buddha – past, present, or future."

Beloved Bhagwan,

The ecstasy of being in Your beautiful presence . . . the thrill of Your love, Your laughter, Your dance, Your silence . . . the agony of realizing the transformation has not yet happened to me. Beloved Master, is it very far away?

Satgyana, the distance between agony and ecstasy, between darkness and light, is so small you can measure it in inches. How much is the distance between your head and your heart? Maybe twelve inches, fifteen inches – and that is the only distance: you have to come down from the head to the heart. It is not even an uphill task; you have just to come down, roll down, towards the heart. And don't feel any agony – agony is also a shadow of the ego.

On one hand, you are saying, "The ecstasy of being in Your beautiful presence . . . the thrill of Your love, Your laughter, Your dance, Your silence" – if this is true, why are you concerned about your own transformation? Let this beautiful presence, this dance, this silence, this ecstasy, overwhelm you. But you remain standing aloof, and you are thinking about your own transformation: that creates agony.

"The agony of realizing the transformation has not yet happened to me" . . . to you, the transformation is never going to happen. You have to disappear, and you will find transformation is there. *You* will never need transformation: either you, or transformation – you can choose.

That is why I say that when there is dance and there is ecstasy and there is a beautiful communion, get lost in it. Don't just stand in the corner; become part of the laughter, part of the ecstasy, part of the mystery that is created by the silence of so many people here.

For a few moments just put aside your concern with yourself, and then you will not take it back up again. Because *you are* the agony, and your absence is ecstasy. And the whole work here is somehow to persuade you not to be the ego, but just a silent presence with no sense of "I."

The distance is very small . . . I am not telling you to go for a thousand miles' pilgrimage – just a few inches, from your head to your heart. And it is so easy, because you are going downwards: you simply stop clinging to the head, where the ego resides, and immediately you will find yourself slipping into a totally new wonderland which you can see happening here, but which is not happening to you.

To you, it cannot happen. It is happening to those who are no longer concerned with themselves, no longer concerned with attainment, no longer concerned with transformation, no longer concerned with enlightenment.

This contradiction has to be understood: unless you forget all about enlightenment, it is not going to happen to you, because it is not an achievement. All achievements are of the ego: they are decorations of the ego, and the ego is interested in decorating itself with enlightenment, too.

There is a beautiful story in the life of Mahavira.

Prasenjita, one of the great kings of those days, had conquered almost the whole known world, and he was very much gratified and very egoistic. But his wife was deeply interested in Mahavira and his teachings.

One night she said to Prasenjita, "Tomorrow morning Mahavira is coming to the city. I am going to meet him and to listen him."

Prasenjita said, "But what has he got that I have not got? He is just a beggar, naked, and I am a world conqueror, a *chakravcrtin*."

His wife laughed and she said, "You have everything; and yet you don't have anything, because you don't have that quality of meditativeness which is the real treasure. All of this kingdom will disappear, will be taken away by death; there is only one thing death cannot destroy, and that is meditativeness. You don't have it."

He could not sleep the whole night. He said to his wife, "I'm coming with you. I will purchase this meditation, whatsoever the cost."

His wife said, "Purchase it . . . ?"

He said, "If it is not available, I will conquer it." Those were the words he understood: everything can be purchased by money; everything can be conquered by power.

His wife said, "You had better come to see Mahavira."

And the same question he raised with Mahavira: "I have come here . . . . Give me your meditation, and I am ready to give you anything you want – you can take my whole kingdom. My wife has shattered my ego, telling me that you have something which I don't have."

Mahavira laughed, and he said, "There was no need to come so far to see me. Just in your city a very poor man, who is my disciple, has what you are asking for. And he is so poor . . . perhaps he may sell it." It was a joke.

Prasenjita said, "I know that man – there is no problem." He turned his chariot towards that poor man's house. His chariot had never been in that part of the city, so a whole crowd gathered. The poor man came out of his house and he said, "What can I do for you?"

Prasenjita said, "You need not do anything. Just give me meditation and whatever you want in return, you will receive ten times more. Just name the price."

The poor man had tears in his eyes, and he said, "I am crying for your poverty. You don't even understand that there are things which cannot be purchased. I can give my life to you, but as far as meditation is concerned, how can I give it to you? Not that I don't want to . . . but it is a quality of egolessness, and you are wanting it just as a decoration for your ego – because your wife has hurt your ego by telling you that Mahavira has something which you don't have."

Meditation is something that you have to grow within yourself. The only condition for growing it is dropping the ego. Just enjoy whatever existence has made available here. Dance it, sing it, laugh it, love it – and forget all about yourself. And it will happen; not to *you* – but it will happen when your idea of yourself is absent.

Beloved Bhagwan,

Every time You move to a new place it gets more beautiful. Every time Your work moves into a new phase it gets more intense. Every night Your words and Your silence are richer than those of the night before. And most of all, every dance You dance with us brings me higher and higher.
I don't know what You're building up to, or where we're going,
but every moment I can feel it getting closer – and I'm so excited!
Beloved Bhagwan, what mischief are You up to this time?

Disha, I have been up to the same mischief all my life. Just it goes on becoming bigger and bigger. And I have to move because when it becomes too bigger, I have to find a new place, new space, new people to participate – but it is the same mischief. I want to destroy you, so that God can be born in you.

I want your death, so that you can be resurrected into a life which is eternal.

Okay, Vimal?

Yes, Bhagwan.

Attention Is Invisible Nourishment

Attention is invisible nourishment: when you look at somebody with love, with joy, with compassion, you are giving that person something which cannot be purchased, something which makes him feel needed, something which makes him feel worthy to exist. When the person is ignored, slowly, slowly the person starts feeling, "I am not needed; nobody even takes note of me. So why go on living?" He starts losing interest in being alive. And the moment you stop being interested in being alive, you cannot be alive for long, even if every physical necessity is fulfilled.

But there is some spiritual necessity. I call it the need to be needed. Somebody needs you and suddenly you feel a new upsurge of energy. The meditator starts feeling as if the whole of existence needs him: the trees need him, the mountains need him, the rivers need him. The ecstatic life of the mystic is based on this experience, that he is needed even by the faraway stars; that when the rose blossoms, it needs somebody to appreciate it.

February 20, 1987,   7 p.m.

Beloved Bhagwan,

Why do You like to make us laugh so much? In those moments it feels as if we are all sharing a cup of divine champagne, and in this rejoicing we lose ourselves and come close to You. Thank you Bhagwan.

Prem Vishva, laughter has never been accepted by any religion of the world as a spiritual quality. As far as I am concerned, it is one of the most important spiritual qualities for the very simple reason that when you are in total laughter your ego disappears. The laughter is: you are not.

And if this is not being spiritual, then nothing else can be. It is because of this that when you laugh together, you melt into each other, and you melt with me.

Small egos disappear like dewdrops in the early morning sun.

The mind has never been able to laugh: it is basically serious; it is basically pathological. The moment you laugh, suddenly you are not functioning from the mind center anymore, you start functioning from the heart center. And if the laughter is really total you can even go deeper than the heart: you can reach to the very center of your being. It can give you a glimpse of truth, of beauty, of the celebrating existence. That's why I love to see you laugh as much as possible.

And you are right: "In those moments it feels as if we are all sharing a cup of divine champagne." It is not "as if" . . . you are really sharing a cup of divine champagne. "And in this rejoicing we lose ourselves and come close to You" – not only close, you can become one with me.

To be close is also to be distant; to be close is also to be separate. Love is never fulfilled by just closeness; it is fulfilled only when boundaries disappear, and merging and melting happens.

Prem Vishva, for you especially, I am telling this joke. A very famous Zulu warrior went to the king of Zululand to ask for the hand of the King's daughter in marriage. The King said, "No man can marry my daughter unless he can first carry out three tasks which I have set."

The warrior said, "Just tell them, O King, and I will do them immediately."

The king said, "I have set aside three tents. In the first tent is a large barrel of alcohol: you must drink it all in one breath. You must immediately go to the second tent, in which there is a seven-foot gorilla who is crazy with toothache; you must find his bad tooth and pull it out with your bare hands. In the third tent, which you must go to immediately after, is an English lady who has been specially trained not to have an orgasm. You must satisfy her totally!"

"Yes, my King," said the warrior. He went inside the first tent and drank the full barrel of alcohol in one mighty effort. He staggered out and went immediately into the next tent containing the mad gorilla. There was a terrible fight, the tent shook and the air was rent with screams and howling, large pieces of fur came flying out of the door, and a human ear.

The roaring and shouting went on for twenty minutes. Then the blood-soaked warrior crawled out, staggered to his feet, and said, "Okay, your kingship, now show me where the English lady with the toothache is."

Beloved Bhagwan,

I feel half-cooked! On the one hand I'm happy, more blessed and blissful, more loving and loved than ever before – and I feel so thrilled about it. And on the other hand my old companions – jealousy, competitiveness, the need to be important, special – they are also still around, in the same pot. I dance and celebrate with lightness and joy, and when the flashes of darkness come I relax and accept as much as I can and I try to remain watchful.

Bhagwan, since supposedly I am both the cook and the cooked, do I need to turn up the fire?
Or would you advise that I continue to simmer slowly?
Somehow, simmering slowly doesn't seem to be our way . . . .

Prem Arup, simmering slowly is certainly not our way. And you are wrong about feeling that you are the cook and the cooked: I am the cook, you are the cooked. So please leave it to me; you just get relaxed and be cooked.

You say: "I feel half-cooked. On the one hand I am happy, more blessed and blissful, more loving and loved than ever before – and I feel so thrilled about it. And on the other hand my old companions – jealousy, competitiveness, the need to be important, special – they are also still around."

Don't be worried about them, don't take them seriously. The more you take them seriously, the more you nourish them. Let them be around: just be playful with them. Your blissfulness, your being more loved and more loving will take care of the whole thing.

Qualities like jealousy exist only when you are not loved, when you are not capable of loving. Competitiveness, the need to be important, special,

they are all part of the same phenomenon: jealousy. They are not separate things, separate aspects. And if you are feeling blissful, happy, loved and loving, then there is no need to be worried: if you have light, the darkness will disappear on its own.

They are your old companions, so just out of habit they still come to see you. Be courteous; don't be angry about them, and don't try to push them away. Just watch – but watch joyously. Your watchfulness can also become serious, and that is a great problem: it should remain part of your playfulness . . . and jealousy cannot exist. And when you are blissful, who cares about being important? – you *are* important. And when you are loved and you are loving, who bothers about being special? These desires arise in people who don't have any taste of bliss, any taste of love.

It is true you are half-cooked – because these things are still coming; but even being half-cooked is a great phenomenon. The rest will also happen. And that is not your responsibility: I am the cook here, and I have | cooked so many people that you can trust me, Arup.

Beloved Bhagwan,

Looking back at this past year-and-a-half since I met You, it seems that I am flying out of control.
People think I am crazy, but I laugh as I tear away the pieces of my old life. And You've told me, that was
just for starters. My meditations are difficult . . . I am so excited and high most of the time.
Maybe You will give me some clue to quiet this bouncing heart.
Beloved Master, I've come this far and given up this much to be here now, to take sannyas and surrender
– what now?

Rich Frank, now you can retire. You have done the last thing – surrender. Now you are no longer there. Now it is my concern – you are completely free, because beyond surrender, there is nothing to be done.

Surrender means that you have dropped the ego, and now "You are flying out of control." It feels out of control because you have remained always *in* control. Now drop that control; now you are no longer the pilot; you have surrendered. And the sky is vast – there is no fear of your falling out of the sky.

You say that people think you are crazy. You are! I attract only crazy people. The so-called saints remain always at a distance.

When I was a student at the university one of my professors told me that it would be a great act of compassion towards him if I didn't come into his class: "As far as your attendance record is concerned, I will give you one hundred percent."

I said, "But what is the matter? I have joined the class, I have paid the fee for it."

He said, "You can take the fee from me, but just the idea of having you for two years in the class drives me crazy. The moment I see you, something in me starts trembling." And he was a very sane person, but people's

sanity is superficial: just a little scratch and they will go insane.

I don't want you to be superficially sane: I want you to drop all superficial sanity. Everybody will think you are crazy, but you are simply being natural; and nature is not crazy. To be natural is the authentic sanity: the more natural you become, the bigger will become the distance with the artificial society and the artificial people – but *you* will be becoming more and more sane.

When you reach to the very core of your being, you have attained the final sanity; but in the eyes of other people you will look absolutely mad. People have created their own game of sanity, and if you break their rules, immediately they condemn you as crazy. I am not here to condemn you, but to transform you. Your craziness is the beginning of your authentic sanity.

Don't be worried about what people say; remember only how you feel yourself. If you are feeling joyous, drunk with blissfulness, there is no need for any control. Control is dangerous, because control means you are not allowing your nature its flow. Control means you are cutting off . . . trying to force yourself to be a certain way, the way others expect you to be. People give respectability and honor to those who are following the rules of their game; they will not give you respectability, and they will not give you honor. But to be crazy and natural is so valuable that these bogus values of honor, respectability, reputation, don't have any meaning.

You cannot fly out of control; it is simply not possible. It is just that you have always remained in control, so just relaxing a little you become afraid.

It happened in the religious class of a small school: the teacher was telling the students to draw, according to them, the concept of God. She had been explaining to them the Christian concept of God. The bishop had come to see how things are going in the class, and she wanted to show something from the small boys and girls.

They had all drawn pictures, and one small boy had drawn a picture of an airplane with four windows. Even the bishop was struck: what kind of an idea of God does he have? And from every window something looking like a man . . . ?

The teacher said, "What is this? This is your idea of God?"

The boy said, "You have told us that God is a trinity: the first is God the Father – you can see . . . with the beard of ancient old age. In the second window is the son – you can even see the cross – Jesus Christ. In the third you don't see any face because it is the holy ghost – just something like a whirlwind."

The bishop and the teacher together asked him, "What about the fourth? From where has the fourth come?"

The little boy said, "The fourth? . . . Pontius the pilot. Without him the airplane will go out of control."

Don't be worried; nature itself takes care of you. You relax . . . and that is the meaning of surrender: that you relax and you allow nature to take you wherever it wants to take you. You don't have any plan, you don't have any guidebook, you don't have a certain goal, you don't have any desire to reach somewhere; wherever nature takes you will be your home, will be your destiny.

You are also worried that "my meditations are difficult . . . I am so excited and high most of the time. Maybe You will give some clue to quiet this bouncing heart." There is no clue; let it bounce as much as it can. And you are excited and high most of the time: enjoy it. Nobody can remain forever excited and high – and the more you are excited and high, the sooner you will be relaxed.

And right now – when you are so excited and high, with a bouncing heart – if you try to meditate, you are just trying something which is against your nature at this moment. Forget meditation for the moment. Meditation will come; first get tired.

When you are calm, you will see that meditation is happening. The heart is bouncing no more; you are not flying high; you are no longer excited; flat on the earth . . . and meditation begins. But first, let this whole energy be exhausted.

I once lived with a friend for a few days. He had a small son so full of energy, that it was impossible to talk. He was jumping into everything, throwing things, putting on the radio. My friend said: "What to do with this boy? He is so full of energy . . . ."

I said, "Don't be worried." I told the boy, "You just go around the house as many times as you can. Then you can ask for any reward, and I will give it to you."

He said, "Promise?"

I said, "Promise." He could go only seven times around the house and then he was flat on the ground.

I said, "What are you doing?"

He said, "Finished!"

I said, "What about your reward?"

He said, "I will think later on. Right now, don't disturb me."

His father said, "Strange . . . I have been telling him continually, not to disturb me! It is the first time *he* has said 'don't disturb me!' "

I said, "He has gone into meditation!"

You will also go into meditation. Everybody who is here is going to go into meditation, but first, jog and jump as high as you can; let your heart bounce . . . and don't be worried: when the energy is moving high, you cannot relax.

Many people asked me about the fact that they cannot sleep – and they have tried all kinds of methods: mantras, chanting, listening to music, but nothing helps.

I said, "These things won't help. You just go for two or three miles of jogging and jumping."

They said, "What? That will make us even more awake."

I said, "You don't understand the dialectics of life: after three miles you will find it is difficult to reach back home; you will start feeling so sleepy and so tired. So don't be worried: I will come with my car and I will pick you up; but I will pick you up only when I see that you are absolutely unable to reach home by walking. You will fall fast asleep anywhere on the street – in deep meditation."

You are new here. Just it will take a little time . . . but soon you will find that every day meditation becomes easier and easier. The energy just has to be exhausted. With so much energy, trying to meditate is just doing something which is impossible. So the clue is simple: allow this energy to have its dance – because when it is gone, then you will ask me, "Now, how to dance, how to sing?"

So while it is there, use it creatively. Meditation can wait a little. And here nobody will think you crazy, because there are far crazier people – you are just a beginner.

I have heard: in one prison, a man entered a cell in which there was another man lying by the side of the wall, resting. This man asked, "How long are you going to be here?" The newcomer said, "I have been sentenced to fifteen years."

The other said, "Then you remain near the door, because you will be getting out first. I have been sentenced to thirty years. So why take the trouble of coming too far inside? Just stay there, near the door. Fifteen years only . . . ?"

You are a newcomer, but you have come to the right place. Here, nobody will think you are crazy if you start jumping and dancing and singing on your own. Nobody is going to think that you are crazy – just a beginner – in the kindergarten.

Exhaust this energy; and then you will not ask how to meditate: you will find yourself flat on the ground and you will find meditation is happening.

Sometimes it has happened that people have thought that perhaps their hearts have stopped, or their breathing has stopped: the energy has been so exhausted that even to breathe or for the heart to beat, very little energy is left. Those are the moments when meditation is the easiest thing in the world. Always wait for the right time, for the right moment.

Beloved Bhagwan,

What's the difference between "letting go," "trusting that everything comes by itself," and "going for it," or "going with your energy"? Most of the time I find myself between not able to trust and unable to go for it. What to do?

Anand Virag . . . then remain in between. Don't do anything. If you find yourself in the middle of these two polarities – one is "let go," another is "go for it" – and you find yourself in between that is even better than either one of them. You have found the golden mean. Just remain there, don't do anything; and all that has to happen to you will happen on its own accord.

It is a very rare question. People find it very easy either to go for it, with effort, with will, with power, or to let go, to surrender, trust and relax. But to find yourself in between is far better than both. There is no need to do anything; there is no need to choose between the two; just remain in between, silent, and watch whatsoever happens. Nature, or existence, or God – any name will do – will take care of you .

If you do something, then it will be forcing, repressing the other, and choosing one against the other. The repressed part will remain within you; and whatever you have chosen is only one half: and there will be moments when you will start thinking, perhaps I have chosen the wrong thing, perhaps the other one was right.

So whatever you choose, if it is only half, you will always repent, because half can never give you fulfillment. The other half will always go on pinching you, it will take revenge, it will not allow you so easily to choose its opposite. It depends on different people.

For you it is not a question of choice: you already understand that you are exactly in between. And you are asking me for my suggestion, what to choose. I am never in favor of choosing anything. Remain choiceless; and wherever you are, relax at that stage, at that step, at that space . . . and remain a watcher. The moment you choose you become a doer – and my whole effort is somehow to hammer it into your head that you are not to be a doer.

Two old ladies went to the zoo. They approached a very dangerous gorilla. As the zoo-attendant was opening the door of the cage, the gorilla reached out and pulled one of the old ladies inside and attacked her savagely. The alarm was raised, and the old lady was rescued. She was taken to the hospital, where she made a slow recovery. After several weeks, her friend was visiting her and consoling her, saying that it was time to forget her ordeal and start living again.

"Ooohh," wailed the old lady, "but he never writes, he never phones."

Half-hearted . . . perhaps somebody has pulled her for the first time in her whole life. She must have been a Catholic nun.

Do not choose. Let your life remain a freedom, without choice. A choiceless freedom and awareness is the very essence of all spiritual growth.

Beloved Bhagwan,

Are You holding my hand or pulling my leg?

Devaprem, if it is me, I must be pulling your leg. Holding your hand is not going to help – because you are not to be pulled out; you have to be completely drowned.

This place is not for stepping higher, this place is for going deeper. And to take you deeper, naturally, I have to pull your leg. You are trying in every possible way to hold on to something, but there is nothing to hold on to. I make sure that there is nothing around you to hold on to – and then I push you. Not even satisfied by that, I start pulling your leg. One day you will be grateful for all the difficult tasks that I had to do for you.

Beloved Bhagwan,

At times the joy, the love, the silence. At other times it seems I've got a lunatic asylum in my head. Bhagwan, what to do?

Satgyana, become friendly with the lunatic in your head. I am against creating any antagonism in you, any kind of split, any schizophrenia.

You are saying, "At times the joy, the love, the silence. At other times it seems I have got a lunatic asylum in my head." Everybody has got that lunatic asylum – that is our heritage.

Your parents have given it to you, your priests have given it to you; your leaders, your teachers, your whole culture has given you only one thing as a heritage – and that is a lunatic asylum in your head.

But they are not responsible. The same has been done to them: every generation goes on giving all kinds of tensions and diseases, superstitions, madnesses, to the new generation. They don't have anything else to give. But you are fortunate that a part of your mind feels joy sometimes, and love, and silence. These are such powerful and potent forces that you need not pay any attention to the lunatic asylum.

Remember that paying attention is giving food. Ignore the lunatic asylum. Pour all the nourishment into your joy and into your love and into your silence. Don't leave anything for all the lunatics that are living in your head. They will start deserting you; they will start entering into somebody else's mind. There are always people who are very receptive; they are only receptive about lunatic things . . . so don't be worried that they will die or starve. They will find their way.

You should simply ignore them. Let them be there, but behave as if they are not, and pour all your energy – without holding anything back – into joy, into love, into silence. So the lunatic part of your mind will start shrinking on its own accord, will die out.

This is the difference between western psychology and the eastern exploration of man's interior being. Western psychology pays too much attention to the lunatic asylum – and that is giving food to it. You will not see Sigmund Freud talking about joy or love or silence or peace or blissfulness. In the whole literature of psychology you will not find these words even mentioned. They have their own vocabulary . . . schizophrenia, neurosis, psychosis.

Whenever a psychoanalyst looks at you, he is looking for the lunatic; he is not looking for anything that is sane in you. He goes on bringing more and more up, digging more and more into the lunatic part of your mind. He makes you convinced that you are completely mad.

The eastern approach is so totally different, and so healthy, that you will not find neurosis, psychosis, schizophrenia, split personality . . . all these words and their complex definitions, explanations . . . and there is not much difference in them either – but they are making so much fuss about all these things.

I have heard: somebody asked a great psychoanalyst, "What is the difference between psychosis and neurosis?" The great psychoanalyst said, "The difference is very subtle but very great. The psychotic thinks that two plus two are five; and the neurotic thinks two plus two are four but is uncomfortable about it." The difference is very subtle, but they are making so much business out of it.

The East has emphasized the healthier part in you, the joyous part in you, the spiritual part in you. My own experience is that whatever you pay attention to, starts growing. Attention is nourishment; and whatever you ignore starts dying out.

In a small experiment one psychoanalyst was trying to find out whether giving someone attention or ignoring them made any difference. The eastern concept is that they make a tremendous difference. So he raised two small monkeys. Both were given sufficient food, medical care, everything that is necessary. But one was ignored: nobody even petted him, nobody hugged him, nobody touched his head with love – this was a deliberate experiment. The other monkey was given so much attention: whoever passed by would say "hello" to him, just pat his head or hug him.

It was a very surprising revelation to the psychoanalyst who was working on it, that the monkey who was not given any attention started shrinking, and the monkey who was given love, attention and friendliness, was growing perfectly well. The ignored monkey died within three months, and the other lived a full life. The experiment has been done many times in different labs, but the same is the result.

Attention is invisible nourishment: when you look at somebody with love, with joy, with compassion, you are giving that person something which cannot be purchased, something which makes him feel needed, something which makes him feel worthy to exist. When the person is ignored, slowly, slowly the person starts feeling, "I am not needed; nobody even takes note of me. So why go on living?" He starts losing interest in being alive. And the moment you stop being interested in being alive, you cannot be alive for long, even if every physical necessity is fulfilled.

But there is some spiritual necessity. I call it the need to be needed. Somebody needs you and suddenly you feel a new upsurge of energy. The meditator starts feeling as if the whole of existence needs him: the trees need him, the mountains need him, the rivers need him. The ecstatic life of the mystic is based on this experience, that he is needed even by the faraway stars; that when the rose blossoms, it needs somebody to appreciate it.

I had a gardener once, absolutely uneducated, illiterate. But he knew something that even great botanists are not aware. He was a poor man, but every year his flowers were winning the competition in the city. I asked him, "What is your secret?"

He was my gardener, so he was looking after my plants. He felt a little embarrassed and said, "It would have been better if you had not asked." He was very shy.

I said, "Don't be worried, whatever it is, you just tell me."

For years nobody has been able . . . and there were many competitors in the city, but that poor gardener was always coming first with his flowers. His roses were so big and so juicy, so red, so fragrant . . . . He said, "I am an uneducated man; I don't know anything. All that I know is that I love my plants and, when there is nobody, I talk with them."

And he asked me, "Don't tell anybody; people will think I am mad. I talk with the roses, I sit with them and I tell them, 'You have to win the competition – this is a question of my whole prestige: for years I have been winning; don't let me down.' They have never failed me. They have always listened to me; and they always remembered that the competition has to be won for this poor old man, who loves them so much."

He has never found in his whole life any garden where he was given total freedom. He was so happy with me that he was writing again and again, " . . . wherever you go, just call me there, I don't ask anything, just food, even once a day will do, and I will grow your roses."

And it was not only roses, all kinds of beautiful flowers he grew. He had one plant which I think does not exist in the West. It is called the "queen of the night": it blossoms in the night, with very small flowers, but thousands of them. When they blossom you cannot see the leaves, only the flowers, just small white flowers.

His nightqueen was so fragrant that the neighbors even complained to me, "We cannot sleep because of the perfume. You have to remove this plant from here. The perfume is so strong that it keeps us awake. It is so beautiful, but we also need rest in the night." I have seen thousands of nightqueens in different places, but I have never known that so much fragrance could come out of a single plant and disturb the whole neighborhood.

I said, "That is not possible. You can move, you can go to hell, but that plant can not be removed, because my gardener does not treat the plants as plants, but as people. He has their names, he calls them by names." Slowly, slowly my gardener became aware that I don't think him crazy. So even in front of me, he will go on talking with his plants – working, watering, and talking.

Now even scientists have come up with the discovery, that plants understand your feelings. They understand your joy, they understand your sadness too. And they understand your ignoring them. If this is true about plants, then man's mind is far more sensitive.

So just remember one thing, ignore the lunatic asylum that you have in your head. Everybody has it, so it is nothing special. Just keep your back towards it. And pour your whole energy in the joy and love and silence and peace, in compassion, into friendliness.

You will be surprised that when your whole energy is transformed into these positive qualities, the negative qualities start disappearing like darkness. One should never make the problem of negative qualities, that is the beginning of a wrong journey. If you have something that you feel should not be there, even this much is giving attention to it, that it should not be there.

When I say, "Ignore!" I am simply saying, "Behave as if it is not there – and pour your whole energy into the positive world, into all those beautiful values, which make you not only human beings, but can even help you to transcend humanity and become a Gautam Buddha.

Okay Vimal,

Yes Bhagwan.

210

Work Can Produce, Silence Can Create

First you have to understand there is no guilt in existence anywhere; there may be mistakes, but no guilt at all. Guilt is a by-product of the idea of sin: that you are committing something sinful. The world wants you to be extroverts – workaholics, it wants you to continuously work and work and work. The world has no need, apparently at least, of those who sit silently, doing nothing. They also are needed – immensely needed – but to see it needs great understanding.

A man of silence, a man who can sit without any movement of his body or his mind, creates a certain vibration all around him which is very infectious. It helps people to be silent, to be relaxed. He is almost like an oasis in the desert. But because it is not visible, the world has never taken note of it.

You always feel guilty when doing nothing – and that is the greatest virtue in the world, not only in your body, but even in your mind. All doing stops: you are simply a presence.

So you have to drop that idea, which has been implanted in you by others. They wanted you to work because work is productive. They could not understand that doing nothing, being silent, has its own way of creating a certain atmosphere – which is far more valuable than any production.

Work can produce, silence can create.

February 21, 1987,   8 a.m.

Beloved Bhagwan,

Moving into aloneness, into such silence, peace and bliss, I suddenly realized that at the same time I was coming closer and closer to You. Dancing with Your love, never before have I been in such a space – coming home at last. But I have to go soon, and I am so afraid to lose it. I feel so fragile, so vulnerable. How can I take care of this treasure, help it to grow and share it at the same time over there?

Prem Vishva, the joy, the love, the blissfulness, the feeling of coming home – if this is true, you need not worry about losing it. The truth can only be found; it cannot be lost. That which can be lost was only your imagination. In any case, going away will be of tremendous help in understanding yourself.

Either you will find that whatever you were feeling here you are feeling wherever you are, or you will find that back in your own world, all that blissfulness and all that love disappears. Then it was just a figment of your imagination. Even to understand that is good, so next time when you come here you can avoid falling into the trap of imagination. As far as I can see, you have come to a space which you cannot lose even if you want to. And the only way to grow deeper into it is to share it with people.

Life needs continuous growth. The moment you stop its growth, it starts dying. So go into the world full of songs, full of dance and abundant love, and give it unconditionally, without any judgment, to anybody who is receptive – and you will go on growing in the experience both deeper and higher.

Something has happened – that much I can say to you. Now it depends on you to let it grow or not to let it grow. And the way of growth is very simple: share it. But the sharing should not be with any judgment on your part; the sharing is not to be done with those who deserve it. Love knows no discrimination between the deserving ones and the nondeserving ones. Love enjoys giving itself – it does not matter to whom. And the miracle of love is that whomsoever you give it to, becomes deserving.

Beloved Bhagwan,

I have a question about guilt. I can't see it, or taste it, or touch it, but somehow it is always there –
especially when I am doing nothing. It only disappears when I am working,
and returns immediately at the thought of dancing, or singing, or meditating.
What is the mechanism of guilt and will I ever be free of it?

P rem Prasado, the mechanism of guilt is very simple. You have been conditioned from your very childhood to believe that doing something is better than doing nothing – and meditation is going into nothingness. The idea has been imposed on you for so long it has taken roots in your mind. But because the idea is basically false, it can be dropped.

First you have to understand there is no guilt in existence anywhere; there may be mistakes, but no guilt at all. Guilt is a byproduct of the idea of sin: that you are committing something sinful. The world wants you to be extroverts – workaholics, it wants you to continuously work and work and work. The world has no need, apparently at least, of those who sit silently, doing nothing. They also are needed – immensely needed – but to see it needs great understanding.

A man of silence, a man who can sit without any movement of his body or his mind, creates a certain vibration all around him which is very infectious. It helps people to be silent, to be relaxed. He is almost like an oasis in the desert. But because it is not visible, the world has never taken note of it.

You always feel guilty when doing nothing – and that is the greatest virtue in the world, not only in your body, but even in your mind. All doing stops: you are simply a presence.

So you have to drop that idea, which has been implanted in you by others. They wanted you to work because work is productive. They could not understand that doing nothing, being silent, has its own way of creating a certain atmosphere – which is far more valuable than any production.

Work can produce, silence can create.

But it is very difficult, because the whole world around you is insisting that you *do* something. Don't just be useless. Remember the words of Rabindranath that we were talking about the other day: "I am useless; I can only sing, and my songs are purposeless." But Rabindranath has enriched this country more than any other individual in this century. Flowers don't have purposes, but a world without flowers will be a very mundane world.

Roses bring something of the beyond into the world – the beauty, the fragrance. They all have no purpose. But purpose is not the only thing life is for. Purpose is necessary for survival, but survival is not living. Living needs songs and dances and love and peace.

Flowers show that existence is so abundant with colors and fragrance, that it goes on sharing. A world without flowers, without poetry, without music, without painting, would not be worth living in. But for centuries the wrong people have ruled over humanity. In Mahatma Gandhi's ashram roses were not allowed. Even in the flower pots wheat was sown – because wheat has a purpose. Roses don't have any purpose. Mahatma Gandhi had the mind of a businessman.

Jesus says, "You cannot live by bread alone; something more is needed." Of course he means God is needed – but if you cannot even enjoy a rose flower, God is very far away from you. Have you ever thought : What is the purpose of God? Is there any utility in God? Even if you find him, what are you going to do with him? Decorate your sitting room?

Life needs work for survival, and to celebrate – silence, songs, music. They are higher values. You want to live for them – the work is for you to survive. But you want to survive because there are roses, and there are songs, and there are meditations, and there are worlds unknown and challenging to be explored. So I am not saying, don't work. But work is the minimum of life, and the state of not doing anything and just being a silent pool of energy is the maximum of living, because out of this silent pool everything that is beautiful arises.

Beloved Bhagwan,

I finally got the courage to expose myself. Help! I am falling apart! My head wants something, my heart something else, my being yet something different, and my body something else. While taking decisions in worldly matters they are not in tune with each other. My head, mind, heart, being and body never agree on one thing. So, beloved Master, when I cannot be in harmony with myself, how can I be in harmony with You and existence?
Bhagwan, please harmonize me!

Yoga Pragya, I can understand that your body, your mind, and your heart are not in harmony. But your being – you have only heard the word; you don't know anything about it. If you had known your being, everything would have been harmonized immediately.

Being is such a great power that neither the heart can go against it, nor the head, nor the body. So leave the being apart – because that is the solution. You have to find your being, and the finding of the being will harmonize your existence.

Right now, when you find body, mind and heart in disharmony, first listen to the body. None of the so-called saints will say this to you : First listen to the body. The body has a wisdom of its own, and the body is uncorrupted by the priests; the body is unpolluted by your teachers, by your education, by your parents. Begin with the body, because right now the body is the purest thing in you. So if the heart and the mind go against it, let them go. You follow the body. The body is the first harmony and the being is the last.

The fight is always between the heart and the head. The body and being are never in conflict – they are both natural. The body is visible nature and the being is invisible nature, but they are part of one phenomenon.

Mind and heart are in conflict, because the mind can be polluted, corrupted – and that's what all the religions and all the cultures have been doing: corrupting your mind. They cannot corrupt your heart. But they have managed a different technique for the heart: they have bypassed it, they have ignored it. They have not nourished it; they have tried in every way to weaken it, condemn it.

So what you have, in fact, is your head, which goes against your body – because all the cultures are against the body – and the body is your home. Your heart is part of the body, and your head is also part of the body – but the head is capable of being influenced, being conditioned. The heart is beyond the reach of other people, only you can reach it.

So begin with the body – first follow the body. The

body will never misguide you, you can trust it – and you can trust it absolutely. Anything that goes against the body is forced upon you by others. That is a good criterion to find out what has been forced on you. Whatever goes against the body is forced on you, it is foreign. You should throw it out.

Your mind is full of foreign elements; your mind is not in its natural state. It can also come into a natural state – and then it will not be against the body, it will be in tune with it. So begin with the body and use it as a criterion.

It is a very simple process; follow the body. Slowly, slowly the mind starts dropping anything that is anti-body. It *has* to drop. It is not its nature, it is carrying it in spite of itself. It is the load that dead humanity has left for you as a heritage.

Following the body, you will be surprised that for the first time you see two things happening: First the head starts dropping conditioning, and second, as the head starts dropping conditioning, you hear for the first time the still small voice of the heart, which was drowned by the noisy head. Because the head is becoming a little more calm, a little more silent, you can hear the heart.

First listen to the body, so all that is gross in your mind will be dropped, and you will start listening to the heart. It is not against the body, because nobody can condition your heart, there is no approach from the outside to the heart. You will be amazed to see that your heart and your body are in harmony. And when this harmony happens, the head is completely finished, it has no power over you. Now you know a new power, purer, more natural, more authentic; and the head drops even its subtle conditioning.

The day the head also becomes silent and comes in tune with the heart and the body, that day you will discover your being – not before it. And once you have discovered your being, you need not try to harmonize anything. The very presence of the being harmonizes everything. The very experience is so vast that your body, your heart, your mind, all lose their identities in the vastness of your being.

But begin with the body. All the religions are saying just the opposite: Oppose the body, don't follow the body, the body is the enemy. That is their strategy to destroy you, because they have taken away the basic element from where you could have grown towards harmony. You will remain always in discord, without harmony. You will never come to know your being, and your whole life will be just anguish, anxiety – tensions of thousands of kinds.

The religions have already given you the clue as to how they have destroyed you: making your mind work against the body has been their strategy. I am saying to you: Start with the body. It is your home. Love it, accept it, and in that very love, in that very acceptance, you are growing towards harmony. This harmony will lead you to being. And once the being is discovered, then you are relieved of all effort. Harmony becomes just your nature – one voice, one organic unity.

Beloved Bhagwan,

How to be with the work and the silence together, friendliness and aloneness, excitement and calmness at the same time?

Deva Majnu, you never ask how to be together with your two eyes, how to be together simultaneously with your two hands, or your two legs. Certainly the same is true about the deeper things of life: work and silence together. What is the problem? You can chop wood – of course there will be the noise of chopping wood, but you can remain silent. Your silence has nothing to do with it. It is not disturbed by chopping the wood. In fact, if your total energy is involved in chopping the wood, you will find you are silent. That's why I insist: Be total when you are doing something. In this totality you will simultaneously find your silence.

You are asking how to be alone and friendly together. Have you ever seen that freak of nature, two children born joined together? Their only use is to be exhibited in museums, in carnivals. Otherwise their life is not a life – they are joined too closely. For friendship a closeness is needed and also a distance; in fact, in a living relationship you are always coming close and going far away, coming close and going far away – without destroying each other's individuality.

Aloneness is individuality. And only individuals can be friends. You cannot be friends with someone you have become identified with, that is not friendship. Either you are dominated by the other or you dominate the other. That is a relationship of the owner and the owned, of the possessor and the possessed.

Friends never possess each other. The most fundamental thing in friendship is to give freedom to the other to be himself. There is a trust, there is no need to dominate the other; there is no need to chain him – through conditions – for tomorrow. Between two friends only one thing exists that bridges them, and that is trust; but it does not bind them.

Your question is meaningless. You don't understand what you are asking. Perhaps that's what happens in the world; even friendship becomes like marriage – expectations, demands . . . .

In the Middle Ages, people of the upper classes in Europe were so concerned with the chastity of their wives that they invented a lock; so if they were going for a few days out of town, they would lock up the wife's sexual organs. She can urinate, but she cannot make love. Those locks are still available and visible in European museums – a great invention!

A warrior was going to war and he was very worried. Finally he locked up his wife. It was just like a belt, which made it impossible for any man to make love to the wife. And then he thought that in the war he might lose the key somewhere, so he went to his best friend and told him, "I am going to war, it may take two, three months for me to come back. I trust you – you keep this key. I have locked up my wife so she cannot make love to anyone. When I come, I will take the key back."

And he was lighthearted, that now there was no problem. As he was getting out of the city he heard the hooves of a horse following him, so he looked back. His friend was rushing, and he said, "Wait! You have given me the wrong key!" Just five minutes have passed . . . ! This is the type of friendship that exists in the world.

Very few people know the joys of friendliness. It makes no demands, it expects nothing – and then there is no problem: you can be alone and you can be full of friendliness. It is one of the most spiritual experiences.

You are also asking how to be in excitement and calmness at the same time. You can try it in two ways:

216

either be excitedly calm or be calmly excited. I don't see any problem in it, I have tried it both ways – it works. Do you think I am not excited about you, your future, your potential, your growth? I am as excited as any gardener about his plants – but that does not disturb my calmness.

These are just like two wings of a bird: they appear to be opposite to each other, but they both are needed for the flight of the bird.

And to know this secret of transforming contradictions into complementaries is one of the most important alchemical mysteries.

So whenever you see two things that are contradictory and you want both, you have just to find a link that transforms them from contradictions into complementaries.

And you will be surprised that there are no contradictions in existence; there are only complementaries – but they look to us like contradictions. The tree grows higher, but its roots go deeper. If the tree was also a philosopher it would be puzzled: how to maintain this contradiction of growing higher and lower simultaneously? But because trees are not philosophers, very simple people, they go on growing higher and they go on growing lower simultaneously.

Beloved Bhagwan,

Would You please speak about the the differences between wanting, desiring, and longing?

Prem Purna, the dictionary meaning of all these three words will be the same, but not the existential meaning. The existential meanings are so different from each other that it is amazing what these linguists, experts in language and grammar, go on doing.

Wanting implies a very clear-cut idea of the object: what you want. It is not vague. You want a house, you want a wife, you want children – the object of wanting is very clear.

Desiring is vague: the object of desire is not clear. You want power – you desire respectability, honor; you desire to be the greatest man in the world.

Wanting is simpler, and there is a possibility you may be able to fulfill it – because it is not an impossible task to have a house, a wife, children. In fact, it is impossible *not* to have them.

But desire is vague: respectability is not an object, but just an idea; honor is not an object, but just an idea;

to be the greatest man is not an object, but just an idea. And even the greatest people – the world may think they are greatest – are unhappy deep down in themselves.

For example, the founder of the Russian Revolution, Lenin, can certainly be called a great man; even his enemies would agree about that. But he was constantly worried, embarrassed, because his legs were short, and his upper body was bigger; they were not in proportion. When he used to sit on a chair, his legs would dangle, they would not reach the ground. So he was always hiding his legs, sitting very close to the table. His table was always covered with cloths, so nobody could see his dangling feet. But whether anybody else saw them or not, he knew . . . .

I don't think that there was any problem – but it remained in his mind as a deep inferiority complex. Perhaps it was this inferiority complex that drove him to become a great revolutionary in the world: if he had

had normal legs, perhaps he would not have been a revolutionary.

Desire is vague; and longing is totally different from wanting and desire. Wanting and desire are both of the head: one is for a clear-cut object, another for vague ideals. Longing is of the heart, not of the mind. It is the heart that longs, and feels the pain of longing. The heart has no business with money or power; the heart's longing is only for love . . . and ultimately for God,

which is the purest form of love, and nothing else. It is a good exercise to contemplate the differences between words which appear to be similar. It will give you clarity.

Longing is just a thirst, and it is beautiful. Desire is ugly, because it is always competitive – jealous of those who have it, when you don't have it. It is ugly because it can do any sort of harm to anybody in order to fulfill itself. It is violent. Wanting is ordinary and mundane – middle class.

Beloved Bhagwan,

When we dissolve into the universal consciousness, and yet retain our individuality,
will we still be able to recognize our friends?
Will I be able to recognize You?
There are some people I just don't want to let go of.

Prem Arup, the people that you just don't want to let go of you will not be able to find because they also need freedom.

In the universal consciousness you can meet only out of freedom, out of pure love. The very idea of not letting them go is anti-freedom. You want to keep the possession in your hands even in the universal consciousness, when individualities have dissolved. Those will be the first people to disappear. They will slip out of your grip.

As far as *I* am concerned, there is no problem. You will be able to recognize me, because between me and you there is no question of possessiveness. The more nonpossessive a friendship you have, the greater the possibility to feel and recognize the essential core of the individual, because all outer forms will have disappeared, will be gone; only the essential core will be there, unembodied. Only out of freedom, out of love, is there a possibility of recognition.

You are asking, "Will we still be able to recognize

our friends?" You are not aware: somebody is a friend today, tomorrow he becomes your enemy; somebody was an enemy yesterday and today he has become your friend. Friends turn into enemies; enemies turn into friends. Unless you have a friendliness which is already eternal, here – now, you will not be able to recognize them.

Whatever you can make eternal, here – now, you will be able to recognize in the hereafter.

And this is good. I have heard about a man who married eight times. Now to get recognized by eight wives simultaneously in the universal consciousness . . . that man will try somehow to fall back into the world! he will not want such universal consciousness, where eight wives are torturing him.

Whatever is pure here will remain pure whatever world you are in. So think of making friendliness completely free of impurity; think of love as only a gratitude, not a demand. All demanding relationships, all expecting relationships will be dissolved. Only the purest relationships – just the sheer joy in the individuality of the other – will be remembered and recognized. And it is good . . . because you have lived so many lives: you have had so many husbands, so many wives, so many friends, so many enemies . . . it has been difficult to deal with them separately. Thousands of lives, and their relationships, in the universal consciousness would crush you, destroy you.

Even Christian theologians have become worried about the last judgment day. Bertrand Russell started the question when he wrote the book, *Why I am Not a Christian*. He pointed out all the fallacies of Christian theology – and one of the fallacies is the last judgment day.

Bertrand Russell was a mathematician. He could not conceive how millions and millions and millions of people can all be judged in one day. And half of them will be women, screaming and trying to find their husbands . . . and they have all had many husbands in many lives and many wives in many lives and they will be quarreling with each other and fighting with each other . . . they will drive God mad. Bertrand Russell says, "That's why the last judgment day goes on being postponed. It is never going to happen."

All the people who are in their graves . . . and they are not a small number: wherever you are sitting there are at least eight people underneath you in their graves. And God will wake all these people up from their graves? First, waking up all these people from their graves will take much time; one day will not do. And people who have been sleeping for centuries . . . even to wake someone up in the morning who has been sleeping for only six or eight hours is a difficult job. People who have been sleeping for millions of years – to wake them up is not going to be simple!

And then the whole gathering will be so big, it will be a real congregation. And everybody will be rushing, finding . . . because in one thousand lives you had one thousand wives, and each of your wives has one thousand husbands – not only you. It is going to be such a quarrelsome day that nobody is going to bother about judgment. And how will God manage?

I agree with Bertrand Russell that the last judgment day is not going to happen, just because it is mathematically impossible.

It is good that you forget all of them; only the purest is remembered – and you don't have much that is pure. So don't just wait for the hereafter; if you want to recognize someone, purify your relationship with the person. Give him absolute freedom – and don't be dominated by him either. Remain absolutely free. Only two freedoms, two alonenesses, two meditators, meeting together for no reason but just sheer joy, will be able to recognize each other.

But Arup, about me you can be certain: whether you recognize me or not, I will recognize you.

Okay, Vimal?

Yes, Bhagwan.

Miracles Are Mostly Fiction

Changing water into wine is a criminal act, not a miracle. But without water I have seen my people so drunk; in their drunkenness they realize their divineness. But I have not been doing anything. I have not been here for many years. The day I disappeared, miracles started happening around me. Love has blossomed, people have become awakened from their sleep of many lives.

But you cannot attribute them to me. At the most my presence is just a catalytic agent. Perhaps it triggers something in you; transforms you, brings to you new dreams, and new realities, and new spaces. But remember, you are not to be grateful to me. You have to be grateful to existence itself, that it has given you the opportunity. The people who claim miracles for themselves are not religious people. They don't know even the taste of spirituality.

The spiritual person is absent as a person and present only as a presence – just a light. It all depends on you to become aflame from that light or not to become aflame. That light is available, you can use it and become light yourself; it is your decision. Hence, if you want to see a miracle, you can see it happening in your own life. All other miracles are mostly fiction.

February 21, 1987,   7 p.m.

Beloved Bhagwan,

You have spoken to us of the raising of Lazarus, and the miracle of Jesus walking on the water.
But what of the miracle that is Yourself?
You have turned tigers into lambs, gorillas into buddhas,
worriers and thinkers into mindlessness, and created an oasis out of a desert.
Please Bhagwan, speak to us of the miracle of miracles that is Yourself!

Zareen, I do not believe in miracles, but still miracles happen. Because I do not believe in them, I cannot claim to be the doer. At the most I am also a watcher.

The miracles that Jesus did are trivia: walking on the water, or turning water into wine, or bringing Lazarus from death back to life. To me they are not miracles.

I am reminded of one of the greatest mystics this land has produced: Ramakrishna. He was one of the simplest men possible. One day a great saint who was well known for his miracles came to see him. Ramakrishna was sitting on the river bank in Dakshineshwar near Calcutta, where the Ganges becomes so huge and so beautiful. The saint was very proud of the miracles that he used to do. And he had come with the specific purpose of showing Ramakrishna that his religiousness is worthless.

He said with great pride and ego in his heart, "What are you doing sitting under a tree? Let us go for a walk on the Ganges, on the waters."

Ramakrishna said, "You have come a long way. Just rest a little and then we can go for a walk on the Ganges."

The man sat down and Ramakrishna said, "Can I ask one thing: how long it took you to learn the art of walking on water?"

The man said, "Almost thirty-six years."

Ramakrisha laughed and he said, "When I want to go to the other shore – just two paise, and that too, the boat-man never takes from me, seeing that I am a poor man. Thirty-six years you have wasted on an art which is only worth two paise. You must be an idiot."

Even if you can walk on water, it does not make you spiritual, it does not give you a glimpse of the divine. On the contrary it takes you further away from God. You become more egoistic, because you can do something which others cannot do.

Jesus brings Lazarus back to life. Naturally it appears to be a great miracle – but it is not, because Lazarus is not transformed, and living a few years more, repeating the old routine again, he has to die. His being brought back to life has not given him anything of the eternal. The same story is repeated in Gautam Buddha's life, and there you can see the difference between a real miracle and a pseudo miracle.

A young son died, and that son was the only hope for his mother. The father had died, his other brothers and sisters had died and the mother was living only for this boy. And this boy too, died. The mother went almost mad. She was crying and weeping and asking everybody, "Tell me the address or the name of a physician who can heal my boy back, because I cannot live, I have no reason to live anymore. I have been carrying so many wounds: my other children died, my husband died. But I kept myself in control, just for this small, beautiful boy, and now he has also gone."

Somebody said, "Don't be worried, Gautam Buddha has come in the town just today. He is staying outside the town in the mango grove. You take the boy to Gautam Buddha."

The woman, with great hope and great longing went to Gautam Buddha, taking the corpse of the dead boy. She put the dead body at Gautam Buddha's feet and said, "If you are really spiritual, if you are awakened, then give my child his life back."

Gautam Buddha said, "That is not difficult. Just one small condition you have to fulfill."

The woman said, "I will fulfill any condition."

He said, "It is not a big condition. I know your whole village grows crops of mustard seed. You go and bring from some home just a handful of mustard seeds."

The woman started running; she said, "I will be coming back within a few minutes."

Buddha said, "You have not heard the whole condition. The condition is: the mustard seed should come from a family where nobody has ever died."

The woman was in such misery, she could not see the point. She rushed from one home to another. And people said, "We can give as many mustard seeds as you want. We can bring the whole village's mustard seeds, if your son's life can come back. But our mustard seeds will not be of any help, because so many people have died in our family, and you cannot find a family where nobody has died."

The number of dead people in every family is more than the number of the living. Your fathers died, your forefathers died, and so on, and so forth – since Adam and Eve people have been doing nothing but dying. The queue is so long behind each person – of dead people.

But she went from house to house and slowly, slowly, by the evening she became aware. Her tears dried up; she came back to Gautam Buddha, touched his feet, and said, "Forget about the boy, in this world everybody has to die. It does not matter when one dies. You initiate me as a sannyasin, so that I can experience something of the deathless, something of the immortal, something of the eternal that lives forever."

Buddha said, "You are intelligent and you have understood my point."

The woman became a sannyasin, and not an ordinary sannyasin. She became enlightened before Buddha died. She was his first woman enlightened disciple, Kisha Gautami was her name. I call this a miracle.

Apparently, it seems, bringing Lazarus back to life is a miracle. But what is the point? He will die again; you have not given him the taste of immortality. Real miracles are invisible to the ordinary mind. I don't believe in these miracles, because they are not miracles.

Zareen, you are asking about my miracle. I have never done anything deliberately, because to do anything deliberately is to go against the natural flow of existence. I am in a total let-go. Yes, things have been happening around me. I cannot take the credit for those things, because I have not *done* anything.

People have come to know for the first time the mysteries of love, the mysteries of life. People have entered into their very interiority, into their subjectivity, where one meets oneself.

And that is the greatest miracle in the world, to meet oneself.

People have become silent, serene, calm and quiet. People have become one organic unity. Such a deep harmony has happened to them that their whole life is resounding with music and poetry.

I have seen the crippled, and almost everybody is crippled by society, gaining strength and dancing in abandon. Dancing to the point where the dancer disappears and only dancing remains. Singing to the point where the singer disappears and only singing remains.

These are the moments which open the doors of the divine. These are the moments you are no more your ordinary self, you become part of the ultimate, of the universal self.

These are miracles. Changing water into wine is a criminal act, not a miracle. But without water I have seen my people so drunk; in their drunkenness they realize their divineness. But I have not been doing anything. I have not been here for many years. The day I disappeared, miracles started happening around me. Love has blossomed, people have become awakened from their sleep of many lives.

But you cannot attribute them to me. At the most my presence is just a catalytic agent. Perhaps it triggers something in you; transforms you, brings to you new dreams, and new realities, and new spaces. But remember, you are not to be grateful to me. You have to be grateful to existence itself, that it has given you the opportunity.

The people who claim miracles for themselves are not religious people. They don't know even the taste of spirituality.

The spiritual person is absent as a person and present only as a presence – just a light. It all depends on you to become aflame from that light or not to become aflame. That light is available, you can use it and become light yourself; it is your decision. Hence, if you want to see a miracle, you can see it happening in your own life. All other miracles are mostly fiction. Nobody has ever walked on water. It is not only about Jesus – it is about anybody; Mahavira, or Buddha, or Bodhidharma, or Zarathustra, many miracles are attributed to them – and those miracles are such trivia. The real miracles remain invisible, unrecorded in history because only the person who goes through the process of the miracle knows it, and even he cannot prove it, he cannot give any evidence for it.

I have been a watcher here. I have seen you change from death to life, I have seen you change from darkness to light, I have seen seen you change from a life of lies to the glory of truth. But I am a watcher, I am not a doer, the whole credit goes to existence itself.

Beloved Bhagwan,

I thought You would like this poem by Rumi.
We are the mirror as well as the face in it,
We are tasting the taste this minute of eternity,
We are pain and what cures pain both,
We are the sweet cold water and the jar that pours.

Prem Prasado, Jalaluddin Rumi is one of the greatest Sufi mystics. He is the only mystic whom Sufis have called Mevlana. Mevlana means, our Beloved Master.

A few people I love immensely. Mevlana Jalaluddin Rumi is one of them, and the reason I love him is that he was not life-negative, but life-affirmative. And the meditation that he has found and which has continued for seven hundred years among a small stream of mystics was the meditation of a certain kind of dance. His followers are called whirling sufis.

You must have seen small children – they like to whirl; and everybody stops them, because the fear of the parents is that the child may fall, may have a fracture, may get hurt. But in spite of all prohibitions, children love to whirl. And nobody has inquired why children love, all over the world, irrespective of race, nation, religion, why children love to whirl.

Jalaluddin Rumi, seeing children whirl, thought that there must be something that the children feel but they cannot express, and perhaps they are not fully aware what it is. So he tried whirling himself, and he was amazed that if you go on whirling there comes a moment when the center of your being remains static and your whole body, mind, brain, everything, whirls.

And that center which does not whirl, is you, the center of the cyclone. The whirling is almost like a cyclone, but exactly in the middle of the cyclone you will find a point which has not moved at all. Every wheel needs a center on which to turn, and the center has to remain unturning. You see in bicycles, in bullock carts, wherever there is a wheel, there is something in the center which is unmoving.

Once Jalaluddin became aware that you can find the unmoving center of your being, he tried for thirty-six hours non-stop, without eating, without drinking – he was determined to whirl to his absolute capacity, not to hold back anything . . . unless he falls, he is not going to stop. Thirty-six hours he whirled, a great crowd watched. The crowd went on changing; people had to go to eat and then they came again. People had to do their work and then they came again; thirty-six hours is a long period. And after thirty-six hours he fell down. And people heard a great laughter.

Jalaluddin was laughing loudly, and he said, "You think *you* have seen me falling, I have also seen myself falling. These thirty-six hours I have not moved a single inch. Now I don't have to go to Mecca in search of God, I have found him. In the unmoving center of my own being, he is."

The followers of Rumi don't have great scriptures, don't have any rituals, except whirling, and a few beautiful poems by Jalaluddin Rumi, which he used to sing after whirling and falling. He will get up and he will be so drunk – in that drunkenness he will sing a song, and those songs have been collected. That is the only literature the followers of Rumi have.

These lines are also from one of the poems of Rumi. Each sentence is impeccable – not only true, but also utterly beautiful.

We are the mirror, that's what I have been saying to you again and again; that we are not the doer, we are

225

only the mirror. Don't get identified with your doings, with your actions; remain a witness, just a watcher. But we are not taught the most essential things of life, we are taught all kinds of stupid things.

The most essential is the art of watchfulness.

I have heard, a drunkard came home in the night. And however drunk you may be, the closer you come to home, as you remember your wife, you almost start becoming sober . . . just the remembrance. And that day was special, because the wife had got so tired . . . in the middle of every night he will come, and she will have to get up and open the door, and then the fight . . . . So she had given him the key that day and told him, "Now behave! When you come home be as silent as possible."

So he was moving very silently – and a policeman was watching. He thought, This is strange, it is his own house, and he is going as if he is a thief. And finally the drunk tried hard to find the lock. Somehow he managed to find the lock, holding the lock in one hand and the key in another, but he could not manage to make the key enter into the lock. Both his hands were shaking. He said, "This is strange. Is there anybody to help me? The house is shaking."

The policeman came and he said, "What is the matter?"

He said, "You just hold the house for a moment, so I can open the lock."

The policeman laughed. He said, "You just give me the key and I will open the lock." So the policeman opened the lock.

The drunkard wanted no trouble that day. The wife had been really very graceful in giving the key. But on the way he had been fighting with another drunkard, and the other drunkard had scratched him, and blood was oozing from many places in his face. So first he entered into the house, very cautiously – but he stumbled, and the wife said, "Who is there?"

Suddenly he remembered his wife's dog, so he just went close to the bed, and started rubbing his nose and his tongue on her feet. So she thought that it was the

dog, turned and went back to sleep. Then he entered the bathroom, looked into the mirror and said, "My God, in the morning she will find out; so many places blood is coming, where that friend of mine has scratched . . . ." So he took some ointment that was there in the bathroom and put the ointment on every scratch, covering it completely, so that in the morning the wife cannot find out.

And in the morning when the wife went into the bathroom, she shouted, "You idiot! You come here. Who has destroyed my mirror? Who has painted it with the ointment?" This was his doing. Seeing the face in the mirror, naturally he went on putting the ointment on the face in the mirror.

You are not a drunkard, but spiritually you are all asleep. And unless you become a watcher of your own actions, of your dreams, of your thoughts, of your desires – there is no way of transformation, of becoming awake, getting out of this rut of sleep which you have continued in for many lives.

Rumi is right when he says, "We are the mirror, as well as the face in it."

We are the watcher and the watched. There is no separation between us and existence. We are part of one whole, just as my two hands are part of one organic unity. I can manage that they fight with each other. I can manage that they are friendly, loving and warm to each other. I can hit one hand with the other hand and wound it.

When you are seeing the tree, or the moon, or the river, or the ocean, you are the mirror and the mirrored too. It is one existence.

This is the basic conclusion of all the mystics, that the whole of existence is one entity, there is no duality. All duality deep down is joined into one existence.

We are the mirror as well as the face in it.

We are tasting the taste this minute of eternity.

Just be watchful this minute. In this silence you are tasting something which is beyond time.

We are tasting the taste of this minute of eternity.
We are pain, and what cures pain, both. We are agony

and we are ecstasy. We are hell and we are heaven, because there is no contradiction in existence. They are all joined together. *We are the sweet cold water and the jar that pours it.*

You can find many contradictions in life. And you can also find that they are all complementaries.

It is something very strange, that all the mystics, whether they were born thousands of years ago, or they are alive today, all fundamentally agree on the essential points of spiritual growth and realization.

For example: the silence, this minute, gives you not an explanation – but it gives you an experience.

Dancing and singing, allow yourself to be so completely overwhelmed that nothing is left behind. And you have entered into the temple of God, where you are the mirror, and you are the face mirrored in it; where you are the seeker and you are the sought; where you are the devotee and you are the God at whose feet you are offering yourself.

It happened in Ramakrishna's life . . . a very strange incident. One great painter wanted to paint the picture of Ramakrishna. After great persuasion Ramakrisha agreed. When the painting was complete, the painter brought it to offer to Ramakrishna. As he gave the painting to Ramakrishna . . . Ramakrishna touched the feet in the painting with his head. The painter could not believe it. He had heard that that man is mad, but now there was no question: he is certainly mad, touching his own feet with his head! Even his disciples became embarrassed. A great silence fell. Finally one disciple asked, "It is your own painting, your own picture – and you are touching its feet with your head? You do such things . . . people think you are mad, and you give them every kind of evidence. Even we become embarrassed when people ask us, 'Why do you go to Ramakrishna, can't you find anybody else who is sane?'"

Ramakrishna said, "Have I committed any wrong? I have not touched my own feet. I have touched the feet – because the painting is of somebody who is in deep silence, in samadhi, in tune with God. You are right, I must be mad, because now I recognize it is my own picture. But at that moment I only felt that the painter has done a great job. He has not only caught the body of the person, but also his spirit." And Ramakrishna kept that painting his whole life, just behind his bed. It is still there.

While his wife was alive she used to make the bed every day, even after his death. She used to bring food to his room. She used to cook all those delicious things that Ramakrishna liked.

People started saying, "One madman is dead, now this mad woman . . . " Sharda was her name. Even disciples of Ramakrishna used to ask her, "When he is dead, what is the point of twice every day making food for him, every night, making his bed?"

She said, "Should I believe you, or should I believe him? Because when he was dying, I asked, 'Are you really dying?' And he said, 'Nobody dies. And you need not change your dress.' " This is the custom among the Hindus, that the widow cannot use colored clothes, she cannot use ornaments, she has to shave her head.

Ramkrishna said, "You are not to do anything, because I am not going to die, I'm simply leaving the body, but I will be here, now, always."

"So whom I am to believe?" Sharda used to say. "And if he is always here now, I cannot resist the temptation of preparing things that he used to like. I may not be able to see him, but he must be able to see me, and that is what is significant – not that I should see him, but that he is watching. And for his whole life his teaching was a simple word: watchfulness."

We are the mirror as well as the face in it.

Beloved Bhagwan,

I can see through Your game: You are giving me enough rope to hang myself. I will gladly do it, but I can't find my neck. But You are not going to get rid of me that easily. I don't know anything about 'being a Buddha,' but I do know the mind-destroying laughter and dance of being Your sannyasin . . . my God, it's the same thing!

Devageet, it is the same thing. You need not know anything about the Buddha. If you can dance totally, if you can laugh totally, if you can surrender yourself to existence – that is what I mean by a sannyasin: one who is surrendered. Then nothing else remains for you to do. That's what makes you divine, that's what makes you a Buddha.

You are saying, "I can see through your game." Just a little bit. If you had seen the whole game, you would not have asked the question. You are saying that I am giving you enough rope to hang yourself, and you are ready to do it gladly – but you can't find your neck. Devageet, you have already hanged yourself. Where can you find your neck? It is gone. You only have the rope.

You are also saying, "You are not going to get rid of me that easily." That's why I say, you are seeing only just a little bit of the game. You are no longer there. In laughing, in dancing, in singing, you have hanged yourself, and now there is no question of getting rid of you.

The problem arises only with those people who dance half-heartedly. Who hang, but hang themselves half-heartedly.

I have heard the story of Mulla Nasruddin, who was going to commit suicide. He always consults me on serious problems, and he said, "I am going to commit suicide."

I said, "That's very good, because one man less – the world is better. And anyway, you have lived long enough, this is time."

He said, "Any suggestions?"

I said, "Don't take any chances. Take a rope, go to the river, you know a high cliff . . . and just on the cliff there is a big tree. So you hang yourself from the tree. Most probably you will succeed, but you are not a great success in life, you have always been a failure, so also take a tin of kerosene oil. Hang yourself first, then pour the oil on yourself. And just now somebody has brought a gift for me: a lighter, so you take this lighter and set fire to yourself. And don't forget to take your gun. If everything fails, shoot yourself in the head."

He said, "That's good. Now there is no chance of missing." I said, "Only one method is enough, and I am coming behind you, if there is some need. I will help you."

He said, "You are a great friend. Because I have asked other friends, and everybody said : Don't talk about such things, never even think of suicide, and you are suggesting all these things. You have presented me with a beautiful cigarette lighter."

So I went with him, I just said, "There, you try."

He put the rope around his neck, but half-heartedly. He had to do it, because I was there watching. And then he poured the kerosene oil; and he went on looking at me, and he put the fire . . . . And then he shot, but not into his head, he shot the rope – so he fell into the river. The fire was gone, because of the river. And I shouted, "It is okay, you drown!"

He said, "I cannot do that because I know swimming." And he came out.

I said, "You are something. When you wanted to die, why did you start swimming?"

He said, "You have never tried such a thing, I did

everything, because of you! And then when I got the chance to swim out of the river I did not miss. Here is your lighter, you keep it. It may help somebody else."

But I said, "What about your suicide?"

He said, "Who wants to commit it?"

But I said, "You had come to ask me."

He said, "Just by the way I wanted to be informed about . . . one never knows. One should collect all kinds of information. But you are such a man, you became so insistent with me, that rather than giving me information, you forced me to have an experience!"

I said, "That's my weakness. People ask me for explanations, and I try to give them experiences."

Devageet, you are finished. You cannot even swim out of the ocean of my dancers and my singers and my musicians, and my sannyasins. There is no hope.

So just relax and drop that rope, it is useless now for you. It may be useful for somebody else, because new people are coming every day.

Beloved Bhagwan,

I'm getting more and more dizzy . . . with trying to follow You up to the sunlit peaks, taking a jump, then suddenly floating down the watercourse way. And before I drown in the ocean, You're dragging me out to dance till the dancer is gone. If we ever pause for breath, should I check that the grass is still growing by itself?

Anand Dhiren, you need not worry about it, that is my business.

The grass is growing by itself perfectly well. You don't worry about the grass, you just dance totally. That's how small things become disturbances. Worrying about the grass, whether it is growing or not, will disturb your dance, will disturb your meditation. You leave this to me.

For what I am sitting here? Just to keep an eye that the grass goes on growing. And I have put a net all around . . . you think it is to prevent the mosquitoes from coming in? You are wrong. It is to prevent dancers from going out and destroying the grass!

Okay, Vimal?

Yes, Bhagwan.

I Am Nothing But Pure Champagne

Your mind has lived within you as the master. You have given it all your respect; you have listened to it against your heart; you have followed it against your nature. It is only natural that it will go on coming back. You will have to learn the art of ignoring it.

And whenever you see something like love, blissfulness, ecstasy, then don't stand apart – be in the midst of those who are dancing. It is contagious. You may not have danced, you may not have sung, you may never have been blissful; don't just be touched by it, but have a good dip in the pool of energy that so many sannyasins create. Then you will not feel isolated amongst friends; you will feel one with them, you will feel a heart-to-heart communion with them.

Nobody is a stranger if you allow a heart-to-heart communion; otherwise, if you remain hung up in your head and he remains hung up in his head, everybody is a stranger. Your heads make you many. Your hearts make you one. Bring your whole energy to the heart....

You have not to do much. Just jump into this atmosphere of ecstasy. There is a saying: Think before jumping . . . . I have changed it; I say, jump before thinking – because thinking is of the head, and it will prevent you from jumping. Jump first! If so many people are not drowned, and they are so drunk . . . you are not different from these people.

So first jump, and then you can think as long as you want – in fact, nobody thinks afterwards. Drink the wine that is available here.

I am nothing but pure champagne.

February 22, 1987,   8 a.m.

Beloved Bhagwan,

I arrived in Poona a few days ago with so many fixed attitudes of cynicism on one hand, and so much hope on the other. All expectations and negativity have vanished, and I feel I am empty of all but a great sadness. I have been touched by Your great love and the compassion of Your sannyasins, but still I keep fighting again and again. I feel my heart close up and become ugly, and I feel isolated among friends. What can I do to be more accepting of Your love and of those around me?

Helen, it happens almost always to newcomers; one comes with fixed ideas, expectations. And those ideas and prejudices are given to you by the world; they are all based on lies. You would have been very happy if your prejudices and ideas had been fulfilled. If you had found this place exactly what you were expecting, there would have been no sadness. The sadness is arising in you because all your negativity has to disappear.

This is not the kind of place that . . . . All over the world—religions, governments and news media are conspiring against us they are spreading all kinds of lies without any foundation – this place is just the opposite of what they are propagating. But they have the power. We have only love.

It is a struggle between power and love. Ultimately love is going to win, but on the way, power may have a few battles – but a battle is not decisive. Those who have never come here, those who have never come in contact with me or my people, can go on living with their prejudices. And their prejudices are not going to make them happy or joyful or blissful; their prejudices are not going to make them blossom, sing and dance and enjoy all the fruits God has given to you.

They are all against me for the simple reason that I am for God, and not for the priests. The priest is the enemy of God, because he is selling God in the marketplace – and God is not for sale. You can surrender to God and he will be yours forever, but you cannot possess God – that is the way to kill him.

When I use the word "god," I mean life, existence. I am not a theologian and I don't believe in any God as a person sitting in heaven creating the world. Just look at this world: look at the madness of humanity. In three thousand years it has fought five thousand wars. If God has created this humanity then he must be mad, because a tree is known by the fruit. You can know everything about God by knowing the highest flowering and fruition of human consciousness.

But the priests are not concerned with life or existence; they are professionals. Their whole effort is how to make you more and more guilty, how to make

232

you feel more and more degraded, humiliated; how to prove to you that you are sinners, you are born in sin. The more your pride and your dignity are taken away, the more you become vulnerable to their exploitation.

You say, "I arrived here a few days ago with so many fixed attitudes of cynicism on the one hand, and so much hope on the other. All expectations and negativity have vanished, and I feel I am empty of all but a great sadness."

This sadness is very significant. It is one of the most important things to understand about human psychology, that even if your misery disappears, you will feel sad. You have become so accustomed to misery, it has been such a good companion for years, that you will feel empty because the old misery is gone – the old pain, the old anguish is no longer there. You have remained engaged with your miserable past. Suddenly you find yourself empty, and a sadness . . . the same sadness which you feel when a friend departs from you.

Once you understand this, you can move through a transformation. This is not the moment to feel empty; this is the moment to feel spacious – -and that's what you are calling empty. The old friends are gone, old prejudices, old negativity, old fixed ideas . . . you are spacious, and to be spacious feels strange in the beginning. But as you become accustomed to it, spaciousness becomes the temple of God. Don't call it empty; words mean much, and whatever you call it, you will start feeling that way.

It happened a few years ago in the Himalayas: There is a beautiful animal which looks like a cow; it is called a blue cow because it has a bluish color. It is a wild animal, and its population grew so much that there was not enough pasture for the animal to remain in the mountains. It started coming to the fields and the gardens on the plains in thousands, and the problem for the Hindus was that they could not kill it because its name is blue cow.

It is not a cow; it just looks like a cow. But the very word cow to the Hindu mind means "the mother."

They have worshiped the cow for thousands of years and the prejudice has gone so deep – they can kill the bull, who is logically their father, if the cow is their mother . . . . They kill the bulls; they save only a few to create more cows and more bulls. The bulls are of no use; they are wild and so strong . . . they castrate their own fathers, and then the bull becomes just a bullock.

In the Indian parliament there was great controversy; something had to be decided. Those blue cows were coming in thousands and destroying people's crops, and all over India, Hindus were writing slogans that those cows should not be killed.

Jawaharlal Nehru, the first prime minister, was an intelligent man; he simply changed the name of those animals. In parliament an act was passed that the "blue horses" should be killed – and no Hindu objected. If it is a horse, then who bothers? It is the same poor animal; and the animal knows nothing about whether she is a blue cow or a blue horse – those names are given by us. The Indian parliament passed the resolution, no Hindu objected, and thousands of blue cows were killed. But if the name had remained blue cow, then there would have been riots all over the country, and thousands of people would have been massacred.

Our minds function through words. Always remember to use the right words. Emptiness is not the right word – it has a negative connotation to it, and to call it spaciousness changes the whole attitude. Spaciousness has a positive feeling about it: the sky is not empty; it is spacious. The word "empty" will make you sad.

The word "spaciousness" will make you glad that at last the rotten furniture of your mind has been thrown out – now you can rearrange your inner house. And in fact, spaciousness has a silence about it – naturally, because there is nothing to create noise. Silence can be misinterpreted as sadness . . . . There are very delicate lines that one has to understand. Language can be a great problem.

Silence and sadness have something in common – the depth, the peace – but sadness is empty, and silence is spaciousness; and to be spacious is one of the great achievements. Because now you can invite the guest, the unknown, the unknowable: you have become a temple.

There is a temple in Japan which is absolutely empty – not even a statue of Buddha inside. But emptiness in Buddhism does not have a negative connotation; it is a spaciousness. That temple attracts pilgrims from thousands of miles away, and there is nothing in the temple. But just to sit in that spaciousness helps you to become part of it – it becomes a meditation.

So change your words. Don't call it great sadness; call it great spaciousness. For the first time you have entered your inner sky; those barriers of prejudices and negativity are all gone.

You say, "I have been touched by Your great love and the compassion of Your sannyasins." Don't just be touched, drown in it! You are not going to lose anything by drowning in love, and compassion, and joy, and song and dance. Your spaciousness will become alive.

You say, "But still I keep fighting again and again." Don't fight, because if you fight you are giving energy to the enemy. Jesus is right when he says, "Love your enemies" – that is a great alchemical secret. If you don't fight, you don't nourish the enemy. If you fight, two things happen: you nourish the enemy, and you have to remain at the same level as the enemy.

I have been telling my people: You can have friendship with anyone, but if you want to have enemies, choose very well. Choose some enemy who is higher than you, better than you, holier than you. Just by becoming his enemy you will have to attain all those qualities – because you cannot fight with an enemy who is on the housetop, while you are crawling on the ground; you will have to come up to the same level.

But I can understand your problem, Helen. It is not your personal problem; it is the problem of the mind as such. The mind has a function if you are miserable, but if you are blissful the mind has no function. The mind has a function if you are full of negative attitudes, but if you are full of affirmations, trust, love, ecstasy, the mind has no function.

The mind is basically the very source of all your negativities. When the negativities disappear, the mind also disappears, and one feels afraid. The mind tries hard to remain in its position; it has been your master for so long that it is not easy for it to leave you alone. It will come back again and again; and if you fight with it, you are still giving it recognition.

Let it come . . . ignore it. That is the key to getting rid of it: ignore it. Let it come, don't take any note of it; don't nourish it by giving it attention. And once the mind comes to know that you have become absolutely inattentive towards it, slowly, slowly, and chunk by chunk, it starts disappearing.

The greatest moment in life comes when the mind has gone forever. This state of mindlessness brings you to your inner being. Mind was keeping you engaged and not allowing you to enter into your interiority. It is always afraid that the moment you go deeper into yourself it will become useless.

I used to stay in Calcutta in the house of the chief justice of the Calcutta High Court. His wife told me two things. She said, "I cannot say these things to anybody. But my husband loves you so much, and respects you so much, that perhaps he may listen to you."

I said, "You need not feel embarrassed; you can simply say whatever is the case."

She said, "The problem with him is that even in bed with me, he remains the chief justice. It is good he should be chief justice in the court, but the children are afraid. The moment his car enters the gate, a sadness falls over the house. The children – who were just laughing and enjoying and dancing – stop; I myself become fearful, because he treats everybody as if they are criminals. He cannot forget that he is the chief justice. So please do something, because our whole family is tortured by his being the chief justice."

I talked to the man. At first he felt very much offended that his wife should say this to me, but I said, "Don't feel offended, because she knows you love me, and you will be able to listen to me. Your being chief justice has become a disease for the whole family. The children cannot laugh, nobody can talk, people start whispering; even your wife has said that in bed, while making love, she is not making love to her husband – she is making love to the chief justice of Calcutta High Court!"

He was very shocked. He told the chauffeur to inform the court that he was not coming in that day. He went with me to a garden, sat there silently and finally said, "You are right. I am not enjoying it either, because I never see my wife happy, I never see my children playing. The moment I enter the house it seems as if death has entered; everything suddenly becomes sad. And I know this is not the truth, because the neighbors have told me the moment I go out of the house, it is full of joy. The children are dancing, singing, playing; my wife is a good singer and poet – she plays many musical instruments – but in front of me she becomes almost a corpse. And I was puzzled: I am not doing anything to anybody, so what is the problem? I am sorry that I felt offended, but you have shown me the problem."

I said, "Come with me to your home. Apologize to everybody – the servants, the chauffeur, the gardener, the children, your wife, your parents – individually. Tell them that from today you will be chief justice only in your high court, and you will leave your chief justice-hood in the court when you come back home."

He said, "Is that necessary? Can I not change silently?"

I said, "They will not understand; they will continue with their old idea. You have to do something. You have harmed them; you have been wounding them continually for years. You owe them at least an apology."

He went with me. With tears in his eyes he touched the feet of his mother and father, and asked, "Just forgive me. I had completely forgotten that being chief justice is only my function, it is not my being. It is just the job that I do – I need not continue to be tense in the house. It is not only that you are all suffering, I am also suffering. I have almost become a foreigner in my own family; even my own children tremble before me. And now, retrospectively, I wonder why I was clinging to this chief justice-hood."

It gave you the mastery. And once you have tasted the poison of being a master, it is very difficult to drop the idea. That's why you are fighting again and again . . . against whom? It is your mind that goes on coming back – your prejudices, your negativities, your cynicism, your expectations. Say goodbye to them forever, because they are not going to give you any meaning, any significance, any celebration.

Let this be the criterion always: Anything that makes you festive, anything that gives you celebration, anything that makes you dance and sing to such an extent that you disappear in your dancing, in your singing, in your celebration . . . is the only true religion I know of. No God is needed, no heaven and hell are needed. All that is needed is a simple understanding that mind is the source of negativities – because those negativities make it the master, and you become a slave. And once the mind has been on the throne for so many years – perhaps for so many lives – it is very natural that it should come back again and again.

I have heard: a man's dog died; he had loved the dog very much – and the dog was very understanding and very loving and very beautiful. He could not live without that dog; the death of that dog had left an empty space within him. He went to purchase another dog, and he told the pet shop owner, "I want something special."

The pet shop owner said, "I have got a very special dog; and the strange thing is that he's the cheapest dog in my shop."

The man said, "This *is* strange. I would like to see the dog."

The pet shop owner took him inside the house; he had put the dog in a special place. The dog was really great . . . and the man said, "Why are you selling him so cheap?"

He said, "You will know tomorrow."

The man could not understand what kind of puzzle this was. There were many dogs – very costly – which bore no comparison with this beautiful dog. He purchased it, and went home.

The next day he found out why the dog was sold at such a cheap price. The dog had disappeared! He went back to the pet shop owner, and said, "The dog has disappeared."

The pet shop owner said, "Do you see now why I sell him at such a cheap price? He always comes back. I have sold him thousands of times, but he is such an intelligent dog, he manages to come back. You can have him again if you want!"

The man said, "But what is the point if he is going to come back again tomorrow? Can I ask why he comes back again?"

The pet shop owner said, "I have given him a special room, and I give him the most delicious food, the best meat. There are two servants to take care of him. Nobody can afford all these comforts and all these luxuries – and nobody even imagines that he needs all these comforts and luxuries. When he sees that his old comforts and luxuries have disappeared, he escapes, he comes back. That dog has given me so much business that just the one dog is enough: even if nothing else is sold, there is no problem."

Your mind has lived within you as the master. You have given it all your respect; you have listened to it against your heart; you have followed it against your nature. It is only natural that it will go on coming back. You will have to learn the art of ignoring it.

And whenever you see something like love, blissfulness, ecstasy, then don't stand apart – be in the midst of those who are dancing. It is contagious. You may not have danced, you may not have sung, you may never have been blissful; don't just be touched by it, but have a good dip in the pool of energy that so many sannyasins create. Then you will not feel isolated amongst friends; you will feel one with them, you will feel a heart-to-heart communion with them.

Nobody is a stranger if you allow a heart-to-heart communion; otherwise, if you remain hung up in your head and he remains hung up in his head, everybody is a stranger.

Your heads make you many. Your hearts make you one. Bring your whole energy to the heart.

All this singing and dancing, and meditations and silence are nothing but simple strategies to bring your energy from the head to the heart. Once the heart starts throbbing with joy, you will have a rejuvenation, a resurrection – and then the mind will never bother you. Once the mind knows you have found the heart, it will not come back.

You are asking me, "What can I do to be more accepting of Your love, and of those around me?" You have not to do much. Just jump into this atmosphere of ecstasy. There is a saying: Think before jumping . . . . I have changed it; I say, jump before thinking – because thinking is of the head, and it will prevent you from jumping. Jump first! If so many people are not drowned, and they are so drunk . . . you are not different from these people.
So first jump, and then you can think as long as you want – in fact, nobody thinks afterwards.

Drink the wine that is available here.

I am nothing but pure champagne.

Beloved Bhagwan,

One sutra from the Shrimad Bhagavadgita I have always avoided sharing with You: "When a man reaches the state where he ceases to have ill will against all living beings, he attains clarity of vision. In that state all directions of the world become joyful for him."
I cannot speak for others, but as far as I am concerned this sutra seems tellingly true. I cannot deny that I am full of ill will against all living beings. And that is exactly why I avoid asking You about it: because I shudder at the thought of exposing myself to You, although I have a vague feeling that You know me much better than I do.
Will You please comment?

Anand Maitreya, you are perfectly right: I know you much better than you know yourself. For example, even this idea that you are full of ill will against all is not right.

Perhaps you may be full of ill will towards a few people – out of five billion people – but I don't see that you are full of ill will against all living beings. Five billion human beings . . . and all living beings? The birds and the animals and the insects . . . there are millions of species of living beings, and their population is far bigger than that of human beings. For example, you can find five billion mosquitoes in Poona alone – so never brag about your population . . . that you have a population of five billion.

The UNO is just about to celebrate . . . . It is strange, that on the one hand we are condemning the population growth, and on the other, the UNO is going to have a celebration one day because mankind has crossed the five billion mark, for the first time in history. Is this a day for celebration, or for crying and weeping? And if it is a day for celebration, then when it crosses six billion – more celebration; seven billion – more celebration. Your celebrations will lead to global suicide. What kind of idiots have gathered in the UNO? They should have declared this day a day of mourning, because it is the beginning of the death of this planet. But this is how man's mind is: on the one hand they are trying to stop the growth of population; on the other

hand they are celebrating it.

You are quoting a sutra from *Shrimad Bhagavadgita*. This is a statement made by Krishna – a beautiful statement: "When a man reaches the state where he ceases to have ill will against all living beings, he attains clarity of vision. In that state, all directions of the world become joyful for him."

You are worried, and you think you are exposing yourself by saying, "I cannot deny that I am full of ill will against all living beings." Impossible – you don't even know all living beings. But first try to understand the sutra . . . .

I am reminded of a story about Gautam Buddha. He used to say to his disciples – and ten thousand sannyasins used to move with him wherever he went – never to forget one thing: after meditation, when you are feeling silent, serene and joyful, shower the whole world with your blessings. Don't hold it within you. And when you have showered it all over the world, without any discrimination, only then is your meditation complete.

One man came to Buddha and he said, "I can follow your direction and guidance about meditation, but I just want one small exception: I will share my blessing, my joy, with the whole world, but I cannot do that with my neighbor. That is impossible."

Buddha said, "Even a single exception will destroy your whole meditation. In fact, your neighbor deserves

237

it more than anybody else: first share with your neighbor, and then share with the whole world."

Neighbors are difficult. Even Jesus had to make two statements: love your enemy as yourself, and love your neighbor as yourself. Very strange statements . . . but as far as I understand it, they are the same people – the neighbors and the enemies.

The question is not that you have ill will towards a few people. The question is: are you not capable of giving water to an enemy who is thirsty and dying? Is your enmity far more important than his thirst and his death? What has he done to you, for you to have any ill will against him? Perhaps he has been angry; perhaps he has cheated you; perhaps he has been dishonest with you, lied to you – but these are very small things. If you can share your compassion and love . . . they are like floods – they will take away all the dirt that has gathered around you.

And Krishna is concerned with you; not with your enemies, or with people with whom you have a relationship of ill will. Having even a single enemy means your heart cannot blossom to its fullness. At least one petal will remain missing.

So the question is not about the object of ill will; the question is of your growth. This is sheer foolishness – to destroy your growth just because there are a few people who have deceived you, or who have insulted you, or who have been destructive towards you.

You are being more destructive towards yourself than anybody else, because you are not allowing your own lotus to blossom in its fullness. Except yourself, there is nobody who is your enemy. They can harm your body, but they cannot harm your soul. But you can harm your soul.

Krishna is saying that having any anger, any enmity, any jealousy, any kind of ill will, is preventing your spiritual growth.

You cannot find another man in the world, who has been condemned, criticized, harassed, in every possible way, more than me. But strangely enough – sometimes I also feel amazed – I don't have any ill will against anybody. The whole world may think I am their enemy, but whatever I am doing, whatever I am saying, is just to help them come out of their sleep. And if in their sleep they shout, and they become angry, it is understandable. You cannot expect them not to be angry with you, when they are having beautiful dreams and you wake them up.

One night, Mulla Nasruddin told his wife, "Quick, bring my glasses – and don't ask any questions. In the morning I will explain."

The wife said, "Strange . . . what are you going to do with your glasses in the middle of the night?"

He said, "Don't waste time! Bring my glasses, immediately." So the wife brought his glasses, and he put them on. He said, "I was seeing such a beautiful woman, but because my eyesight is not good . . . ." And with his glasses on, he tried hard to persuade her, "Come back again. Don't be worried, there is nobody; my wife has gone to sleep again, she is snoring . . . ." But nobody came.

Once a dream is broken, it is very difficult – almost impossible – to continue it. It is not like a novel: that you stop reading, and the next day you start reading from the place you had stopped before. But if somebody is dreaming of a beautiful woman, or of a beautiful man, or of a great treasure; or is thinking that he has reached paradise, and you wake him up – naturally he is going to throw tantrums.

Attempts on my life have been made; I have been harassed, imprisoned, treated as if I am a murderer; almost all the countries of the world have passed resolutions in their parliaments that I cannot enter their lands. Still, I only have a good laugh at the whole madness of humanity – but no ill will. They need all the compassion, all the love, all the sympathy they can get.

Basically it is a question of understanding: if somebody has insulted you, it is his problem, not your problem. It was his tongue, his words, his body. And he is free to use them, why should you be worried?

There is a story that I have been telling again and again, because it remains so fresh: Gautam Buddha passed by a village, and the villagers were against him – which was to be expected. They all gathered round and started abusing him, using ugly four-letter words. Even most silent followers became so enraged, but because Buddha was present they could not say anything.

Buddha listened silently, very patiently, and then said, "If your conversation is complete, now it is time for me to go – because I have to reach to another village where people must be waiting. But if your conversation is not complete, I will come back by the same route, and I will have enough time for you."

One man said, "Conversation? Do you think it was conversation?"

Buddha said, "Yes. You expressed your feelings, you exposed yourselves; I never thought that the people of this village trusted me so much that they would expose their hearts without being afraid that it may look ugly. I will come back; then if something has remained, you can complete it. And before I go, I want to ask one question only: In the village before, people came with sweets and flowers, but we had taken our food – and we take food only one time a day, and we do not carry any with us – so we said, 'We are sorry, but we are grateful that you came with such beautiful food.' I want to ask you, what should they have done with the food, and the sweets and the flowers?"

Somebody in the crowd said, "What! They should have distributed them in the village. The villagers would have enjoyed it."

Buddha said, "You are very intelligent. Just do the same: I do not accept whatever you have brought – food or four-letter words; respect or insult. You have come a little late; you should have met me ten years ago

– I would have cut off all of your heads. But at that time I was asleep, and now I am awake.

"I can understand that in your sleep you are shouting, crying, saying things; but these things don't offend me, unless I accept them. You can go on shouting, and these things will keep coming back to you. So now go back to the village, and distribute them to your friends, wives, children."

And Buddha moved on.

His chief disciple, Ananda, said, "This was too much" – they all came from the warrior race – and he said, "I had completely forgotten that I am a sannyasin. If you had not been in front of me, I would have killed a few of them. The were really nasty."

Buddha said, "Hearing them, I felt compassion; but hearing you, I feel sad. It is not expected of you; you are on the path of awakening. They are poor people, fast asleep."

Anand Maitreya, the first thing is you are not full of ill will for all living beings – that is impossible. One would die if he was so full of ill will; that means he would be so full of poison. And certainly you are not a man who has even a few enemies; you have such a loving and nice heart.

I have given you the name Anand Maitreya, which means blissful friend – and I don't give a name without meaning. I have never seen you angry, violent; I have never heard from you a single word against anybody – and you have been with me for more than twenty years; you are one of the most advanced sannyasins on this campus.

So only one thing is right in your question: that I know more about you than you know.

Beloved Bhagwan,

Dancing with You in Chuang Tzu every day I find that I am more and more mad. Still, most of the time,
I can clearly see a subtle line within me that is holding me back.
Bhagwan, what is this fear of losing oneself all about?

Prem Azima, it is natural. Thousands of years are behind the fear that you may go beyond control, and you may not be able to come back. There is a very hidden fear of madness; but this is not the madness you are afraid of. This is divine madness. It is not that you are going into a nervous breakdown: it is a breakthrough, not a breakdown.

But everybody feels afraid. It is almost like learning to swim. You cannot jump immediately into deep waters – first you have to learn in shallow water, in a swimming pool. And once you have learned swimming, which is not something difficult . . . .

In fact the experts say that every child is born with the art of swimming; and one great expert in Japan has been experimenting for years. First he taught six-month-old babies to swim; then he taught three-month-old babies. You know perfectly well that if somebody dies in water, he will start floating on top of the water.

You are alive and you are afraid that you will be drowned: the man who is dead is no longer afraid – he is floating on top of the water. He knows something more than you know.

You are drowning because you go on struggling and fighting with the water. It just takes a little time, two or three days, to learn how to have a harmony between the water and your body.

In the beginning you have to start where you are certain that you cannot be drowned, where the water is shallow. Once you have learned, then you can go . . . it does not matter how deep the water is, because you are always on the top. It may be the five-miles-deep Pacific Ocean – it does not matter. Five feet or five miles are equal; you are always on the surface.

Mulla Nasruddin also wanted to learn to swim. He went to the teacher, who used to teach the boys of the school to swim. He said, "Although I am not a boy . . . I have always been afraid of water, and before I die, I want to learn to swim so that this fear can be dropped."

He said, "It will not be difficult. You come with me to the river." Afraid, inside he must have been trembling . . . and when they reached the river, he slipped, just on the ground; it was muddy and he slipped. He got up and ran away towards his house.

The teacher said, "What are you doing, Mulla Nasruddin? Don't you want to learn to swim?"

He said, "I will, but first I will practice."

The teacher said, "Where will you practice?"

He said, "First I will practice on my mattress: I will throw my hands and legs . . . and I will do everything. When I have become an expert I will come; otherwise, I am not going to come close to water – it is dangerous."

You cannot learn swimming on your bed. If you try too much, you may even get some fractures or something, but you will not learn swimming.

It is perfectly right. Azima, you say, "Dancing with You in Chuang Tzu every day I find that I am becoming more and more mad." You are going very slowly. But there are people . . . . Some people are accustomed to purchasing things retail, and a few people purchase things wholesale – wholesale is cheaper and better. Don't go slowly, more and more mad – inch by inch. I assure you: Go totally mad, because for thirty years, I have pushed thousands of people into total madness; they never came back to complain, so you need not be worried.

Otherwise, you will continue to have this fear: "Still

most of the time, I can clearly see a subtle line within me that is holding me back." Everybody is afraid of going mad. What will people say? But here, this is a communion of the mad people. Here, if you go slowly, people will laugh, "Look at that idiot, he is going so slowly."

You are not in the ordinary world. Here, things are done totally and wholesale. So today, you jump the line – and the line will disappear, and you will disappear. And you will not come to complain – that much I can assure you – because nobody has ever complained, "Bhagwan, I have gone completely mad."
These slow-goers – these are the people who go on asking about fear, about a line to cross. Just close your eyes and take a jump; it has done no harm to anybody.

What appears to be insanity, you will find to be the greatest sanity in the world, because it is divine madness – this totality and intensity of dancing, singing and praying that makes you absolutely alert. The ego disappears, the mind disappears, and all that is rubbish within you is burnt. Only the pure gold, twenty-four carat gold, remains. That is your authentic being, and that is the only present you can take as an offering to God.

Okay, Vimal?

Yes, Bhagwan.

Silence Is Always Louder Than Any Scream

Silence is always louder than any scream. A scream has a beginning and an end; silence is eternal.

Silence is the scream of the whole existence.

But I would not prevent you from screaming, because the people you are screaming at are so deaf that it is compassionate towards them to scream as loudly as possible; and they are so insane that they cannot understand silence.

Silence can be understood only by those who know what silence is, who have experienced silence. Perhaps your scream may reach the insane minds of the politicians and the bureaucrats and the theologians and the religious leaders–because they are full of mad noises themselves. They don't know what silence is.

If they had known silence, I would have been welcomed by them.

February 22, 1987,　7 p.m.

Beloved Bhagwan,

Would You say this is not love?
For behind the tears of absence
is a serene memory
as a constant presence in my center
always, always in the center
of my heart, of my feet,
all the directions of the earth,
the words and the silences,
the embraces and the songs,
but most of all
in the center of my sorrowing smile
sometimes pained with rage.

So would You say this is not love?
Because I shout: "You bastards!"
For I cannot accept in silence or with joy
that they gag Your mouth
and they fetter Your feet.
Would You say this is not love?
The divine rage that screams within me
singing its furious song
for the thousands and thousands of hearts
who would have loved to meet You
but are hindered by boundaries of fear,
by bureaucracy, passports and masked manners.

Would You say if I could ask You
my eternal question
that I do not love You?
Because I feel to scream to them
that I love You, I love You,
and because I want them all to love You,
to be free
to love You and to meet You
under every tree,
in every country,
on every street around the earth,
and because I wish for every wretch
You could reach out Your hand
or Your infinite silence.

I would be dead by now
forgotten of myself
if I had not met You.
And so I weep for all of those
who died in forgetfulness
of their own soul
without having met You.
And again and again I scream:
"You bastards!"
into the faces of those
who try to chain You close
in order to keep You
from the thirsty and the lost.

So would You say this is not love?
For the scream is louder still
than the silence.
For the heart is turmoil and the rage
whets the intelligence
like a sword to cut the chains,
to cut the heads of the parasites,
and to open a door
for intuition to enter.

I cannot take this any more,
the fear and the meanness of those who decide
what is right and what is wrong.
Nor the fear of those who are afraid
of the songs,
of the dance,
of the music that springs up
when a living being
meets You.
So, oh, my love, would You say
this is not love?

Sarjano I am reminded of a beautiful statue of Gautam Buddha, which was sent to me from Japan by a friend. It was no ordinary statue; it was the samurai conception of Gautam Buddha. In one of his hands was ~~a burning torch~~ and in the other hand was ~~a naked sword.~~ And the beauty and the strangeness of the statue was this: that ~~half of his face was lighted by the torch – serene, silent, peaceful,~~ and ~~the other side of his face had the same sharpness as the sword~~ he was holding in his hand.

~~Silence can also be a song.~~
~~Love can also be a sword.~~

These great experiences of life – ~~silence or love~~ or ~~blissfulness~~ – are not limited to only one meaning. They include the whole spectrum of the rainbow: all the colors between black and white also belong to them. ~~Love can be as soft as a rose flower,~~ and ~~love can be as hard as a bullet~~ – these are all aspects. One has to remember only one thing: that ~~they are coming out of a loving space. Your revolution has to come from a loving space; your rebellion has to have the flavor of love.~~ Then it is a totally different phenomenon: it is no longer political, it starts taking on a spiritual dimension.

I can understand, Sarjano, you love me too much. You cannot bear to see what the religions, the organized churches of the world are doing to me. You cannot tolerate it; it is impossible for your love to tolerate what the politicians and the bureaucrats have been doing to me.

I have been teaching only silence and love to people, and I have been treated as if I am a murderer!

The U.S. attorney of Oregon said at a press conference, "We could not put Bhagwan into jail because we don't have any evidence that he has committed any crime." And the same man, in the federal court, produced a long list of crimes, and blackmailed my attorneys, threatened them. They came to see me in the jail, they had tears in their eyes – and they were professional attorneys, they were not concerned about me the way you are concerned about me.

But those twelve days in American jails . . . . They arrested me without any arrest warrant. And the way the judges behaved . . . they would not allow me even to inform my attorneys that I had been arrested; they would not indicate even verbally the reason why I had been arrested. The magistrate before whom I first had to appear was a woman magistrate. For three days continuously the U.S. attorney argued and could not prove anything against me. He had to accept, himself – in his closing statement on the third day – that "I have failed to prove any crime against Bhagwan, and I don't have anything else to say." Still the magistrate did not allow me to be released on bail.

Even the jailer could not believe what was happening. He had brought my things with him, thinking that I would be released. They did not have any arrest warrant, they did not have any cause to show; for three days he had been listening and there was not a single point that proved me guilty or criminal.

When bail was refused, he said, "I have never in my life seen such injustice. The reason why your bail has not been given is something nobody will ever know." The reason was that the government had threatened the magistrate, "If you give Bhagwan bail, you will always remain a state magistrate; you will never move into the position of federal judge. And if you don't give bail, you will soon be promoted to federal judge." And within three weeks she was promoted.

My attorneys were watching all this happening, and the final thing that they could not believe was that the U.S. attorney did not want the trial. He said to them, "We know and you know that there is no case at all – you are going to win. But it is in our hands not to give him bail, and to go on prolonging the case for ten years, twelve years . . . so you have to choose. If you insist on a trial, then don't blame us. You will win, but Bhagwan could be in jail for twenty years. If you want him to be released without trial then you have to accept at least two crimes. The choice is clear for you."

For twelve days my attorneys had been running from one jail to another – because they were taking me from one jail to another every day, changing the jails, trying to find some indirect way to kill me.

They put me in a cell with a man who was going to die of herpes and AIDS. The cell was meant for two, but for six months nobody had shared it because the doctor had ordered that he should remain alone. They put me in that cell. And while the doctor was present, the jailer was present, the U.S. marshal was present, as they moved me, the man – who was almost counting his last breaths – told me, "Bhagwan, you don't know me, but I have been watching You on television, and I have fallen in love with You.

"Don't come into the cell; just stand near the door, because I am suffering from herpes and AIDS and I am dying. And they have put you knowingly here – because for six months they have not put anybody else in here. Everything in the cell is contaminated. You just remain by the door, and knock on the door, because it will take hours of knocking for anybody to turn up."

It took almost one hour before the jailer came. I asked him, "For six months this cell has not been given to another person. You know perfectly well this man is dying . . . why have you put me here?"

Immediately I was changed. They had no answer. I asked the doctor, "You must have taken the Hippocratic Oath to save people's lives. If you have any shame, any dignity . . . . You were present – you have been preventing even murderers from being put in this cell – and you did not say anything."

He said to me, "We cannot do anything. Orders came from the top that every indirect method should be used – so if the person dies, we are not responsible."

As I entered in another jail, in the middle of the night, the U.S. marshal wanted me to sign my name as 'David Washington.' I said, "But that is not my name."

He said, "That we don't know. This is the order we have received from the top: you cannot write your own name on the form. In the jail, you will be known as David Washington."

I said, "I see written on your coat in beautiful letters 'U.S. Department of Justice.' At least take this coat off. What kind of justice is this? – and do you think I am an idiot that I can't see your game? – if I sign under the name 'David Washington' you can kill me, and nobody will be able even to find a trace of where I disappeared because I never entered your jail."

I said, "I am not going to write anybody else's name. But if you are feeling tired – I can see it is the middle of the night, the whole day working . . . you must be feeling tired – you can leave me here on this bench in the office. I will wait. Or you can do one thing: you can fill in the form and I will sign it."

He could not understand a simple strategy. He filled in the form with David Washington and

247

everything as he wanted. It was all fiction: my father's name was fiction, my place of residence was fiction – but I signed *my* signature. He looked at my signature and said, "What does it mean?"

I said, "It must mean 'David Washington.' And tomorrow you will see in the newspapers and on television . . . my signature is known all over the world."

My attorneys were watching continuously, running from one city to another city, from one jail to another jail. They were worried that if they did not accept two crimes, the trial would mean my torture and perhaps my death. And if I have to live for twenty years in jail, what is the point of winning? They came with tears in their eyes, and they said, "We are asking you something which we should not ask. We are here to defend you, and to defend your innocence, but the government is blackmailing us." And they told me that this was their strategy.

And he has made it clear, the same U.S. attorney "If you want Bhagwan alive, you must immediately accept two crimes . . . and within fifteen minutes Bhagwan has to leave America."

Seeing their tears, and thinking of the millions of my people around the world, who were telephoning and sending so many letters and telegrams and flowers that every jail was full of flowers . . . . The jailers were asking me, "What to do with these flowers? Where to keep them? – because we don't have space."

I said to them, "There is no need to worry; I am a nonserious person. I can accept any crime they want. Outside the court the whole world media is waiting, and outside the court I will say, "Under the oath of truth, I have lied. The government forced me to lie." On one hand they force you to take the oath that you will not lie, and on the other hand they blackmail you into lying.

So I said, "Don't be worried," – I accepted, without even bothering what those crimes were. They had not said that if I accept the crimes, there is going to be a huge fine – four hundred thousand dollars, which is

nearabout sixty lakh rupees – and that for five years I cannot enter America. And fifteen years of suspended sentence – so that even if after five years I enter the country and the government thinks that I am committing any crime, I will have to go to jail for ten years, and there will be no trial for it and no question about it.

These are their protections, so I cannot go to a higher court and appeal: that this is blackmail. So in fact they have prevented me from entering America for fifteen years.

And my attorneys were perfectly right: as I left the jail, a bomb was found under my seat. The bomb was a time bomb. Now, nobody else can put a bomb inside the jail except the jail authorities, except the government.

The case finished within five minutes, because I accepted – there was no question of argument, and I said, "Any crime they say . . . I have committed. No need to waste the time of the court. You simply give your judgment." My people immediately produced four hundred thousand dollars, and within ten minutes I was out of the jail. My plane had been kept ready, so that within fifteen minutes I could leave America.

I was wondering why they were in such a hurry, why fifteen minutes? My attorneys said, "They are worried that if you are allowed to stay here for two days or five days, you may go to a higher court and appeal that you have been blackmailed – so you have to leave America immediately."

These are the democratic governments. These are the people who go on saying that their ideals are democracy, liberty, freedom of expression, freedom for the individual to be himself. So I can understand if you call these politicians, these popes, these shankaracharyas, "the bastards." It is simply that your love is too much for me and your love for freedom, individuality, and respect for life is too much.

My whole teaching can be reduced to a simple concept: reverence for life and freedom.

So Sarjano, you need not be worried. You must be

feeling that I may say this is not love. This *too* is love –
love on fire, love aflame. And ~~love has to learn not to be
just a rose flower. It has to know that if the time comes,
it can become a sword.~~

You are asking me, "Would You say this is not love?"
No, I would not say that.

> "For behind the tears of absence
> is a serene memory
> as a constant presence in my center
> of my heart, of my feet,
> all the directions of the earth,
> the words and the silences,
> the embraces and the songs,
> but most of all
> in the center of my sorrowing smile
> sometimes pained with rage."

~~Love knows to roar like a lion too.
Love is not just sweet poetry.
If love were just sweet poetry, it could not exist in
this insane world. It has to be strong enough – stronger
than hate, stronger than anger – it has to be a lion's roar.~~
"So would You say this is not love?" No, Sarjano, this
is love in its purity, in its utter genuineness, in its
absolute authenticity.

> "Because I shout: 'You bastards!'
> For I cannot accept in silence or with joy
> that they gag Your mouth
> and they fetter Your feet.
> Would You say this is not love?"

I have knocked on the doors of twenty-one
countries, but no country was courageous enough to
allow me even a tourist visa for three or four weeks.

In Greece they allowed me a four-week visa, but the
archbishop of Greece started making a great noise,
sending telegrams to the president and to the prime
minister, and writing threatening letters to the owner
of the house in which I was staying, saying that if he
wants to save his house, I should be thrown out.
Because if I am not thrown out within thirty-six hours,
he is going to burn down the whole house with all the
people in it; burn them alive. And this is the archbishop
of the most ancient Christian church. He represents
Jesus Christ!

The government became afraid. They had no
reason . . . because I had not even left the house in two
weeks. I was asleep in the afternoon when the police
came. My legal secretary, Anando, was telling the
officers, "Sit down, have some tea, and I will wake Him
up." But they threw her from a four-foot porch down
onto the gravel, and dragged her over the gravel to the
jeep, and took her away to the police station: she was
trying to prevent government action.

And as I was awakened by John, I heard noises as if
dynamite was being exploded. The police started
throwing rocks at the house from all sides, destroying
the beautiful ancient windows and doors . . . and they
also had dynamite. They said, "You have to wake him
up this very moment, otherwise we will dynamite the
house."

No arrest warrant . . . no reason to be so
furious . . . just because the archbishop had told the
government that if I was allowed to stay in Greece, the
morality, the religion, the culture, everything would be
in danger. In just two weeks I would corrupt the minds
of the young people. I had not even left my house, and
I had not met anybody. The people who had come to
see me had all come from outside Greece.

But I wondered: they have built up this morality
and this religion and this culture over two thousand
years . . . what kind of culture and what kind of morality
is it which can be destroyed in two weeks by an
individual man? It does not deserve to exist if it is so
weak, so impotent.

The American government has been telling all the
governments of the world that I should not be allowed,
even as a tourist, in their countries. One small country,
Uruguay, in South America, was very happy that I had
come there, because the president had been reading

my books, and he had not dreamt that I would ever come to Uruguay. So he said, "We will make every effort to give You land, so that You can create a community. Because not only will we be enriched by Your presence and Your disciples, but thousands of pilgrims will start coming; and we are a poor country – it will be a financial gain too." And he immediately managed a one-year residence visa for me.

But when the American president, Ronald Reagan, became aware of it – the American ambassador in Uruguay informed him – he threatened the president of Uruguay: "Within thirty-six hours Bhagwan should leave the country. Otherwise you will have to return all the loans that we have given you in the past, and all the loans – billions of dollars – which we were going to give you in the coming two years will not be given. So you can choose."

Now, Uruguay cannot manage to return the money and cannot afford not to take billions of dollars in the coming two years, because her whole planning is based on those billions of dollars. The whole economy of the country would collapse.

The president had tears in his eyes when he told me, "Your coming to our country has at least made me aware of one thing: that we are *not* independent. We have been living under a delusion.

"You will have to leave. It is illegal – because you have a valid residence visa for one year; and you have not committed any heinous crime – that is the only reason that a residence visa can be canceled." And I had only been there one month. And he said, "It is unfortunate that I have to do it. I am doing it against my own conscience."

Even this much the American president was not willing to concede: that I should simply leave the country. My plane was standing at the airport . . . I said, "There is no problem; I can leave the country. I will not put your country into such jeopardy."

He said, "The American president insists that You should be deported; You should not leave the country without being deported. I am forced to commit crimes:

first, to tell You for no reason to leave the country, You have done nothing. Second, to deport You. But I am absolutely helpless. Still, I want one thing: that on Your passport there should be no stamp of deportation from Uruguay. We have a small airport – so move Your airplane to that airport, and in the evening leave without informing us; so we can say, 'He left without informing us. There was no time to deport him.' "

But he was wrong. As my jet moved to the small airport – the American embassy must have been watching – the American ambassador was there with all the stamps and the official whose business it is to deport people. I was delayed there, because they had to fill in all the forms, and as I left the country, I said, "It doesn't matter . . . ." In fact, my passport has become a historical document: I have been deported from so many countries without any reason.

When I left Uruguay the president was invited to America immediately, and Ronald Reagan gave him thirty-six million dollars as a "gesture of friendship." That was a reward because I was thrown out within thirty-six hours: exactly thirty-six million dollars, one million dollars per hour! In fact, I should start asking these governments for my percentage: You are getting billions of dollars because of me – I should get at least two percent.

America has been informing all the governments . . . I have seen the documents that they are sending to every government. All that those documents say is: "This man is dangerous. He can corrupt the morality of the country, the culture of the country; he can corrupt the youth of the country. He can destroy the religion of the country."

It is such a strange world. One day the German parliament decided that I should not be allowed into Germany – not only that I should not be allowed into Germany, but my airplane should not be allowed to land at any airport, even for refueling. I cannot understand how I can corrupt their morality, sitting in my airplane for just fifteen minutes.

In England I was not allowed to stay in the airport

lounge for just six hours during the night–which was my right. It is an international airport, and my pilots had finished their flying hours and they could not fly any more – it would have been against the law.

And just in case they refused, saying that the first-class lounge is not for private air jet travelers, but only for commercial flights, we purchased two tickets also. Just to show them, "If that is the problem, we also have tickets for a commercial flight tomorrow morning."

But the airport official had a file, and every other moment he was phoning the prime minister, "What shall I say now? What shall I do now?" – because it was something he had never done before. To tell somebody, "Your staying in the lounge will corrupt the country's morality" does not look reasonable. And finally he came to me and he said, "There is no point in arguing. They have decided that you can stay only if you want to stay in jail for six hours. We will not allow you to stay anywhere else." So for no crime, I had to stay six hours in jail in England.

The U.S. attorney general has been saying again and again in press conferences, "I don't want to hear Bhagwan's name again, and I don't want any news media to report his ideas. I want him to be completely silenced."

This is their strategy to silence me: that I should not be allowed in any country; and no sannyasins should be allowed into India. That's why I have withdrawn your orange clothes and your malas; otherwise you would not have been able to enter India. Now they cannot figure out who is a sannyasin and who is not a sannyasin. Now the whole world is my sannyasin.

"The divine rage that screams within me
singing its furious song
for the thousands and thousands of hearts
who would have loved to meet You
but are hindered by boundaries of fear,
by bureaucracy, passports and masked manners."

Sarjano understands it perfectly well – he is from Italy. He and other Italian sannyasins have been trying continually for one year just to get a three-week tourist visa for me, and the Italian government goes on saying next week . . . and one year has passed. Because the pope has put an embargo on the government: in no case should Bhagwan be allowed into Italy. These cowards are your religious leaders. And just now, Sarjano went there again to enquire, how many more weeks? They said, "Because one year has passed, that application is invalid; put in a new application." So he has put in a new application, and I think that again it will take one year – before it becomes invalid again.

When the pope was in India, he was opposed by everybody: Hindus, Mohammedans, Jainas, Buddhists – wherever he went he was opposed. I was the only man in the whole country who opposed the people who were opposing the pope, and said to them, "This is ugly and this simply shows weakness. Welcome him: invite him for a public, open discussion. In every city he enters, he should have to face a public discussion on the fundamentals of religion; that will be something valuable. Let us see how much he understands about the fundamentals of religion."

For ten thousand years this country has been pouring its whole genius into religious experiments. There is no other place in the world where religion has been so intensely and insistently explored. Christianity looks so childish compared to Buddhism that there is no need to oppose the pope. It is a good opportunity that he himself has come here; and if he had faced intellectual discussions all over the country, I think that he would never have come back again.

I can understand your rage against bureaucracy, passports, and masked manners.

"Would You say if I could ask You
my eternal question
that I do not love You?"

Sarjano, my eternal answer is that you love me too much.

"Because I feel to scream to them
that I love You, I love You,
and because I want them all to love You,
to be free
to love You and to meet You
under every tree,
in every country,
on every street around the earth,
and because I wish for every wretch
You could reach out Your hand
or Your infinite silence.

I would be dead by now,
forgotten of myself
if I had not met You.
And so I weep for all of those
who died in forgetfulness
of their own soul
without having met You.
And again and again I scream:
"You bastards!"
into the faces of those
who try to chain You close
in order to keep You
from the thirsty and the lost.

So would You say this is not love?
For the scream is louder still
than the silence."

Sarjano, there I don't agree with you. Silence is
always louder than any scream. A scream has a
beginning and an end; silence is eternal.
Silence is the scream of the whole existence.

But I would not prevent you from screaming,
because the people you are screaming at are so deaf
that it is compassionate towards them to scream as
loudly as possible; and they are so insane that they
cannot understand silence.

Silence can be understood only by those who know
what silence is, who have experienced silence. Perhaps
your scream may reach the insane minds of the
politicians and the bureaucrats and the theologians
and the religious leaders – because they are full of mad
noises themselves. They don't know what silence is. If
they had known silence, I would have been welcomed
by them.

The first man from outside America to protest
against my arrest was a Zen master from Japan. He
immediately phoned Ronald Reagan and phoned to
me, informing me, "I have phoned Ronald Reagan, and
I have told him that he is committing a great sin, he will
suffer for it." He has never met me, but in his monastery
my books are read as scriptures – his disciples know
about Zen from *my* books. Zen was born in Japan, but
he has found a better expression, a more profound
meaning in *my* words; so rather than teaching them
through Japanese scriptures, he is teaching them from
my books.

I told him on the phone, "I am grateful that you
protested, but there was no need to tell him that he
should repent, that he has committed a sin."

He said, "I am enraged. I am a man of silence. My
whole life I have been simply meditating and doing
nothing. But seeing you on television, in chains,
handcuffed, being treated as if you are a murderer, I
could not remain silent." And that old Zen monk's
prediction is coming true. Ronald Reagan and the
attorney general of America, Mr. Meese, are both going
down the drain. Irangate is going to finish them
completely.

And just today Neelam has brought to me the news
that in the White House, Ronald Reagan's daughter and
his son-in-law have seen a ghost – they think it is the
ghost of Lincoln. But why should Lincoln be wearing
red clothes? Now even Ronald Reagan is afraid to be in
the White House – because many other people have
seen it, even his dog starts barking when others see the
ghost. It seems some old sannyasin is just playing a
joke! . . . Soon the White House will be a ghost house;
nobody will be ready to live in it. Only dead sannyasins
will enjoy living in the White House.

But Ronald Reagan and this Mr. Meese are absolutely finished; they don't have any future. So don't be angry. Even if you scream, your scream should come out of your love, out of your compassion – so that the deaf can hear and the blind can see.

> "For the heart is turmoil and the rage
> whets the intelligence
> like a sword to cut the chains,
> to cut the heads of the parasites,
> and to open a door
> for intuition to enter.
> I cannot take this any more,
> the fear and the meanness of those who decide
> what is right and what is wrong.
> Nor the fear of those who are afraid
> of the songs,
> of the dance,
> of the music that springs up
> when a living being
> meets You.
> So, oh, my love, would You say
> this is not love?"

Again, Sarjano, I say: This is too much love. Just don't forget in your anger and rage that it is love that is roaring like a lion. Basically it is love. Whatever they have done, and whatever they are doing, is just out of unconsciousness. You cannot be too angry about them: they need more pity and more compassion.

Now, here it is going to happen, everywhere it is going to happen . . . . We have had this property since 1974 – we purchased it. But the government has not transferred it to our name. So we have paid the money, but the property belongs still to the original owners.

The municipal corporation goes on asking for taxes from us, and we are paying those taxes.

Because I had gone to America for five years, one structure was demolished by our people – because it was of no use anymore. One hall was enough. When I was here before, then ten thousand people used to be here. Soon they will be coming again . . . so we have started to raise the structure again. It is an old structure – we are simply putting it back together – but the municipal commissioner is so enraged about it that he has threatened that he will come on the twenty-eighth of February with bulldozers and demolish the structure. And it is our temple.

So the twenty-eighth is going to be a really festive day! You have to lie down across the whole width of the road, with all the musicians playing and dancers dancing, and tell them, "First you will have to bulldoze our people, and then you can bulldoze the whole property – because we will not be here, it will not be of any use. But unless you bulldoze all the people who are here, you cannot move one inch into the ashram land." Now we will see how much guts that municipal commissioner has got.

We are not going to be violent; we will be singing songs of love, we will be playing music, we will be dancing with joy. Let the whole world know that to be joyful, to be peaceful, to be loving, to be nonviolent, to be festive is criminal. Perhaps it may raise the whole consciousness of humanity.

So you have to be ready for your great celebration. And, Sarjano, it will be a good opportunity, so that I can teach you that you can die for truth – even dancing and singing, with joy, with no anger, just love and compassion.

Beloved Bhagwan,

I don't know how You do it! One minute I think I am in the deepest depths of sadness, the blackest fog of despair, a total blot on the landscape, a complete mistake on the part of existence. The next minute You come dancing in my direction, a huge laugh bubbles up inside of me, and I am utterly in love with the world again – at least until my next premenstrual crisis. What amazes me is that I am still amazed every time You do something like this, even after ten years. Will I ever learn?

Never!

Anando, there are things you should never learn. Being amazed again and again, remaining available for wonder, is one of the most significant spiritual qualities.

I know it is not only your question; perhaps it is the question of everyone who is here. One minute you are in "the deepest depths of sadness, the blackest fog of despair, a total blot on the landscape, a complete mistake on the part of existence. The next minute You come dancing in my direction, a huge laugh bubbles up inside of me, and I am utterly in love with the world again. I don't know how you do it." Neither do *I* know. I just see it happening.

I know only one thing: that I am never sad, never in dark spaces, never miserable, never depressed. Whatever happens, I remain untouched by it. Perhaps that may be the reason that even when you are in a sad state and I come dancing towards you, your sadness disappears and your whole being becomes a laughter. It is only a question of coming in contact with someone who is overflowing with blissfulness. Your darkness disappears just as any darkness disappears when the light comes. Just a small ray of sun and the darkness disappears, just a small candle with its flame and the darkness disappears.

I have always loved this beautiful story: In the very beginning when God made the world, one day darkness approached God and said, "You have to do something. Your sun has been harassing me continuously; from the morning till evening, he goes on chasing me. I cannot rest even for a moment before he comes again. And I have not done him any wrong. Still, for some unknown reason, he is being so antagonistic towards me. You have to say something to him. It has to be stopped."

God said, "This is strange; why should he do that? Call the sun immediately." The sun was called and God said, "Why do you torture darkness?"

He said, "Darkness? I have never met her. How can I torture somebody whom I have never met, have never even seen? It is the first time I have ever heard that there is something like darkness."

God said, "But darkness herself has complained against you."

The sun said, "I am ready to apologize, to tell her I am sorry. Call her!"

And God sent messenger after messenger, but darkness would not come. When the sun was gone, darkness came, and God said, "So late . . . ? You both have to be present together; only then can this matter be settled."

The matter still remains unsettled, because both cannot be present together. The complaint from darkness is still in the files of God. But since then darkness has not come back to complain, because again the same question will arise, that they both have to be present in front of God. Only then is any judgment possible.

Darkness cannot be present when light is present. Why? – because darkness has no existence of its own; it is only absence of light. Light has a positive existence of its own, darkness is only absence. When light is not there, darkness is; when light is there, darkness is not.

Anando, perhaps the same is happening to you. When I come dancing towards you suddenly your sadness, your misery, disappears. Misery also is nothing but an absence – an absence of blissfulness. Sadness is nothing but an absence of joy. And when I come with a flood of joy, suddenly you find you are laughing, you are smiling, you are dancing – you have forgotten completely that great depth of sadness.

I don't do it. If you are available to me and open to me, it is going to happen. It is a happening, not a doing, so I cannot take the credit for it. The credit goes to existence itself.

And you have made one point: "I am utterly in love with the world again – at least until my next premenstrual crisis." It used to be thought that only women have premenstrual crises. That is wrong. The latest findings are that men also have them. For centuries they were not aware of it, because it has no physical expression. But if you want to find out, just go on noting in your diary or on your calendar every day for three months, whether you have been sad or not. You will be surprised to discover that every twenty-eight days, suddenly for four or five days you are sad and melancholy. But because there is no physical expression, humanity has remained unaware of it.

Just recently psychologists became aware that it is not possible that man does not have a cycle parallel to woman. And as they explored, they found it: after exactly four weeks, for four or five days every man goes into depression. And it is very good to know which days you will be suffering from your monthly period – whether you are a man or a woman – because when somebody is suffering from their menstrual period, you have to be more compassionate and more loving towards the person. He is not his usual self.

And if you remember that your wife is going through her period, don't fight with her. Just take it for granted that she will be angry, she will nag, she will throw plates, she will throw pillows, she will do all kinds of nasty things to you. All you have to do is to save yourself from being hit, and enjoy – because what can the poor woman do? She is suffering from her period; she is under the influence of her hormones. She is not doing it – these cunning hormones are making her do things!

And if you can be patient, loving, then she also has to remember that when her husband is suffering from his period, she should not get in his way. He will drive fast, he will honk the horn, necessary or unnecessary – he will put the radio on full blast. Just don't get in his way. Let him do whatever he is doing: he will take apart and repair a television set which was working perfectly . . . . The poor boy is going through a crisis. But it is chemistry; nobody can do anything about it.

The only thing to be remembered is that if you both have menstrual crises on the same date, then one of you has to go for a honeymoon – just one. Each month you can alternate – next month the other one can go for the honeymoon. But don't remain together, because that will be a very explosive situation.

Man has lived for millions of years without being aware of the fact, simply because it has no physical expression. But they both go through the same psychological changes.

Unless you become a watcher, unless you become a witness to your own mental states . . . . This is what I call meditation. And these are great opportunities: when you are feeling sad, just watch it. It is chemistry . . . you are consciousness. Don't get mixed up with chemistry; don't get identified with chemistry; it is physiology, it is chemistry, it is biology – you are consciousness, a watcher.

Slowly, slowly, even when your whole chemistry is going berserk, you will remain centered, grounded, unaffected – and this is true for both, man or woman.

Okay, Vimal?

Yes, Bhagwan.

Your Existence Is Just A Carbon Copy

Your existence is just a carbon copy and you are clinging to it. Unless you drop it, the original, the real face of your being, will not show. And it is one of the most important things to remember: that if you can drop your ego, your personality, and allow existence to take its place, all the best and most beautiful qualities will follow on their own accord. You will not have to be good, you will find you *are* good. You will not have to be loving, you will find you *are* love.

You will not have to meditate, you will find you *are* meditation.

Just say goodbye to your ego, which is nothing but the opinions of others – press clippings, which you are holding as if they are your soul. Drop them! And immediately you become so clean, so pure, so spacious, that God cannot resist entering into you. You become a temple.

My whole effort here is to transform you from ordinary houses into sacred temples. When you can become the residence of the divine, why go on carrying secondhand opinions of people who themselves are just carbon copies?

February 23, 1987,   8 a.m.

Beloved Bhagwan,

There is the love between man and woman – active, sensual and playful; and the love between master and disciple – passive, cool and silent; and there is the possibility of simply being love every moment. Is love something that is always changing, coming and going, taking on different flavors and colors, or is love simply everything that is and every moment that is?

Anand Sadhyo, love that comes and goes is only a reflection of the real love. A full moon reflected in the lake looks exactly like the moon, but the reflection can be disturbed very easily by a small wind. It shatters into thousands of pieces of silver all over the lake, and as the lake settles back, it again appears as the moon.

But the real moon in the sky is not disturbed by winds, by seasons, by anything. It is even there in the day, although you cannot see it because the sunlight is too bright.

Love is in the exact same situation. Real love is just to be love; it is not a relationship, it is your state of being. It has nothing to do with anybody, you are simply full of love. Many can share it; those who are thirsty can quench their thirst.

This state of being love is the ultimate peak of consciousness, called the awakened state or the enlightened state, the state of a Gautam Buddha. He does not love – he *is* love. He is doing nothing on his part – just his presence radiates love. This love is not addressed to anyone in particular, just as the sunrays are not addressed to any particular flower, any particular tree. It reaches all those who are available to receive it.

Love as a state of being is only an availability. You can take as much as you can contain; it is abundant, overflowing. A man in this state, even if he is sitting alone, goes on radiating love. This love is reflected in many kinds of love, but those are only reflections.

"The love between man and woman – active, sensual, and playful; the love between master and disciple – passive, cool and silent"; the love between friends: it can have many manifestations, but they are always changing. They have to change, because they are only reflections, shadows, and in their wake they bring much misery.

When the moon is reflected in the lake, there is joy, there is beauty; and when it is shattered by the wind, or just by a small pebble thrown into the lake, it is all gone – shattered. And you know in your experience that your love relationships with friends, with husbands, with wives, with masters, are all very fragile. Any small thing and the whole love disappears. Not only does it disappear, it changes into its opposite. Friends become enemies; husband and wife need not become enemies because they are already enemies; disciples betray their masters. There are always Judases who can sell their masters.

We are acquainted with all these loves; they are all conditional. Even the love of parents for their children is conditional: if you obey them, if you are not a rebel, if you are going to become what they want you to become, you will be loved; but if you go on your own way – parents even abandon their children, disinherit their children.

But these reflections indicate that there must be a reality which is reflected. Without something real, there cannot be any reflections.

In the enlightened man, love becomes his very nature, his very breath, his very heartbeat. Wherever he is, he goes on showering his love. It is unconditional – it does not ask anything from you, hence it cannot be disturbed. And unless you know *this* love, you have only been dreaming about love. All those reflections are nothing but dreams, and they bring great misery, anxiety, anguish. In between they give you a few moments of joy – those moments are nothing but consolations.

Authentic love is a tremendous contentment in yourself; it is a settling of your energies at the center of your being. This centeredness brings an alchemical change to your energies. Then wherever you are – with the trees, with the ocean, with the mountains, with the stars, with people, with animals, with birds – you cannot do anything, love simply radiates from you. It is your very life. You cannot prevent it. Preventing it will be committing suicide.

From your so-called love affairs, learn only one thing: that there must be something authentic and real and eternal which is reflected in the mirrors of your relationships. Unless you know *that* love, you will suffer much, and you will gain nothing. And it can be known because it is your intrinsic capacity; you are born with the seed. You just have to take a little care

with it, and it will start growing. Soon you will be full of flowers – the spring has come. And once it comes, it never goes. To the very last moment it remains there.

A very beautiful story is told about Gautam Buddha. He informed his disciples that on a particular day, the coming full moon night, he was going to die. As the full moon disappeared, he would also disappear.

It is a rare coincidence that Gautam Buddha was born on a full moon night, he became enlightened on a full moon night, and he died on a full moon night.

Thousands of his disciples rushed from all over the place just to see him for the last time. There was great sadness, but people were holding back their tears, not to make his departure difficult. And Buddha asked, "If you have any questions – because tomorrow I will not be here – if in your heart there is some question still which you have not exposed, just ask me. Before I leave I want all my disciples to be completely alert, without any questions. I want my disciples to become answers, not questions."

Nobody said anything. Only Ananda said, "You have answered us for forty-two years continually, day in, day out – we don't have any questions. We have come just to be near you when you dissolve into the universal consciousness.

"We have heard from the ancient days, that whenever an enlightened man dies, as he leaves his body, his consciousness spreads all over the universe. We want to be close to you just to have a taste of your consciousness."

And at that moment Buddha said, "Okay, then I say goodbye to you. I will die in four steps. First I will leave my body; then I will leave my mind; then I will leave my heart; and in the fourth, the *turiya*, I will dissolve into the ocean of existence."

He closed his eyes, and just that very moment a man came running and he said, "I have to ask something. For thirty years I have been postponing it. Buddha has been coming to my town many times in these thirty years, and I have always thought that this time I am going to see him and ask my question. But something

259

or other . . . and I went on postponing. Just human stupidity – a guest has come, I was engaged with customers, there was a marriage ceremony I had to participate in. So I went on postponing, thinking that there is no hurry, that when he comes next time, then I will ask. But sometimes my wife was sick, sometimes I was sick . . . and these thirty years have passed. Just now I heard that Buddha is dying. Now I cannot postpone. No reason can prevent me."

But Ananda said, "You have come a little late. He has begun his inner journey; he has already moved two steps: we can see his body has become utterly silent, and as far as dropping the mind . . . it is just an empty mind, he must have dropped it. It may take a little while for him to drop the heart, because it was the heart that he was using continuously to radiate his love, his joy, his silence. It is not right to disturb him at this moment. Forty-two years he has been speaking; now it is your fault if in thirty years you could not find the time – it is *your* question."

But Buddha returned. His breathing, which had disappeared, came back again, his heart started beating again. He opened his eyes and he said, "Ananda, do you want it to be remembered by the coming generations that Buddha's love was so small that he could not come two steps back when a thirsty man had come? And I am still alive – I would be blamed forever. Don't prevent him, let him ask his question."

The man was seeing Buddha for the first time, and in a very strange situation: thousands of people were sitting silently, their eyes full of tears. And Buddha was almost half dead: he had taken two steps inwards; just two steps more and he would become part of the oceanic consciousness.

But a man who *is* love even in such a situation will radiate love. Ananda and all the disciples could not believe that for an ordinary man, who is not even a disciple, who has postponed for thirty years . . . . But Buddha's love and his compassion are infinite – he asked the man . . . but the man was so overwhelmed by the situation, he forgot his question.

He said, "I am fulfilled enough. Just your love has answered all my questions. You were half-dead and still you came back just to answer an ordinary man who has been avoiding you for thirty years, always finding different excuses." He touched Buddha's feet and he said, "Let me be your last disciple; initiate me. I had come to ask a question, but now there is no question – before your love, all questions disappear. And I don't want to miss this opportunity to be initiated by you."

Buddha initiated the man. And he asked again, "Is there anyone still holding some question? Because it will be very difficult for me . . . if I pass the third stage, if I have left the heart and moved into pure consciousness, the fourth state, it will be difficult for me – even if I want to return. So please, if you have any questions, don't feel shy – ask them."

They said, "We are already feeling very sad and sorry because this man unnecessarily disturbed you. This is not a moment to disturb you, this is a moment to be silent – so silent that when you dissolve your consciousness, something of it becomes part of us, too." He said goodbye again and entered into the fourth state.

The story is very symbolic . . . . Up to this point it is absolutely historical. But in the East it is a tradition that what cannot be said in ordinary ways, can be related in parables, in stories. The story is:

As Buddha died, the trees that were dying, the trees whose leaves had become pale, suddenly became green; out of season, bushes and plants and trees burst into flower. There was a tremendous impact from his death – people who had been with him for decades and had not become enlightened, became enlightened in that moment.

Just as he dropped the body and his consciousness became unimprisoned, it spread all over. Whoever was receptive, according to his receptivity, he was fulfilled. Even the trees were not unaware. When he was dying the birds were silent, and when he died they started singing their songs of joy.

Whenever an enlightened man dies, the whole

world feels a rain of love, of consciousness, of blissfulness, of peace. So don't waste your time just in reflections. Those reflections are good as fingers pointing to the real moon. Use those reflections to find the real which is reflected, and you will reach home from this strange land of insane people.

Beloved Bhagwan,

I am puzzled that I feel in your presence a beautiful absence, not in the sense of emptiness, but rather a quality of overflowingness.
Can you say something about this sense of absence?

Deva Nartan, you need not be puzzled about it, because you are feeling something which is absolutely true.

I am absent, as a person. I have been absent for a long time. But the moment I became absent – the person disappeared – a miracle happened. The disappearance of the person did not create emptiness. On the contrary, when the person was there I was empty; as the person disappeared I became absolute fullness, a presence.

When I was there, God was not there. When I evaporated, in that space a new quality – I call it godliness – a new presence, a new light, a new love, which belonged to eternity, slowly, slowly became more and more clear to me.

I used to be a house; now I am a temple. Everything from the outside has remained the same, but inside the sacred has descended.

So what you are feeling is absolutely the truth. On one hand I am absent, on another hand I am too much presence. If you can allow yourself just a little bit of space, my presence will enter into you. But you are so full of yourself that there is no way for God to enter in you, and you are keeping all your windows and doors closed out of fear that something from within you may fall out, may disappear, may be stolen; and there is nothing but crap.

The spiritual revolution can be reduced to a simple maxim:

You disappear and let God be.

You cannot find God. You and God cannot co-exist. If you exist, you are filling the whole space – and you are a false entity. Your name is false, whatever opinions you have collected about yourself are just opinions of people who themselves are fast asleep.

When I left the university, I approached the education minister directly, and I told him, "These are my qualifications: I have been top in my subject in the whole university; I need an appointment in a university."

He said, "This is strange. No application, nothing – you have just come directly to me."

I said, "In the application you would not have been able to feel me. I have come because my qualifications are just acquired from the outside, they are not inborn. I want you to face my inborn qualities."

There was a moment of silence. He said, "I can see and I can understand; but still the formalities have to be fulfilled."

So I said, "Just give me a piece of paper and I will write the application."

He said, "The application alone will not do; you have to attach a character certificate. Have you brought a character certificate?"

I said, "That is one of the most difficult things, because I have not come across a man to whom *I* can give a character certificate; how can I ask him to give me a character certificate?"

He said, "This is very difficult, but without a character certificate the formalities will not be fulfilled."

Then I said, "I can write a character certificate myself, because who knows me more than I know myself? My vice-chancellor was giving me a character certificate, I refused because I know the man – he has no character at all. And what is the meaning of having a character certificate from a man who has no character at all?

"I had certainly asked one of my professors to give me a character certificate, but he refused. He said, 'It is impossible to describe you, because I have known you for two years . . . you do not come into any category, and I don't know what to say about you. I would have loved to give you a character certificate, I have tried many times to write it, but nothing seemed to be adequate. I have dropped the idea.' "

The education minister said, "But a character certificate by your own hand is a strange thing."

I said, "I will do it properly. You accept this as an original character certificate, and I will get exactly the same from my professor – so that will be a carbon copy of the original; the original I am giving to you. I will not sign it, I will put my professor's signature, and because I have loved his handwriting, even he himself cannot make a distinction, whether he has signed it or I have signed it."

He said, "Finish it somehow, just do it."

So I signed the character certificate in the name of my professor, Dr. S. S. Roy, and I made a copy of it, and I went to S. S. Roy and I said, "The original I have given to the education minister. Now you give me a carbon copy of it."

He said, "What do you mean? I have heard always that the original has to be signed by me."

I said, "I have signed for you. Now, there cannot be two originals; that's why I am telling you to give me one carbon copy, as a proof."

I dictated it to him, he signed it, and he told me, "In my whole life, I don't think such a thing is going to happen again: that somebody writes a character certificate for himself, signs it with *my* signature, in the presence of the education minister. He is committing a crime . . . ."

I said, "You don't be worried; if you see both certificates, you will feel *your* signature is not so good."

He said, "That I can believe, because I have seen . . . you have signed my signature in many places. Before I had even reached the philosophy department, you had already signed the register and when I saw it the first time I could not believe what had happened. I had just arrived, and my signature was there! And I could not see any fault in it. I enquired, 'Who has signed it?'"

I said, "I have signed it, because it was getting late, and it has to be signed in time. Just to save you lying I managed to sign it. Now you need not be worried; you can come at any time, I will always sign it exactly at the time it has to be signed – that you have entered into the department. Even if you don't come, it does not matter; the signature will be there."

Your existence is just a carbon copy and you are clinging to it. Unless you drop it, the original, the real face of your being, will not show. And it is one of the most important things to remember: that if you can drop your ego, your personality, and allow existence to take its place, all the best and most beautiful qualities will follow on their own accord.

You will not have to be good, you will find you *are* good.

You will not have to be loving, you will find you *are* love.

You will not have to meditate, you will find you *are* meditation.

Just say goodbye to your ego, which is nothing but the opinions of others – press clippings, which you are holding as if they are your soul. Drop them! And immediately you become so clean, so pure, so spacious, that God cannot resist entering into you. You become a temple.

My whole effort here is to transform you from ordinary houses into sacred temples. When you can become the residence of the divine, why go on carrying secondhand opinions of people who themselves are just carbon copies?

Knowing the reality is such a benediction that one feels in every breath nothing but prayer – without any words, but full of gratitude.

Be absent as you are, so that God can be present in you with all his fragrance, with all his beauty, with all his glory, with all his eternity.

Beloved Bhagwan,

What is this longing to be sitting close to You, to rest my head on Your feet, to dance so wildly that the Rolls Royce stops, to play the guitar and sing so loudly, to look into and drown in Your eyes, to stop breathing when You move Your hand? What is this irresistible pull to be physically close to You?

Anand Masta, whenever and wherever you feel the presence of the divine, you may not be able intellectually to understand it – you may be an atheist who does not believe that there is anything divine – but if you are open, available, you will be pulled with a magnetic force and that pull will be expressed in all these longings.

You are asking, "What is this longing to be close to You?" Translated rightly, it is the longing to be close to yourself.

I am no more than a mirror. You see something of your originality reflected, something of your beauty reflected, something that you are missing, and missing very deeply. It is like a wound in you. You want it to be healed, and you know if you come closer, it will be healed. It is not knowledge gathered from books, it is your intrinsic wisdom.

It is almost like: a moth finds it irresistible to go close whenever it sees a beautiful flame, although it knows that by going closer to the flame it will be consumed. But moths are not skeptical, not doubting – they trust in their longing. Knowing that their death is sure, they also know somewhere deep within their consciousness that after death is resurrection. Nobody has told them.

This longing to be close to me is the longing of a moth to be close to the flame.

"To rest my head on Your feet" – this is something very strange, of which the West is absolutely unaware. The East, for thousands of years, has understood the longing; it is an energy phenomenon.

The master is almost like a river that is coming down from the hills, with all the coolness, with all the songs of the forest, with all the beauty of the wild animals.

The East has understood it, that if you put your head on the feet of the master, his energy will start flowing into you. It can flow only from his feet.

Energy cannot go upwards. It follows exactly the same law as water: it goes downwards.

Friedrich Nietzsche, in his masterpiece *Thus Spoke Zarathustra*, starts the book: This is how the downgoing of Zarathustra started. He was living in the mountains for a long time where very rare birds make their nests. To reach to that height is not possible.

He has lived on the heights and now he is so

overfull of silence, of love, of blessings, of blissfulness, that a *downward* flow starts. It is a very symbolic statement: Thus Zarathustra started going down; just like a river, because that is the only way to reach to the people who live in the valleys.

Masta, your longing to rest your head on my feet is coming from a very deep source of wisdom and understanding. And I have given you the name Anand Masta. The day I initiated you I could see in your eyes the possibility of divine madness: Masta means "mad," Anand Masta means "blissfully mad." And now it seems the spring has come and flowers have started blossoming.

"What is this longing to be close to you, to rest my head on your feet, to dance so wildly that the Rolls Royce stops, to play the guitar and sing so loudly, to look into and drown in your eyes, to stop breathing when you move your hand? What is this irresistible pull to be physically close to you?"

Just a natural longing of every disciple to be drowned in the blissful energy, loving energy, in the ecstasy of the master. And to be drowned in the ecstasy of the master, one wants to dance madly so that the ego disappears and only dance remains – because the ego cannot dissolve into the master, but the dance can dissolve. To sing so loudly and so madly that the singer disappears; only then the song can dissolve into the master.

And because you are not yet aware of the whole phenomenon, you think it is "a pull to be physically close to You." There you are not understanding your own longing clearly, only very vaguely. It is not a question of physical closeness, it is a question of spiritual closeness. But because you have known yourself only as body, you are absolutely unaware of the treasures of your soul.

The body is there today, tomorrow it may not be; but your soul is going to be forever. The irresistible urge is to let your soul, your consciousness, become one with the master. I have called that state the state of a devotee.

The student is only intellectually interested; the disciple comes closer – he is not only intellectually interested, it is not only his curiosity to know more and more – the disciple wants to *be* more and more. But there comes a limit, when the disciple cannot resist the urge to be one with the master, to be one with the beloved. This is a spiritual urge.

But everybody feels it first as if it is an urge to be physically close. My intuition was perfectly right when I gave you the name "blissful madness." Now the time has come, the time of maturity. And when your madness matures, it moves from disciplehood to a higher stage of devotion.

In the West it is very much misunderstood: that people touch the feet of their elders, of their mothers, of their fathers, of their masters. They think it seems to be a little humiliating. It is not.

If you have loved and if touching the feet of your master is nothing but an expression of your devotion, you will not be humiliated. On the contrary, you will be raised to the highest consciousness you are capable of.

Anand Masta, you are fortunate, you are blessed. Let this longing grow into a sweet pain. Let it deepen. Don't be afraid. And you will find that which you have come here to find. In this humbleness, in this loving devotion, you are coming closer to the divine.

And there is an old, very old saying which seems to be very significant, that if you move one step towards God, he moves one thousand steps towards you.

Beloved Bhagwan,

While sitting with You my heart is in pain, but this pain is so blissful and sweet that I can only rejoice in it. Please tell me, what is this blissful pain while being close to You?

Sadhan, you are just a little ahead of Anand Masta. Your longing to be one with the master, to be one with the beloved, has ripened even more. That is why you feel your heart is full of pain, but the pain is very sweet.

When the pain is very sweet and blissful, so that you can rejoice in it, the pain is not of this world. Who can rejoice in pain? This pain has a totally different quality from ordinary pain. That's why it is sweet, it is blissful, and you feel like rejoicing in it.

Rejoice! Let this sweet pain become a song, a dance. Let this sweet pain drown you completely – disappear in it. And your disappearance is the greatest thing that can happen to a person, because your disappearance is the beginning of the finding of the divine.

Okay, Vimal?

Yes, Bhagwan.

Silence Has Its Own Fragrance

It will appear absurd to the logical mind, but the fact is that blissfulness has its own perfume, silence has its own fragrance, just as love has its own taste, its own sweetness. Although you cannot eat love and you cannot taste love, you know perfectly well that love has a sweetness. Silence also has its own flowers, its own fragrance. And the enlightened man's consciousness can be approached through any of your senses. You can see it in his presence, in his grace, in his eyes; in his gestures you can smell it. You can hear it, just a small whisper, as if a breeze has passed through the pine trees – subtle, but absolutely certain. You can taste it . . . .

When I go out, you have been through a great shower of love, peace, silence, song, music and dance. Your whole being is cleansed. You feel the freshness, you feel the profundity, so tangible that if your eyes are closed you may think I am still present here – but in a certain way nothing changes, only my body moves away from here.

I am always present – wherever love longs for me and a heart beats for me, wherever a consciousness searches for me, I am available there.

February 23, 1987,   7 p.m.

Beloved Bhagwan,

Last year in Bombay, You said that since I've met You there has never been a no in me. Yes, Bhagwan, that is true. And yet, the other night, I saw my head shaking in a deep no to Your words. When You said I love you too much, I felt for the first time a no in me, so total, so deep. For a moment I heard my heart singing, No, no, no – it is not too much, there is space in my being to love You much more. So I guess You were joking, or using poetic license, or a metaphor. I don't like to say no to You, but if You dare to repeat that I love You too much I will start to laugh and say, "No, Bhagwan, no," again and again, "No, Bhagwan."

Sarjano, words like yes and no are very flexible. They are not opposites, they are two extremes of one single energy. Hence sometimes a very strange phenomenon happens. It is said about women that when they say no they mean yes – the flexibility is so great – and when you were saying no, you were meaning yes.

I can understand why the no arose in you, because love knows no limits. For those who love, even too much love is too little. You wanted to say no, because you are capable of loving more. But that capacity is infinite: at no point does love feel that it has come to a full stop – there are always possibilities, potentialities, and space available to grow more. Your no is not no, it is really a preparation for a greater yes.

So I want to say to you: Sarjano, you love me too much. And even if you say no, it does not matter. It simply means even too much is too little – and you can see that you can love more. Too much is not the end, so

your no is, in a disguised form, nothing but yes. You cannot deceive me by words.

You are saying, "Last year in Bombay You said that since I have met You there has never been a no in me." I still say so. But you are puzzled, because you feel, "Yes, Bhagwan, that is true. And yet, the other night I saw my head shaking in a deep no to Your words." It is because your love is greater than any words can contain. But your no is not negative, it is another form of saying yes.

"When You said I love You too much, I felt for the first time a no in me, so total, so deep. For a moment I heard my heart singing, No, no, no – it is not too much . . . ." You were not saying no to me, you were simply saying no to my statement that you love me too much.

Suddenly you became aware that you are capable of loving more – this is not too much. I agree with you: you are capable of loving more. Still, it is too much. It will become even vaster, deeper, greater; but that is not going to change my statement. And you have understood yourself, without being clearly aware of it, when you said, "It is not too much. There is space in my being to love you much more. So I guess You were joking, or using poetic license, or a metaphor."

No, I was neither joking, nor using metaphors, nor poetic license. I was simply describing the simple fact that your love is too much for me. But for you, it may appear too little. That is the perennial experience of all lovers. The loved one feels it is too much, but the lover feels it is nothing: "I have not put my whole being into it yet."

"I don't like to say no to You . . . ." You have never said no to me. Even when yesterday, the no was arising in you, it was nothing but preparing ground for a bigger yes.

You are challenging me, that "If You dare to repeat that I love You too much, I will start to laugh and say, 'No, Bhagwan, no!' Again and again, 'No, Bhagwan!' "

You can laugh, and you can still say, "No, Bhagwan, no." But it will mean only "Yes, Bhagwan, yes." And I repeat again and again that you love me too much, Sarjano. Language is a very slippery matter.

I am reminded of a small incident. In a monastery, only one hour was given to the monks who lived in the monastery, to go out in the garden. But it was called one hour for praying in the open, under the sky. Two friends were very much troubled by one thing – both were smokers, and since they had entered the monastery they had not smoked: it was prohibited.

One of them said to the other, "Perhaps it is prohibited inside the monastery, but in the garden . . . ? I think we should ask the abbot, the chief monk." Both agreed, and the next day one came out angry, enraged, humiliated, insulted, because the abbot had refused absolutely. He had used the words, "absolutely no." As he came out, he became even more furious, because he saw the other sitting under a tree smoking so joyfully. He could not believe it.

He said, "Have you asked, or are you smoking without asking?" He said, "I asked – but why are you looking so red with anger?" He said, "This is strange: has he agreed?" The monk who was smoking said, "Yes – he said, 'Yes, absolutely yes!' " The other man said, "This abbot seems to be crazy. To me he said, 'No, absolutely no!' "

Still the other man went on laughing and he said, "Just cool down, sit down, and tell me what you have asked." He said, "I have asked simply, 'While outside in the garden, can I smoke?' And he said, 'No, absolutely no!' " The one who was smoking said, "Now things are clear. You asked a wrong question. I asked 'Can I pray while smoking?' He said, 'Yes, absolutely yes!' "

Your no, Sarjano, is nothing but yes. You are not satisfied with too much, you want more. And now you cannot laugh, and you cannot say, "No, Bhagwan no" – you will have to say, "Yes, Bhagwan yes."

Even when you were saying no, you were saying yes – you were just not alert why that no was arising in you.

Beloved Bhagwan,

In the discourses after You have danced with us and left the hall, something seems to linger in the air in this mandir that is not unlike the fragrance of a rare flower, ephemeral, and yet so tangible to the senses. Sometimes the silence is so profound that were my eyes closed I would never know that You were physically no more among us. Would You please say something about this phenomenon?

Milarepa, it will appear absurd to the logical mind, but the fact is that blissfulness has its own perfume, silence has its own fragrance, just as love has its own taste, its own sweetness. Although you cannot eat love and you cannot taste love, you know perfectly well that love has a sweetness.

Silence also has its own flowers, its own fragrance. And the enlightened man's consciousness can be approached through any of your senses. You can see it in his presence, in his grace, in his eyes, in his gestures you can smell it. You can hear it, just a small whisper, as if a breeze has passed through the pine trees – subtle, but absolutely certain. You can taste it.

The night Jesus departed from his disciples – you must all remember the last supper – he talked to them for the last time. And what he said seems to be very strange. He said, "You have to eat me and you have to drink me. And unless you eat me and drink me and digest me, unless I become your blood, your bones, your marrow, you will not be able to find me." Certainly he was not speaking to cannibals. He was talking about this subtle phenomenon which is available only to disciples and devotees.

When I go out, you have been through a great shower of love, peace, silence, song, music and dance. Your whole being is cleansed. You feel the freshness, you feel the profundity, so tangible that if your eyes are closed you may think I am still present here – but in a certain way nothing changes, only my body moves away from here. I am always present – wherever love longs for me and a heart beats for me, wherever a consciousness searches for me, I am available there.

Both Gautam Buddha and Mahavira, the greatest masters the Indian tradition has produced, made it a rule that their sannyasins should move in groups of five. In the beginning I could not figure it out – why five? And for twenty-five centuries Jaina monks and Buddhist monks and nuns have moved . . . the group cannot be less than five – it can be more. Now it is a dead tradition: they follow it, they don't know its meaning. I have asked many Jaina monks, many Buddhists; they say, "We are simply following the scriptures."

But as I became aware that the enlightened consciousness has all the qualities which your five senses can experience, then I had a clue. Buddha himself, and Mahavira himself, too, used to make up the groups of five sannyasins – to move, to spread the message. It was not at random, it was not any five, just because they were friends. They were chosen by Gautam Buddha and Mahavira themselves.

And my own experience is, they were chosen for this simple reason: that one was more sensitive as far as his eyes were concerned, and another was more sensitive as far as his ears were concerned, and another was more sensitive as far as his taste was concerned. Those five people were almost the five senses, together the most sensitive five, so whenever they will meditate in silence, it will be far easier for the consciousness of Gautam Buddha or Mahavira to be present amongst them.

Their senses became the doors. It is very difficult to find a person whose every sense is functioning at the maximum. We know it perfectly well: there are people who cannot smell anything, their nose is dead; there are people who are called "color-blind."

For example, George Bernard Shaw did not realize until the age of sixty that he was color-blind. It was just a coincidence that on his sixtieth birthday some friend sent him a suit as a present, but he had forgotten to add a matching tie. And Bernard Shaw liked the suit very much. He wanted to wear it on his birthday when all his friends were going to be there. So he asked his secretary, a young woman, to go with him to find a matching tie.

The secretary was puzzled, because the suit was green and Bernard Shaw chose a yellow tie. She did not think that this was a good match; it would look very odd and awkward. Even the shopkeeper said, "Sir, this tie won't go with this suit." Bernard Shaw said, "Why not? They are of the same color."

That day he realized that between green and yellow he could not make any distinction. He was blind to the color yellow: it looked like green. You will be surprised to know that almost ten percent of people are color-blind. It is not a small percentage: out of every ten persons, one person is color-blind. He may not know his whole life – and eyes are the most important factors.

Musicians know perfectly well that there are people who have an ear for music; all people don't have the ear. In a factual way everybody has an ear, but to have an ear for music is a totally different thing. You need a very deep sensitivity about sound and about silence.

There are many people who don't have much sensitivity about taste, or about touch. You may have come across people . . . if you shake hands with them it feels as if you are shaking hands with the dead branch of a tree: you don't feel any energy, any warmth, any love being transferred. And with other people, when you shake hands with them, you know there has been a dialogue: your hands have spoken to each other things which you cannot say.

Buddha and Mahavira, were both very alert in choosing people to make small groups of five; each was perfect in at least one sense. The five together were perfect in all five senses. Buddha promised his disciples : Whenever five of you are together in deep silence and meditation, the sixth also will be present – I am the sixth.

So if you are sensitive – and meditation makes you more and more sensitive – then even when I am gone and it's only my physical body that is no longer here, your sensitivity will not let my consciousness go away so easily. I will remain amongst you for a little while.

There are many of you who don't want to go away from Chuang Tzu immediately, because it is an experience in itself – in my absense you are still feeling my presence. So people linger on a little, laughing, dancing, or sometimes singing, or sometimes just sitting surrounded by an unknown energy, an unnamed energy . . . but yet somehow familiar.

It all depends on your love, on how much you love. Love destroys distance, and if love is total, it destroys distance totally. Then even when you are alone – no need for five persons – you will feel me with you.

Just today I received a letter from Emerson. Emerson is Hasya's son; Hasya is my international secretary. I was feeling that something is bound to be strange about Emerson, because Hasya was phoning continually to many friends here, giving them the same message, that Emerson was coming, take care of him. It is perfectly okay, Hasya is a Jewish mama: although Emerson is thirty years old, for almost two weeks she has been phoning continually and not to one person . . . the same instructions to many different persons: "Take care. Emerson is coming."

When I heard this – that so many people are receiving the message – I said, "What is his age?" And when I came to know that he was thirty, I said, "My God!" I used to think that Hasya must have gone beyond her Jewish mind. She has dropped all Judaism – that is one thing – but to drop being a Jewish mama . . . that is difficult. There are mothers and mothers in the world, but no mother comes close to the Jewish mother.

Now, a thirty year-old son – and also, she is coming to take care of him in just three days. Yesterday I saw him and I felt really sorry for him and sorry for Hasya.

Hasya deep down wanted him to understand me, but he was so dead, so insensitive. Today he wrote me a letter. He is in love with Kendra, one of my sannyasins. The letter was long, but the essential part was, "Bhagwan, I hate you." The reason for his hate is that, first, I have taken his mother. Now he is in love with Kendra, and he says, "I know perfectly well that Kendra has you as her first priority. I'm not even her second priority . . . her second priority is another sannyasin." – I think he must be thinking of John – "I am the third priority: it hurts." And he wanted me to say to Kendra that she should go with Emerson.

I have replied, that all my sannyasins live in absolute freedom. I don't say to anybody to do something or not to do something. If Kendra wants to be here, it is her choice; if she wants to be with John, it is her choice; if she wants to go with you, that is her choice. Whatever she chooses, my blessings are with her. As far as you are concerned, I cannot say anything to you, because a man who says, "I hate you," will not be able to understand anything. Hate is the most difficult barrier for understanding, just as love is the greatest opening for understanding.

He is puzzled – because he is very rich, a billionaire – about why Kendra wants to be here, even when she cleans the floors, does manual work. It is beyond his comprehension – because he thinks money can buy everything, and he can give Kendra everything she wants. But it will be a great problem: even if Kendra goes with him out of compassion, he knows deep down that he is the third on the laundry list. How long can he tolerate Kendra? He will take revenge. Right now he will be very persuasive – but he cannot forgive her for putting him into third place.

And his puzzle is, why are people here? He was asking my personal physician, Amrito, "Why are you all here? I cannot understand." One has to be somewhere or other. The same question can be asked, "Why are you in Hollywood? Why are you in L.A.?" One has to be somewhere or other.

I wanted to tell him a story: once Mulla Nasruddin was caught in the cupboard of the bedroom of one of his friends. The friend was very angry, but Mulla is a man who has his own logic. The man was very angry, and he could see . . . because he had been out when Mulla was with his wife, and when he came in Mulla was hiding in the cupboard. But he could not ask the right thing, he simply asked, "Why are you here?" Mulla said, "This is a strange question – one has to be somewhere! Do you want me to be nowhere? – you are asking an absurd question. One can ask me anywhere, 'Why are you here?' "

But Emerson must be very insensitive. He could not see your joy, he could not see your songs, he could not see your blissfulness, he could not see your silence, he could not see your love, he could not see anything: he was simply asking, "What are these people doing here?" And what is he doing in Hollywood? Earning more money? These people are certainly not earning more money; they are earning more being, earning more love, they are earning more sensitivity, they are earning more spiritual growth, they are earning more life – and finally, they are earning God.

They have a thousand and one reasons to be here, and to be in Hollywood you have only one reason: earning more money. But what are you going to do with money? At the age of thirty he is as dead as someone should be at the age of ninety; all his senses are gone. Perhaps he is only available to more money and more money. And if he thinks that by having more money, he can have love, he can purchase love, he can purchase truth, virtue . . . . Anything that is really valuable is not purchasable, anything that is valuable has no price on it and anything that has a price on it, is only for very mediocre minds.

For those who don't know the flight of an eagle because they can only hop on the ground, the question arises, "What is that eagle doing far away there in the sky?" Hopping here on the earth is enough for them; flying from place A to B, from B to C, and going far away beyond the horizon, and disappearing into the sky, is beyond their imagination and their dreams.

Looking at him I was afraid about Kendra, because if you live with anybody who has been dead so long, you are going to be dead. Never be in the company of the dead! Seek out the company of the more joyful, the more dancing, the more living – because life is infectious, just as death is infectious.

I am happy to see that he has not been able to affect Kendra; she is still happy and dancing and singing and joyous. Kendra, help him. He is not completely dead, but soon he will be – because thirty is the age when people start dying. He has almost died before his time. And I am worried and concerned about Hasya. She will be coming here, and she is very alive, very joyful – a very happy human being. It seems Emerson is copying his father. Hasya had to leave her husband . . . now I know what must have been the cause; that man must have been a dead weight on her soul. She needs a dancing partner, not a dead weight or a golden cross hanging around her neck.

Emerson has chosen to be with his father, and not to be with his mother, because the father is very rich, and all his money is going to be in his hands. He will be one of the richest men in America when the father is gone. But I am concerned about the son; the son is going before the father.

If he can be here just for a few months, perhaps seeing so many alive people, living in this dancing vibe, in the presence of all these meditators, something that is dormant within him may start growing. He may be born again. This place can become a rebirth for him – but for that he will have to be a little courageous, and Kendra will have to be a little stronger. If she can keep him here, his hate for me I will change to love. That is not a problem, that is a very simple thing, because hate is the same energy. He hates me because I have taken his mother and now I'm taking his girlfriend. But being here he can have both the girlfriend and the mother, and more important is that he can save himself from dying.

Money kills people, becomes a weight on their heart. I'm not saying that people should not have money. They should always remember only that there are higher values than money. Use the money to reach to the higher values; make money the stepping stone. It cannot purchase those values, but it can become a stepping stone.

Beloved Bhagwan,

Several years ago my wife saw your picture and said, "There is an enlightened man."
I said, "They are all fake, and India's caste system and poverty are evidence of that."
I am a four-year-old sannyasin, and she is not. What happened?

Antar Rituraj, your wife recognized me too soon. Seeing the picture, she said, "There is an enlightened man." And that's where she stopped. She did not bother to understand what enlightenment is. If she has recognized someone as an enlightened man, then she should have come, at least once, to be with me. But she seems to be very knowledgeable.

You were critical, you said, "They are all fake" – and you are 99.9 percent right – "and India's caste system and poverty are evidence of that," – that too, is a hundred percent true. Now you are asking, "I am a four-year-old sannyasin, and she is not. What happened?" You made a statement which became a question mark in your being. Her statement became a full stop: "There is an enlightened man," – and things are finished. But you were critical: "They are all fake, and India's caste system and poverty are evidence of that."

It became a question mark in you, because you were making a very cynical, very skeptical, very negative statement. You wanted to come and see whether your statement was true about me too, or not. Your question mark brought you here; she had no questions. Being with me you found that there is a 0.1 percent possibility of an enlightened man, of a man who has an awakened consciousness, and is not the cause of the caste system and poverty in India, but is fighting against it, and is suffering because of that fight.

You are not aware, how many summonses from how many courts go on coming . . . that somebody's religious feelings are hurt, and I have to be present in the court in Bengal, in North India, in Himachal Pradesh. All these thirty years the same people – whom I have been trying to awaken: You are suffering unnecessarily from the caste system, rebel against it! – these same people have tried to kill me many times. They have disturbed my meetings, they have thrown stones at me, they have even stopped my train. They would not allow the train to go ahead unless I was thrown out of the train.

The same poor people are so conditioned . . . . They are suffering from their conditioning, and I am fighting against that conditioning, and they think I am fighting against them! I am fighting *for* them *against* their conditioning, but they are so identified with their conditioning that it is almost impossible to make them aware of the distinction: that your conditioning is not you. And by birth nobody is a Brahmin.

I am reminded of a beautiful old story: One great seer in the Upanishads is Uddalak. His father sent Uddalak to a forest university where only seers were the teachers, and meditation was the basic teaching. And when Uddalak came bach home after ten, twelve years, his father – who was a learned scholar, well-respected and well-known – saw him coming and he ran away out of the back door.

His wife asked, "Where are you going? Your son is coming." He said, "I cannot face him; moreover, I cannot allow him to touch my feet; it will look very awkward. He has really become a Brahmin. He has become a Brahmin because he has known the Brahma." Brahma is the ultimate life source. "I am only a Brahmin by birth; he has earned it. If he does not touch my feet, that will look awkward, if he does touch my feet, *that* will look awkward, if I touch his feet that too will look awkward. It is better that I should escape. I am not leaving you alone – your son is back. I will come back home only when I am also a Brahmin not only by birth, but by experience, by my own realization."

Nobody is born a Brahmin, and nobody is born a warrior, and nobody is born a *sudra*, an untouchable.

The poverty in this country is there because the religions of this country have been consoling the poor, just as they have been consoling the poor in other countries. Their explanations may be different, but the ultimate result is to console them: your poverty is not something bad; if you can patiently go through this fire test, in the afterlife you will be rewarded a millionfold.

So when you came to me, you found an enlightened man who was not fitting your definition. You cannot say to me that I am responsible for the caste system in India, you cannot say that I am responsible for the poverty in India. You had to change your definition. Your question became a quest. You became a sannyasin, a pilgrim, to find out the truth that makes one enlightened.

Your wife will remain in darkness, in unconscious-ness. Now it is your responsibility and your love, that your wife should also become a seeker. Just seeing a picture and saying, Here is an enlightened man, is not going to help her. But she has a certain sensibility, a certain alertness – howsoever little. If you love her, don't go on the path along : help her also to be on the path. It will help you in return. Whenever your love is great you want the beloved also to come to know the ultimate joy, bliss and benediction. It may be your wife, it may be your son, it may be your daughter, it may be your husband, whomever you love. Your love is just a word . . . what else you can you give, if you cannot give an urge, a thirst for truth?

Invite your wife. If she can recognize me in my picture, there is every possibility she will recognize me looking into my eyes. Just don't be jealous of her – she is going to fall in love; you will become priority number two.

Okay, Vimal?

Yes, Bhagwan.

When Buddhas Rebel

If you want to be really a rebel, first you have to find your being. Then each of your acts will be not only an act of love and devotion, it will also be an act of tremendous revolution – in your life and in other people's lives. Your love is true, but very small.

I want your love to be as big as possible – bigger than the sky. It should have no limits to it. And out of that love arises the true rebel, the true rebellion.

The whole of history is full of the failures of revolutions; and the reason for their failure is that they were not coming from being – they were only coming from doing. Neither Karl Marx had any idea of being, nor Lenin, nor Mao Tse-tung.

All these great revolutionaries have done much. But because they themselves were very superficial their revolutions have remained superficial, just a kind of whitewash – not a revolution which comes from the very roots.

My sannyasins are going to be rebels, but rebels not in the ordinary sense of the word. Before they become rebels they have to become buddhas. Only then will the world know true revolution – when buddhas rebel.

February 24, 1987,   8 a.m.

Beloved Bhagwan,

I was first attracted to You through the mind. I loved what You had to say. It has been almost ten years since You gave me sannyas and I'm afraid I'm still connected through the mind.
In these years there have been but few instances when I have known the feelings of love, of trust, and openness. My mind usually comes in and ends these moments. I like to hide behind the words of the old Sufi song – "I love you whether I know it or not." Do You see any possibility for me to jump from my mind into my heart and stay there? Is it possible for me to know love?

Nitin, your coming to me was from the very beginning not right. Those who come to me through their intellect only *think* they have come to me; they never arrive.

You were attracted because you were intellectually convinced of what I was saying. You have never been in love with me, but only with the words, arguments. And the words and arguments are not my being. Because of this wrong beginning, ten years have passed, but you have not moved a single inch.

You think that there are moments of trust, love and openness; those are your imagination, because there are never moments of trust. When trust comes, it never goes. There are no moments of love – when love comes, it stays, forever and forever.

There are no moments of openness – and if you have known a single moment of openness, you will not close yourself again. Because closed, you are in darkness, cut off from existence and cut off from all that is valuable. For what should you close? You can remain closed if you have not known a moment of openness. Once you have tasted the moment of openness, it is impossible to go back.

So, the first thing you say is: "I was first attracted to You through the mind." You are still attracted through the mind. And mind never creates any bridge; when you are attracted through the mind you are falling in love with your own mind. You are using me as a support for your own arguments, for your own philosophy, for your own religion, and you are deceiving yourself that you are falling in love with me.

Mind never falls in love; it is the deadly enemy of love. It is so egocentric that it will always take anything that is supportive to it, that is nourishment to it.

These ten years I have been watching you, and I have been really surprised. You are amongst so many lovers – you see their joy, you see their songs, you see their dance, you hear their laughter – but nothing stirs within you, because everything goes into your head. And the head is the most superficial thing in your being.

So it is not that "in the beginning" you were attracted through the mind; I am afraid even in the end you will remain attracted through the mind. It is good to be aware of it, because then a change is possible.

You say, "I loved what You had to say." That could have been listened to from a tape recorder. Do you think you will fall in love with the tape recorder? You are in love with your own ego so much that you go on gathering everything that supports it, nourishes it, makes it stronger – and this is not the place to make your ego stronger! This is the place where you should lose your ego, and hopefully will not find it again.

The head-oriented approach to me has been destructive to your ten years; it can destroy your ten lives. You are saying, "It has been almost ten years since You gave me sannyas." I never give sannyas to anybody – you take sannyas. Just see the cunningness of the mind: you have taken sannyas, I have not given it to you. And you can drop sannyas any moment because *you* have taken it. If I had given it, then only I can take it back; you cannot drop it.

I did not knock on your door saying, "Nitin, please become a sannyasin." You came to me. You asked for sannyas. It was just out of compassion that I gave you sannyas, knowing perfectly well it was not going to change anything in you. You came here following your wife – she is an authentic sannyasin; she is not in love with my words.

When you love me, it does not matter what I say. To the loving heart, words don't mean anything; but the presence of the person, his love, his abundant readiness to share his bliss – this is a totally different approach.

But I know your problem: you are a poor chartered accountant. Accountants are not known to be lovers, and lovers never account. Your mind is full of your accountings: how much you are gaining. You must be keeping inside you all the records. But that is not the way of love. So first you have to drop your false ideas. One is, that in the beginning you came through the mind. I insist again: you are still here because of the mind. You have a trained mind.

Secondly, you say, "You gave me sannyas." That is unnecessarily blaming me. You took sannyas; you asked for it. If these false ideas disappear – then perhaps there is a possibility of transformation. And you are also unconsciously aware of what I am saying because you say, "And I am afraid I am still connected through the mind."

Mind never connects; it disconnects.

If you are all here, enclosed in your minds, then there are five hundred people. But if you are here, singing and dancing and celebrating through the heart, then there is only one consciousness.

Mind divides, and particularly the mind of a chartered accountant. You are spoilt by your accountancy. You are a good accountant, you have a good mind, a sharp intellect – but these are not of any use in sannyas. You are clinging to them, and you are with me because you feel I agree with you. You will have to change the whole thing: *you* have to agree with *me*; I do not have to be in agreement with you. And when I say you have to agree with me, that agreement is not going to be of the mind, but only of the heart. When your heart agrees with me there is a harmony and a bridge and things start taking mysterious, miraculous changes.

You say, "In these years there have been but few instances when I have known the feelings of love, of trust and openness." Absolutely wrong! You are trying to console yourself; because people are living here in trust, in love, in openness, and you don't want to appear an absolute beggar who has not known any moment of love, of trust, or of openness.

Because the basic principle about love, trust or openness is: they come but they never go. Why should one leave the joy of love and fall into the misery of lovelessness? Why should one know the beauty of trust and still go back to his mind, to his arithmetic and accountancy?

I am not saying that you have to drop your accounting. Mind can do that, but through that you cannot be connected with me. If you can drop these ideas it will be a shock to you – that you have not known even moments of love, moments of trust, moments of openness – but this shock is going to be of immense value. It will heal you. This shock will awaken you.

You say, "My mind usually comes in and ends these moments." Mind has not the power to end love; this simply shows you have not known anything of love or trust. When people fall in love, however great a mind they may have, the love is going to be victorious, not the mind.

Mind is juiceless, dry bones. It is a bio-computer; it is not your soul. And unless you start from the heart you cannot arrive at the being; heart is the gate to the being. Mind does not allow you to go out of itself – just out of the fear that you may come across the heart, which is so juicy, so beautiful, so lovely and so loving, that meeting the heart, mind has no way to pull you back.

You can use the mind as an instrument, but it cannot remain your master; and, Nitin, it is still your master. You are quoting a Sufi saying which you cannot understand. The only person alive on the earth who can understand it is Ajit Saraswati. He was in the same trap in which you are – he approached me from his mind. Because I was saying things which he had not the courage to say, or was not articulate enough to say, he came closer to me, and as he became more and more articulate, listening, he asked me, "Many Rotary Clubs, Lions Clubs ask me to speak about You – should I go?"

I never prevent people; I knew that this was going to be his downfall. I said, "If they are inviting you, you can go." And he started talking to the Rotary Clubs in Poona and Kholapur and Sholapur – in different places. He had come with me to America too, and when he found that he could say the same words, he could manage to argue in the same way, he came back to Poona.

There was a celebration in the ashram and everybody thought that he had come directly from the commune, he must have brought some flavor with him – so they asked him to speak. And I was informed that:

"It was such a surprise to us that he was not speaking about You, he was speaking himself – and he knows nothing."

And since I have come here he has not come to the ashram, he has not come to any meetings, he has not come even to see me once – and he has been related to me almost for twenty years. But that relation was the same as your relation: of the mind. Now he has become a parrot. He runs small classes where he teaches – not even mentioning my name; he teaches as if he has experienced.

Zareen asked him, "You have not come to see Bhagwan?"

He said, "I love him very much. He is in my heart; I need not come to see him." Can you see the cunningness of the mind? It means lovers should stop seeing each other, because what is the point? "I love you too much. You are in my heart; there is no need to see you."

In the ashram it has become a joke – if somebody wants to avoid somebody else he says, "I love you too much. You are in my heart; we need not meet. There is no need." This is a great way!

Anando was telling me that some sannyasin was interested in her, but she was feeling utterly disgusted by the man, so she said, "I love you too much. You are in my heart; we need not see each other."

You are quoting a Sufi song, "I love you whether I know it or not." It is a very mysterious statement, and only a mystic can make it – not you, Nitin; you cannot even understand the meaning of it. The Sufi mystic is saying, "I love you whether I know it or not." He is giving expression to the idea that whether the trees know about their roots or not, those roots are their very life; without them the trees cannot exist at all. The Sufi mystic is saying about God that, "I must be loving you, otherwise why I am alive? Without your love nourishing me continuously, life is impossible."

But he is a humble man. He says, "It does not matter whether I know it or not, but one thing is certain: love must be happening, because I am still alive.

Not only I must be in love with you, you are also in love with me – whether I know it or not." Those who know it become enlightened. Those who don't know it – they also are nourished by the same source as any Gautam Buddha; but *you* cannot say that to me.

I am not an invisible God and love is not something that comes through the back door, you sometimes know it and sometimes don't know it. Love comes through the front door and comes like a flood. It drowns you: how you can avoid knowing it?

Love is the only thing, perhaps, which does not make any sound, does not speak, but is still heard. It does not become your knowledge, but still there is a knowing far higher than knowledge. Your love for me is because of the words I say to you. You hear in those words echoes of your own ideas, but basically your love is for your own ideas. Because I am also expressing them – perhaps you were not so clear, things were vague, my statements have made them clear – you think you owe to me your love, your trust, your openness. But these are all mind games. Be clear that you have never loved anybody except yourself.

"Do you see any possibility for me to jump from my mind into my heart and stay there? Is it possible for me to know love?" It is everybody's birthright – but one has to claim it. And love is so precious, unless you claim it, you are going to miss it.

There is every possibility for you to shift your energy from the head to the heart, and I would like to add also from the heart to the being – because the heart is only a half-way station. You can have a little stopover, change trains; you can have some breakfast, and rest a little before the train that goes to the being leaves the platform.

The heart is not the goal, the heart is only a means to attain the being. All these are possible for you, Nitin, just as they are possible for anybody else; but you have to put your conceptions in the right order. It may hurt, it may be painful – all surgery is painful – but if you are courageous enough, you can move through the surgery and you will come out of it healed, healthier, more wholesome.

You came because your wife came; you simply followed her. And you tried, deep in your unconscious, to compete with her – but the head cannot win in any competition with the heart. But nothing is lost; even if after ten years you recognize the reality, the change will start happening.

The greatest problem in life is to go on living with false notions. Then you are so full of false notions that the truth has no space for itself. First destroy the false notions. Create space for the guest, and once your space is ready – your silence, your peace, your serenity – the guest comes without delay. He is standing just outside your door. He has been waiting for many lives for you to open your doors and let the sun and the wind and the rain come in, because God comes with the sun, with the rain, with the wind. And throw out all the junk that you have gathered inside you.

The moment you are spacious, you have not to do anything else – that space will be filled with the presence of the divine. And then you will know what love is, what trust is, what openness is: the greatest treasures in life.

Beloved Bhagwan,

I am still so much in doing. To me, doing is much more natural than being, and in this way I feel to express my love and devotion to You. But is it true love? Many years ago I told You that I felt like being a warrior in the West. Also now I have the same feeling. Does that mean that I don't move much on the path to become a meditator?

Deva Majid, I am aware that you are still "so much in doing," and you are expressing and exposing yourself very authentically. You are saying to me, "Doing is much more natural than being." Just one thing you are not aware of: you can compare two things only if you know them both.

You know doing, but you don't know being; hence, please don't compare. Being is only an empty word for you – doing is full of excitement. But this is how people go on living: in deceptions.

Doing can give you excitement.

Being can give you ecstasy.

Excitement is very mundane, very ordinary – any idiot can afford it. You are not an idiot, you are an intelligent being. So first, I am not saying that you have to change from doing to being; I am saying, first at least have a little taste of being, and then you are free to choose. I am certain that nobody has ever chosen doing, once he has known being.

It does not mean that the man of being becomes useless, that he stops doing things. No; the man of being does things more beautifully, more gracefully, more aesthetically. The man of being transforms his doings from their mundane quality into something sacred. So there is no opposition; it is not a question of choosing – it is not a question of to be or not to be.

When you know only doing, you are unaware of your great potential. I want you to know being, too. And it will not destroy your doing, it will simply beautify it; it will make each act a prayer, each act an art, each act a deep fulfilment. Being will flow through your doings, it will make your life more colorful. Otherwise, soon you will get fed up with your doings, because they are the same, again and again, again and again – how long can you remain excited about them? But if your doing flows from your being, then each doing has a different flavor, a different individuality, a different fragrance.

You are saying, Majid, "To me doing is much more natural than being" – because doing is superficial. And the whole society teaches you to be a doer, nobody is concerned with your being. Otherwise being is your deeper nature. There is no antagonism between doing and being, just that being will bring depth, significance, to your doings.

So if you really want to be a doer, you have to enter into the realm of being. You are saying, "And in this way I feel to express my love and devotion to you." It is true: through your doings you express your love and your devotion to me – but you don't know that there are greater things possible in you.

The same acts of love, of devotion, will have such profundity, such eternity, that you will be amazed that you were satisfied only with the surface and never dived deep into the water. But without diving deeper into the water you cannot find the pearls. On the surface you can find the white foam on top of the waves, shining in the sun, and it looks beautiful – but it is nothing but air bubbles. If you take the foam in your hand, soon you will find it has disappeared, just leaving your hand wet.

You are asking me, "But is it true love?" It is. But love has many, many depths. It is only the beginning, the first rung of the ladder. When you are capable of reaching to the highest rung, why be satisfied with a poorer state of your consciousness?

I know you are a rebel – and that is what you are excited about, rebellious acts – but your rebellion cannot be more than a little excitement; it cannot transform you, and it cannot transform society. If you want to be really a rebel, first you have to find your being. Then each of your acts will be not only an act of love and devotion, it will also be an act of tremendous revolution – in your life and in other people's lives. Your love is true, but very small.

I want your love to be as big as possible – bigger than the sky. It should have no limits to it. And out of that love arises the true rebel, the true rebellion.

The whole of history is full of the failures of revolutions; and the reason for their failure is that they were not coming from being – they were only coming from doing. Neither Karl Marx had any idea of being, nor Lenin, nor Mao Tse-tung. All these great revolutionaries have done much. But because they themselves were very superficial their revolutions have remained superficial, just a kind of whitewash – not a revolution which comes from the very roots.

My sannyasins are going to be rebels, but rebels not in the ordinary sense of the word. Before they become rebels they have to become buddhas. Only then will the world know true revolution – when buddhas rebel.

In Hindi, we have a very beautiful word; it has the same root as 'buddha' – it is *'buddhu.'* *'Buddhu'* means the idiot, and 'buddha' means the highest peak of consciousness. Strange people! the same root – the same word – becomes 'buddha,' and the same root becomes the word 'buddhu.' All the revolutions that have happened in the world have happened through the 'buddhus.' I would like revolutions to come from the deepest core of the 'buddhas.' I will not take your doing away; I only want to enrich it, to intensify it, to transform it from excitement to ecstasy.

You are saying, "Many years ago, I told You that I felt to be like a warrior in the West. Also now I have the same feeling. Does that mean that I don't move much on the path to become a meditator?" You are misunderstanding; I am not against the warrior – I want you all to be warriors. But before you become a warrior, you must be.

Who is going to become a warrior? You don't know even who you are. This ignorance in the center . . . and you become a warrior? Then naturally your being a warrior is going to be destructive, not creative. It is arising out of ignorance. I would like you to be warriors out of silence, purity, innocence.

But you have a fixed idea, Majid, as if the meditator and the warrior are two different parts. It has been so in the past, because the past has not been able to create the whole man. My effort is to give you wholeness in all the dimensions possible.

Be a meditator, and then whatever you do – you can be a rebel, you can be a warrior – the world will not be harmed by you, the world will be beautified by you. And that is the only gratitude we can show to existence. When you leave the world, leave it a little better than when you entered into it – just a little better, just a little more beautiful, a little more humane, a little more loving, a little more colorful, a little more holy.

To me there is no contradiction between a meditator and a warrior, but the priority is for the meditator. Only a meditator can be relied upon – that the sword in his hand is not going to destroy but to save; that the power that he has come to feel through meditation is going to be a creative energy, so whatever he touches is going to become gold.

I want you all to become magicians – magicians in the sense that your meditation will transform everything that you touch.

Without meditation, whatever you do is futile.

Okay, Vimal?

Yes, Bhagwan.

Pregnant With Enlightenment

You may create a beautiful statue, but still it is dead. You may create great music, but it is ephemeral; it comes like the wind and goes away. You may create great dance, but it cannot be a living child, a smiling child – a child who sees wonders, breathes, whose heart beats.

All your art and all your creativity seem to be a poor substitute to the woman. I have been asked many times why women are not great poets, great musicians, great painters, great sculptors. The reason is that because they can give birth to life, they don't feel any need to create anything else.

Only on one point, in one place, man and woman meet, and that I call the space of meditation – where man and woman are really equal, because both can give birth to themselves. They can be reborn; both can be pregnant with enlightenment.

Except in the space of meditation, man and woman are two different species. They meet only in deep meditation. And unless the whole of humanity is meditative, men and women will go on fighting with each other. Their love is always going up and down – there are moments of beauty, and there are moments of ugliness; there are moments of joy, and there are moments of misery.

But in meditation – if two meditators share their energies – love is a constant phenomenon, it does not change. It has the quality of eternity; it becomes divine.

The meeting of love and meditation is the greatest experience in life.

February 24, 1987,   7 p.m.

Beloved Bhagwan,

Something is happening to me – a feeling of fullness, richness, and expansion in my upper body. It's pushing on my throat. It's not gripping me, it's embracing me, and everyone and everything around me. I don't know if they can feel it, but I can. It's a touchless touch, like a sweet hello, not addressed to anyone or anything – but rather everyone and everything. And it is silently following me around. This is like a strange pregnancy, which I know nothing about. How could I? I am a man. What is it, Bhagwan? Can men get pregnant? Have You been visiting me in the night, Bhagwan?

Dhyan John, man also gets pregnant – not in the same way as woman; his pregnancy is far superior. The woman can produce more human beings but, when man gets pregnant, he produces either music, painting, sculpture, poetry – all that makes life worth living and all that gives life value.

But very few people feel this kind of pregnancy. They are so involved in their mundane affairs – in money, in honor, in power, in prestige – that they never care that they can also produce something which will outlive them.

The woman's child will have a life of seventy or eighty years, but what about the poetry of the *Upanishads?* Five thousand years, and it is still vibrant and still alive – and the people who gave birth to it could not have avoided feeling pregnant. Every great poet knows that when some poetry is striving to be born he feels almost feminine, almost like a womb in which the poetry is taking shape and growing.

The same is true of all creative arts; but it is more true about those who are meditating, because they are pregnant with a Gautam Buddha. They are going to give birth to themselves. It is a very mysterious phenomenon, but very like the pregnancy of a woman.

You are saying, "Something is happening to me – a feeling of fullness, richness, and expansion." Those are the symptoms that your old life is going to disappear and a new life is taking shape within you. Where there was emptiness, now there is fullness. Where there was a poverty . . . because all that man desires, wants, proves only one thing: that he is poor. And you cannot find even the richest man who is not poor in this sense; he may have everything, still he is wanting more. He is a rich poor man, a rich beggar. Your poverty is disappearing and a richness is taking its place.

Everybody lives a closed life. Out of fear – the fear of exposure, the fear of becoming vulnerable, the fear of one's nakedness – one goes on hiding oneself, creating walls and walls around oneself. But as one starts meditating those walls start collapsing, because consciousness needs expansion. It cannot be confined in a small space – even the whole sky is too small for it.

You are going through a great transformation. This is the transformation everyone is here for. You are saying, "It is embracing me and everyone and everything around me. It is a touchless touch, like a sweet hello, not addressed to anyone or anything – but rather everyone and everything. And it is silently following me around. This is like a strange pregnancy, which I know nothing about."

Now you will know more and more about it. Just avoid abortion! And as far as man is concerned, and his creativity is concerned, no birth control is needed. More and more people have to be in the same state of creativity.

You are wondering, "How could I? I am a man." That's why you can be – because you are a man. There is a deep psychological background to it which has to be understood. Man has always felt inferior in comparison to woman, because woman can give birth and man cannot. Woman can become a mother – the beginning of a new life; man cannot do it. To substitute for it man started finding in what ways he could also be creative and productive. It was a deep spiritual need to destroy that inferiority.

He has given birth to great paintings, to great poetry, to great dances, to great music – they are all substitutes. That is why women have not bothered about creating poetry, music, literature. You will be surprised to know that women are not even the best cooks in the world; and they have not even written a book about the art of cooking. The best cooks in all the great hotels of the world are men. It is strange . . . .

The woman feels satisfied – she knows she can give birth to life. You may create a beautiful statue, but still it is dead. You may create great music, but it is ephemeral; it comes like the wind and goes away. You may create great dance, but it cannot be a living child, a smiling child – a child who sees wonders, breathes, whose heart beats.

All your art and all your creativity seem to be a poor substitute to the woman. I have been asked many times why women are not great poets, great musicians, great painters, great sculptors. The reason is that because they can give birth to life, they don't feel any need to create anything else.

Only on one point, in one place, man and woman meet, and that I call the space of meditation – where man and woman are really equal, because both can give birth to themselves. They can be reborn; both can be pregnant with enlightenment.

Except in the space of meditation, man and woman are two different species. They meet only in deep meditation. And unless the whole of humanity is meditative, men and women will go on fighting with each other. Their love is always going up and down – there are moments of beauty, and there are moments of ugliness, there are moments of joy, and there are moments of misery.

But in meditation – if two meditators share their energies – love is a constant phenomenon, it does not change. It has the quality of eternity; it becomes divine.

The meeting of love and meditation is the greatest experience in life.

To have love without meditation is to live in a very troubled, anxiety-ridden state – in anguish, angst, always in a turmoil. There are moments of silence, but that silence is nothing but cold war – preparation for another war, that's all. Obviously, to prepare for another war, for a few days, for a few moments, you have to be silent.

But it has not been possible up to now, because all the religions have decided on a wrong path. They have decided to separate men and women; they have decided to make them enemies. And they are all against me because I am trying for a single thing: that as far as meditation is concerned it is nobody's monopoly – neither male nor female. It is the only meeting point, where man is no more a man, nor a woman is a woman; both are just human beings, potential gods, seeds of godliness.

Neither love alone can do it – because it is too much

trouble – nor meditation alone can do it, because without love, meditation becomes more like the silence of a cemetery, of a graveyard. It is no longer dancing, it is no longer flowering. Yes, there is peace, but the peace is deathlike – it is not alive. The peace is no longer breathing, the peace no longer has a heartbeat.

My whole life has been devoted to only one single program: how to bring love and meditation together – because only through that meeting a new humanity is possible. And only in the meeting of love and meditation, the duality of man and woman – the inequality of man and woman – disappears.

The women's liberation movement cannot deliver the goods. I am not directly concerned with women's liberation, I am concerned with the liberation of all – because if woman is not liberated, man is also not liberated. They are functioning with each other as the jailer and the jailed; they are in bondage to each other. Neither man is liberated, nor woman – both are living under a slavery imposed by each other in the hope that perhaps if they enslave the other, they will be free. But the other has its own ways of enslaving you.

Only in meditation, in silence, where love blossoms, there is – without any struggle, without any fight – a natural harmony, equality, a natural equilibrium. And when it is natural, it has a beauty of its own.

Dhyan John, you are asking, "Can men get pregnant?" The whole culture, all that is civilization, is nothing but the result of a few men getting pregnant. Every man has the capacity to be pregnant; but very few people take the challenge, move on the arduous path. The woman's pregnancy is only biological. Man cannot be pregnant biologically, but spiritually he can be pregnant. And woman can also be pregnant spiritually as well as biologically.

And you are asking, "Have you been visiting me in the night, Bhagwan?" Dhyan John, do you think I am a holy ghost, making virgin girls pregnant – and now, getting tired of girls, I have started making men, virgin men like Dhyan John, pregnant? I am not a holy ghost – I am not a Christian at all. But it is true, you are pregnant. Feel blessed, rejoice in it! And allow it as much nourishment as possible. It is going to give birth to you – a new you!

Beloved Bhagwan,

I can sense some mysteries which You never speak of. Is it that we must come in the night and take them?
Or are some mysteries simply revealed once we are drowned in them?
Beloved, beloved Bhagwan, what does *understanding* mean?

Devageet, it is true, there are mysteries which I never speak of. Not that I don't want to speak about them, but their very nature is – they cannot be spoken of. You will have to listen to them while I am silent. You will have to listen them between the gaps of my words. Words cannot indicate towards them, but silence continuously shouts about them. You just need the right way of listening – just as you understand a language because you have learned it.

Silence is also a language, the language of existence. Trees use it, and the stars use it, and the mountains use it, and the mystics use it. I am saying that which can be said; I am also saying, through my silence, that which cannot be said. Now it is up to you whether you can get a silent whisper, and allow it into your deepest being – because only there its full meaning will be revealed to you. Your mind is incapable, inadequate. The mind has no way to understand silence, it can understand only language, only words; but the wordless . . . .

You cannot complain about mind – it is beyond its capacity. It is just like – my eyes can see the light, my ears cannot see the light. That does not mean that I should complain about my ears: "Why don't you see the light?" They are not meant for it. They can listen to music – eyes cannot listen to music. Mind can understand words. If you want to understand that which is beyond words, then mind has to be transcended; you have to enter into the space called no-mind. It is just above your mind, beyond your mind. No-mind only understands silence; words don't reach there.

You are saying, "Is it that we must come in the night and take them?" It is not a question of your coming in the night or in the day and taking them, because I am not hiding them; I am throwing them at you continually every morning, every evening. But you go on picking up only the words, and you go on dropping the wordless – the gaps.

Only in Sufism is there a book which I can call holy. I cannot call the *Bible* holy, and I cannot call *Gita* holy. But the book of the Sufis I *can* call holy – for a simple reason: because nothing is written in it. It is empty. It has been coming down for almost one thousand years from the master to the disciple; and it is given only when the disciple is so ready that he can read that which is not written.

When it was given for the first time by a mystic . . . . He was dying, and for his whole life it had been a mystery to his disciples; his whole library was available to everybody, but one book he used to keep under his pillow. He would read it only when he had closed the doors, locked the doors, taken a good look that nobody was hiding inside the room; and then he would take the book out of his bed and read it for hours. Naturally there was great curiosity. People were even hiding on the roof, looking, by moving the tiles, to see what was happening. But they could not figure it out – what kind of book this was.

They asked him again and again, and he would say, "When the time is ripe, I will give you the book." And the day came when he was dying, and all the disciples had gathered, and it was only a question of a few more moments and he would be gone. They were feeling a little embarrassed to ask about the book, "Now that you are going, at least tell us something about the book." To ask an old dying master looked very ungentlemanly.

But one man gathered courage and he said, "Master, you have forgotten one thing, that book!" He said, "I have not forgotten. It is just under my pillow, and before I take my last breath, I will give it to my successor."

And he called one of his disciples – nobody had ever thought that this man was going to be the successor of their master. Certainly he was a strange man, utterly silent. He had no friends, he would never participate in the mass prayers, he would never go into the library to look into the ancient scriptures; but he would sit under the trees by the side of the river. Sometimes the whole night he was lying down on the lawn and looking at the stars. Everybody thought he was a little bit crazy. He never asked the master a question.

There were learned scholars, even more learned than the master himself, very well acquainted with all the old scriptures; but the master called that strange man, that star-gazer, that silent one – the one who had no friends, who was alone amidst the crowd of disciples, but who had the eyes of an innocent child, and his heart full of unsung songs.

He pulled out the book and gave it to the disciple, and said, "This book will be symbolic. Whoever possesses it will be the successor, so remember, be very careful, don't let anybody else read it. Only you can read it, and before you die you can give it to the right person, who is capable of reading it."

This way for one thousand years the book has passed from one hand to another hand – and the book is absolutely empty. When for the first time, just fifty years ago, the mystic who was now the successor wanted to publish it, he could not find a publisher – because whomsoever he showed it to would look at it and say, "But there is nothing to publish in it. It is just a notebook, and nothing is written in it." But now it has been published; some daring publisher in England has published it: *The Book of Nothing.* But they have destroyed it a little because they have put an introduction to it: the whole history of the book – in one thousand years, how many mystics have possessed it, and how it was transferred from one teacher to another teacher, and this is the first time it is being published. This is simple foolishness – that book does not need any introduction. But that is how man's mind functions – every book needs an introduction, so that book also needs an introduction; and inside there is nothing – one thousand pages, empty.

And they have destroyed it by publishing it, because now people are using it as a notebook, they are writing things in it. It was not meant for that purpose. It was meant that the master should give it to a disciple when he can understand the gaps between the words, between the lines; when words and lines become meaningless, then the empty paper . . . . Just watching it, and you also become empty. Just deeply looking at it, you move from mind to no-mind – and suddenly that empty page becomes a door into the mysteries of life.

Devageet, try to listen to my silences. You will not find any speaker in the whole world speaking the way I speak. Just in the middle of the sentence, there is a gap. It is deliberate, it is significant, it has more meaning than all the words. In fact, I use all the words so that I can create a gap. Otherwise how to create a gap?

Listen to the gaps, listen to my silence, listen to the silence of the trees and the stars – because silence is nobody's monopoly, it is neither Hindu, nor Mohammedan, nor Christian; it is the only thing which is not monopolized by anybody – and you will start finding the mysteries that I want to speak about. But just the words are not capable of expressing them.

And, lastly, you are asking, "Bhagwan, what does 'understanding' mean?" This English word "understanding" is a little strange, but significant. Whenever you know something, you are standing above it, and that which you know is standing under. You have gone higher. To say it in other words: as your consciousness starts moving higher, more and more things are standing under. Things that are standing under, you have understood them. Things that are standing above you, you have still to go higher – only the higher can understand the lower, the lower cannot understand the higher.

So the basic thing is to go as high in your consciousness as possible. And consciousness goes on becoming higher as you go on dropping unnecessary knowledge, which is a load. Anything borrowed is a load, is a hindrance. You have to be so light that you can become an eagle and can fly to the faraway sky.

The first man who walked on the moon – when he came back he was asked what was his first idea? Standing on the moon, looking at the sky, looking at the earth, what was his first idea? And what he said is very significant.

He said, "My first idea was, my beloved earth! For the first time I understood that there is no America, there is no Russia, there is no China, there is no India – it is one earth, my earth. There are no lines, no divisions, all are man-manufactured. And the strangest thing I saw was that the earth was looking like the moon, radiating light." It is eight times bigger than the moon, so just to see the moon eight times bigger, with eight times more light . . . . And the moon itself was looking just like dry desert, not even a single drop of water has fallen on it, never has even grass grown on it – no life anywhere, utter silence. And this silence I call the silence of death.

Our earth is also silent, but the wind passes through

the trees . . . and there is life . . . and the birds sing, and there is light, and deep in the middle of the night when everything is silent a cuckoo starts singing – do you think it disturbs the silence? No, it deepens it, it makes it more musical; and as the cuckoo becomes silent, the night is more deeply silent than it was before. This is a living silence. Always remember, any quality that has no life in it is not worth having. Unless a saint can also dance, he is not a saint; he is just a dead fossil.

When you start seeing that even truth, meditation, beauty or virtue – all have their own songs, sung or unsung, you will be moving into the mysteries. Death has no mystery, death is a dead-end street. Life is an ongoing process, forever and forever. Just raise your consciousness, and your understanding will become wider and bigger; when your consciousness reaches to the highest point, everything is below it. That is exactly the meaning of understanding. Now you understand.

Beloved Bhagwan,

Is it possible that I know myself less and less?

Prem Pradeepa, it is not only possible that you know yourself less and less: the more you are here, the closer you come to me, the more your knowledge will evaporate; the more you will become innocent, not knowing, but full of wonder – just like a small child wondering about each and everything. This is absolute freedom and liberation from mind.

Socrates is reported to have said, "When I was young I thought I knew everything; when I became a little more mature I also became aware that there is much that I don't know. When I became still older I was puzzled because I used to know more when I was young – and now I know less and less every day. And finally, before he died, he said, 'I know nothing.' "

The day he said, "I know nothing . . . ." In Greece there was a temple in Delphi, and there was an oracle in the temple who used to predict many things in trance. The day Socrates said, "I know nothing," the same day, the same time, in Delphi, the oracle declared that Socrates was the wisest man in the world.

People who had come from Athens to listen to the oracle rushed back to inform Socrates, because such an honor had never been given to anyone by the oracle – the wisest man in the world. And when they reported it to Socrates he laughed; he said, "I used to be, when I was very young, when I was very arrogant, when I was very egoistic. Now I know nothing."

But the people said, "The oracle has never been wrong." They returned to Delphi, and they reported, "This time you are wrong, because Socrates himself denies it; he says, 'I know nothing.' "

The oracle laughed now, and said, "That is the reason why I have declared him the wisest man in the world. Only the wisest man in the world has the courage and the innocence and the humbleness to declare 'I know nothing.' "

Pradeepa, here you are all not to know more and more, but to know less and less. My work is not to load you with more knowledge; my work is to unload you, unburden you, make you so light that you can fly. So what is happening is exactly the right thing that is expected to happen. This is a mystery school; those who enter the gateless gate of this mystery school should come with a clear understanding that when they return they will be reborn again as small children, knowing nothing. But to know nothing is the beginning of knowing oneself. You know so may things that you have completely forgotten to know yourself. When you know nothing, your whole capacity for knowing turns upon yourself; and to know oneself is the only authentic wisdom there is, a wisdom that liberates, a wisdom that makes you aware of your immortality, a wisdom that makes you aware that you are not an island, but part of the whole.

Beloved Bhagwan,

A few days ago it happened, and You must know it; the one who can find words for everything now has no words to describe this experience. I only say what it was not:
there were no angels playing their trumpets, there was no celestial music, nor smell of incense, nor flowers, nor colors of thousands of rainbows . . . .
The experience came from the back, with velvet feet like a thief, so unknown and so familiar . . . .
My arms grasped the sky searching for Your hand while my feet walked on their own towards Lao Tzu gate, and my being was only a riverlike whisper, murmuring, "Bhagwan, Bhagwan, Bhagwan."
But Your hand was not there, or didn't I see it, didn't I feel it?
Oh Bhagwan, my Beloved Ocean, haven't You promised me that You would take hold of my hand?

Sarjano, I have promised you, and I have been fulfilling my promise. But I will not hold your hand from outside, I will hold your hand from your inside – your hand will be my hand. That is true holding; from the outside it is very superficial, but from the inside, it is as deep as it can be. And who do you think was following you with velvet feet? Feet are never made of velvet but my shoes are. But in the night a small misunderstanding is possible.

You are saying, "A few days ago it happened, and You must know it." Yes, I know it. "The one who can find words for everything now has no words to describe his experience. I only say what it was not." But this is the only way to describe a few experiences. All the great experiences have to be described negatively – what it is not. With a negative description there is a beauty . . . . The positive description confines a thing, the negative description only indicates – it does not confine. So it is absolutely right to describe it by what

it is not.

"There were no angels playing their trumpets." There are no angels anywhere; and anyway, trumpets are so costly nowadays . . . . Forget those old days of the *Old Testament,* when every angel was given trumpets and harps – even people who had reached heaven by mistake.

I have heard about one person certainly, a man from Munich, Germany. He was a porter at the station, and by some mistake, angels carried him to heaven. He tried many times, "You must be mistaken, I am just a porter, I am not a saint; why are you dragging me towards heaven? This is my time to go to the pub, and I tell you frankly, I am a sinner, just don't harass me." But they went on with their trumpets and their harps, and nobody listened to the poor porter. He said, "This is strange." And then he was presented to the chief of the angels, and he was given a harp, and he said, "What? What I am supposed to do?"

He said, "There is nothing to be done, you just sit on any cloud, and play the harp."

He said, "I am a porter, I have never played on any instrument."

They said, "Don't be worried, in the beginning every saint says so."

He said, "But I am not a saint! And I am concerned that pub may be closed! In all this nonsense, do you think me an idiot, sitting on a cloud, playing on the harp, when it is time to go to the pub?"

But they told him "You will have to behave, because soon God will be coming here. He always comes when new arrivals enter into paradise."

He said, "My God, so it means tonight I cannot go to the pub?"

They said, "You stop talking about the pub."

So he had to sit on a cloud. He felt very embarrassed, that this was not a place to sit; but he saw angels and saints were sitting on all the clouds and playing on their harps, "Hallelujah, hallelujah." He has never done any such thing. But then he heard God is coming, so he started doing anything that he managed to do and shouting loudly, "Hallelujah, hallelujah." But again and again he remembered the pub.

God was sitting on his golden throne, on a big white cloud. Just silently the porter was saying in between, "You son of a bitch, hallelujah, hallelujah."

He thought that God would not hear what he was saying very silently, but God heard it. He asked the other angels, "Why are you torturing that porter? It is an accident, he is not supposed to be here, and he is very unhappy, just look at his face. He is saying, 'Hallelujah, hallelujah,' but inside he is saying something else that only I can hear! Just send him back, let him go to his pub."

So he was thrown back to the earth. Although he fell with a thump on the ground he said, "At least there is still time! All those idiots sitting on the clouds, look like clowns, and for eternity you have just to play on your harp, and go on singing, 'Hallelujah, hallelujah.' "

He got up and went into the pub and the people said, "You are very late."

He said, "I got into such trouble. By accident people took me to heaven. It was just my old habit of telling people 'You son of a bitch' that helped me. When God heard it, he thought it was better to send this man away; otherwise he will corrupt the other saints."

In the old days it was okay, Sarjano. Nowadays there are "no angels, no trumpets, no celestial music nor smell of incense, nor flowers, nor colors of thousands of rainbows . . . ." The mystics have been talking about these things, because they could not find words to relate the experience, just as you cannot.

There are just ways of describing something; thousands of lotus flowers, thousands of rainbows, thousands of suns rising all around – these are all simply indications that language has failed. And what they want to say they cannot say, but there is a tremendous urge to say it. So they are caught in a dilemma. They cannot say it and they cannot resist not saying it. So something has to be said.

One great German thinker – perhaps one of the greatest thinkers of this century – Ludwig Wittgenstein, in one of his most rare books: *Logico Tractatus Philosophicus,* has one statement. He does not write in the ordinary way people write, he writes only maxims. But each of his maxims he numbers one, two, three. Each of his maxims has tremendous value and is pregnant with meaning; he has condensed paragraphs, pages or perhaps books into one sentence.

One of the sentences in this *Tractatus* is: "That which cannot be said, should not be said." I wrote him a letter, "You have not followed your own dictum. You have said something about it. 'That which cannot be said should not be said.' You have said something about it."

I received a letter from one of his friends; Wittgenstein had died. I was not aware that he is dead – I was only a student in the university. The friend wrote, "Wittgenstein is dead. I am sorry that he could not see your letter because he was such a sincere and honest man, he may have removed his statement from the book – because what you are saying is absolutely right. If nothing should be said about that which cannot be said, even this sentence should not be there – just an empty place."

"The experience came from the back." It almost always comes from the back. Because anything coming from the front can make you tense, can make you closed, can make you defensive. All great experiences come from the back, because from the back . . . until they have overwhelmed you, you are not aware and you cannot be defensive. And by the time you become aware, it is too late – you cannot do anything. You are possessed.

". . . with velvet feet, like a thief." In Hindi, one of the names of God is "Hari" and "Hari" means a thief. India has a longer experience of the mysterious than any other country in the world. It has even chosen names with a very deep awareness that they should not be just names, but they should also contain the experience.

"The experience came from the back like a thief, so unknown and so familiar." Whenever any one of you will come to know something of the unknown, you will always find it both; unknown on the one hand, and so familiar – as if you have always known it. And it is both, because it is not something that is coming from the outside. It is something that is really growing within you. It is something that in your unconscious you have always felt, but your consciousness has not been aware of it, and now the consciousness becomes aware. So you have both contradictory statements together, "unknown" and "so familiar."

"My arms grasp the sky searching for Your hand." Sarjano, that's where you were not clear. You were searching for my hand as though it were something outside. But slowly, slowly, as more and more experiences of this type become available to you, you will see that you are seeing through my eyes; and you are trying to search – and it is not your hand but my hand. There is a state of immense attunement, when the master is not outside, but inside you.

You are not so small as you appear. You are not confined to the body. You are vast enough, you can contain all. Your capacity for containing is oceanic.

"While my feet walked on their own towards Lao Tzu Gate and my being was only a river-like whisper, murmuring: 'Bhagwan, Bhagwan, Bhagwan . . . .' But Your hand was not there." It was there. And next time something like this happens, just look at your hand and you will not find your own hand – but you will find my hand.

"Or didn't I see it; didn't I feel it?" No, it was just your first experience. And you were looking, very naturally, on the outside. You must have seen one of the great paintings of Michaelangelo in which God is creating the world and his hand is touching the hand of Adam. He's hanging in the sky, downwards, and Adam is on the earth. It is one of the most beautiful paintings.

But Michaelangelo has no experience – that God's hand cannot come from outside, and anything that comes from outside is not God's. God can only blossom from your innermost being. He can see through your eyes and he can spread his hand in your hand. He can walk with your feet and he can breathe with your lungs, and he can beat from your heart.

Never think of God as something outside. It is always your interior, your subjective experience.

"Oh Bhagwan! My Beloved Bhagwan! Haven't You promised me that You would take hold of my hand?"

I had promised you, Sarjano; and I was holding it.

Okay, Vimal?

Yes, Bhagwan.

Let Everything Pass

The East has never fought with the mind; it has found a totally different method. Its method is just to be a watcher on the hills.

Let everything pass.

Don't judge, don't condemn, don't evaluate.

You are only a mirror; these are not your functions. You simply reflect – and they will all pass. If you don't take any note of them, if you can ignore them, they will stop coming to you; they don't want to be uninvited guests. Perhaps because of the old habit, for a few days they may continue; but you will be able to see that the traffic is becoming less and less; otherwise it is twenty-four-hour rush hour.

Once the mind is silent, empty, spacious, you have found the golden key, the master key, which opens all the mysteries of love, of truth, of eternal life.

February 25, 1987,   8 a.m.

Beloved Bhagwan,

In Plato's *The Symposium* Socrates says that, "A man who practices the mysteries of love
will be in contact not with a reflection, but with truth itself.
To know this blessing of human nature, one can find no better helper than love."
Please comment.

Milarepa, I have been commenting my whole life on love, in thousands of different ways. But the message is the same. Just one most fundamental thing has to be remembered, that is: it is not the love that *you* think is love. Neither Socrates is speaking about it, nor I am speaking about it.

The love you know is nothing but a biological urge, it depends on your chemistry and your hormones. It can be changed very easily, by a small change in your chemistry – and the love that you thought is the ultimate truth will simply disappear. You have been calling lust, love. This distinction should be remembered. Socrates says, "a man who practices the mysteries of love . . . ." Lust has no mysteries, it is a plain biological game. Every animal, every bird, every tree knows about it. Certainly, the love which has mysteries is going to be totally different from the love with which you are ordinarily acquainted. "A man who practises the mysteries of love will be in contact not with the reflection, but with truth itself."

This love that can become a contact with truth itself arises only out of your consciousness, not out of your body, but out of your innermost being. Lust arises out of your body. Love arises out of your consciousness. But people don't know their consciousness, and the misunderstanding goes on and on – their bodily lust is taken for love.

Very few people in the world have known love. Those are the people who have become so silent, so peaceful . . . and out of that silence and peace they come in contact with their innermost being, their soul. Once you are in contact with your soul, your love becomes not a relationship, but simply a shadow to you. Wherever you move, with whomsoever you move, you are loving.

Right now, what you call love is addressed to someone, and confined to someone; and love is not a phenomenon that can be confined. You can have it in your open hands, but you cannot have it in your fist. The moment your hands are closed – they are empty. The moment they are open – the whole of existence is available to you.

Socrates is right: one who knows love also knows truth, because they are only two names of one experience. And if you have not known the truth, remember that you have not known love either. "To know this blessing of human nature, one can find no better helper than love."

There is only one thing I would like to say about Socrates: his whole approach was logical and argumentative. His method is known as Socratic dialogue. It is a very lengthy process, like psychoanalysis. He will discuss and discuss, and destroy all your false arguments and false ideas. This was his contention, which has a truth in it: When all false ideas are demolished, that which remains behind and cannot be argued about, is your being. And from that being arises the fragrance of love.

But Socrates knew nothing of meditation. He came to know truth through the long, unnecessary route of arguments. He was one of the best arguers the world has produced; there is no parallel. But what he was doing by argument cannot become a universal phenomenon; the path is long, and unnecessarily long.

The false can disappear if you sit silently, whenever you have time, and just watch your thoughts. No need to argue, no need to fight, no need to push them out, just watch – as if you are seeing something on the TV – screen.

The East has known a greater miracle than Socrates. Socrates was not acquainted with the East at all. And the obvious reason was: he has found love, he has found truth – and he never thought that there could be a shortcut. His process is torturous. If you read the dialogues of Socrates you will feel that the process is long, and each argument creates new problems – new problems create new arguments . . . he is fighting with shadows.

But it was not his fault. In his time Athens was one of the most sophisticated, intellectual cities in the world. He was unaware that exactly at the same time Buddha was teaching meditation in India, Lao Tzu was teaching meditation in China, Mahavira was teaching meditation . . . . It was at exactly the same time, twenty-five centuries ago.

Socrates had inherited logic from his forefathers; Greece was full of sophists. Sophists were strange people, their philosophy was that there is no truth, there is no untruth – it all depends who has the better argument. If you can argue better than your opponent, you are right. And if you come across another person who can argue better than you, then you are wrong.

So it was only the gymnastics of argument that Socrates inherited. He changed the whole process: sophistry became philosophy. The word 'philo' means love, and 'sophia' means wisdom. Sophistry was simply argumentativeness. He did a great job, but it almost always happens – the people you are fighting with, even if you are victorious, leave a great impact on you.

Just by fighting with them you have to use their own methods, otherwise you cannot fight. If one country is piling up nuclear weapons, then those who fight them have to pile up nuclear weapons. Because Socrates was continually fighting with the sophists . . . . He wanted to destroy this idea that better argument is all, that there is no truth and there is no untruth – and he succeeded. He was a discontinuity with his past. But the people he had been fighting, he had to fight with arguments. So although the sophists were defeated, the argumentativeness remained with Socrates himself.

He used it in a better way. He used it in discovering the truth. But he was absolutely unaware that in another part of the world, in the East, in China, in India, people had a different inheritance: almost ten thousand years of sitting silently and doing nothing.

And as silence descends on you, as thoughts start leaving, and all disturbances disappear, and the lake of your consciousness becomes almost a mirror:

You know you are the truth; you know you are love; you know you are divine. In a single step – from mind to no-mind – all the treasures, all the mysteries of love, life, truth, blissfulness, open their doors. There is no need to argue against the false.

My contention is: even to argue against the false is to give some credit to the false, and that has been the eastern contention for thousands of years. You don't argue with your shadow: Don't come with me today, I don't like you, when I don't want you, why do you go on following me? You don't run away from your shadow – because the shadow will run too.

A Sufi story says: A man was afraid of his shadow, because he had read in a book that death was almost like a shadow – that when it comes, it comes like a shadow. And it became such an obsession in his mind, that he became afraid even of ordinary shadows.

He would run, and he would do everything . . . he would try to fight – and he was a warrior! But even your sword cannot do any harm to a shadow – the shadow does not exist. He was so tired that he asked a mystic, "What to do with the shadow? I have done everything that can be done, but nothing happens. I have broken my sword. I have been running so much to avoid it that my feet are oozing blood."

The mystic laughed, he said, "You do one thing. Under that tree, just sit down, and then tell me, where is your shadow?"

Under the tree there was much shadow. To have a shadow you need the sun, the light. But when he went under the tree, and sat there and looked all around, there was no shadow. He said, "What a miracle you have done! You have not even moved from your place, and my shadow is gone." The mystic said, "Your very approach was unnecessary. To fight with the false is to give credibility to the false. In your fight you have accepted that the false also has some reality."

The East has never fought with the mind; it has found a totally different method. Its method is just to be a watcher on the hills.

Let everything pass.

Don't judge, don't condemn, don't evaluate.

You are only a mirror; these are not your functions. You simply reflect – and they will all pass. If you don't take any note of them, if you can ignore them, they will stop coming to you; they don't want to be uninvited guests. Perhaps because of the old habit, for a few days they may continue; but you will be able to see that the traffic is becoming less and less; otherwise it is twenty-four- hour rush hour.

Once the mind is silent, empty, spacious, you have found the golden key, the master key, which opens all the mysteries of love, of truth, of eternal life.

Socrates' idea is basically right, but about his method I do not agree. His method is unnecessary. If you are going to come home, why run miles away and then come back home? You are already there. Just close your eyes and be silent, and relax. But the conclusion is right: "A man who practises the mysteries of love will be in contact, not with a reflection, but with truth itself. To know this blessing of human nature, one can find no better helper than love."

Either you can start by increasing your love, expanding your love . . . but where will you expand it? Your mind is standing like a China wall all around you. First that China wall has to disappear – and that is the function of meditation.

Socrates could have been for the West their Gautam Buddha, and the whole history of the West would have been totally different. He has created the basic path for the western mind: argument. And argument by and by, rather than discovering love, has discovered atom bombs, nuclear weapons, science, technology.

The East has not been able to discover these things because it has never given any credit to argumentation, to reason. Its whole concentration has been on expanding consciousness – and to give it space, it has to get rid of the mind. Once the mind is not there you don't have any boundaries, even the sky is not the boundary. You are all over the place. This feeling of being all over the place is love; and knowing it, that it is arising from the very center of your being, is truth.

But, Milarepa, Socrates is not talking in California. He is not talking to so-called lovers all over the world. He is talking to a few disciples who have come in search of truth. He helped a few people; he could not help many, for the simple reason that with everybody the process was so long.

But the East has been fortunate to discover a single-step pilgrimage: from mind to no-mind – and you have arrived home.

You have always been there. You have never left it for a single moment! Just, your mind has been wandering all over the world, but you have never been anywhere else; you are exactly where you should be.

If the wandering of the mind stops, suddenly – the revelation.

Beloved Bhagwan,

At the age of thirty-seven I feel as if I'm starting a new life. Knowing nothing, unsophisticated and childish, dreams and ambitions are being shattered, and the future is totally unknown. I feel that you are stripping me naked; is this Your work?

Ram Fakeer, this is my work: to take away from you all that is false.

I cannot give you anything, I can only take away – because that which you need, you already have. But it is covered with so many lies, so many falsities, so many superstitions, that although my basic attitude is creative, ninety-nine percent of my work is destructive.

To create that which you already have – to make you aware of it – everything false has to be removed. And you have so much junk! Your mind is so full of rotten furniture . . . .

I used to stay in one place in India, Sagar, in the house of the richest man of that city. He was a collector of things. Anything that came onto the market, whether he needed it or not, had to be in his house. His house was so full of absolutely useless, out-of-date, unnecessary things, that it was difficult even to move in the house.

The room where I used to stay, was so full of furniture! Furniture belonging to different ages, Victorian . . . . Radio sets, and television has not come to that city yet – but in his room there was a television set.

I said, "What is the purpose of this television set?"
He said, "Some day, television will come."
I said, "Have you ever thought of one thing, that in the room where you put me – and you put me in the room which has all your great treasures – even to move one has to be very cautious not to stumble, even in the daylight." I told him, "You have destroyed this room."

He said, "What are you saying? I have decorated it."
I said, "Your decoration is nothing but destruction."
The English word 'room' is very significant. It simply means 'roominess,' 'spaciousness.' The more things you put in the room the more you are destroying it. Then it is no longer a room, it has become a warehouse.

I asked him, "Have you another room in the house?"
He said, "This is the best. If you call this a warehouse, then you will be even more unsatisfied with the other rooms. They are even more full. In this room I keep the latest things; this is my guest room."

I said, "Great guestroom you have created!"
Your mind always reminds me of his guestroom – so much rubbish, junk, so much furniture that there is no space even for yourself.

The life of meditation is: to create room in you, to create space in you. Throw out all the nonsense that others have given to you. You will be aware of yourself only when the mind is utterly empty. On the one hand, it will become empty; on the other hand, it will become full of you, your pure being.

Growth needs space. Your consciousness is starving. Give it a sky to fly in – and it is in your hands, because whatever you have in your mind, you have collected it. Now you don't know how to get rid of it. Meditation is only a technique for getting rid of it. The greatest day in your life is when deep silence overwhelms you.

Yes, Ram Fakeer, your observation is true: "At the age of thirty-seven I feel as if I am starting a new life." You are starting a new life – but don't think that before this you had an old life too. You were dead. Because your statement can have the implication that the old life is finished, the new is beginning.

I want to say to you: Life is always new, only death is old. You were dead, and I have been calling you, "Lazarus, come out of the grave." And it is not late, thirty-seven years old is not late. You have wasted only half of your life; half is still there. And this half can be lived so intensely and so totally that what has gone unlived will not be missed.

Even a single moment, lived totally and intensely, is equal to eternity. Otherwise you can go on vegetating for the whole of eternity; you don't have any taste of life, and the nectar of life. It is a beginning. Let us say, Ram Fakeer, you are born now.

There is a beautiful story in Gautam Buddha's life: one of the great emperors of his time, Prasenjita, had come to see him. Naturally he wanted to have a private conversation, because people who are rich, people who are in power, are always afraid to expose themselves. If people know that they are also as human as you are, with all the frailities, with all the weaknesses, it will be humiliating.

So Buddha gave him a private audience. He was talking to the emperor, and at that moment an old sannyasin, who must have been seventy or seventy-five, approached and said, "Forgive me. I don't want to disturb your conversation, I just want to touch the feet of Gautam Buddha and I will go. I will not say a single word. I am going for a long journey, to spread the message of my master; and I have to start now, because before the sun sets I have to reach the next village. Once the sun sets, Buddhist monks don't travel, so it is just out of compulsion; please forgive me." And he touched Buddha's feet.

Buddha asked a very strange question – at least it sounded strange to Prasenjita. He said, "Bhikkhu," that is Buddha's word for sannyasin, "how old are you?" And the old man said, "Don't make me feel embarrassed before the emperor, because I am only four years old."

The emperor could not believe it; he looked again, this man four years old? It is possible he may be seventy, seventy-five, eighty – that much difference is possible; but four years old is absolutely unbelievable. He said to Buddha, "It is none of my business to interfere, but I cannot resist the temptation. This man is lying so flatly, and you are not even objecting. Do you think he is four years old?"

Gautam Buddha said, "Yes, but you are puzzled because you don't know how we count age. When a man starts authentic life, a life of love and silence and meditation, when he gets initiated into the mysteries of existence – life is counted from that day. Physically this man is seventy-five years old, but it is only four years ago that he found the door out of death into life."

Ram Fakeer, forget those thirty-seven years in exactly the way you forget in the morning all the dreams and the nightmares of the night. Not that you have not lived them; when they were present, they were as real as anything. Start totally fresh.

You are saying, "I feel as if I am starting a new life." You are starting your first life. "Knowing nothing," – that is a great beginning, the most blissful beginning – because knowing nothing means mind has been put aside; knowing nothing means ego has been dropped; knowing nothing means your eyes are again fresh, innocent, full of wonder. You can again understand the songs of the birds, you can again see clearly the psychedelic colors of the flowers, you can again run after butterflies, you can again collect seashells on the beach. A man who has come out of his grave finds this whole existence so alluring, so beautiful, so attractive, that there is no need to find any God. He has found God in the flowers, in the birds, in the trees, in people. In fact there is no other God except this singing life, this dancing life, this green foliage, these colorful flowers.

God is not a creator – God is creativity; and the whole existence is continuously engaged in creativity. That old idea that God created the world in six days and then got tired, and on the seventh day rested, and he is still resting . . . . His Sunday has not ended yet, I don't think Monday will ever start . . . the whole idea is idiotic. This beautiful existence cannot be created in six days.

I used to have a tailor, a very beautiful old Mohammedan. I was going for a long trip, so I asked him, "Saturday evening I want my clothes to be ready, and there are six days still, and don't play tricks!" Because all over the world for some reason, tailors cannot be relied upon. That is part of their profession.

He said, "If you want, I will make them in six days. But before you ask it, have a look at the world."

I said, "What do you mean?"

He said, "I mean God created this world in six days – what a mess! Then don't tell me that the sleeves are long, or the robe is short, or the neck is too tight – it will be a mess. If even God could not manage . . . . I am a poor old man."

So I said, "Okay, you take your time, but my clothes should not be a mess. I can postpone the trip."

But the whole idea of God creating the world is absolutely without evidence. There is not a single eyewitness. By the very nature of the case there cannot be any eyewitness, because if an eyewitness was there, that means the world was already there. And it is also stupid, because Christians think God created the world exactly four thousand and four years before Jesus Christ was born. Certainly it must have been the first of January, Monday, when he started. But one wonders what he had been doing before that . . . the whole of eternity in the past.

What kind of God, what kind of creator? And if he had waited so long, what was the necessity to create it now, and make people unnecessarily miserable? He could have waited still longer. The people who believe in that story – and they have to believe, because it is in their holy scriptures – cannot provide a single reason why he suddenly decided to create the world. And if the cause of creating the world came from outside, that means the world was already there. It must have come from his own inner being; hence I want to change the whole structure of the story.

To me God is creation itself: it has always been here, and it will always be here. God is not a person separate from existence; God is in every particle, in every cell, in every atom of existence. He is our existence, our life, our love, our truth.

Ram Fakeer, you have started with a great beginning, knowing nothing. Nothing can be greater than that. In this not-knowing many, many flowers will blossom; in this not-knowing an authentic humbleness will grow; in this not-knowing you will find tremendous gratitude. Just that you are here, in this moment . . . . The knowledgeable person is covered with so much dust – and dirty dust. His mirror is covered with so many layers of knowledge that it stops reflecting.

Not knowing means all dust has been removed, your mirror is clean. Now you can reflect the farthest stars in the sky.

"Knowing nothing, unsophisticated and childish, dreams and ambitions are being shattered and the future is totally unknown." That is the beauty of the future. If it was known, it would be very ugly. If you knew that tomorrow morning your wife would kiss you . . . . The kiss in itself is enough of a torture, but to know it beforehand – you cannot sleep the whole night because the morning is coming.

If you knew the future, life would lose all adventure, all ecstasy, all mystery. It is the unknown that, every moment, keeps you surprised and again surprised. A man who knows everything about the future – just think of his misery. He knows that on a particular date after thirty years, "I am going to die." He knows that on a particular date, to a certain woman, "I am going to be married." He knows what is going to happen after marriage . . . every day a quarrel, every day a fight.

Still, people are strange; they go to the astrologers, to the palmists to know about the future. They are not satisfied with knowing the past. That has tortured them enough, they have suffered enough – still they want more suffering.

One astrologer was brought to me in Calcutta; he is very famous in that part of the country. I was staying with a very beautiful man – rarely one comes across such a man – his name was Sohanlal Dugar. We had come to know each other in a strange encounter in Jaipur. I was talking to a gathering and he was present. I had no idea who he was – he was one of the richest men in the country, and certainly the richest in Calcutta.

After listening to me he came with a big bundle of notes, touched my feet, and put the notes at my feet. I said, "I accept your love, your respect, but notes I don't need. If I need money sometime . . . you can just leave your address with me."

As I refused – the man was almost seventy-five or eighty years old – tears, big tears started coming out of his eyes. I said, "Have I hurt you?"

He said, "You don't understand my misery and my poverty. I am one of the richest men in the country, but I have got only money and nothing else. So when somebody refuses my money, he has refused me. I don't have anything else to give to you. You can just accept it and burn it in front of me – that is your business. Once you have accepted, what you do with the money is not my concern, but you cannot reject it. I am a very poor man, because I don't have anything else than money."

It was so difficult; I accepted the money and gave it to the organization which had arranged the lectures for me, but the old man became a great friend to me. The difference in my age and his age was great at that time.

He said, "If you have really accepted the money, whenever you come to Calcutta you have to stay at my house." I said, "There is no problem, I will be staying at your house."

He was really a great soul. The whole house was centrally air-conditioned; it was a palace. When Calcutta was the capital of India, before New Delhi, it used to be the palace of the governor general. There were no mosquitoes, no flies – still when I was eating he would sit in front of me in the old Indian way, with a small bamboo fan in his hand, moving it. I said, "There are no flies, no mosquitoes, and the house is centrally air-conditioned, it is absolutely cool; your waving the fan over me is absolutely unnecessary, just sit by my side."

He said, "No, because I am a gambler. Today I am the richest man, but tomorrow I may not be. This palace may be gone, this air-conditioning may be gone. But you have promised me that you will stay at my house, so I don't take any note of this air-conditioning and this palace. Then, only this fan will be there to give you a little coolness and to drive away the mosquitoes."

I said, "This is too much concern for the future. If it happens, then you can do it; but right now?"

He said, "I live according to palmistry, astrology – and I have called my best astrologer to see your birth-chart and your hand."

I could not hurt the old man, so I said, "Okay, when he comes . . . ." The astrologer came, and I told him, "I don't believe in astrology. Even if it is true, I want sciences that make the future known to people destroyed. The future should remain unknown. But there is no need to destroy, because it is a bogus science, and I will prove to you that it is bogus."

He said, "You don't know . . . I am the biggest astrologer in Bengal. I will see how you can prove it." He said many things about my future and then he asked for his fee. His fee was one thousand rupees, and I had told Sohanlal Dugar, "You are not going to give him the fee. I will settle the matter."

So the old man remained silent. The astrologer asked about his fee. I said, "You should have known that this man is not going to give you the fee. You don't even know the future that is so close – within five minutes this man is going to refuse . . . and you are talking about my whole life. You don't even know about your own life: that one thousand rupees are gone. This is my evidence that this is a pseudo science. You can cheat people because people are so interested in knowing the future. They don't understand that if they knew, life would lose all juice. When you were born, you could have brought with you a small card, with everything that is going to happen printed on it. And do you think then life would be worth living?"

Life has excitement and ecstasy because the future is unknown. The unknowability of the future is the most beautiful phenomenon; one does not know about the next moment.

Ram Fakeer, you are saying, "I feel that you are stripping me naked. Is this Your work?"

I repeat, Yes, this is my work. The moment you are naked, you have come home. All falsities dropped, all cover-ups dropped, all masks dropped, you are simply yourself, a naked consciousness.

Yes, that is my very profession.

Okay, Vimal?

Yes, Bhagwan.

BIOGRAPHY

The Childhood Years

1931   Bhagwan Shree Rajneesh was born in Kuchwada, Madhya Pradesh, India, on December 11, 1931, the eldest son of a modest cloth merchant who belonged to the Jain religion. He spent His first seven years with His grandparents who allowed Him absolute freedom to do exactly as He liked, and who fully supported His early and intense investigations into the truth about life.

1938   After the death of His grandfather, He went to live with His parents at Gadawara, a town of 20,000. His grandmother moved to the same town and remained His most generous friend until she died in 1970, declaring herself to be a disciple of her grandson.

1946   Bhagwan experienced His first satori at 14 years of age. Over the years, His experiments with meditation deepened. The intensity of His spiritual search took its toll on His physical condition. His parents and friends feared He might not live long.

The University Years

1953   At the age of 21, on March 21, 1953, Bhagwan attained enlightenment, the highest peak of human consciousness. Here, He said, His outer biography ended, and He has since lived in an egoless state of at-oneness with the inner laws of life. Outwardly, He continued to pursue His studies at the University of Saugar, from which He graduated with First Class Honors in Philosophy in 1956. He was All-India Debating Champion and won the Gold Medal in His graduating class.

1957   Bhagwan taught at the Sanskrit College, Raipur. A year later, He became philosophy professor at the University of Jabalpur. He gave up this post in 1966 in order to dedicate Himself entirely to the task of teaching modern man the art of meditation. Throughout the sixties, He traveled the length and breadth of India as the "Acharya (teacher) Rajneesh," arousing the wrath of the Establishment wherever He went. He exposed the hypocrisy of the vested interests and their attempts to obstruct man's access to his greatest human right –

the right to be himself. He addressed audiences of tens of thousands of people, touching the hearts of millions.

The Bombay Years

1968   He settled in Bombay, living and teaching there. Regularly, He held "meditation camps," mostly in hill stations, where He introduced His revolutionary Dynamic Meditation, a technique that helps to stop the mind by first allowing it to cathart. From 1970 He started initiating people into Neo-Sannyas, a path of commitment to self-exploration and meditation, helped by His love and personal guidance. He began to be called "Bhagwan" – "The Blessed One."

1970   The first seekers from the West arrived, among them many professional people. Bhagwan's fame began to spread throughout Europe, America, Australia and Japan. The monthly Meditation Camps continued and in 1974 a new place was found in Poona, where the teaching could be intensified.

The Poona Years

1974   On the 21st anniversary of Bhagwan's enlightenment, the ashram in Poona opened. The radius of Bhagwan's influence became worldwide. At the same time, His health began to fail seriously. Bhagwan retreated more and more into the privacy of His room, emerging only twice daily: lecturing in the morning and initiating and advising seekers in the evenings. Therapy groups combining Eastern insight into meditation with Western psychotherapy were created. Within two years, the ashram earned a reputation as "the world's finest growth and therapy

center." Bhagwan's lectures encompassed all the great religious traditions of the world. At the same time, His vast erudition in Western science and thought, His clarity of speech and depth of argument made the time-honored gap between East and West disappear for His listeners. His lectures, taped and transcribed into books, fill hundreds of volumes and have been absorbed by hundreds of thousands of readers. By the late seventies, Bhagwan's ashram in Poona had become a mecca to modern seekers of truth.

Indian Prime Minister Morarji Desai, a devout traditional Hindu, thwarted all attempts of Bhagwan's disciples to move their ashram to a remote corner of India where they would be able to experiment with applying Bhagwan's teachings to create a self-sufficient community living in meditation, love, creativity and laughter.

1980   An attempt was made to murder Bhagwan at one of His lectures by a member of a traditional Hindu sect. While the official religions and churches opposed Him East and West, Bhagwan by then had over a quarter of a million disciples worldwide.

A New Phase – Rajneeshpuram, USA

1981   On May 1st Bhagwan stopped speaking and entered a phase of "silent heart-to-heart communion" while His body, now seriously ill from a back condition, was resting. He was taken to the USA by His doctors and caretakers in view of possible emergency surgery. His American disciples purchased a 64,000 acre ranch in the Central Oregon desert. They invited Bhagwan there – where He recovered rapidly. A model agricultural commune evolved around Him with breathtaking speed and impressive results, reclaiming overgrazed and depleted land from the desert and turning it into a green oasis feeding a city of 5,000.

At yearly summer festivals held for Bhagwan's friends from all over the world, up to 20,000 visitors were housed and fed at this new city of Rajneeshpuram.

Parallel to the rapid growth of the commune in Oregon, large communes sprang up in all major Western countries, including Japan, living on their own independent businesses. Bhagwan had by then applied for permanent residence in the U.S. as a religious leader, but was refused by the American government; one of the reasons given was His vow of public silence. At the same time the new city was under increasing legal attack from the Oregon government and the Christian majority in the state. Oregon's land use laws, meant to protect the environment, became a major weapon in the fight against a city that had put enormous effort into reclaiming barren land and enhancing the environment – in fact a city which had become an ecological model for the world.

In October 1984, Bhagwan started speaking to small groups in His residence, and in July 1985 He started giving public discourses every morning to thousands of seekers in Rajneesh Mandir.

1985   On September 14, Bhagwan's personal secretary and several members of the commune's management suddenly left, and a whole pattern of illegal acts committed by them came to light. Bhagwan invited the American authorities to the city to fully investigate the matter. The authorities used this opportunity to accelerate their fight against the commune.

On October 29, Bhagwan was arrested without a warrant in Charlotte, NC. At the bail hearings He was put in chains. The trip back to Oregon where He was to appear in court – normally a five hour flight – took eight days. For a few days there was no trace of Bhagwan. Later He revealed that in the Oklahoma State Penitentiary He was signed in under the name of "David Washington" and put into an isolation cell with a prisoner suffering from infectious herpes, a disease that could have proven fatal for Bhagwan. Just an hour before being finally released, after a 12-day ordeal in prisons and chains, a bomb was discovered at the Portland, Oregon maximum security jail in which Bhagwan was kept. Everybody was evacuated except Bhagwan, who was kept inside for an hour.

In mid-November His lawyers urged Him to plead guilty to two of thirty-four minor "immigration violations" with which He had been charged, so as to avoid further risks to His life in the hands of the American judicial system. Bhagwan acquiesced and entered an "Alfred plea," a plea peculiar to the US judicial system, whereby He could accept the contention of guilt while at the same time maintain His innocence. He was fined four hundred thousand dollars and ordered to leave the USA, not to return for five years. He left by private jet the same day and flew to India, where He rested in the Himalayas. A week later, the Oregon commune decided to disperse. In a press conference, U.S. Attorney Charles Turner made three telling points in answering the question: Why weren't the charges brought against His secretary also brought against Bhagwan? Turner said that the government's first priority was to destroy the commune and that the authorities knew that the removal of Bhagwan would precipitate this. Second, they did not want to make Bhagwan a martyr. Third, there was no evidence whatsoever implicating Him in any of the crimes.

The World Tour – A Study In Human Rights

Dec. 85   Bhagwan's new secretary, His companion and His doctor were ordered out of India, their visas cancelled. Bhagwan left for Kathmandu, Nepal, where He resumed His daily discourses.

Feb. 86   Bhagwan went to *Greece* on a 30-day tourist visa, where He lived in the villa of a Greek film producer and started to speak twice daily. Disciples flocked to hear Him. The Greek Orthodox clergy threatened the Greek government that blood would flow unless Bhagwan was thrown out of the country.

Mar. 5 1986   Police broke into the villa and arrested Bhagwan without warrant, shunting Him off to Athens where only a twenty-five thousand dollar sum could move the authorities not to put Him on the boat to India.

Mar. 6 1986   He left in a private jet for *Switzerland* where His 7-day visa was cancelled by armed policemen upon arrival. He was declared 'persona non grata' because of "immigration offenses in the United States" and asked to leave.

He moved on to *Sweden* where He was met the same way – surrounded by rifled policemen. He was told He was "a danger to national security," and ordered to leave

immediately.

He moved on to *England*. His pilots were now legally bound to rest for eight hours. Bhagwan wanted to wait in the First Class Transit Lounge, but He was not allowed; nor was He allowed to stay in a hotel overnight. Instead, He and His companions were locked up in a small, dirty cell crowded with refugees.

Mar. 7 1986   Bhagwan and His group flew to *Ireland*, where they were given tourist visas. They went to a hotel near Limerick. The next morning police arrived and ordered them to leave immediately. However, this was not possible because *Canada* had by then refused Bhagwan's plane permission to land at Gander for refuelling on the intended flight to *Antigua* in the Caribbean.

This extraordinary denial of the right to refuel was made in spite of a bond from Lloyds of London guaranteeing that Bhagwan would not step outside the plane.

On the condition that there was no publicity that might embarrass the authorities, He was allowed to remain in Ireland until other arrangements could be made.

During the wait, Antigua withdrew permission for Bhagwan to go there. *Holland*, when asked, also refused Bhagwan. *Germany* had already passed a 'preventive decree' not to allow Bhagwan to enter their country. In *Italy*, His tourist application remained stalled – and is still stalled 15 months later . . . .

Mar. 19   At the last moment, *Uruguay* turned up

with an invitation, and so, on March 19th, Bhagwan, His devotees and fellow travelers flew to Montevideo via Dakar, Senegal. Uruguay even opened up the possibility of permanent residence. However, in Uruguay it was discovered why He was being denied access to every country He tried to enter – telexes with "diplomatic secret information" (all from NATO government sources) mentioning INTERPOL rumors of "smuggling charges, drug dealing and prostitution" concerning Bhagwan's circle had invariably preceded them in their prospective host countries just in time for the police to be alerted. Uruguay soon came under the same pressure.

May 14 1986
The government planned to announce at a press conference that Bhagwan had been granted permanent residence in Uruguay.

That night Sanguinetti, the President of Uruguay, received a call from Washington, DC, saying that if Bhagwan stayed in Uruguay, current US loans of six billion dollars would be called in, and no future loans given. Bhagwan had to leave Uruguay on June 18th.

The next day, Sanguinetti and Reagan announced from Washington a new US loan to Uruguay of one hundred and fifty million dollars.

Jun. 19 1986
Jamaica granted Bhagwan a 10-day visa. Moments after He landed there, a US navy jet landed next to Bhagwan's private jet, and two civilians descended. The next morning, the visas of Bhagwan and His group were cancelled.

Bhagwan flew on to Lisbon via Madrid, and remained "undiscovered" for some time. A few weeks later policemen were placed around the villa where He was resting. Bhagwan decided to return back to India the next day.

In all, twenty-one countries had either deported Him or denied Him entry.

Jul. 29 1986
Bhagwan arrived in Bombay, India, where He settled for six months as a personal guest of an Indian friend. In the privacy of His host's home, He resumed His daily discourses.

Jan. 4 1987
Bhagwan moved into the house at the ashram in Poona where He had lived for the major part of the seventies.

Immediately upon Bhagwan's arrival, the police chief of Poona ordered Him to leave on the grounds that He was a "controversial person" who may "disturb the tranquility of the city." The order was revoked the same day by the Bombay High Court. The same Hindu fanatic who, in May 1980, tried to murder Bhagwan by throwing a knife at Him during a public lecture began making aggressive threats about forcing his way into the ashram with 200 commandoes trained in martial arts – unless Bhagwan was expelled from Poona.

May 21 1987
At the time of writing, despite the attempts of the governments of the "free world" to isolate Bhagwan in virtual internal exile, thousands of disciples have traveled to Poona to be with their Master once again.

BOOKS BY BHAGWAN SHREE RAJNEESH

ENGLISH LANGUAGE EDITIONS
Rajneesh Publishers
Recent Releases

Sermons in Stones
The Rajneesh Bible *(Volumes 1-4)*
Bhagwan Shree Rajneesh On Basic Human Rights
The Last Testament *(Volume 1)*
        (Interviews with the World Press)
The Rajneesh Upanishad
Beyond Enlightenment
The Book *An Introduction to the Teachings of*
        Bhagwan Shree Rajneesh
        Series I from A-H
        Series II from I -O
        Series III from R-Z

Biographies

Books I have Loved
Glimpses of a Golden Childhood
Notes of a Madman

Photobiographies

The Sound of Running Water - *Bhagwan Shree*
        Rajneesh and His work 1974-1978
This Very Place The Lotus Paradise - *Bhagwan*
        Shree Rajneesh and His Work 1978-1984

The Bauls

The Beloved *(Volumes 1 & 2)*

Buddha

The Book of the Books *(Volumes 1-4)*
        - *the Dhammapada*
The Diamond Sutra - *the Vajrachchedika*
        Prajnaparamita Sutra
The Discipline of Transcendence *(Volumes 1-4)*
        - *the Sutra of 42 Chapters*
The Heart Sutra
        - *the Prajnaparamita Hridayam Sutra*

Buddhist Masters

The Book of Wisdom *(Volumes 1 & 2)*
        - *Atisha's Seven Points of Mind Training*
The White Lotus - *the Sayings of Bodhidharma*

Early Discourses and Writings

A Cup of Tea - *Letters to Disciples*
From Sex to Superconsciousness
And Now, and Here *(Volumes 1&2)*
Beware of Socialism
Krishna: The Man and His Philosophy
The Long and the Short and the All
The Perfect Way
In Search of the Miraculous *(Volume 1)*

Hassidism

The Art of Dying
The True Sage

Jesus

Come Follow Me *(Volumes 1-4)*
    - *the Sayings of Jesus*
I Say Unto You *(Volumes 1&2)*
    - *the Sayings of Jesus*
The Mustard Seed - *the Gospel of Thomas*

Kabir

The Divine Melody
Ecstasy: The Forgotten Language
The Fish in the Sea is Not Thirsty
The Guest
The Path of Love
The Revolution

Meditation

The Orange Book - *the Meditation Techniques
    of Bhagwan Shree Rajneesh*

Responses to Questions

Be Still and Know
The Goose is Out
My Way: The Way of the White Clouds
Walk Without Feet, Fly Without Wings and
    Think Without Mind
The Wild Geese and the Water
Zen: Zest, Zip, Zap and Zing

Sufism

Just Like That

The Perfect Master *(Volumes 1&2)*
The Secret
Sufis: The People of the Path *(Volumes 1&2)*
Unio Mystica *(Volumes 1&2)*
    - *the Hadiqa of Hakim Sanai*
Until You Die
The Wisdom of the Sands *(Volumes 1&2)*

Tantra

The Book of the Secrets *(Volumes 4&5)*
    - *Vigyana Bhairava Tantra*
Tantra, Spirituality and Sex
    - *Excerpts from The Book of the Secrets*
Tantra: The Supreme Understanding
    - *Tilopa's Song of Mahamudra*
The Tantra Vision *(Volumes 1&2)*
    - *the Royal Song of Saraha*

Tao

The Empty Boat - *the Stories of Chuang Tzu*
The Secret of Secrets *(Volumes 1&2)*
    - *the Secret of the Golden Flower*
Tao: The Golden Gate *(Volumes 1&2)*
Tao: The Pathless Path
    - *the Stories of Lieh Tzu*
Tao: The Three Treasures *(Volumes 1-4)*
    - *the Tao Te Ching of Lao Tzu*
When the Shoe Fits
    - *the Stories of Chuang Tzu*

The Upanishads

I Am That - *Isa Upanishad*
The Ultimate Alchemy *(Volumes 1&2)*
    - *Atma Pooja Upanishad*
Vedanta: Seven Steps to Samadhi
    - *Akshya Upanishad*
Philosophia Ultima - *Mandukya Upanishad*

Western Mystics

The Hidden Harmony
- *the Fragments of Heraclitus*
The New Alchemy: To Turn You on
- *Mabel Collins' Light on the Path*
Philosophia Perennis (Volumes 1&2)
- *the Golden Verses of Pythagoras*
Guida Spirituale - *the Desiderata*
Theologia Mystica
- *the Treatise of St. Dionysius*

Yoga

Yoga: The Alpha and the Omega *(Volumes 1-10)*
- *the Yoga Sutras of Patanjali*
Yoga: The Science of the Soul *(Volumes 1-3)*
- *Originally titled Yoga: The Alpha and the Omega*

Zen

Ah, This!
Ancient Music in the Pines
And the Flowers Showered
Dang Dang Doko Dang
The First Principle
The Grass Grows By Itself
Nirvana: The Last Nightmare
No Water, No Moon
Returning to the Source
A Sudden Clash of Thunder
The Sun Rises in the Evening
Zen: The Path of Paradox *(Volumes 1-3)*
Zen: The Special Transmission - *Zen Stories*

Zen Masters

Hsin Hsin Ming: The Book of Nothing
- *Discourses on the Faith-Mind of Sosan*
The Search - *the Ten Bulls of Zen*

Take It Easy *(Volumes 1&2) - Poems of Ikkyu*
This Very Body the Buddha
- *Hakuin's Song of Meditation*

Darshan Diaries
Talks between Master and Disciple

Hammer on the Rock
(December 10, 1975 - January 15, 1976)
Above All Don't Wobble *(January 16 - February 12, 1976)*
Nothing to Lose But Your Head
(February 13 - March 12, 1976)
Be Realistic: Plan For a Miracle *(March 13 - April 6, 1976)*
Get Out of Your Own Way *(April 7 - May 2, 1976)*
Beloved of My Heart *(May 3 - 28, 1976)*
The Cypress in the Courtyard *(May 29 - June 27, 1976)*
A Rose is a Rose is a Rose *(June 28 - July 27, 1976)*
Dance Your Way to God *(July 28 - August 20, 1976)*
The Passion for the Impossible
(August 21 - September 18, 1976)
The Great Nothing *(September 19 - October 11, 1976)*
God is Not for Sale *(October 12 - November 7, 1976)*
The Shadow of the Whip
(November 8 - December 3, 1976)
Blessed are the Ignorant *(December 4 - 31, 1976)*
The Buddha Disease *(January 1977)*
What Is, Is, What Ain't, Ain't *(February 1977)*
The Zero Experience *(March 1977)*
For Madmen Only (Price of Admission: Your Mind)
(April 1977)
This is It *(May 1977)*
The Further Shore *(June 1977)*
Far Beyond the Stars *(July 1977)*
The No Book (No Buddha, No Teaching, No Discipline)
(August 1977)
Don't Just Do Something, Sit There *(September 1977)*
Only Losers Can Win in this Game *(October 1977)*
The Open Secret *(November 1977)*
The Open Door *(December 1977)*
The Sun Behind the Sun Behind the Sun *(January 1978)*

Believing the Impossible Before Breakfast
(February 1978)
Don't Bite My Finger, Look Where I'm Pointing
(March 1978)
Let Go! *(April 1978)*
The 99 Names of Nothingness *(May 1978)*
The Madman's Guide to Enlightenment *(June 1978)*
Don't Look Before You Leap *(July 1978)*
Hallelujah! *(August 1978)*
God's Got a Thing About You *(September 1978)*
The Tongue-Tip Taste of Tao *(October 1978)*
The Sacred Yes *(November 1978)*
Turn On, Tune In, and Drop the Lot *(December 1978)*
Zorba the Buddha *(January 1979)*
Won't You Join the Dance? *(February 1979)*
You Ain't Seen Nothin' Yet *(March 1979)*
The Shadow of the Bamboo *(April 1979)*
Just Around the Corner *(May 1979)*
Snap Your Fingers, Slap Your Face & Wake Up!
(June 1979)
The Rainbow Bridge *(July 1979)*
Don't Let Yourself Be Upset by the Sutra, Rather Upset
the Sutra Yourself *(August/September 1979)*
The Sound of One Hand Clapping *(March 1981)*

Other Publishers
UNITED KINGDOM

The Book of the Secrets *(Volume 1, Thames & Hudson)*
Roots and Wings *(Routledge & Kegan Paul)*
The Supreme Doctrine *(Routledge & Kegan Paul)*
Tao: The Three Treasures *(Volume 1, Wildwood House)*

Books on
Bhagwan Shree Rajneesh

The Way of the Heart: the Rajneesh Movement
*by Judith Thompson and Paul Heelas, Department of
Religious Studies, University of Lancaster
(Aquarian Press)*

UNITED STATES OF AMERICA

The Book of the Secrets *(Volumes 1-3, Harper & Row)*
The Great Challenge *(Grove Press)*
Hammer on the Rock *(Grove Press)*
I Am the Gate *(Harper & Row)*
Journey toward the Heart
(Original title: Until You Die, Harper & Row)
Meditation: The Art of Ecstasy *(Harper & Row)*
The Mustard Seed *(Harper & Row)*
My Way: The Way of the White Clouds *(Grove Press)*
The Psychology of the Esoteric *(Harper & Row)*
Roots and Wings *(Routledge & Kegan Paul)*
The Supreme Doctrine *(Routledge & Kegan Paul)*
Words Like Fire *(Original title: Come Follow Me, Volume 1)*
(Harper & Row)

Books on
Bhagwan Shree Rajneesh

The Awakened One: The Life and Work of Bhagwan Shree
Rajneesh *by Swami Satya Vedant (Harper & Row)*
The Rajneesh Story: The Bhagwan's Garden
by Dell Murphy (Linwood Press, Oregon)

FOREIGN LANGUAGE EDITIONS

Chinese

I Am The Gate (Woolin)

Danish

The Book of the Secrets (Volume 1, Borgens)
(Hemmelighedernes Bog)
Hu-Meditation and Cosmic Orgasm (Borgens)
(Hu-Meditation Og Kosmik Orgasme)

Dutch

Bhagwan Shree Rajneesh On Basic Human Rights
(Stichting Rajneesh Publikaties) (Bhagwan Shree
Rajneesh Over de Rechten van de Mens)
The Book of Secrets (Volumes 1-5, Mirananda)
(Het Boek der Geheimen)
No Water, No Moon (Volumes 1&2, Mirananda)
(Geen Water, Geen Maan)
I am the Gate (Ankh-Hermes) (Ik Ben de Poort)
Meditation: The Art of Inner Ecstasy (Mirananda)
(Meditatie: De Kunst van Innerlijke Extase)
My Way: The Way of the White Clouds (Arcanum)
(Mijn Weg, De Weg van de Witte Wolk)
The Mustard Seed (Volumes 1&2, Mirananda)
(Het Mosterdzaad)
The New Man (Volumes 1&2, Zorn/Altamia) (Excerpts from
The Last Testament, Volume 1) (De Nieuwe Mens)
The Orange Book (Ankh-Hermes)
(Het Oranje Meditatieboek)
The Psychology of the Esoteric (Ankh-Hermes)
(Psychologie en Evolutie)
Tantra: The Supreme Understanding (Ankh-Hermes)
(Tantra: Het Allerhoogste Inzicht)
Tantra, Spirituality & Sex (Ankh-Hermes)
(Tantra, Spiritualiteit en Seks)
Tantra Vision (Volumes 1&2, Arcanum) (De Tantra Visie)
Tao: The Three Treasures (Volume 1, Ankh-Hermes)(Tau)

Just Like That (Mirananda)(Heel Eenvoudig)
Until You Die (Ankh-Hermes) (Totdat Je Sterft)
The Hidden Harmony (Mirananda) (De Verborgen Harmonie)
Come Follow Me (Volume 1, Ankh-Hermes) (Volg Mij)
Come Follow Me (Volume 2, Ankh-Hermes)
(Gezaaid in Goede Aarde)
Come Follow Me (Volume 3, Ankh-Hermes) (Drink Mij)
Come Follow Me (Volume 4, Ankh-Hermes)
(Ik Ben de Zee Die Je Zoekt)
10 Zen Stories (Ankh-Hermes) (Zoeken naar de Stier)

French

The Psychology of the Esoteric (Dangles)
(L'eveil a la Conscience Cosmique)
I am the Gate (EPI) (Je Suis la Porte)
The Book of the Secrets (Volume 1, Soleil Orange)
(Le Livre des Secrets)
Meditation: The Art of Inner Ecstasy (Dangles)
(La Meditation Dynamique)

German

Bhagwan Shree Rajneesh On Basic Human Rights
(Rajneesh Verlags GmbH) (Bhagwan Shree Rajneesh:
Über die Grundrechte des Menschen)
The Search (Sambuddha) (Auf der Suche)
The Book of the Secrets (Volume 1, Heyne)
(Das Buch der Geheimnisse)
The Sound of One Hand Clapping (Edition Gyandip)
(Das Klatschen der einen Hand)
The Orange Book (Rajneesh Verlag/RFE)
(Das Orangene Buch)
A Cup of Tea (Sannyas) (Der Freund)
The Goose Is Out! (Rajneesh Verlag) (Die Gans ist raus!)
Roots and Wings (Volume 1, Edition Lotus)
(Mit Wurzeln und Flügeln)
Roots and Wings (Volume 2, Edition Lotus)
(Die Schuhe auf dem Kopf)

The Hidden Harmony (Sannyas)
(Die verborgene Harmonie)
The Mustard Seed (Rajneesh Verlag/Heyne)
(Die verbotene Wahrheit)
Ecstasy: The Forgotten Language (Herzschlag)
(Ekstase: Die vergessene Sprache)
The Psychology of the Esoteric (Sannyas)
(Esoterische Psychologie)
Glimpses of a Golden Childhood (Goldmann)
(Goldene Augenblicke: Portrait einer Jugend
in Indien)
I am the Gate (Sannyas) (Ich bin der Weg)
Intelligence of the Heart (Compilation only in German,
Herzschlag) (Intelligenz des Herzens)
Come Follow Me (Volume 1, Sannyas/Droemer Knaur)
(Komm und Folge Mir)
Come Follow Me (Volume 2, Sannyas)
(Jesus aber schwieg)
Come Follow Me (Volume 3, Sannyas)
(Jesus - der Menschensohn)
No Water, No Moon (Herzschlag)
(Kein Wasser, Kein Mond)
Tantra, Spirituality & Sex (Rajneesh Verlag)
(Tantra, Spiritualität und Sex)
Meditation: The Art of Inner Ecstasy (Heyne)
(Meditation: Die Kunst, zu sich selbst zu finden)
My Way: The Way of the White Clouds (Herzschlag)
(Mein Weg: Der Weg der weißen Wolke)
Until You Die (Edition Gyandip) (Nicht bevor du stirbst)
Nirvana: The Last Nightmare (Rajneesh Verlag/RFE)
(Nirvana: Die letzte Hürde auf dem Weg)
The Great Challenge (Sannyas) (Rebellion der Seele)
Sexualität and Aids (Excerpts, Rajneesh Verlag)
(Sexualität und Aids)
Spiritual Development & Sexuality (Fischer)
(Spirituelle Entwicklung und Sexualität)
Hammer on the Rock (Fischer)
(Sprengt den Fels der Unbewußtheit)
Dimensions Beyond the Known (Sannyas)
(Sprung ins Unbekannte)

Tantra: The Supreme Understanding (Sannyas)
(Tantra: Die höchste Einsicht)
Tantra, Spirituality & Sex (Sannyas)
(Tantrische Liebeskunst)
The Tantra Vision (Volume 1, Heyne) (Tantrische Vision)
From Sex to Superconsciousness (New Age/Thomas
Martin) (Vom Sex zum kosmischen Bewusstsein)
Beware of Socialism (Rajneesh Verlag)
(Vorsicht Sozialismus)
What is Meditation? (Compilation, Sannyas)
(Was ist Meditation?)
Yoga: The Alpha and the Omega (Volume 1, Edition
Gyandip)(Yoga: Alpha und Omega)
Above All Don't Wobble (Fachbuchhandlung für
Psychologie) (Und Vor Allem: Nicht Wackeln)
The True Sage (Edition Lotus) (Alchemie der Verwandlung)
Der Höhepunkt des Lebens (Excerpts only in German –
Rajneesh Verlag)
Kunst kommt nicht von Können (Excerpts only in German –
Rajneesh Verlag)
Liebe beginnt nach den Flitterwochen (Excerpts only in
German – Rajneesh Verlag)

Greek

The Hidden Harmony (PIGI/Rassoulis) (I Krifi Armonia)

Hebrew

Tantra: The Supreme Understanding (Massada)
(Tantra: Ha'havana Ha'eelaeet)

Italian

Bhagwan Shree Rajneesh On Basic Human Rights
(Rajneesh Services Corporation)
(Bhagwan Shree Rajneesh I Dritti Dell'Uomo)
The Hidden Harmony (Volumes 1&2, Re Nudo)
(L'Armonia Nascosta)

No Water, No Moon (Mediterranee) (Dieci Storie Zen di
    Bhagwan Shree Rajneesh: Ne Acqua, Ne Luna)
The Supreme Doctrine (Rizzoli) (La Dottrina Suprema)
Dimensions Beyond the Known (Mediterranee/Re Nudo)
    (Dimensioni Oltre il Conosciuto)
Ecstasy: The Forgotten Language (Riza Libri)
    (Estasi: Il Linguaggio Dimenticato)
Guida Spirituale (Mondadori) (Guida Spirituale)
I am the Gate (Mediterranee) (Io Sono La Soglia)
The Orange Book (Mediterranee) (Il Libro Arancione)
The Book of the Secrets (Volume 1, Bompiani)
    (Il Libro dei Segreti)
Meditation: The Art of Inner Ecstasy (Mediterranee)
    (Meditazione Dinamica: L'Arte dell'Estasi Interiore)
My Way: The Way of the White Clouds (Mediterranee)
    (La Mia Via: La Via delle Nuvole Bianche)
Nirvana: The Last Nightmare (Basaia)
    (Nirvana: L'Ultimo Incubo)
The New Alchemy: To Turn You On (Psiche)
    (La Nuova Alchimia)
Philosophia Perennis (Ecig) (Philosophia Perennis)
The Psychology of the Esoteric (Mediterranee)
    (La Rivoluzione Interiore)
The Search (La Salamandra) (La Ricerca)
The Mustard Seed (Volumes 1-3, Rajneesh Foundation Italy)
    (Il Seme della Ribellione)
Tantra: The Supreme Understanding (Bompiani)
    (Tantra: La Comprensione Suprema)
Tantra, Spirituality & Sex (Rajneesh Foundation Italy)
    (Tantra, Spiritualita e Sesso)
Tao: The Three Treasures (Volumes 1-3, Re Nudo)
    (Tao: I Tre Tesori)
Techniques of Liberation (La Salamandra)
    (Tecniche di Liberazione)
Seeds of Revolution (Suga Co) (Semi di Saggezza)
The Rajneesh Bible (Volume 1, Bompiani)
    (La Bibbia di Rajneesh)
From Sex to Superconsciousness (Basaia)
    (Dal Sesso all'Eros Cosmico)

Japanese

Bhagwan Shree Rajneesh On Basic Human Rights
    (Meisosha Ltd.)
Dance Your Way to God (Rajneesh Publications)
The Diamond Sutra (Meisosha Ltd./LAF Mitsuya)
The Empty Boat (Volumes 1&2, Rajneesh Publications)
From Sex to Superconsciousness (Rajneesh Publications)
The Grass Grows by Itself (Fumikura)
The Heart Sutra (Merkmal)
Meditation: The Art of Inner Ecstasy (Merkmal)
The Mustard Seed (Volumes 1&2, Merkmal)
My Way: The Way of the White Clouds
    (Rajneesh Publications)
The Orange Book (Wholistic Therapy Institute)
The Search (Merkmal)
The Beloved (Volumes 1&2, Merkmal)
Tantra: The Supreme Understanding (Merkmal)
Tao: The Three Treasures (Volumes 1-4, Merkmal)
Until You Die (Fumikura)

Korean

The Art of Dying (Chung Ha)
The Grass Grows by Itself (Chung Ha)
The Empty Boat (Chung Ha)

Portuguese

The Cypress in the Courtyard (Cultrix)
    (O Cipreste No Jardim)
The Divine Melody (Cultrix) (A Divina Melodia)
Dimensions Beyond the Known (Cultrix)
    (Dimensoes Alem do Conhecido)
The Book of the Secrets (Volumes 1&2, Maha Lakshmi
    Editora) (O Livro Dos Segredos)
I am the Gate (Pensamento) (Eu Sou A Porta)
The Hidden Harmony (Pensamento) (A Harmonia Oculta)
Meditation: The Art of Inner Ecstasy (Cultrix)
    (Meditacao: A Arte Do Extase)

My Way: The Way of the White Clouds
   (Tao Livraria & Editora)
   (Meu Caminho: O Cominho Das Nuvens Brancas)
No Water, No Moon (Pensamento) (Nem Agua, Nem Lua)
Come Follow Me (Volume 1, Global/Ground)
   (Palavras De Fogo)
The Psychology of the Esoteric (Tao Livaria & Editora)
   (A Psicologia Do Esoterico)
The Mustard Seed (Volumes 1&2, Tao Livraria & Editora)
   (A Semente De Mostarda)
Sufis: The People of the Path (Maha Lakshmi Editora)
   (Sufis: O Povo do Caminho)
From Sex to Superconsciousness (Cultrix)
   (Do Sexo A Supersciencia)
The New Alchemy To Turn You On (Cultrix)
   (A Nova Alquimia)
Roots and Wings (Cultrix) (Raizes E Asas)
The Orange Book (Pensamento) (O Livro Orange)
Tantra, Spirituality & Sex (Agora)
   (Tantra: Sexo E Espiritualidade)
Tantra: The Supreme Understanding (Cultrix)
   (Tantra: A Suprema Comprensao)
Ecstasy: The Forgotten Language (Global)
   (Extase: A Linguagem Esquecida)
The Art of Dying (Global) (Arte de Morrer)
Unio Mystica (Maha Lakshmi) (Unio Mystica)

Serbo-Croat

Bhagwan Shree Rajneesh (Compilation of various
   quotations, Swami Mahavira)

Spanish

Tao: The Three Treasures (Editorial Sirio)
   (Tao: Los Tres Tesoros)
Meditation: The Art of Inner Ecstasy (Rosello Impresiones)
   (Meditacion: El Arte del Extasis)
The Psychology of the Esoteric (Editorial Cuatro Vientos)
   (Psicologia de lo Esoterico: La Nueva Evolucion
   del Hombre)
What is Meditation? (Koan/Rosello
   Impresiones/Pastanaga) (Que Es Meditacion?)
I am The Gate (Editorial Diana) (Yo Soy La Puerta)
Tantra: The Supreme Understanding
   (Volumes 1&2, Rosello Impresiones)
   (Introduccion al Mundo del Tantra)
The Heart Sutra (Sarvogeet) (El Sutra del Corazon)
Come Follow Me (Volume 1, Sagaro) (Ven, Sigueme)
My Way: The Way of the White Clouds
   (Editorial Cuatro Vientos)
   (El Camino de las Nubes Blancas)
The Ultimate Risk (Editorial Martinez Roca)
   (El Riesgo Supremo)
Only One Sky (Collection Tantra) (Solo Un Cielo)

Swedish

The Great Challenge (Livskraft)
   (Den Vaeldiga Utmaningen)

RAJNEESH MEDITATION CENTERS, ASHRAMS AND COMMUNES

Argentina

Niketana Rajneesh Meditation Center
Combate de los Pozos 764
1222 Buenos Aires
Argentina

Austria

Deepa Rajneesh Meditation Center
Kripstrasse 31
6060 Absam
Austria

Australia

Kalika Rajneesh Meditation Center
25 Martin Street
Cairns 4870
Australia

Prabhakar Rajneesh Meditation Center
c/o Post Office
Innot Hot Springs
North Queensland 4872
Australia

Rajneeshgrad Neo-Sannyas Commune
P.O. Box 1097
160 High Street
Fremantle WA 6160
Australia

Belgium

Suryodaya Rajneesh Meditation Center
Rue de Drapieres 12
1050 Bruxelles
Belgium

Brazil

Anurag Rajneesh Meditation Center
Avenida Recife 4282
Modulo 4, Apto. 314 ES
Tancia-Recife 50000
Brazil

Jwala Rajneesh Meditation Center
Avenida Nico Pecanta 50
Sala 2315, Edificio Rodoefo
De Padi Centro
Rio de Janeiro
Brazil

Premadhara Rajneesh Medition Center
Av. Dep. Paulino Rocha 1001
Apto. 402, Sqn. Bloco H
Castelao, Fortaneza-Ceara 60000
Brazil

Purnam Rajneesh Meditation Center
Caixa Postal 1946
Rio Grande do Sul
Porto Alegre 90000
Brazil

Sudhakar Rajneesh Meditation Center
Rua Pereira da Silva 493
Laranjeiras
Rio de Janeiro 22210 RJ
Brazil

Canada

Grada Rajneesh Neo-Sannyas Commune
5161 Avenue de Parc
Montreal, Quebec H2V 4G3
Canada

Samaroha Rajneesh Meditation Center
1774 Tolmie Street
Vancouver, B.C. V6R 4B8
Canada

Chile

Pramada Rajneesh Meditation Center
Genaro Prieto 2363
Providencia
Santiago
Chile

Colombia

Padma Rajneesh Meditation Center
Apartado Aereo 4128
Medellin
Colombia

Denmark

Khalaas Rajneesh Meditation Center
Museumsstien 8
9990 Skagen
Denmark

Rajneesh Institute for Spiritual Creativity
Bogballevey 3, Tonning
8740 Braeostrup
Denmark

Sahajo Rajneesh Medition Center
Sudergade 26, 1
3000 Helsinger
Denmark

Ecuador

Moulik Rajneesh Meditation Center
Eustorgio Salgado 197, piso 3
Miraflores Quito
Ecuador

Finland

Leela Rajneesh Meditation Center
Merimiehenkatu 16B 24
00150 Helsinki 15
Finland

Great Britain

Purnima Rajneesh Meditation Center
3 Annette Road
Holloway
London N7 6EX
Great Britain

Greece

Darshan Rajneesh Meditation Center
20 Aribou Street
11633 Athens
Greece

India

Rajneeshdham Neo-Sannyas Commune
17 Koregaon Park
411 001 Poona
India

Rajyoga Rajneesh Meditation Center
C5/44 Safdarjang Development Area
Opposite ITT, Palam Road
110016 New Delhi
India

Italy

Devamani Rajneesh Meditation Center
Via Basilica 5
10122 Torino
Italy

Miasto Rajneesh Neo-Sannyas Commune
Podere San Giorgio
Cotorniano
53010 Frosini (Siena)
Italy

Japan

Eer Rajneesh Neo-Sannyas Commune
Mimura Building 6-21-34 Kikuna
Kohoku-ku
Yokohama 222
Japan

Mahamani Rajneesh Meditation Center
105 Country Heights
635 Shimabukuro
Kitanakagusuku-son
Okinawa 901-23
Japan

Sitara Rajneesh Meditation Center
498-218, Teine-miyanosawa
Nishi-ku
Sapporo-shi
Hokkaido
Japan

Kenya

Archana Rajneesh Meditation Center
P.O. Box 82501
Mombasa
Kenya

Preetam Rajneesh Meditation Center
P.O. Box 10256
Nairobi
Kenya

Mexico

Madhu Rajneesh Meditation Center
Rancho Cutzi Minzicuri
San Juan de Vina
Tacambaro
Michoacan
Mexico

Nepal

Asheesh Rajneesh Meditation Center
P.O. Box 278
Pulchowk
Kathmandu
Nepal

Rajneesh Teerth Neo-Sannyas Commune
Masina Patan
P.O. Box 91
Pokhara
Nepal

Satmarga Rajneesh Meditation Center
Mahendra Pul
Pokhara
Nepal

Netherlands

Amaltas Rajneesh Meditation Center
Staalwijklaan 4
3763 LG Soest
Netherlands

Arvind Rajneesh Meditation Center
Hoge Larenseweg 168
1221 AV Hilversum
Netherlands

De Nieuwe Mens
Enschedesestraat 305
7552 CV Hengelo (O)
Netherlands

De Stad Rajneesh Mystery School
Cornelis Troostplein 23
1072 JS Amsterdam
Netherlands

Mudita Rajneesh Meditation Center
Veldhuizenstraat 2
Gein
1072 Amsterdam
Netherlands

Prakash Rajneesh Meditation Center
Dykhuizenweg 70
9903 AE Appingedam
Netherlands

Rajneesh Humaniversity Foundation
Dr. Wiardi Beckmanlaan 4
1931 BW Egmond aan Zee
Netherlands

Wajid Rajneesh Meditation Center
Prins Hendrikplein 1
2518 JA Den Haag
Netherlands

New Zealand

Shunyadeep Rajneesh Meditation Center
42 Park Road
Mirimar, Wellington
New Zealand

Norway

Devananda Rajneesh Meditation Center
P.O. Box 177
Vinderen
0319 Oslo 3
Norway

Peru

Adityo Rajneesh Meditation Center
Paseo de la Republica 4670 Depto E
Miraflores
Lima 18
Peru

Spain

Kamli Rajneesh Meditation Center
Apartado de Correos 607
Ibiza
Spain

Sweden

Madhur Rajneesh Meditation Center
Forfattarvagen 40
16142 Bromma
Sweden

Switzerland

Almasta Rajneesh Meditation Center
9 Av. des Arpilleres
1224 Chene-Bougerie – Geneva
Switzerland

Mingus Rajneesh Meditation Center
Asylstrasse 11
8032 Zürich
Switzerland

Nisargam Rajneesh Meditation Center
16 Rue Etienne Dumont
1204 Geneva
Switzerland

USA

Bhagwatam Rajneesh Meditation Center
P.O. Box 2886 (Altos)
Old San Juan, PR 00905
USA

Devadeep Rajneesh Meditation Center
1430 Longfellow Street NW
Washington, DC 20011
USA

Devadeep Rajneesh Meditation Center
Dicob Road
P.O. Box 1
Lowville, NY 13367
USA

Devatara Rajneesh Meditation Center
155 Spencer Ave.
Lynbrook, L.I., NY 11563
USA

Dharmadeep Rajneesh Meditation Center
2455 6th Avenue N.
St. Petersburg, FL 33713
USA

Fulwari Rajneesh Meditation Center
1726 Hillmont Drive
Nashville, TN 37215
USA

Mahima Rajneesh Meditation Center
P.O. Box 1863
Makawao, HI 96768
USA

Nanda Rajneesh Meditation Center
31486 West St.
South Laguna, CA 92677
USA

Neeraj Rajneesh Meditation Center
2493 McGovern Drive
Scenectady, NY 12309
USA

Premsindhu Rajneesh Meditation Center
214 Beryl Street
Mill Valley, CA 94941
USA

Rajneesh Institute for Meditation and Therapy
P.O. Box 13515
Boulder, CO 80308
USA

Rajneesh Institute for Tao
201 North Ave.
Weston, MA 02193
USA

Sangit Rajneesh Meditation Center
2920 Healy Ave.
Far Rockaway, NY 11691
USA

Sudhakar Rajneesh Meditation Center
1511 7th Street
Wansau, WI 54401
USA

Sukhdhama Rajneesh Meditation Center
1546 28th Street No. 412
Boulder, CO 80303
USA

Suravi Rajneesh Meditation Center
P.O. Box 20026
Seattle, WA 98102
USA

Surdham Rajneesh Meditation Center
The Nest, 75-111
Indian Wells, CA 92210
USA

Tara Rajneesh Meditation Center
2240 S. Patterson Blvd. 4
Dayton, OH 45409
USA

Vibhakara Rajneesh Meditation Center
P.O. Box 5161
Woodland Park, CO 80866
USA

Yakaru Rajneesh Meditation Center
P.O. Box 130
Laytonville, CA 95454
USA

Venezuela

Dana Rajneesh Meditation Center
Edif. La Vera Piso 7 Apto 74
Resid. Sans-Souci
Chacaito
Caracas
Venezuela

West Germany

Ansumala Rajneesh Meditation Center
Kaps 1
8219 Rimsting
West Germany

Dharmadeep Rajneesh Institute for Meditation
and Spiritual Growth
Karolinenstrasse 7-9
2000 Hamburg 6
West Germany

Doerfchen Rajneesh Institute for Spiritual
Therapy and Meditation
Dahlmannstrasse 9
1000 Berlin 12
West Germany

Geha Rajneesh Meditation Center
Winterstetten 44
7970 Leutkirch
West Germany

Mani Rajneesh Meditation Center
Johannes-Buell Weg 13 II
2000 Hamburg 65
West Germany

Nityam Rajneesh Meditation Center
Villa Roedelstein
6551 Altenbamberg
West Germany

Nishant Rajneesh Meditation Center
c/o Tassy Family
Hoer Rain 6, Weichendorf
8608 Memmelsdorf
West Germany

Prabha Rajneesh Meditation Center
Husarenstrasse 38
3300 Braunschweig
West Germany

...suna Rajneesh Meditation Center
...enekinger Weg 60
5880 Luedenscheid
West Germany

Premapara Rajneesh Meditation Center
Asternweg 4
8900 Augsburg 1
West Germany

Purnam Rajneesh Neo-Sannyas Commune
Graf-Adolf-Strasse 87
4000 Duesseldorf 1
West Germany

Rajneesh Academy for Harmonious Integration
and Meditation (RAHIM)
Rahim/Rast e.V.
Merianstrasse 12
7800 Freiburg
West Germany

Rajneeshstadt
Strickhauserstrasse 39
2882 Ovelgoenne
West Germany

Sampat Rajneesh Meditation Center
Mendelweg 5
7900 Ulm/Lehr
West Germany

Sirat Rajneesh Meditation Center
Hochbuchstrasse 50
7410 Reutlingen
West Germany

Tao Rajneesh Zentrum
Klenzestrasse 41
8000 Muenchen 5
West Germany

Uta Rajneesh Institute fuer Spirituelle
Therapie und Meditation
Venloerstrasse 5-7
5000 Koeln 1
West Germany